I0091801

Samuel Smiles

Self-Help with illustrations of character, conduct and

perseverance

Samuel Smiles

Self-Help with illustrations of character, conduct and perseverance

ISBN/EAN: 9783742866912

Manufactured in Europe, USA, Canada, Australia, Japa

Cover: Foto ©Suzi / pixelio.de

Manufactured and distributed by brebook publishing software
(www.brebook.com)

Samuel Smiles

**Self-Help with illustrations of character, conduct and
perseverance**

SELF-HELP;

WITH ILLUSTRATIONS OF

CHARACTER, CONDUCT, AND PERSEVERANCE.

By SAMUEL SMILES,

AUTHOR OF 'LIVES OF THE ENGINEERS.'

"This above all,—To thine own self be true;
And it must follow, as the night the day,
Thou canst not then be false to any man."
SHAKESPEARE.

"Might I give counsel to any young man, I would say to him, try
to frequent the company of your betters. In books and in life,
that is the most wholesome society; learn to admire rightly; the
great pleasure of life is that. Note what great men admired:
they admired great things; narrow spirits admire basely, and
worship meanly."—W. M. THACKERAY.

A NEW EDITION.

LONDON:

JOHN MURRAY, ALBEMARLE STREET.

1868.

The right of Translation is reserved.

BY THE SAME AUTHOR.

'SELF-HELP,' OU CARACTÈRE, CONDUITE ET PER-
SÉVÉRANCE, Illustrés à l'aide de Biographie. Traduit de l'Anglais par
ALFRED TALANDIER sur le texte revu et corrigé par l'Auteur. Post 8vo.
5s.

INDUSTRIAL BIOGRAPHY: IRON-WORKERS and
TOOL-MAKERS. A companion Volume to 'Self-Help.' Post 8vo. 6s.

JAMES BRINDLEY AND THE EARLY ENGI-
NEERS. With Illustrations. Post 8vo. 6s.

LIFE OF THOMAS TELFORD, CIVIL ENGINEER;
with an Introductory History of Roads and Travelling in Britain. Post
8vo. 6s.

THE STORY OF THE LIFE OF GEORGE
STEPHENSON; INCLUDING A MEMOIR OF HIS SON ROBERT STEPHEN-
SON. With Illustrations. Post 8vo. 6s.

LIVES OF BRITISH ENGINEERS, from the Earliest
Times to the Death of Robert Stephenson; with an Account of their
Principal Works, and a HISTORY OF INLAND COMMUNICATION IN BRITAIN.
With Portraits and 270 Woodcuts. 3 Vols. 8vo. 63s.

LIVES OF BOULTON AND WATT; comprising
a History of the Invention and Introduction of the Steam-Engine; principally from the Soho MSS. With Portraits and 72 Woodcuts. 8vo. 21s.

THE HUGUENOTS: THEIR SETTLEMENTS, CHURCHES,
and INDUSTRIES, in ENGLAND and IRELAND. 8vo. 16s.

WORKMEN'S EARNINGS,—SAVINGS,—AND
STRIKES: Reprinted from the 'Quarterly Review.' Post 8vo. 1s. 6d.

LONDON : PRINTED BY W. CLOWES AND SONS, STAMFORD STREET,
AND CHARING CROSS.

PREFACE.

———

THIS is a revised edition of a book which has already been received with considerable favour at home and abroad. It has been reprinted in various forms in America; translations have appeared in Dutch and French, and others are about to appear in German and Danish. The book has, doubtless, proved attractive to readers in different countries by reason of the variety of anecdotal illustrations of life and character which it contains, and the interest which all more or less feel in the labours, the trials, the struggles, and the achievements of others. No one can be better aware than the author, of its fragmentary character, arising from the manner in which it was for the most part originally composed,—having been put together principally from jottings made during many years,—intended as readings for young men, and without any view to publication. The appearance of this edition has furnished an opportunity for pruning the volume of some superfluous matter, and introducing various new illustrations, which will probably be found of general interest.

In one respect the title of the book, which it is now too late to alter, has proved unfortunate, as it has led some, who have judged it merely by the title, to suppose that it consists of a eulogy of selfishness: the very opposite of what it really is,—or at least of what the author intended it to be. Although its chief object unquestionably is to stimulate youths to apply themselves diligently to right pursuits,—sparing neither labour, pains, nor self-denial in prosecuting them,—and to rely upon their own efforts in life, rather than depend upon the help or patronage of others, it will also be found, from the examples given of literary and scientific men, artists, inventors, educators, philanthropists, missionaries, and martyrs, that the duty of helping one's self in the highest sense involves the helping of one's neighbours.

It has also been objected to the book that too much notice is taken in it of men who have succeeded in life by helping themselves, and too little of the multitude of men who have failed. "Why should not Failure," it has been asked, "have its Plutarch as well as Success?" There is, indeed, no reason why Failure should not have its Plutarch, except that a record of mere failure would probably be found excessively depressing as well as uninstructive reading. It is, however, shown in the following pages that Failure is the best discipline of the true worker, by stimulating him to renewed efforts, evoking his best powers, and carrying him onward in self-culture, self-control, and growth in knowledge and wisdom. Viewed in this light, Failure, conquered by Perseverance, is always full of interest and instruction, and this we have endeavoured to illustrate by many examples.

As for Failure *per se*, although it may be well to find consolations for it at the close of life, there is reason to doubt whether it is an object that ought to be set before youth at the beginning of it. Indeed, "how *not* to do it" is of all things the easiest learnt : it needs neither teaching, effort, self-denial, industry, patience, perseverance, nor judgment. Besides, readers do not care to know about the general who lost his battles, the engineer whose engines blew up, the architect who designed only deformities, the painter who never got beyond daubs, the schemer who did not invent his machine, the merchant who could not keep out of the Gazette. It is true, the best of men may fail, in the best of causes. But even these best of men did not try to fail, or regard their failure as meritorious ; on the contrary, they tried to succeed, and looked upon failure as misfortune. Failure in any good cause is, however, honourable, whilst success in any bad cause is merely infamous. At the same time success in the good cause is unquestionably better than failure. But it is not the result in any case that is to be regarded so much as the aim and the effort, the patience, the courage, and the endeavour with which desirable and worthy objects are pursued ;—

> " 'Tis not in mortals to command success ;
> We will do more—deserve it."

The object of the book briefly is, to re-inculcate these old-fashioned but wholesome lessons—which perhaps cannot be too often urged,—that youth must work in order to enjoy,—that nothing creditable can be accomplished without application and diligence,—that the student must not be daunted by difficulties, but conquer them by patience and perseverance,—and that, above all, he must seek elevation of character, without which capacity is worthless and worldly success is naught. If the author has not succeeded in illustrating these lessons, he can only say that he has failed in his object.

Among the new passages introduced in the present edition, may be mentioned the following :—Illustrious Foreigners of humble origin (pp. 10-12), French Generals and Marshals risen from the ranks (14), De Tocqueville and Mutual Help (24), William Lee, M.A., and the Stocking-loom (42), John Heathcoat, M.P., and the Bobbin-net machine (47), Jacquard and his Loom (55), Vaucanson (58), Joshua Heilmann and the Combing-machine (62), Bernard Palissy and his struggles (69), Böttgher, discoverer of Hard Porcelain (80), Count de Buffon as Student (104), Cuvier (128), Ambrose Paré (134), Claude Lorraine (160), Jacques Callot (162), Benvenuto Cellini (164), Nicholas Poussin (168), Ary Scheffer (171), the Strutts of Belper (214), Francis Xavier (238), Napoleon as a man of business (276), Intrepidity of Deal Boatmen (400), besides numerous other passages which it is unnecessary to specify.

London, May, 1866.

INTRODUCTION TO THE FIRST EDITION.

THE origin of this book may be briefly told.

Some fifteen years since, the author was requested to deliver an address before the members of some evening classes, which had been formed in a northern town for mutual improvement, under the following circumstances :—

Two or three young men of the humblest rank resolved to meet in the winter evenings, for the purpose of improving themselves by exchanging knowledge with each other. Their first meetings were held in the room of a cottage in which one of the members lived ; and, as others shortly joined them, the place soon became inconveniently filled. When summer set in, they adjourned to the cottage garden outside ; and the classes were then held in the open air, round a little boarded hut used as a garden-house, in which those who officiated as teachers set the sums, and gave forth the lessons of the evening. When the weather was fine, the youths might be seen, until a late hour, hanging round the door of the hut like a cluster of bees ; but sometimes a sudden shower of rain would dash the sums from their slates, and disperse them for the evening unsatisfied.

Winter, with its cold nights, was drawing near, and what were they to do for shelter? Their numbers had by this time so increased, that no room of an ordinary cottage could accommodate them. Though they were for the most part young men earning comparatively small weekly wages, they resolved to incur the risk of hiring a room; and, on making inquiry, they found a large dingy apartment to let, which had been used as a temporary Cholera Hospital. No tenant could be found for the place, which was avoided as if a plague still clung to it. But the mutual improvement youths, nothing daunted, hired the cholera room at so much a week, lit it up, placed a few benches and a deal table in it, and began their winter classes. The place soon presented a busy and cheerful appearance in the evenings. The teaching may have been, as no doubt it was, of a very rude and imperfect sort; but it was done with a will. Those who knew a little taught those who knew less—improving themselves while they improved the others; and, at all events, setting before them a good working example. Thus these youths—and there were also grown men amongst them—proceeded to teach themselves and each other, reading and writing, arithmetic and geography; and even mathematics, chemistry, and some of the modern languages.

About a hundred young men had thus come together, when, growing ambitious, they desired to have lectures delivered to them; and then it was that the author became acquainted with their proceedings. A party of them waited on him, for the purpose of inviting him to deliver an introductory address, or, as they expressed it, "to talk to them a bit;" prefacing the request by a modest statement of what they had done and what they were doing. He could not fail to be touched by the admirable self-helping spirit which they had displayed; and, though entertaining but slight faith in popular lecturing, he felt that a few words of encouragement, honestly and sincerely uttered, might not be without some good effect. And in this spirit he addressed them on more than one occasion, citing examples of what other men had done, as illustrations of what each might, in a greater or less degree, do for himself; and pointing out that their happiness and well-being as individuals in after life, must necessarily depend mainly upon themselves—upon their own diligent self-culture, self-discipline, and self-control—and, above all, on that honest and upright performance of individual duty, which is the glory of manly character.

. There was nothing in the slightest degree new or original in this counsel, which was as old as the Proverbs of Solomon, and possibly quite as familiar. But old-fashioned though the advice may have been, it was welcomed. The youths went forward in their course; worked on with energy and resolution; and, reaching manhood, they went forth in various directions into the world, where many of them now occupy positions of trust and usefulness. Several years after the incidents referred to, the subject was unexpectedly recalled to the author's recollection by an evening visit from a young man—apparently fresh from the work of a foundry—who explained that he was now an employer of labour and a thriving man; and he was pleased to remember with gratitude the words spoken in all honesty to him and to his fellow-pupils years before, and even to attribute some measure of his success in life to the endeavours which he had made to work up to their spirit.

The author's personal interest having in this way been attracted to the subject of Self-Help, he was accustomed to add to the memoranda from which he had addressed these young men ; and to note down occasionally in his leisure evening moments, after the hours of business, the results of such reading, observation, and experience of life, as he conceived to bear upon it. One of the most prominent illustrations cited in his earlier addresses, was that of George Stephenson, the engineer; and the original interest of the subject, as well as the special facilities and opportunities which the author possessed for illustrating Mr. Stephenson's life and career, induced him to prosecute it at his leisure, and eventually to publish his biography. The present volume is written in a similar spirit, as it has been similar in its origin. The illustrative sketches of character introduced, are, however, necessarily less elaborately treated—being busts rather than full-length portraits, and, in many of the cases, only some striking feature has been noted ; the lives of individuals, as indeed of nations, often concentrating their lustre and interest in a few passages. Such as the book is, the author now leaves it in the hands of the reader ; in the hope that the lessons of industry, perseverance, and self-culture, which it contains, will be found useful and instructive, as well as generally interesting.

London, September, 1859.

CONTENTS.

CHAPTER I.

SELF-HELP—NATIONAL AND INDIVIDUAL.

CHAPTER II.

LEADERS OF INDUSTRY—INVENTORS AND PRODUCERS.

CHAPTER III.

Three great Potters—Pallissy, Böttgher, Wedgwood.

CHAPTER IV.

APPLICATION AND PERSEVERANCE.

CHAPTER V.

HELPS AND OPPORTUNITIES—SCIENTIFIC PURSUITS.

CHAPTER VI.

WORKERS IN ART.

CHAPTER VII.

INDUSTRY AND THE PEERAGE.

CHAPTER VIII.

Energy and Courage.

CHAPTER IX.

Men of Business.

CHAPTER X.

MONEY—ITS USE AND ABUSE.

CHAPTER XI.

SELF-CULTURE—FACILITIES AND DIFFICULTIES.

CHAPTER XII.

EXAMPLE—MODELS.

b

CHAPTER XIII.

Character—The True Gentleman.

SELF-HELP, &c.

CHAPTER I.

SELF-HELP—NATIONAL AND INDIVIDUAL.

"The worth of a State, in the long run, is the worth of the individuals composing it."—*J. S. Mill.*

"We put too much faith in systems, and look too little to men."—*B. Disraeli.*

"HEAVEN helps those who help themselves" is a well-tried maxim, embodying in a small compass the results of vast human experience. The spirit of self-help is the root of all genuine growth in the individual; and, exhibited in the lives of many, it constitutes the true source of national vigour and strength. Help from without is often enfeebling in its effects, but help from within invariably invigorates. Whatever is done *for* men or classes, to a certain extent takes away the stimulus and necessity of doing for themselves; and where men are subjected to over-guidance and over-government, the inevitable tendency is to render them comparatively helpless.

Even the best institutions can give a man no active help. Perhaps the most they can do is, to leave him free to develop himself and improve his individual condition. But

B

in all times men have been prone to believe that their happiness and well-being were to be secured by means of institutions rather than by their own conduct. Hence the value of legislation as an agent in human advancement has usually been much over-estimated. To constitute the millionth part of a Legislature, by voting for one or two men once in three or five years, however conscientiously this duty may be performed, can exercise but little active influence upon any man's life and character. Moreover, it is every day becoming more clearly understood, that the function of Government is negative and restrictive, rather than positive and active; being resolvable principally into protection— protection of life, liberty, and property. Laws, wisely administered, will secure men in the enjoyment of the fruits of their labour, whether of mind or body, at a comparatively small personal sacrifice; but no laws, however stringent, can make the idle industrious, the thriftless provident, or the drunken sober. Such reforms can only be effected by means of individual action, economy, and self-denial; by better habits, rather than by greater rights.

The Government of a nation itself is usually found to be but the reflex of the individuals composing it. The Govern- ment that is ahead of the people will inevitably be dragged down to their level, as the Government that is behind them will in the long run be dragged up. In the order of nature, the collective character of a nation will as surely find its befitting results in its law and government, as water finds its own level. The noble people will be nobly ruled, and the ignorant and corrupt ignobly. Indeed all experience serves to prove that the worth and strength of a State depend far less upon the form of its institutions than upon the character of its men. For the nation is only an aggregate of indi- vidual conditions, and civilization itself is but a question of the personal improvement of the men, women, and children of whom society is composed.

National progress is the sum of individual industry, energy, and uprightness, as national decay is of individual idleness, selfishness, and vice. What we are accustomed to decry as great social evils, will, for the most part, be found to be but the outgrowth of man's own perverted life; and though we may endeavour to cut them down and extirpate them by means of Law, they will only spring up again with fresh luxuriance in some other form, unless the conditions of personal life and character are radically improved. If this view be correct, then it follows that the highest patriotism and philanthropy consist, not so much in altering laws and modifying institutions, as in helping and stimulating men to elevate and improve themselves by their own free and independent individual action.

It may be of comparatively little consequence how a man is governed from without, whilst everything depends upon how he governs himself from within. The greatest slave is not he who is ruled by a despot, great though that evil be, but he who is the thrall of his own moral ignorance, selfishness, and vice. Nations who are thus enslaved at heart cannot be freed by any mere changes of masters or of institutions; and so long as the fatal delusion prevails, that liberty solely depends upon and consists in government, so long will such changes, no matter at what cost they may be effected, have as little practical and lasting result as the shifting of the figures in a phantasmagoria. The solid foundations of liberty must rest upon individual character; which is also the only sure guarantee for social security and national progress. John Stuart Mill truly observes that " even despotism does not produce its worst effects so long as individuality exists under it ; and whatever crushes individuality *is* despotism, by whatever name it be called."

Old fallacies as to human progress are constantly turning up. Some call for Cæsars, others for Nationalities, and others for Acts of Parliament. We are to wait for Cæsars, and when they are found, " happy the people who recognise and follow them."* This doctrine shortly means, everything *for* the people, nothing *by* them,—a doctrine which, if taken as a guide, must, by destroying the free conscience of a community, speedily prepare the way for any form of despotism. Cæsarism is human idolatry in its worst form—a worship of mere power, as degrading in its effects as the worship of mere wealth would be. A far healthier doctrine to inculcate among the nations would be that of Self-Help; and so soon as it is thoroughly understood and carried into action, Cæsarism will be no more. The two principles are directly antagonistic; and what Victor Hugo said of the Pen and the Sword alike applies to them, " Ceci tuera cela." [*This will kill that.*]

The power of Nationalities and Acts of Parliament is also a prevalent superstition. What William Dargan, one of Ireland's truest patriots, said at the closing of the first Dublin Industrial Exhibition, may well be quoted now. " To tell the truth," he said, " I never heard the word independence mentioned that my own country and my own fellow townsmen did not occur to my mind. I have heard a great deal about the independence that we were to get from this, that, and the other place, and of the great expectations we were to have from persons from other countries coming amongst us. Whilst I value as much as any man the great advantages that must result to us from that intercourse, I have always been deeply impressed with the feeling that our industrial independence is dependent upon ourselves. I believe that with simple industry and careful exactness in the utilization of our energies, we never had a fairer chance nor a brighter prospect than the present. We have made a step, but perseverance is the great agent of success; and if we but go on zealously, I believe in my conscience that in a short period we shall arrive at a position of equal comfort, of equal happiness, and of equal independence, with that of any other people."

* Napoleon III., ' Life of Cæsar.'

All nations have been made what they are by the thinking and the working of many generations of men. Patient and persevering labourers in all ranks and conditions of life, cultivators of the soil and explorers of the mine, inventors and discoverers, manufacturers, mechanics and artisans, poets, philosophers, and politicians, all have contributed towards the grand result, one generation building upon another's labours, and carrying them forward to still higher stages. This constant succession of noble workers—the artisans of civilisation—has served to create order out of chaos in industry, science, and art; and the living race has thus, in the course of nature, become the inheritor of the rich estate provided by the skill and industry of our forefathers, which is placed in our hands to cultivate, and to hand down, not only unimpaired but improved, to our successors.

The spirit of self-help, as exhibited in the energetic action of individuals, has in all times been a marked feature in the English character, and furnishes the true measure of our power as a nation. Rising above the heads of the mass, there were always to be found a series of individuals distinguished beyond others, who commanded the public homage. But our progress has also been owing to multitudes of smaller and less known men. Though only the generals' names may be remembered in the history of any great campaign, it has been in a great measure through the individual valour and heroism of the privates that victories have been won. And life, too, is " a soldiers' battle,"—men in the ranks having in all times been amongst the greatest of workers. Many are the lives of men unwritten, which have nevertheless as powerfully influenced civilisation and progress as the more fortunate Great whose names are recorded in biography. Even the humblest person, who sets before his fellows an example of industry, sobriety, and upright honesty of purpose in life, has a present as well as a future influence upon the well-being of his country ; for his life and character pass unconsciously into the lives of others, and propagate good example for all time to come.

Daily experience shows that it is energetic individualism which produces the most powerful effects upon the life and action of others, and really constitutes the best practical education. Schools, academies, and colleges, give but the merest beginnings of culture in comparison with it. Far more influential is the life-education daily given in our homes, in the streets, behind counters, in workshops, at the loom and the plough, in counting-houses and manufactories, and in the busy haunts of men. This is that finishing instruction as members of society, which Schiller designated " the education of the human race," consisting in action, conduct, self-culture, self-control,—all that tends to discipline a man truly, and fit him for the proper performance of the duties and business of life,—a kind of education not to be learnt from books, or acquired by any amount of mere literary training. With his usual weight of words Bacon observes, that " Studies teach not their own use ; but that is a wisdom without them, and above them, won by observation ;" a remark that holds true of actual life, as well as of the cultivation of the intellect itself. For all experience serves to illustrate and enforce the lesson, that a man perfects himself by work more than by reading,—that it is life rather than literature, action rather than study, and character rather than biography, which tend perpetually to renovate mankind.

Biographies of great, but especially of good men, are nevertheless most instructive and useful, as helps, guides, and incentives to others. Some of the best are almost equivalent to gospels—teaching high living, high thinking, and energetic action for their own and the world's good. The valuable examples which they furnish of the power of self-help, of patient purpose, resolute working, and steadfast integrity, issuing in the formation of truly noble and manly character, exhibit in language not to be misunderstood, what it is in the power of each to accomplish for himself; and eloquently illustrate the efficacy of self-respect and self-reliance in enabling men of even the humblest rank to work out for themselves an honourable competency and a solid reputation.

Great men of science, literature, and art—apostles of great thoughts and lords of the great heart—have belonged to no exclusive class nor rank in life. They have come alike from colleges, workshops, and farmhouses,—from the huts of poor men and the mansions of the rich. Some of God's greatest apostles have come from " the ranks." The poorest have sometimes taken the highest places; nor have difficulties apparently the most insuperable proved obstacles in their way. Those very difficulties, in many instances, would even seem to have been their best helpers, by evoking their powers of labour and endurance, and stimulating into life faculties which might otherwise have lain dormant. The instances of obstacles thus surmounted, and of triumphs thus achieved, are indeed so numerous, as almost to justify the proverb that "with Will one can do anything." Take, for instance, the remarkable fact, that from the barber's shop came Jeremy Taylor, the most poetical of divines; Sir Richard Arkwright, the inventor of the spinning-jenny and founder of the cotton manufacture; Lord Tenterden, one of the most distinguished of Lord Chief Justices; and Turner, the greatest among landscape painters.

No one knows to a certainty what Shakespeare was; but it is unquestionable that he sprang from a humble rank. His father was a butcher and grazier; and Shakespeare himself is supposed to have been in early life a woolcomber; whilst others aver that he was an usher in a school, and afterwards a scrivener's clerk. He truly seems to have been "not one, but all mankind's epitome." For such is the accuracy of his sea phrases that a naval writer alleges that he must have been a sailor; whilst a clergyman infers, from internal evidence in his writings, that he was probably a parson's clerk; and a distinguished judge of horse-flesh insists that he must have been a horse-dealer. Shakespeare was certainly an actor, and in the course of his life "played many parts," gathering his wonderful stores of knowledge from a wide field of experience and observation. In any event, he must have been a close student and a hard worker; and to this day his writings continue to exercise a powerful influence on the formation of English character.

The common class of day labourers has given us Brindley the engineer, Cook the navigator, and Burns the poet. Masons and bricklayers can boast of Ben Jonson, who worked at the building of Lincoln's Inn, with a trowel in his hand and a book in his pocket, Edwards and Telford the engineers, Hugh Miller the geologist, and Allan Cunningham the writer and sculptor; whilst among distinguished carpenters we find the names of Inigo Jones the architect, Harrison the chronometer-maker, John Hunter the physiologist, Romney and Opie the painters, Professor Lee the Orientalist, and John Gibson the sculptor.

From the weaver class have sprung Simson the mathematician, Bacon the sculptor, the two Milners, Adam Walker, John Foster, Wilson the ornithologist, Dr. Livingstone the missionary traveller, and Tannahill the poet. Shoemakers have given us Sir Cloudesley Shovel the great Admiral, Sturgeon the electrician, Samuel Drew the essayist, Gifford the editor of the 'Quarterly Review,' Bloomfield the poet, and William Carey the missionary; whilst Morrison, another laborious missionary, was a maker of shoe-lasts. Within the last few years, a profound naturalist has been discovered in the person of a shoemaker at Banff, named Thomas Edwards, who, while maintaining himself by his trade, has devoted his leisure to the study of natural science in all its branches, his researches in connexion with the smaller crustaceæ having been rewarded by the discovery of a new species, to which the name of " Praniza Edwardsii " has been given by naturalists.

Nor have tailors been undistinguished. John Stow, the historian, worked at the trade during some part of his life. Jackson, the painter, made clothes until he reached manhood. The brave Sir John Hawkswood, who so greatly distinguished himself at Poictiers, and was knighted by Edward III. for his valour, was in early life apprenticed to a London tailor. Admiral Hobson, who broke the boom at Vigo in 1702, belonged to the same calling. He was working as a tailor's apprentice near Bonchurch, in the Isle of Wight, when the news flew through the village that a squadron of men-of-war was sailing off the island. He sprang from the shopboard, and ran down with his comrades to the beach, to gaze upon the glorious sight. The boy was suddenly inflamed with the ambition to be a sailor; and springing into a boat, he rowed off to the squadron, gained the admiral's ship, and was accepted as a volunteer. Years after, he returned to his native village full of honours, and dined off bacon and eggs in the cottage where he had worked as an apprentice. But the greatest tailor of all is unquestionably Andrew Johnson, the present President of the United States—a man of extraordinary force of character and vigour of intellect. In his great speech at Washington, when describing himself as having begun his political career as an alderman, and run through all the branches of the legislature, a voice in the crowd cried, "From a tailor up." It was characteristic of Johnson to take the intended sarcasm in good part, and even to turn it to account. "Some gentleman says I have been a tailor. That does not disconcert me in the least; for when I was a tailor I had the reputation of being a good one, and making close fits; I was always punctual with my customers, and always did good work."

Cardinal Wolsey, De Foe, Akenside, and Kirke White were the sons of butchers; Bunyan was a tinker, and Joseph Lancaster a basket-maker. Among the great names identified with the invention of the steam-engine are those of Newcomen, Watt, and Stephenson; the first a blacksmith, the second a maker of mathematical instruments, and the third an engine-fireman. Huntingdon the preacher was originally a coalheaver, and Bewick, the father of wood-engraving, a coalminer. Dodsley was a footman, and Holcroft a groom. Baffin the navigator began his seafaring career as a man before the mast, and Sir Cloudesley Shovel as a cabin-boy. Herschel played the oboe in a military band. Chantrey was a journeyman carver, Etty a journeyman printer, and Sir Thomas Lawrence the son of a tavern-keeper. Michael Faraday, the son of a blacksmith, was in early life apprenticed to a bookbinder, and worked at that trade until he reached his twenty-second year: he now occupies the very first rank as a philosopher, excelling even his master, Sir Humphry Davy, in the art of lucidly expounding the most difficult and abstruse points in natural science.

Among those who have given the greatest impulse to the sublime science of astronomy, we find Copernicus, the son of a Polish baker; Kepler, the son of a German public-house keeper, and himself the "garçon de cabaret;" d'Alembert, a foundling picked up one winter's night on the steps of the church of St. Jean le Rond at Paris, and brought up by the wife of a glazier; and Newton and Laplace, the one the son of a small freeholder near Grantham, the other the son of a poor peasant of Beaumont-en-Auge, near Honfleur. Notwithstanding their comparatively adverse circumstances in early life, these distinguished men achieved a solid and enduring reputation by the exercise of their genius, which all the wealth in the world could not have purchased. The very possession of wealth might indeed have proved an obstacle greater even than the humble means to which they were born.   The father of Lagrange, the astronomer and mathematician, held the office of Treasurer of War at Turin ; but having ruined himself by speculations, his family were reduced to comparative poverty.   To this circumstance Lagrange was in after life accustomed partly to attribute his own fame and happiness.   " Had I been rich," said he, " I should probably not have become a mathematician."

The sons of clergymen and ministers of religion generally, have particularly distinguished themselves in our country's history.   Amongst them we find the names of Drake and Nelson, celebrated in naval heroism ; of Wollaston, Young, Playfair, and Bell, in science ; of Wren, Reynolds, Wilson, and Wilkie, in art ; of Thurlow and Campbell, in law ; and of Addison, Thomson, Goldsmith, Coleridge, and Tennyson, in literature.   Lord Hardinge, Colonel Edwardes, and Major Hodson, so honourably known in Indian warfare, were also the sons of clergymen.   Indeed, the empire of England in India was won and held chiefly by men of the middle class—such as Clive, Warren Hastings, and their successors—men for the most part bred in factories and trained to habits of business.

Among the sons of attorneys we find Edmund Burke, Smeaton the engineer, Scott and Wordsworth, and Lords Somers, Hardwick, and Dunning.   Sir William Blackstone was the posthumous son of a silk-mercer.   Lord Gifford's father was a grocer at Dover ; Lord Denman's a physician ; Judge Talfourd's a country brewer; and Lord Chief Baron Pollock's a celebrated saddler at Charing Cross. Layard, the discoverer of the monuments of Nineveh, was an articled clerk in a London solicitor's office; and Sir William Armstrong, the inventor of hydraulic machinery and of the Armstrong ordnance, was also trained to the law and practised for some time as an attorney.   Milton was the son of a London scrivener, and Pope and Southey were

the sons of linendrapers. Professor Wilson was the son of
a Paisley manufacturer, and Lord Macaulay of an African
merchant. Keats was a druggist, and Sir Humphry Davy a
country apothecary's apprentice. Speaking of himself, Davy
once said, "What I am I have made myself: I say this
without vanity, and in pure simplicity of heart." Richard
Owen, the Newton of Natural History, began life as a
midshipman, and did not enter upon the line of scientific
research in which he has since become so distinguished,
until comparatively late in life. He laid the foundations of
his great knowledge while occupied in cataloguing the magnificent museum accumulated by the industry of John
Hunter, a work which occupied him at the College of Surgeons during a period of about ten years.

Foreign not less than English biography abounds in
illustrations of men who have glorified the lot of poverty by
their labours and their genius. In Art we find Claude, the
son of a pastrycook; Geefs, of a baker; Leopold Robert,
of a watchmaker; and Haydn, of a wheelwright; whilst
Daguerre was a scene-painter at the Opera. The father of
Gregory VII. was a carpenter; of Sextus V., a shepherd;
and of Adrian VI., a poor bargeman. When a boy, Adrian,
unable to pay for a light by which to study, was accustomed
to prepare his lessons by the light of the lamps in the streets
and the church porches, exhibiting a degree of patience and
industry which were the certain forerunners of his future
distinction. Of like humble origin were Hauy, the mineral-
ogist, who was the son of a weaver of Saint-Just; Haute-
feuille, the mechanician, of a baker at Orleans; Joseph
Fourier, the mathematician, of a tailor at Auxerre; Durand,
the architect, of a Paris shoemaker; and Gesner, the naturalist, of a skinner or worker in hides, at Zurich. This last
began his career under all the disadvantages attendant on
poverty, sickness, and domestic calamity; none of which,
however, were sufficient to damp his courage or hinder his

progress. His life was indeed an eminent illustration of the truth of the saying, that those who have most to do and are willing to work, will find the most time. Pierre Ramus was another man of like character. He was the son of poor parents in Picardy, and when a boy was employed to tend sheep. But not liking the occupation he ran away to Paris. After encountering much misery, he succeeded in entering the College of Navarre as a servant. The situation, however, opened for him the road to learning, and he shortly became one of the most distinguished men of his time.

The chemist Vauquelin was the son of a peasant of Saint-André-d'Herbetot, in the Calvados. When a boy at school, though poorly clad, he was full of bright intelligence; and the master, who taught him to read and write, when praising him for his diligence, used to say, " Go on, my boy; work, study, Colin, and one day you will go as well dressed as the parish churchwarden!" A country apothecary who visited the school, admired the robust boy's arms, and offered to take him into his laboratory to pound his drugs, to which Vauquelin assented, in the hope of being able to continue his lessons. But the apothecary would not permit him to spend any part of his time in learning; and on ascertaining this, the youth immediately determined to quit his service. He therefore left Saint-André and took the road for Paris with his havresac on his back. Arrived there, he searched for a place as apothecary's boy, but could not find one. Worn out by fatigue and destitution, Vauquelin fell ill, and in that state was taken to the hospital, where he thought he should die. But better things were in store for the poor boy. He recovered, and again proceeded in his search of employment, which he at length found with an apothecary. Shortly after, he became known to Fourcroy the eminent chemist, who was so pleased with the youth that he made him his private secretary; and many years after, on the death of that great philosopher, Vauquelin succeeded him as Professor of Chemistry. Finally, in 1829, the electors of the district of Calvados appointed him their representative in the Chamber of Deputies, and he re-entered in triumph the village which he had left so many years before, so poor and so obscure.

England has no parallel instances to show, of promotions from the ranks of the army to the highest military offices, which have been so common in France since the first Revolution. " La carrière ouverte aux talents " has there received many striking illustrations, which would doubtless be matched among ourselves were the road to promotion as open. Hoche, Humbert, and Pichegru, began their respective careers as private soldiers. Hoche, while in the King's army, was accustomed to embroider waistcoats to enable him to earn money wherewith to purchase books on military science. Humbert was a scapegrace when a youth ; at sixteen he ran away from home, and was by turns servant to a tradesman at Nancy, a workman at Lyons, and a hawker of rabbit skins. In 1792, he enlisted as a volunteer ; and in a year he was general of brigade. Kleber, Lefèvre, Suchet, Victor, Lannes, Soult, Massena, St. Cyr, D'Erlon, Murat, Augereau, Bessières, and Ney, all rose from the ranks. In some cases promotion was rapid, in others it was slow. Saint Cyr, the son of a tanner of Toul, began life as an actor, after which he enlisted in the Chasseurs, and was promoted to a captaincy within a year. Victor, Duc de Belluno, enlisted in the Artillery in 1781 : during the events preceding the Revolution he was discharged ; but immediately on the outbreak of war he re-enlisted, and in the course of a few months his intrepidity and ability secured his promotion as Adjutant-Major and chief of batallion. Murat, " le beau sabreur," was the son of a village innkeeper in Perigord, where he looked after the horses. He first enlisted in a regiment of Chasseurs, from which he was dismissed for insubordination ; but again enlisting, he shortly rose to the rank of Colonel. Ney enlisted at eighteen in a hussar regiment, and gradually advanced step by step: Kleber soon discovered his merits, surnaming him "The Indefatigable," and promoted him to be Adjutant-General when only twenty-five. On the other hand, Soult * was six years from the date of his enlistment before he reached the rank of sergeant. But Soult's advancement was rapid compared with that of Massena, who served for fourteen years before he was made sergeant ; and though he afterwards rose successively, step by step, to the grades of Colonel, General of Division, and Marshal, he declared that the post of sergeant was the step which of all others had cost him the most labour to win. Similar promotions from the ranks, in the French army, have continued down to our own day. Changarnier entered the King's bodyguard as a private in 1815. Marshal Bugeaud served four years in the ranks, after which he was made an officer. Marshal Randon, the present French Minister of War, began his military career as a drummer boy ; and in the portrait of him in the gallery at Versailles, his hand rests upon a drum-head, the picture being thus painted at his own request. Instances such as these inspire French soldiers with enthusiasm for their service, as each private feels that he may possibly carry the baton of a marshal in his knapsack.

The instances of men, in this and other countries, who, by dint of persevering application and energy, have raised themselves from the humblest ranks of industry to eminent positions of usefulness and influence in society, are indeed so numerous that they have long ceased to be regarded as exceptional. Looking at some of the more remarkable, it

---

* Soult received but little education in his youth, and learnt next to no geography until he became foreign minister of France, when the study of this branch of knowledge is said to have given him the greatest pleasure.—' Œuvres, &c., d'Alexis de Tocqueville. Par G. de Beaumont.' Paris, 1861. I. 52.

might almost be said that early encounter with difficulty and adverse circumstances was the necessary and indispensable condition of success. The British House of Commons has always contained a considerable number of such self-raised men—fitting representatives of the industrial character of the people; and it is to the credit of our Legislature that they have been welcomed and honoured there. When the late Joseph Brotherton, member for Salford, in the course of the discussion on the Ten Hours Bill, detailed with true pathos the hardships and fatigues to which he had been subjected when working as a factory boy in a cotton mill, and described the resolution which he had then formed, that if ever it was in his power he would endeavour to ameliorate the condition of that class, Sir James Graham rose immediately after him, and declared, amidst the cheers of the House, that he did not before know that Mr. Brotherton's origin had been so humble, but that it rendered him more proud than he had ever before been of the House of Commons, to think that a person risen from that condition should be able to sit side by side, on equal terms, with the hereditary gentry of the land.

The late Mr. Fox, member for Oldham, was accustomed to introduce his recollections of past times with the words, " when I was working as a weaver boy at Norwich;" and there are other members of parliament, still living, whose origin has been equally humble. Mr. Lindsay, the well-known ship owner, until recently member for Sunderland, once told the simple story of his life to the electors of Weymouth, in answer to an attack made upon him by his political opponents. He had been left an orphan at fourteen, and when he left Glasgow for Liverpool to push his way in the world, not being able to pay the usual fare, the captain of the steamer agreed to take his labour in exchange, and the boy worked his passage by trimming the coals in the coal hole. At Liverpool he remained for seven weeks before he could obtain employment, during which time he lived in sheds and fared hardly; until at last he found shelter on board a West Indiaman. He entered as a boy, and before he was nineteen, by steady good conduct he had risen to the command of a ship. At twenty-three he retired from the sea, and settled on shore, after which his progress was rapid : " he had prospered," he said, " by steady industry, by constant work, and by ever keeping in view the great principle of doing to others as you would be done by."

The career of Mr. William Jackson, of Birkenhead, the present member for North Derbyshire, bears considerable resemblance to that of Mr. Lindsay. His father, a surgeon at Lancaster, died, leaving a family of eleven children, of whom William Jackson was the seventh son. The elder boys had been well educated while the father lived, but at his death the younger members had to shift for themselves. William, when under twelve years old, was taken from school, and put to hard work at a ship's side from six in the morning till nine at night. His master falling ill, the boy was taken into the counting-house, where he had more leisure. This gave him an opportunity of reading, and having obtained access to a set of the ' Encyclopædia Britannica,' he read the volumes through from A to Z, partly by day, but chiefly at night. He afterwards put himself to a trade, was diligent, and succeeded in it. Now he has ships sailing on almost every sea, and holds commercial relations with nearly every country on the globe.

Among like men of the same class may be ranked the late Richard Cobden, whose start in life was equally humble. The son of a small farmer at Midhurst in Sussex, he was sent at an early age to London and employed as a boy in a warehouse in the City. He was diligent, well conducted, and eager for information. His master, a man of the old school, warned him against too much reading;

but the boy went on in his own course, storing his mind with the wealth found in books. He was promoted from one position of trust to another—became a traveller for his house—secured a large connection, and eventually started in business as a calico printer at Manchester. Taking an interest in public questions, more especially in popular education, his attention was gradually drawn to the subject of the Corn Laws, to the repeal of which he may be said to have devoted his fortune and his life. It may be mentioned as a curious fact that the first speech he delivered in public was a total failure. But he had great perseverance, application, and energy; and with persistency and practice, he became at length one of the most persuasive and effective of public speakers, extorting the disinterested eulogy of even Sir Robert Peel himself. M. Drouyn de Lhuys, the French Ambassador, has eloquently said of Mr. Cobden, that he was " a living proof of what merit, perseverance, and labour can accomplish; one of the most complete examples of those men who, sprung from the humblest ranks of society, raise themselves to the highest rank in public estimation by the effect of their own worth and of their personal services; finally, one of the rarest examples of the solid qualities inherent in the English character."

In all these cases, strenuous individual application was the price paid for distinction; excellence of any sort being invariably placed beyond the reach of indolence. It is the diligent hand and head alone that maketh rich—in self-culture, growth in wisdom, and in business. Even when men are born to wealth and high social position, any solid reputation which they may individually achieve can only be attained by energetic application; for though an inheritance of acres may be bequeathed, an inheritance of knowledge and wisdom cannot. The wealthy man may pay others for doing his work for him, but it is impossible to get his thinking done for him by another, or to purchase any kind of self-

culture. Indeed, the doctrine that excellence in any pursuit
is only to be achieved by laborious application, holds as true
in the case of the man of wealth as in that of Drew and
Gifford, whose only school was a cobbler's stall, or Hugh
Miller, whose only college was a Cromarty stone quarry.

Riches and ease, it is perfectly clear, are not necessary
for man's highest culture, else had not the world been so
largely indebted in all times to those who have sprung from
the humbler ranks. An easy and luxurious existence does
not train men to effort or encounter with difficulty; nor
does it awaken that consciousness of power which is so
necessary for energetic and effective action in life. Indeed,
so far from poverty being a misfortune, it may, by vigorous
self-help, be converted even into a blessing; rousing a man
to that struggle with the world in which, though some may
purchase ease by degradation, the right-minded and true-
hearted find strength, confidence, and triumph. Bacon
says, " Men seem neither to understand their riches nor
their strength : of the former they believe greater things
than they should; of the latter much less. Self-reliance
and self-denial will teach a man to drink out of his own
cistern, and eat his own sweet bread, and to learn and labour
truly to get his living, and carefully to expend the good
things committed to his trust."

Riches are so great a temptation to ease and self-indulgence, to which men are by nature prone, that the glory is all
the greater of those who, born to ample fortunes, nevertheless
take an active part in the work of their generation—who
" scorn delights and live laborious days." It is to the
honour of the wealthier ranks in this country that they are
not idlers; for they do their fair share of the work of the
state, and usually take more than their fair share of its ·
dangers. It was a fine thing said of a subaltern officer in
the Peninsular campaigns, observed trudging alone through
mud and mire by the side of his regiment, " There goes

15,000*l.* a-year!" and in our own day, the bleak slopes of Sebastopol and the burning soil of India have borne witness to the like noble self-denial and devotion on the part of our gentler classes; many a gallant and noble fellow, of rank and estate, having risked his life, or lost it, in one or other of those fields of action, in the service of his country.

Nor have the wealthier classes been undistinguished in the more peaceful pursuits of philosophy and science. Take, for instance, the great names of Bacon, the father of modern philosophy, and of Worcester, Boyle, Cavendish, Talbot, and Rosse, in science. The last named may be regarded as the great mechanic of the peerage; a man who, if he had not been born a peer, would probably have taken the highest rank as an inventor. So thorough is his knowledge of smith-work that he is said to have been pressed on one occasion to accept the foremanship of a large workshop, by a manufacturer to whom his rank was unknown. The great Rosse telescope, of his own fabrication, is certainly the most extraordinary instrument of the kind that has yet been constructed.

But it is principally in the departments of politics and literature that we find the most energetic labourers amongst our higher classes. Success in these lines of action, as in all others, can only be achieved through industry, practice, and study; and the great Minister, or parliamentary leader, must necessarily be amongst the very hardest of workers. Such was Palmerston; and such are Derby and Russell, Disraeli and Gladstone. These men have had the benefit of no Ten Hours Bill, but have often, during the busy season of Parliament, worked "double shift," almost day and night. One of the most illustrious of such workers in modern times was unquestionably the late Sir Robert Peel. He possessed in an extraordinary degree the power of continuous intellectual labour, nor did he spare himself. His career, indeed, presented a remarkable example of how much a man of comparatively moderate powers can accomplish by means of assiduous application and indefatigable industry. During the forty years that he held a seat in Parliament, his labours were prodigious. He was a most conscientious man, and whatever he undertook to do, he did thoroughly. All his speeches bear evidence of his careful study of everything that had been spoken or written on the subject under consideration. He was elaborate almost to excess; and spared no pains to adapt himself to the various capacities of his audience. Withal, he possessed much practical sagacity, great strength of purpose, and power to direct the issues of action with steady hand and eye. In one respect he surpassed most men : his principles broadened and enlarged with time ; and age, instead of contracting, only served to mellow and ripen his nature. To the last he continued open to the reception of new views, and, though many thought him cautious to excess, he did not allow himself to fall into that indiscriminating admiration of the past, which is the palsy of many minds similarly educated, and renders the old age of many nothing but a pity.

The indefatigable industry of Lord Brougham has become almost proverbial. His public labours have extended over a period of upwards of sixty years, during which he has ranged over many fields—of law, literature, politics, and science,—and achieved distinction in them all. How he contrived it, has been to many a mystery. Once, when Sir Samuel Romilly was requested to undertake some new work, he excused himself by saying that he had no time ; "but," he added, " go with it to that fellow Brougham, he seems to have time for everything." The secret of it was, that he never left a minute unemployed ; withal he possessed a constitution of iron. When arrived at an age at which most men would have retired from the world to enjoy their hard-earned leisure, perhaps to doze away their time in an easy chair, Lord Brougham commenced and prosecuted a series of elaborate investigations as to the laws of Light, and he

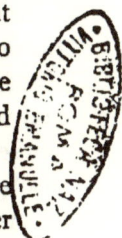

submitted the results to the most scientific audiences that Paris and London could muster. About the same time, he was passing through the press his admirable sketches of the ' Men of Science and Literature of the Reign of George III.,' and taking his full share of the law business and the political discussions in the House of Lords. Sydney Smith once recommended him to confine himself to only the transaction of so much business as three strong men could get through. But such was Brougham's love of work—long become a habit—that no amount of application seems to have been too great for him ; and such was his love of excellence, that it has been said of him that if his station in life had been only that of a shoe-black, he would never have rested satisfied until he had become the best shoe-black in England.

Another hard-working man of the same class is Sir E. Bulwer Lytton. Few writers have done more, or achieved higher distinction in various walks — as a novelist, poet, dramatist, historian, essayist, orator, and politician. He has worked his way step by step, disdainful of ease, and animated throughout by the ardent desire to excel. On the score of mere industry, there are few living English writers who have written so much, and none that have produced so much of high quality. The industry of Bulwer is entitled to all the greater praise that it has been entirely self-imposed. To hunt, and shoot, and live at ease,—to frequent the clubs and enjoy the opera, with the variety of London visiting and sight-seeing during the "season," and then off to the country mansion, with its well-stocked preserves, and its thousand delightful out-door pleasures,—to travel abroad, to Paris, Vienna, or Rome,—all this is excessively attractive to a lover of pleasure and a man of fortune, and by no means calculated to make him voluntarily undertake continuous labour of any kind. Yet these pleasures, all within his reach, Bulwer must, as compared with men born to similar estate, have denied himself in assuming the position and pursuing the career of a literary man. Like Byron, his first effort was poetical ('Weeds and Wild Flowers'), and a failure. His second was a novel ('Falkland'), and it proved a failure too. A man of weaker nerve would have dropped authorship; but Bulwer had pluck and perseverance; and he worked on, determined to succeed. He was incessantly industrious, read extensively, and from failure went courageously onwards to success. 'Pelham' followed 'Falkland' within a year, and the remainder of Bulwer's literary life, now extending over a period of thirty years, has been a succession of triumphs.

Mr. Disraeli affords a similar instance of the power of industry and application in working out an eminent public career. His first achievements were, like Bulwer's, in literature; and he reached success only through a succession of failures. His 'Wondrous Tale of Alroy' and 'Revolutionary Epic' were laughed at, and regarded as indications of literary lunacy. But he worked on in other directions, and his 'Coningsby,' 'Sybil,' and 'Tancred,' proved the sterling stuff of which he was made. As an orator too, his first appearance in the House of Commons was a failure. It was spoken of as "more screaming than an Adelphi farce." Though composed in a grand and ambitious strain, every sentence was hailed with "loud laughter." 'Hamlet' played as a comedy were nothing to it. But he concluded with a sentence which embodied a prophecy. Writhing under the laughter with which his studied eloquence had been received, he exclaimed, "I have begun several times many things, and have succeeded in them at last. I shall sit down now, but the time will come when you will hear me." The time did come; and how Disraeli succeeded in at length commanding the attention of the first assembly of gentlemen in the world, affords a striking illustration of what energy and determination will do; for Disraeli earned his position by dint of patient industry. He did not, as many young men do, having once failed, retire dejected, to mope and whine in a corner, but diligently set himself to work. He carefully unlearnt his faults, studied the character of his audience, practised sedulously the art of speech, and industriously filled his mind with the elements of parliamentary knowledge. He worked patiently for success ; and it came, out slowly : then the House laughed with him, instead of at him. The recollection of his early failure was effaced, and by general consent he was at length admitted to be one of the most finished and effective of parliamentary speakers.

Although much may be accomplished by means of individual industry and energy, as these and other instances set forth in the following pages serve to illustrate, it must at the same time be acknowledged that the help which we derive from others in the journey of life is of very great importance. The poet Wordsworth has well said that "these two things, contradictory though they may seem, must go together—manly dependence and manly independence, manly reliance and manly self-reliance." From infancy to old age, all are more or less indebted to others for nurture and culture ; and the best and strongest are usually found the readiest to acknowledge such help. Take, for example, the career of the late Alexis de Tocqueville, a man doubly well-born, for his father was a distinguished peer of France, and his mother a granddaughter of Malesherbes. Through powerful family influence, he was appointed Judge Auditor at Versailles when only twenty-one ; but probably feeling that he had not fairly won the position by merit, he determined to give it up and owe his future advancement in life to himself alone. "A foolish resolution," some will say; but De Tocqueville bravely acted it out. He resigned his appointment, and made arrangements to leave France for the purpose of travelling through the United States, the results of which were published in his great book on ' Democracy in America.' His friend and travelling companion, Gustave de Beaumont,

has described his indefatigable industry during this journey.
" His nature," he says, " was wholly averse to idleness, and
whether he was travelling or resting, his mind was always at
work. . . . With Alexis, the most agreeable conversation
was that which was the most useful. The worst day was
the lost day, or the day ill spent; the least loss of time
annoyed him." Tocqueville himself wrote to a friend—
" There is no time of life at which one can wholly cease
from action; for effort without one's self, and still more
effort within, is equally necessary, if not more so, when we
grow old, as it is in youth. I compare man in this world
to a traveller journeying without ceasing towards a colder
and colder region; the higher he goes, the faster he ought
to walk. The great malady of the soul is cold. And in
resisting this formidable evil, one needs not only to be
sustained by the action of a mind employed, but also by
contact with one's fellows in the business of life." *

Notwithstanding de Tocqueville's decided views as to the
necessity of exercising individual energy and self-dependence,
no one could be more ready than he was to recognise the
value of that help and support for which all men are indebted to others in a greater or less degree. Thus, he
often acknowledged, with gratitude, his obligations to his
friends De Kergorlay and Stofells,—to the former for intellectual assistance, and to the latter for moral support and
sympathy. To De Kergorlay he wrote—" Thine is the
only soul in which I have confidence, and whose influence
exercises a genuine effect upon my own. Many others have
influence upon the details of my actions, but no one has so
much influence as thou on the origination of fundamental
ideas, and of those principles which are the rule of conduct." De Tocqueville was not less ready to confess the

* ' Œuvres et Correspondance inédite d'Alexis de Tocqueville.   Par
Gustave de Beaumont.'   I. 398.

great obligations which he owed to his wife, Marie, for
the preservation of that temper and frame of mind which
enabled him to prosecute his studies with success.   He
believed that a noble-minded woman insensibly elevated the
character of her husband, while one of a grovelling nature
as certainly tended to degrade it.*

In fine, human character is moulded by a thousand subtle
influences; by example and precept; by life and literature;
by friends and neighbours; by the world we live in as well
as by the spirits of our forefathers, whose legacy of good
words and deeds we inherit.   But great, unquestionably,
though these influences are acknowledged to be, it is nevertheless equally clear that men must necessarily be the active
agents of their own well-being and well-doing; and that,
however much the wise and the good may owe to others,
they themselves must in the very nature of things be their
own best helpers.

* "I have seen," said he, "a hundred times in the course of my life,
a weak man exhibit genuine public virtue, because supported by a wife
who sustained him in his course, not so much by advising him to such and
such acts, as by exercising a strengthening influence over the manner
in which duty or even ambition was to be regarded.   Much oftener,
however, it must be confessed, have I seen private and domestic life
gradually transform a man to whom nature had given generosity, disinterestedness, and even some capacity for greatness, into an ambitious,
mean-spirited, vulgar, and selfish creature who, in matters relating to
his country, ended by considering them only in so far as they rendered
his own particular condition more comfortable and easy."—' Œuvres
de Tocqueville.'   II. 349.

CHAPTER II.

LEADERS OF INDUSTRY—INVENTORS AND PRODUCERS.

" Le travail et la Science sont désormais les maîtres du monde."—*De Salvandy.*
" Deduct all that men of the humbler classes have done for England in the way of inventions only, and see where she would have been but for them."—*Arthur Helps.*

O N E of the most strongly-marked features of the English people is their spirit of industry, standing out prominent and distinct in their past history, and as strikingly characteristic of them now as at any former period. It is this spirit, displayed by the commons of England, which has laid the foundations and built up the industrial greatness of the empire. This vigorous growth of the nation has been mainly the result of the free energy of individuals, and it has been contingent upon the number of hands and minds from time to time actively employed within it, whether as cultivators of the soil, producers of articles of utility, contrivers of tools and machines, writers of books, or creators of works of art. And while this spirit of active industry has been the vital principle of the nation, it has also been its saving and remedial one, counteracting from time to time the effects of errors in our laws and imperfections in our constitution.

— The career of industry which the nation has pursued, has also proved its best education. As steady application to work is the healthiest training for every individual, so is it the best discipline of a state. Honourable industry travels the same road with duty; and Providence has closely linked both with happiness. The gods, says the poet, have placed labour and toil on the way leading to the Elysian fields. Certain it is that no bread eaten by man is so sweet as that earned by his own labour, whether bodily or mental. By labour the earth has been subdued, and man redeemed from barbarism; nor has a single step in civilization been made without it. Labour is not only a necessity and a duty, but a blessing : only the idler feels it to be a curse. The duty of work is written on the thews and muscles of the limbs, the mechanism of the hand, the nerves and lobes of the brain—the sum of whose healthy action is satisfaction and enjoyment. In the school of labour is taught the best practical wisdom ; nor is a life of manual employment, as we shall hereafter find, incompatible with high mental culture.

Hugh Miller, than whom none knew better the strength and the weakness belonging to the lot of labour, stated the result of his experience to be, that Work, even the hardest, is full of pleasure and materials for self-improvement. He held honest labour to be the best of teachers, and that the school of toil is the noblest of schools—save only the Christian one,—that it is a school in which the ability of being useful is imparted, the spirit of independence learnt, and the habit of persevering effort acquired. He was even of opinion that the training of the mechanic,—by the exercise which it gives to his observant faculties, from his daily dealing with things actual and practical, and the close experience of life which he acquires,—better fits him for picking his way along the journey of life, and is more favourable to his growth as a Man, emphatically speaking, than the training afforded by any other condition.

The array of great names which we have already cursorily cited, of men springing from the ranks of the industrial classes, who have achieved distinction in various walks of life—in science, commerce, literature, and art—shows that at all events the difficulties interposed by poverty and labour are not insurmountable. As respects the great contrivances and inventions which have conferred so much power and wealth upon the nation, it is unquestionable that for the greater part of them we have been indebted to men of the humblest rank. Deduct what they have done in this particular line of action, and it will be found that very little indeed remains for other men to have accomplished.

Inventors have set in motion some of the greatest industries of the world. To them society owes many of its chief necessaries, comforts, and luxuries; and by their genius and labour daily life has been rendered in all respects more easy as well as enjoyable. Our food, our clothing, the furniture of our homes, the glass which admits the light to our dwellings at the same time that it excludes the cold, the gas which illuminates our streets, our means of locomotion by land and by sea, the tools by which our various articles of necessity and luxury are fabricated, have been the result of the labour and ingenuity of many men and many minds. Mankind at large are all the happier for such inventions, and are every day reaping the benefit of them in an increase of individual well-being as well as of public enjoyment.

Though the invention of the working steam-engine—the king of machines—belongs, comparatively speaking, to our own epoch, the idea of it was born many centuries ago. Like other contrivances and discoveries, it was effected step by step—one man transmitting the result of his labours, at the time apparently useless, to his successors, who took it up and carried it forward another stage,—the prosecution of the inquiry extending over many generations. Thus the idea promulgated by Hero of Alexandria was never altogether lost; but, like the grain of wheat hid in the hand of the Egyptian mummy, it sprouted and again grew vigorously when brought into the full light of modern science. The steam-engine was nothing, however, until it emerged from the state of theory, and was taken in hand by practical mechanics; and what a noble story of patient, laborious investigation, of difficulties encountered and overcome by heroic industry, does not that marvellous machine tell of! It is indeed, in itself, a monument of the power of self-help in man. Grouped around it we find Savary, the military engineer; Newcomen, the Dartmouth blacksmith; Cawley, the glazier; Potter, the engine-boy; Smeaton, the civil engineer; and, towering above all, the laborious, patient, never-tiring James Watt, the mathematical-instrument maker.

Watt was one of the most industrious of men; and the story of his life proves, what all experience confirms, that it is not the man of the greatest natural vigour and capacity who achieves the highest results, but he who employs his powers with the greatest industry and the most carefully disciplined skill—the skill that comes by labour, application, and experience. Many men in his time knew far more than Watt, but none laboured so assiduously as he did to turn all that he did know to useful practical purposes. He was, above all things, most persevering in the pursuit of facts. He cultivated carefully that habit of active attention on which all the higher working qualities of the mind mainly depend. Indeed, Mr. Edgeworth entertained the opinion, that the difference of intellect in men depends more upon the early cultivation of this *habit of attention*, than upon any great disparity between the powers of one individual and another.

Even when a boy, Watt found science in his toys. The quadrants lying about his father's carpenter's shop led him to the study of optics and astronomy; his ill health induced him to pry into the secrets of physiology; and his solitary walks through the country attracted him to the study of botany and history. While carrying on the business of a mathematical-instrument maker, he received an order to build an organ ; and, though without an ear for music, he undertook the study of harmonics, and successfully constructed the instrument. And, in like manner, when the little model of Newcomen's steam-engine, belonging to the University of Glasgow, was placed in his hands to repair, he forthwith set himself to learn all that was then known about heat, evaporation, and condensation,—at the same time plodding his way in mechanics and the science of construction,—the results of which he at length embodied in his condensing steam-engine.

For ten years he went on contriving and inventing—with little hope to cheer him, and with few friends to encourage him. He went on, meanwhile, earning bread for his family by making and selling quadrants, making and mending fiddles, flutes, and musical instruments ; measuring mason-work, surveying roads, superintending the construction of canals, or doing anything that turned up, and offered a prospect of honest gain. At length, Watt found a fit partner in another eminent leader of industry—Matthew Boulton, of Birmingham ; a skilful, energetic, and far-seeing man, who vigorously undertook the enterprise of introducing the condensing-engine into general use as a working power; and the success of both is now matter of history.*

Many skilful inventors have from time to time added new power to the steam-engine ; and, by numerous modifications, rendered it capable of being applied to nearly all the purposes of manufacture—driving machinery, impelling ships, grinding corn, printing books, stamping money, hammering, planing, and turning iron; in short, of performing every description of mechanical labour where power is required. One of the most useful modifications in the engine was that

---

* Since the original publication of this book, the author has in another work, ' The Lives of Boulton and Watt,' endeavoured to portray in greater detail the character and achievements of these two remarkable men.

devised by Trevithick, and eventually perfected by George
Stephenson and his son, in the form of the railway locomotive, by which social changes of immense importance have
been brought about, of even greater consequence, considered in their results on human progress and civilization,
than the condensing-engine of Watt.

One of the first grand results of Watt's invention,—which
placed an almost unlimited power at the command of the
producing classes,—was the establishment of the cotton-
manufacture. The person most closely identified with the
foundation of this great branch of industry was unquestionably Sir Richard Arkwright, whose practical energy and
sagacity were perhaps even more remarkable than his mechanical inventiveness. His originality as an inventor has
indeed been called in question, like that of Watt and
Stephenson. Arkwright probably stood in the same relation
to the spinning-machine that Watt did to the steam-engine
and Stephenson to the locomotive. He gathered together
the scattered threads of ingenuity which already existed, and
wove them, after his own design, into a new and original
fabric. Though Lewis Paul, of Birmingham, patented the
invention of spinning by rollers thirty years before Arkwright,
the machines constructed by him were so imperfect in their
details, that they could not be profitably worked, and the
invention was practically a failure. Another obscure mechanic, a reed-maker of Leigh, named Thomas Highs, is
also said to have invented the water-frame and spinning-
jenny; but they, too, proved unsuccessful.

When the demands of industry are found to press upon
the resources of inventors, the same idea is usually found
floating about in many minds ;—such has been the case with
the steam-engine, the safety-lamp, the electric telegraph, and
other inventions. Many ingenious minds are found labouring
in the throes of invention, until at length the master mind, the
strong practical man, steps forward, and straightway delivers

them of their idea, applies the principle successfully, and the thing is done. Then there is a loud outcry among all the smaller contrivers, who see themselves distanced in the race; and hence men such as Watt, Stephenson, and Arkwright, have usually to defend their reputation and their rights as practical and successful inventors.

Richard Arkwright, like most of our great mechanicians, sprang from the ranks. He was born in Preston in 1732. His parents were very poor, and he was the youngest of thirteen children. He was never at school: the only education he received he gave to himself; and to the last he was only able to write with difficulty. When a boy, he was apprenticed to a barber, and after learning the business, he set up for himself in Bolton, where he occupied an underground cellar, over which he put up the sign, "Come to the subterraneous barber--he shaves for a penny." The other barbers found their customers leaving them, and reduced their prices to his standard, when Arkwright, determined to push his trade, announced his determination to give "A clean shave for a halfpenny." After a few years he quitted his cellar, and became an itinerant dealer in hair. At that time wigs were worn, and wig-making formed an important branch of the barbering business. Arkwright went about buying hair for the wigs. He was accustomed to attend the hiring fairs throughout Lancashire resorted to by young women, for the purpose of securing their long tresses; and it is said that in negotiations of this sort he was very successful. He also dealt in a chemical hair dye, which he used adroitly, and thereby secured a considerable trade. But he does not seem, notwithstanding his pushing character, to have done more than earn a bare living.

The fashion of wig-wearing having undergone a change, distress fell upon the wig-makers; and Arkwright, being of a mechanical turn, was consequently induced to turn machine inventor or "conjurer," as the pursuit was then popularly

D

termed. Many attempts were made about that time to invent a spinning-machine, and our barber determined to launch his little bark on the sea of invention with the rest. Like other self-taught men of the same bias, he had already been devoting his spare time to the invention of a perpetual-motion machine; and from that the transition to a spinning-machine was easy. He followed his experiments so assiduously that he neglected his business, lost the little money he had saved, and was reduced to great poverty. His wife—for he had by this time married—was impatient at what she conceived to be a wanton waste of time and money, and in a moment of sudden wrath she seized upon and destroyed his models, hoping thus to remove the cause of the family privations. Arkwright was a stubborn and enthusiastic man, and he was provoked beyond measure by this conduct of his wife, from whom he immediately separated.

In travelling about the country, Arkwright had become acquainted with a person named Kay, a clockmaker at Warrington, who assisted him in constructing some of the parts of his perpetual-motion machinery. It is supposed that he was informed by Kay of the principle of spinning by rollers; but it is also said that the idea was first suggested to him by accidentally observing a red-hot piece of iron become elongated by passing between iron rollers. However this may be, the idea at once took firm possession of his mind, and he proceeded to devise the process by which it was to be accomplished, Kay being able to tell him nothing on this point. Arkwright now abandoned his business of hair collecting, and devoted himself to the perfecting of his machine, a model of which, constructed by Kay under his directions, he set up in the parlour of the Free Grammar School at Preston. Being a burgess of the town, he voted at the contested election at which General Burgoyne was returned; but such was his poverty, and such the tattered state of his dress, that a number of persons subscribed a sum sufficient to have him put in a state fit to appear in the poll-room. The exhibition of his machine in a town where so many workpeople lived by the exercise of manual labour proved a dangerous experiment; ominous growlings were heard outside the school-room from time to time, and Arkwright,—remembering the fate of Kay, who was mobbed and compelled to fly from Lancashire because of his invention of the fly-shuttle, and of poor Hargreaves, whose spinning-jenny had been pulled to pieces only a short time before by a Blackburn mob,—wisely determined on packing up his model and removing to a less dangerous locality. He went accordingly to Nottingham, where he applied to some of the local bankers for pecuniary assistance ; and the Messrs. Wright consented to advance him a sum of money on condition of sharing in the profits of the invention. The machine, how-ever, not being perfected so soon as they had anticipated, the bankers recommended Arkwright to apply to Messrs. Strutt and Need, the former of whom was the ingenious inventor and patentee of the stocking-frame. Mr. Strutt at once appreciated the merits of the invention, and a partner-ship was entered into with Arkwright, whose road to fortune was now clear. The patent was secured in the name of " Richard Arkwright, of Nottingham, clockmaker," and it is a circumstance worthy of note, that it was taken out in 1769, the same year in which Watt secured the patent for his steam-engine. A cotton-mill was first erected at Nottingham, driven by horses ; and another was shortly after built, on a much larger scale, at Cromford, in Derbyshire, turned by a water-wheel, from which circumstance the spinning-machine came to be called the water-frame.

Arkwright's labours, however, were, comparatively speak-ing, only begun. He had still to perfect all the working details of his machine. It was in his hands the subject of constant modification and improvement, until eventually it was rendered practicable and profitable in an eminent degree. But success was only secured by long and patient labour: for some years, indeed, the speculation was disheartening and unprofitable, swallowing up a very large amount of capital without any result. When success began to appear more certain, then the Lancashire manufacturers fell upon Arkwright's patent to pull it in pieces, as the Cornish miners fell upon Boulton and Watt to rob them of the profits of their steam-engine. Arkwright was even denounced as the enemy of the working people ; and a mill which he built near Chorley was destroyed by a mob in the presence of a strong force of police and military. The Lancashire men refused to buy his materials, though they were confessedly the best in the market. Then they refused to pay patent-right for the use of his machines, and combined to crush him in the courts of law. To the disgust of right-minded people, Arkwright's patent was upset. After the trial, when passing the hotel at which his opponents were staying, one of them said, loud enough to be heard by him, " Well, we've done the old shaver at last;" to which he coolly replied, " Never mind, I've a razor left that will shave you all." He established new mills in Lancashire, Derbyshire, and at New Lanark, in Scotland. The mills at Cromford also came into his hands at the expiry of his partnership with Strutt, and the amount and the excellence of his products were such, that in a short time he obtained so complete a control of the trade, that the prices were fixed by him, and he governed the main operations of the other cotton-spinners.

Arkwright was a man of great force of character, indomitable courage, much worldly shrewdness, with a business faculty almost amounting to genius. At one period his time was engrossed by severe and continuous labour, occasioned by the organising and conducting of his numerous manufactories, sometimes from four in the morning till nine at night. At fifty years of age he set to work to learn English grammar, and improve himself in writing and orthography. After overcoming every obstacle, he had the satisfaction of reaping the reward of his enterprise. Eighteen years after he had constructed his first machine, he rose to such estimation in Derbyshire that he was appointed High Sheriff of the county, and shortly after George III. conferred upon him the honour of knighthood. He died in 1792. Be it for good or for evil, Arkwright was the founder in England of the modern factory system, a branch of industry which has unquestionably proved a source of immense wealth to individuals and to the nation.

All the other great branches of industry in Britain furnish like examples of energetic men of business, the source of much benefit to the neighbourhoods in which they have laboured, and of increased power and wealth to the community at large. Amongst such might be cited the Strutts of Belper; the Tennants of Glasgow; the Marshalls and Gotts of Leeds; the Peels, Ashworths, Birleys, Fieldens, Ashtons, Heywoods, and Ainsworths of South Lancashire, some of whose descendants have since become distinguished in connection with the political history of England. Such pre-eminently were the Peels of South Lancashire.

The founder of the Peel family, about the middle of last century, was a small yeoman, occupying the Hole House Farm, near Blackburn, from which he afterwards removed to a house situated in Fish Lane in that town. Robert Peel, as he advanced in life, saw a large family of sons and daughters growing up about him; but the land about Blackburn being somewhat barren, it did not appear to him that agricultural pursuits offered a very encouraging prospect for their industry. The place had, however, long been the seat of a domestic manufacture—the fabric called "Blackburn greys," consisting of linen weft and cotton warp, being chiefly made in that town and its neighbourhood. It was then customary—previous to the introduction of the factory system—for industrious yeomen with families to employ the time not occupied in the fields in weaving at home; and Robert Peel accordingly began the domestic trade of calico-making. He was honest, and made an honest article; thrifty and hardworking, and his trade prospered. He was also enterprising, and was one of the first to adopt the carding cylinder, then recently invented.

But Robert Peel's attention was principally directed to the *printing* of calico—then a comparatively unknown art— and for some time he carried on a series of experiments with the object of printing by machinery. The experiments were secretly conducted in his own house, the cloth being ironed for the purpose by one of the women of the family. It was then customary, in such houses as the Peels, to use pewter plates at dinner. Having sketched a figure or pattern on one of the plates, the thought struck him that an impression might be got from it in reverse, and printed on calico with colour. In a cottage at the end of the farm-house lived a woman who kept a calendering machine, and going into her cottage, he put the plate with colour rubbed into the figured part and some calico over it, through the machine, when it was found to leave a satisfactory impression. Such is said to have been the origin of roller printing on calico. Robert Peel shortly perfected his process, and the first pattern he brought out was a parsley leaf; hence he is spoken of in the neighbourhood of Blackburn to this day as "Parsley Peel." The process of calico printing by what is called the mule machine— that is, by means of a wooden cylinder in relief, with an engraved copper cylinder—was afterwards brought to perfection by one of his sons, the head of the firm of Messrs. Peel and Co., of Church. Stimulated by his success, Robert Peel shortly gave up farming, and removing to Brookside, a village about two miles from Blackburn, he devoted himself exclusively to the printing business. There, with the aid of his sons, who were as energetic as himself, he successfully carried on the trade for several years; and as the young men grew up towards manhood, the concern branched out into various firms of Peels, each of which became a centre of industrial activity and a source of remunerative employment to large numbers of people.

From what can now be learnt of the character of the original and untitled Robert Peel, he must have been a remarkable man—shrewd, sagacious, and far-seeing. But little is known of him excepting from tradition, and the sons of those who knew him are fast passing away. His son, Sir Robert, thus modestly spoke of him :—" My father may be truly said to have been the founder of our family ; and he so accurately appreciated the importance of commercial wealth in a national point of view, that he was often heard to say that the gains to individuals were small compared with the national gains arising from trade."

Sir Robert Peel, the first baronet and the second manufacturer of the name, inherited all his father's enterprise, ability, and industry. His position, at starting in life, was little above that of an ordinary working man; for his father, though laying the foundations of future prosperity, was still struggling with the difficulties arising from insufficient capital. When Robert was only twenty years of age, he determined to begin the business of cotton-printing, which he had by this time learnt from his father, on his own account. His uncle, James Haworth, and William Yates of Blackburn, joined him in his enterprise ; the whole capital which they could raise amongst them amounting to only about 500*l.*, the principal part of which was supplied by William Yates. The father of the latter was a householder in Blackburn, where he was well known and much respected ; and having saved money by his business, he was willing to advance sufficient to give his son a start in the lucrative trade of cotton-printing, then in its infancy. Robert Peel, though comparatively a mere youth, supplied the practical knowledge of the business; but it was said of him, and proved true, that he "carried an old head on young shoulders." A ruined corn-mill, with its adjoining fields, was purchased for a comparatively small sum, near the then insignificant town of Bury, where the works long after continued to be known as " The Ground;" and a few wooden sheds having been run up, the firm commenced their cotton-printing business in a very humble way in the year 1770, adding to it that of cotton-spinning a few years later. The frugal style in which the partners lived may be inferred from the following incident in their early career. William Yates, being a married man with a family, commenced housekeeping on a small scale, and, to oblige Peel, who was single, he agreed to take him as a lodger. The sum which the latter first paid for board and lodging was only 8*s.* a week; but Yates, considering this too little, insisted on the weekly payment being increased a shilling, to which Peel at first demurred, and a difference between the partners took place, which was eventually compromised by the lodger paying an advance of sixpence a week. William Yates's eldest child was a girl named Ellen, and she very soon became an especial favourite with the young lodger. On returning from his hard day's work at "The Ground," he would take the little girl upon his knee, and say to her, "Nelly, thou bonny little dear, wilt be my wife?" to which the child would readily answer "Yes," as any child would do. "Then I'll wait for thee, Nelly; I'll wed thee, and none else." And Robert Peel did wait. As the girl grew in beauty towards womanhood, his determination to wait for her was strengthened; and after the lapse of ten years— years of close application to business and rapidly increasing prosperity—Robert Peel married Ellen Yates when she had completed her seventeenth year; and the pretty child, whom her mother's lodger and father's partner had nursed upon his knee, became Mrs. Peel, and eventually Lady Peel, the mother of the future Prime Minister of England. Lady Peel was a noble and beautiful woman, fitted to grace any station in life. She possessed rare powers of mind, and was, on every emergency, the high-souled and faithful counsellor of her husband. For many years after their marriage, she acted as his amanuensis, conducting the principal part of his business correspondence, for Mr. Peel himself was an indifferent and almost unintelligible writer. She died in 1803, only three years after the Baronetcy had been conferred upon her husband. It is said that London fashionable life—so unlike what she had been accustomed to at home—proved injurious to her health; and old Mr. Yates afterwards used to say, "if Robert hadn't made our Nelly a 'Lady,' she might ha' been living yet."

The career of Yates, Peel, & Co., was throughout one of great and uninterrupted prosperity. Sir Robert Peel himself was the soul of the firm; to great energy and application uniting much practical sagacity, and first-rate mercantile abilities—qualities in which many of the early cotton-spinners were exceedingly deficient. He was a man of iron mind and frame, and toiled unceasingly. In short, he was to cotton printing what Arkwright was to cotton-spinning, and his success was equally great. The excellence of the articles produced by the firm secured the command of the market, and the character of the firm stood pre-eminent in Lancashire. Besides greatly benefiting Bury, the partnership planted similar extensive works in the neighbourhood, on the Irwell and the Roch; and it was cited to their honour, that, while they sought to raise to the highest perfection the quality of their manufactures, they also endeavoured, in all ways, to promote the well-being and comfort of their workpeople; for whom they contrived to provide remunerative employment even in the least prosperous times.

Sir Robert Peel readily appreciated the value of all new processes and inventions; in illustration of which we may allude to his adoption of the process for producing what is called *resist work* in calico printing. This is accomplished by the use of a paste, or resist, on such parts of the cloth as were intended to remain white. The person who discovered the paste was a traveller for a London house, who sold it to Mr. Peel for an inconsiderable sum. It required the experience of a year or two to perfect the system and make it practically useful; but the beauty of its effect, and the extreme precision of outline in the pattern produced, at once placed the Bury establishment at the head of all the factories for calico printing in the country. Other firms, conducted with like spirit, were established by members of the same family at Burnley, Foxhill bank, and Altham, in Lancashire; Salley Abbey, in Yorkshire; and afterwards at Burton-on-Trent, in Staffordshire; these various establishments, whilst they brought wealth to their proprietors, setting an example to the whole cotton trade, and training up many of the most successful printers and manufacturers in Lancashire.

Among other distinguished founders of industry, the Rev. William Lee, inventor of the Stocking Frame, and John Heathcoat, inventor of the Bobbin-net Machine, are worthy of notice, as men of great mechanical skill and perseverance, through whose labours a vast amount of remunerative employment has been provided for the labouring population of Nottingham and the adjacent districts. The accounts which have been preserved of the circumstances connected with the invention of the Stocking Frame are very confused, and in many respects contradictory, though there is no doubt as to the name of the inventor. This was William Lee, born at Woodborough, a village some seven miles from Nottingham, about the year 1563. According to some accounts, he was the heir to a small freehold, while according to others he was a poor scholar,* and had to struggle with poverty from his earliest years.   He entered as a sizar at Christ College, Cambridge, in May, 1579, and subsequently removed to St. John's, taking his degree of B.A. in 1582-3.   It is believed that he commenced M.A. in 1586; but on this point there appears to be some confusion in the records of the University.   The statement usually made that he was expelled for marrying contrary to the statutes, is incorrect, as he was never a Fellow of the University, and therefore could not be prejudiced by taking such a step.

At the time when Lee invented the Stocking Frame he was officiating as curate of Calverton, near Nottingham; and it is alleged by some writers that the invention had its origin in disappointed affection.   The curate is said to have fallen deeply in love with a young lady of the village, who failed to reciprocate his affections; and when he visited her, she was accustomed to pay much more attention to the process of knitting stockings and instructing her pupils in the art, than to the addresses of her admirer.   This slight is said to have created in his mind such an aversion to knitting by hand, that he formed the determination to invent a machine that should supersede it and render it a gainless employment.   For three years he devoted himself to the prosecution of the invention, sacrificing everything to his new idea.   As the prospect of success opened before him, he abandoned his curacy, and devoted himself to the art of stocking making by machinery.   This is the version of the story given by Henson† on the authority of an old

---

* The following entry, which occurs in the account of monies disbursed by the burgesses of Sheffield in 1573 [?] is supposed by some to refer to the inventor of the stocking frame :—" Item gyven to Willm Lee, a poore scholler in Sheafield, towards the settyng him to the Universitie of Chambrydge, and buying him bookes and other furnyture [which money was afterwards returned] xiii iiii [13*s*. 4*d*.].—Hunter, ' History of Hallamshire,' 141.

† ' History of the Framework Knitters.'

stocking-maker, who died in Collins's Hospital, Nottingham, aged ninety-two, and was apprenticed in the town during the reign of Queen Anne. It is also given by Deering and Blackner as the traditional account in the neighbourhood, and it is in some measure borne out by the arms of the London Company of Frame-Work Knitters, which consists of a stocking frame without the wood-work, with a clergyman on one side and a woman on the other as supporters.*

Whatever may have been the actual facts as to the origin of the invention of the Stocking Loom, there can be no doubt as to the extraordinary mechanical genius displayed by its inventor. That a clergyman living in a remote village, whose life had for the most part been spent with books, should contrive a machine of such delicate and complicated movements, and at once advance the art of knitting from the tedious process of linking threads in a chain of loops by three skewers in the fingers of a woman, to the beautiful and rapid process of weaving by the stocking frame, was indeed an astonishing achievement, which may be pronounced almost unequalled in the history of mechanical invention. Lee's merit was all the greater, as the handicraft arts were then in their infancy, and little attention had as yet been

---

* There are, however, other and different accounts. One is to the effect that Lee set about studying the contrivance of the stocking-loom for the purpose of lessening the labour of a young country-girl to whom he was attached, whose occupation was knitting; another, that being married and poor, his wife was under the necessity of contributing to their joint support by knitting; and that Lee, while watching the motion of his wife's fingers, conceived the idea of imitating their movements by a machine. The latter story seems to have been invented by Aaron Hill, Esq., in his 'Account of the Rise and Progress of the Beech Oil manufacture,' London, 1715; but his statement is altogether unreliable. Thus he makes Lee to have been a Fellow of a college at Oxford, from which he was expelled for marrying an innkeeper's daughter; whilst Lee neither studied at Oxford, nor married there, nor was a Fellow of any college; and he concludes by alleging that the result of his invention was to "make Lee and his family happy;" whereas the invention brought him only a heritage of misery, and he died abroad destitute.

given to the contrivance of machinery for the purposes of manufacture. He was under the necessity of extemporising the parts of his machine as he best could, and adopting various expedients to overcome difficulties as they arose. His tools were imperfect, and his materials imperfect; and he had no skilled workmen to assist him. According to tradition, the first frame he made was a twelve gauge, without lead sinkers, and it was almost wholly of wood; the needles being also stuck in bits of wood. One of Lee's principal difficulties consisted in the formation of the stitch, for want of needle eyes; but this he eventually overcame by forming eyes to the needles with a three-square file.* At length, one difficulty after another was successfully overcome, and after three years' labour the machine was sufficiently complete to be fit for use. The quondam curate, full of enthusiasm for his art, now began stocking weaving in the village of Calverton, and he continued to work there for several years, instructing his brother James and several of his relations in the practice of the art.

Having brought his frame to a considerable degree of perfection, and being desirous of securing the patronage of Queen Elizabeth, whose partiality for knitted silk stockings was well known, Lee proceeded to London to exhibit the loom before her Majesty. He first showed it to several members of the court, among others to Sir William (afterwards Lord) Hunsdon, whom he taught to work it with success; and Lee was, through their instrumentality, at length admitted to an interview with the Queen, and worked the machine in her presence. Elizabeth, however, did not

---

* Blackner, 'History of Nottingham.' The author adds, "We have information, handed down in direct succession from father to son, that it was not till late in the seventeenth century that one man could manage the working of a frame. The man who was considered the workman employed a labourer, who stood behind the frame to work the slur and pressing motions; but the application of traddles and of the feet eventually rendered the labour unnecessary."

give him the encouragement that he had expected ; and she
is said to have opposed the invention on the ground that it
was calculated to deprive a large number of poor people of
their employment of hand knitting. Lee was no more successful in finding other patrons, and considering himself and
his invention treated with contempt, he embraced the offer
made to him by Sully, the sagacious minister of Henry IV.,
to proceed to Rouen and instruct the operatives of that
town—then one of the most important manufacturing centres
of France—in the construction and use of the stocking-
frame. Lee accordingly transferred himself and his machines
to France, in 1605, taking with him his brother and seven
workmen. He met with a cordial reception at Rouen, and
was proceeding with the manufacture of stockings on a
large scale—having nine of his frames in full work,—when
unhappily ill fortune again overtook him. Henry IV., his
protector, on whom he had relied for the rewards, honours,
and promised grant of privileges, which had induced Lee to
settle in France, was murdered by the fanatic Ravaillac ; and
the encouragement and protection which had heretofore
been extended to him were at once withdrawn. To press
his claims at court, Lee proceeded to Paris ; but being a
protestant as well as a foreigner, his representations were
treated with neglect ; and worn out with vexation and grief,
this distinguished inventor shortly after died at Paris, in a
state of extreme poverty and distress.

Lee's brother, with seven of the workmen, succeeded in
escaping from France with their frames, leaving two behind.
On James Lee's return to Nottinghamshire, he was joined
by one Ashton, a miller of Thoroton, who had been instructed in the art of frame-work knitting by the inventor
himself before he left England. These two, with the workmen and their frames, began the stocking manufacture at
Thoroton, and carried it on with considerable success. The
place was favourably situated for the purpose, as the sheep

pastured in the neighbouring district of Sherwood yielded a kind of wool of the longest staple. Ashton is said to have introduced the method of making the frames with lead sinkers, which was a great improvement. The number of looms employed in different parts of England gradually increased; and the machine manufacture of stockings eventually· became an important branch of the national industry.

One of the most important modifications in the Stocking Frame was that which enabled it to be applied to the manufacture of lace on a large scale. In 1777, two workmen, Frost and Holmes, were both engaged in making point net by means of the modifications they had introduced in the stocking frame; and in the course of about thirty years, so rapid was the growth of this branch of production, that 1500 point-net frames were at work, giving employment to upwards of 15,000 people. Owing, however, to the war, to change of fashion, and to other circumstances, the Nottingham lace manufacture rapidly fell off; and it continued in a decaying state until the invention of the Bobbin-net Machine by John Heathcoat, late M.P. for Tiverton, which had the effect of at once re-establishing the manufacture on solid foundations.

John Heathcoat was the son of a cottage farmer at Long Whalton, Leicestershire, where he was born in 1784. He was taught to read and write at the village school, but was shortly removed from it to be put apprentice to a framesmith in a neighbouring village. The boy soon learnt to handle tools with dexterity, and he acquired a minute knowledge of the parts of which the stocking frame was composed, as well as of the more intricate warp machine. At his leisure he studied how to introduce improvements in them, and his friend Mr. Bazley, M.P., states that as early as the age of sixteen, he conceived the idea of inventing a machine by which lace might be made similar to Buckingham or French lace, then all made by hand. The first practical improvement he succeeded in introducing was in the warp frame ; when, by means of an ingenious apparatus, he succeeded in producing "mitts" of a lacey appearance; and it was this success which determined him to pursue the study of mechanical lace-making.   The stocking frame had already, in a modified form, been applied to the manufacture of point-net lace, in which the mesh was *looped* as in a stocking ; but the work was slight and frail, and therefore unsatisfactory. Many ingenious Nottingham mechanics had during a long succession of years been labouring at the problem of inventing a machine by which the mesh of threads should be *twisted* round each other on the formation of the net. Some of these men died in poverty, some were driven insane, and all alike failed in the object of their search.   The old warp machine held its ground.

When a little over twenty-one years of age, Heathcoat married, and went to Nottingham in search of work. .He there found employment as a smith and "setter-up" of hosiery and warp-frames.   He also continued to pursue the subject on which his mind had before been occupied, and laboured to compass the contrivance of a twist traverse-net machine.   He first studied the art of making the Buckingham or pillow-lace by hand, with the object of effecting the same motions by mechanical means.   It was a long and laborious task, requiring the exercise of great perseverance and no little ingenuity.   His master, Elliott, described him at that time as plodding, patient, self-denying, and taciturn, undaunted by failures and mistakes, full of resources and expedients, and entertaining the most perfect confidence that his application of mechanical principles would eventually be crowned with success.*   During this time his wife

---

* Memoir by Mr. Felkin in the 'Nottingham Journal,' to which, as well as to Mr. Bazley, M.P., we are indebted for most of the above facts. We are glad to learn that Mr. Felkin is preparing a complete history of the branches of industry above referred to.

was kept in almost as great anxiety as himself. She well knew of his struggles and difficulties; and she even began to feel the pressure of poverty on her household. For while he was labouring at his invention, he was frequently under the necessity of laying aside the work that brought in the weekly wage. Many years after, when all difficulties had been successfully overcome, the conversation which took place between husband and wife one eventful Saturday evening, was vividly remembered. "Well, John," said the anxious wife, looking in her husband's face, "will it work?" "No, Anne," was the sad answer, "I have had to take it all in pieces again." Though he could still speak hopefully and cheerfully, his poor wife could restrain her feelings no longer, but sat down and cried bitterly. She had, however, only a few more weeks to wait; for success, long laboured for and richly deserved, came at last; and a proud and happy man was John Heathcoat when he brought home the first narrow strip of bobbin-net made by his machine, and placed it in the hands of his wife.

It is difficult to describe in words an invention so complicated as the bobbin-net machine. It was indeed a mechanical pillow for making lace; imitating in an ingenious manner the motions of the lace-maker's fingers in intersecting or tying the meshes of the lace upon her pillow. On analysing the component parts of a piece of hand-made lace, Heathcoat was enabled to classify the threads into longitudinal and diagonal. He began his experiments by stretching common packing-threads across his room for the warp, and then passing the weft-threads between them by common plyers, delivering them to other plyers on the opposite side; then, after giving them a sideways motion and twist, the threads were repassed back between the next adjoining cords, the meshes being thus tied in the same way as upon pillows by hand. He had then to contrive a mechanism that should accomplish all these nice and deli-

E

cate movements ; and to do this cost him no small amount
of bodily and mental toil. Long after, he said : " The single
difficulty of getting the diagonal threads to twist in the
allotted space was so great, that if it had now to be done,
I should probably not attempt its accomplishment."* His
next step was to provide thin metallic discs, to be used as
bobbins for conducting the thread backwards and forwards
through the warp. These discs, being arranged in carrier-
frames, placed on each side of the warp, were moved by
suitable machinery, so as to conduct the threads from side
to side in forming the lace. He eventually succeeded in
working out his principle with extraordinary skill and success ;
and, at the age of twenty-four, he was enabled to secure his
invention by a patent.

As in the case of nearly all inventions which have proved
productive, Heathcoat's rights as a patentee were disputed,
and his claims as an inventor called in question. On the
supposed invalidity of the patent, the lace-makers boldly
adopted the bobbin-net machine, and set the inventor at
defiance. But other patents were taken out for alleged improvements and adaptations ; and it was only when these
new patentees fell out and went to law with each other that
Heathcoat's rights became established. One lace-manufacturer having brought an action against another for an alleged
infringement of his patent, the jury brought in a verdict for
the defendant, in which the judge concurred, on the ground
that *both* the machines in question were infringements of
Heathcoat's patent. It was on the occasion of this trial,
"Boville *v.* Moore," that Sir John Copley (afterwards Lord
Lyndhurst), who was retained for the defence in the interest
of Mr. Heathcoat, learnt to work the bobbin-net machine
in order that he might master the details of the invention.
On reading over his brief, he confessed that he did not

* Mr. Felkin's Memoir.

quite understand the merits of the case; but, as it seemed
to him to be one of great importance, he offered to go
down into the country forthwith and study the machine until
he understood it; "and then," said he, "I will defend you
to the best of my ability." He accordingly put himself into
that night's mail, and went down to Nottingham to get up
his case as perhaps counsel never got it up before. Next
morning the learned sergeant placed himself in a lace-loom,
and he did not leave it until he could deftly make a piece
of bobbin-net with his own hands, and thoroughly understood the principle as well as the details of the machine.
When the case came on for trial, the learned sergeant was
enabled to work the model on the table with such ease
and skill, and to explain the precise nature of the invention with such felicitous clearness, as to astonish alike judge,
jury, and spectators; and the thorough conscientiousness and
mastery with which he handled the case had no doubt its
influence upon the decision of the court.

After the trial was over, Mr. Heathcoat, on inquiry, found
about six hundred machines at work after his patent, and
he proceeded to levy royalty upon the owners of them,
which amounted to a large sum. But the profits realised
by the manufacturers of lace were very great, and the use
of the machines rapidly extended; while the price of the
article was reduced from five pounds the square yard to
about five pence in the course of twenty-five years. During
the same period the average annual returns of the lace-trade
have been at least four millions sterling, and it gives remunerative employment to about 150,000 workpeople.

To return to the personal history of Mr. Heathcoat. In
1809 we find him established as a lace-manufacturer at
Loughborough, in Leicestershire. There he carried on a
prosperous business for several years, giving employment to
a large number of operatives, at wages varying from 5*l.* to
10*l.* a week. Notwithstanding the great increase in the

E 2

number of hands employed in lace-making through the introduction of the new machines, it began to be whispered about
among the workpeople that they were superseding labour,
and an extensive conspiracy was formed for the purpose of
destroying them wherever found.   As early as the year 1811
disputes arose between the masters and men engaged in the
stocking and lace trades in the south-western parts of Nottinghamshire and the adjacent parts of Derbyshire and
Leicestershire, the result of which was the assembly of a
mob at Sutton, in Ashfield, who proceeded in open day to
break the stocking and lace-frames of the manufacturers.
Some of the ringleaders having been seized and punished,
the disaffected learnt caution ; but the destruction of the
machines was nevertheless carried on secretly wherever a
safe opportunity presented itself.   As the machines were of
so delicate a construction that a single blow of a hammer
rendered them useless, and as the manufacture was carried
on for the most part in detached buildings, often in private
dwellings remote from towns, the opportunities of destroying
them were unusually easy.   In the neighbourhood of Nottingham, which was the focus of turbulence, the machine-
breakers organized themselves in regular bodies, and held
nocturnal meetings at which their plans were arranged.
Probably with the view of inspiring confidence, they gave
out that they were under the command of a leader named
Ned Ludd, or General Ludd, and hence their designation
of Luddites.   Under this organization machine-breaking was
carried on with great vigour during the winter of 1811,
occasioning great distress, and throwing large numbers of
workpeople out of employment.   Meanwhile, the owners of
the frames proceeded to remove them from the villages
and lone dwellings in the country, and brought them into
warehouses in the towns for their better protection.

The Luddites seem to have been encouraged by the
lenity of the sentences pronounced on such of their con-

federates as had been apprehended and tried; and, shortly after, the mania broke out afresh, and rapidly extended over the northern and midland manufacturing districts. The organization became more secret; an oath was administered to the members binding them to obedience to the orders issued by the heads of the confederacy; and the betrayal of their designs was decreed to be death. All machines were doomed by them to destruction, whether employed in the manufacture of cloth, calico, or lace; and a reign of terror began which lasted for years. In Yorkshire and Lancashire mills were boldly attacked by armed rioters, and in many cases they were wrecked or burnt; so that it became necessary to guard them by soldiers and yeomanry. The masters themselves were doomed to death; many of them were assaulted, and some were murdered. At length the law was vigorously set in motion; numbers of the misguided Luddites were apprehended; some were executed; and after several years' violent commotion from this cause, the machine-breaking riots were at length quelled.

Among the numerous manufacturers whose works were attacked by the Luddites, was the inventor of the bobbin-net machine himself. One bright sunny day, in the summer of 1816, a body of rioters entered his factory at Loughborough with torches, and set fire to it, destroying thirty-seven lace-machines, and above 10,000*l.* worth of property. Ten of the men were apprehended for the felony, and eight of them were executed. Mr. Heathcoat made a claim upon the county for compensation, and it was resisted; but the Court of Queen's Bench decided in his favour, and decreed that the county must make good his loss of 10,000*l.* The magistrates sought to couple with the payment of the damage the condition that Mr. Heathcoat should expend the money in the county of Leicester; but to this he would not assent, having already resolved on removing his manufacture elsewhere. At Tiverton, in Devonshire, he found a large building which had been formerly used as a woollen

manufactory; but the Tiverton cloth trade having fallen
into decay, the building remained unoccupied, and the
town itself was generally in a very poverty-stricken condition. Mr. Heathcoat bought the old mill, renovated
and enlarged it, and there recommenced the manufacture of lace upon a larger scale than before; keeping
in full work as many as three hundred machines, and employing a large number of artisans at good wages. Not
only did he carry on the manufacture of lace, but the various
branches of business connected with it—yarn-doubling, silk-
spinning, net-making, and finishing. He also established at
Tiverton an iron-foundry and works for the manufacture of
agricultural implements, which proved of great convenience to
the district. It was a favourite idea of his that steam power
was capable of being applied to perform all the heavy
drudgery of life, and he laboured for a long time at the
invention of a steam-plough. In 1832 he so far completed
his invention as to be enabled to take out a patent for it;
and Heathcoat's steam-plough, though it has since been
superseded by Fowler's, was considered the best machine
of the kind that had up to that time been invented.

Mr. Heathcoat was a man of great natural gifts. He
possessed a sound understanding, quick perception, and
a genius for business of the highest order. With these
he combined uprightness, honesty, and integrity—qualities which are the true glory of human character. Himself a diligent self-educator, he gave ready encouragement
to deserving youths in his employment, stimulating their
talents and fostering their energies. During his own busy
life, he contrived to save time to master French and Italian,
of which he acquired an accurate and grammatical knowledge. His mind was largely stored with the results of a
careful study of the best literature, and there were few subjects on which he had not formed for himself shrewd and
accurate views. The two thousand workpeople in his employment regarded him almost as a father, and he carefully

provided for their comfort and improvement. Prosperity did not spoil him, as it does so many ; nor close his heart against the claims of the poor and struggling, who were always sure of his sympathy and help. To provide for the education of the children of his workpeople, he built schools for them at a cost of about 6000*l*. He was also a man of singularly cheerful and buoyant disposition, a favourite with men of all classes, and most admired and beloved by those who knew him best.

In 1831 the electors of Tiverton, of which town Mr. Heathcoat had proved himself so genuine a benefactor, returned him to represent them in Parliament, and he continued their member for nearly thirty years. During a great part of that time he had Lord Palmerston for his colleague, and the noble lord, on more than one public occasion, expressed the high regard which he entertained for his venerable friend. On retiring from the representation in 1859, owing to advancing age and increasing infirmities, thirteen hundred of his workmen presented him with a silver inkstand and gold pen, in token of their esteem. He enjoyed his leisure for only two more years, dying in January, 1861, at the age of seventy-seven, and leaving behind him a character for probity, virtue, manliness, and mechanical genius, of which his descendants may well be proud.

We next turn to a career of a very different kind, that of the illustrious but unfortunate Jacquard, whose life also illustrates in a remarkable manner the influence which ingenious men, even of the humblest rank, may exercise upon the industry of a nation. Jacquard was the son of a hardworking couple of Lyons, his father being a weaver, and his mother a pattern reader. They were too poor to give him any but the most meagre education. When he was of age to learn a trade, his father placed him with a bookbinder. An old clerk, who made up the master's accounts, gave Jacquard some lessons in mathematics. He very shortly began to display a remarkable turn for mechanics, and some of his contrivances quite astonished the old clerk, who advised Jacquard's father to put him to some other trade, in which his peculiar abilities might have better scope than in bookbinding. He was accordingly put apprentice to a cutler; but was so badly treated by his master, that he shortly afterwards left his employment, on which he was placed with a type-founder.

His parents dying, Jacquard found himself in a measure compelled to take to his father's two looms, and carry·on the trade of a weaver. He immediately proceeded to improve the looms, and became so engrossed with his inventions that he forgot his work, and very soon found himself at the end of his means. He then sold the looms to pay his debts, at the same time that he took upon himself the burden of supporting a wife. He became still poorer, and to satisfy his creditors, he next sold his cottage. He tried to find employment, but in vain, people believing him to·be an idler, occupied with mere dreams about his inventions. At length he obtained employment with a line-maker of Bresse, whither he went, his wife remaining at Lyons, earning a precarious living by making straw bonnets.

We hear nothing further of Jacquard for some years, but in the interval he seems to have prosecuted his improvement in the drawloom for the better manufacture of figured fabrics; for, in 1790, he brought out his contrivance for selecting the warp threads, which, when added to the loom, superseded the services of a draw-boy. The adoption of this machine was slow but steady, and in ten years after its introduction, 4000 of them were found at work in Lyons. Jacquard's pursuits were rudely interrupted by the Revolution, and, in 1792, we find him fighting in the ranks of the Lyonnaise Volunteers against the Army of the Convention under the command of Dubois Crancé. The city was taken; Jacquard fled and joined the Army of the Rhine, where he rose to the rank of sergeant. He might have remained a soldier, but that, his only son having been shot dead at his side, he deserted and returned to Lyons to recover his wife. He found her in a garret, still employed at her old trade of straw-bonnet making. While living in concealment with her, his mind reverted to the inventions over which he had so long brooded in former years ; but he had no means wherewith to prosecute them. Jacquard found it necessary, however, to emerge from his hiding-place and try to find some employment. He succeeded in obtaining it with an intelligent manufacturer, and while working by day he went on inventing by night. It had occurred to him that great improvements might still be introduced in looms for figured goods, and he incidentally mentioned the subject one day to his master, regretting at the same time that his limited means prevented him from carrying out his ideas. Happily his master appreciated the value of the suggestions, and with laudable generosity placed a sum of money at his disposal, that he might prosecute the proposed improvements at his leisure.

In three months Jacquard had invented a loom to substitute mechanical action for the irksome and toilsome labour of the workman. The loom was exhibited at the Exposition of National Industry at Paris in 1801, and obtained a bronze medal. Jacquard was further honoured by a visit at Lyons from the Minister Carnot, who desired to congratulate him in person on the success of his invention. In the following year the Society of Arts in London offered a prize for the invention of a machine for manufacturing fishing-nets and boarding-netting for ships. Jacquard heard of this, and while walking one day in the fields according to his custom, he turned the subject over in his mind, and contrived the plan of a machine for the purpose. His friend, the manufacturer, again furnished him with the means of carrying out his idea, and in three weeks Jacquard had completed his invention.

Jacquard's achievement having come to the knowledge of the Prefect of the Department, he was summoned before that functionary, and, on his explanation of the working of the machine, a report on the subject was forwarded to the Emperor. The inventor was forthwith summoned to Paris with his machine, and brought into the presence of the Emperor, who received him with the consideration due to his genius. The interview lasted two hours, during which Jacquard, placed at his ease by the Emperor's affability, explained to him the improvements which he proposed to make in the looms for weaving figured goods. The result was, that he was provided with apartments in the Conservatoire des Arts et Métiers, where he had the use of the workshop during his stay, and was provided with a suitable allowance for his maintenance.

Installed in the Conservatoire, Jacquard proceeded to complete the details of his improved loom. He had the advantage of minutely inspecting the various exquisite pieces of mechanism contained in that great treasury of human . ingenuity. Among the machines which more particularly attracted his attention, and eventually set him upon the track of his discovery, was a loom for weaving flowered silk, made by Vaucanson the celebrated automaton-maker.

Vaucanson was a man of the highest order of constructive genius. The inventive faculty was so strong in him that it may almost be said to have amounted to a passion, and could not be restrained. The saying that the poet is born, not made, applies with equal force to the inventor, who, though indebted, like the other, to culture and improved opportunities, nevertheless contrives and constructs new combinations of machinery mainly to gratify his own instinct. This was peculiarly the case with Vaucanson; for his most elaborate works were not so much distinguished for their utility as for the curious ingenuity which they displayed. While a mere boy attending Sunday conversations with his mother, he amused himself by watching, through the chinks of a partition wall, part of the movements of a clock in the adjoining apartment. He endeavoured to understand them, and by brooding over the subject, after several months he discovered the principle of the escapement.

From that time the subject of mechanical invention took complete possession of him. With some rude tools which he contrived, he made a wooden clock that marked the hours with remarkable exactness; while he made for a miniature chapel the figures of some angels which waved their wings, and some priests that made several ecclesiastical movements. With the view of executing some other automata he had designed, he proceeded to study anatomy, music, and mechanics, which occupied him for several years. The sight of the Flute-player in the Gardens of the Tuileries inspired him with the resolution to invent a similar figure that should *play;* and after several years' study and labour, though struggling with illness, he succeeded in accomplishing his object. He next produced a Flageolet-player, which was succeeded by a Duck—the most ingenious of his contrivances,—which swam, dabbled, drank, and quacked like a real duck. He next invented an asp, employed in the tragedy of 'Cléopâtre,' which hissed and darted at the bosom of the actress.

Vaucanson, however, did not confine himself merely to the making of automata. By reason of his ingenuity, Cardinal de Fleury appointed him inspector of the silk manufactories of France; and he was no sooner in office, than with his usual irrepressible instinct to invent, he proceeded to introduce improvements in silk machinery. One of these was his mill for thrown silk, which so excited the anger of the Lyons operatives, who feared the loss of employment through its means, that they pelted him with stones and had nearly killed him. He nevertheless went on inventing, and next produced a machine for weaving flowered silks, with a contrivance for giving a dressing to the thread, so as to render that of each bobbin or skein of an equal thickness.

When Vaucanson died in 1782, after a long illness, he bequeathed his collection of machines to the Queen, who seems to have set but small value on them, and they were shortly after dispersed. But his machine for weaving flowered silks was happily preserved in the Conservatoire des Arts et Métiers, and there Jacquard found it among the many curious and interesting articles in the collection. It proved of the utmost value to him, for it immediately set him on the track of the principal modification which he introduced in his improved loom.

One of the chief features of Vaucanson's machine was a pierced cylinder which, according to the holes it presented when revolved, regulated the movement of certain needles, and caused the threads of the warp to deviate in such a manner as to produce a given design, though only of a simple character. Jacquard seized upon the suggestion with avidity, and, with the genius of the true inventor, at once proceeded to improve upon it. At the end of a month his weaving-machine was completed. To the cylinder of Vaucanson, he added an endless piece of pasteboard pierced with a number of holes, through which the threads of the warp were presented to the weaver ; while another piece of mechanism indicated to the workman the colour of the shuttle which he ought to throw. Thus the drawboy and the reader of designs were both at once superseded. The first use Jacquard made of his new loom was to weave with it several yards of rich stuff which he presented to the Empress Josephine. Napoleon was highly gratified with the result of the inventor's labours, and ordered a number of the looms to be constructed by the best workmen, after Jacquard's model, and presented to him ; after which he returned to Lyons.

There he experienced the frequent fate of inventors.

He was regarded by his townsmen as an enemy, and treated by them as Kay, Hargreaves, and Arkwright had been in Lancashire. The workmen looked upon the new loom as fatal to their trade, and feared lest it should at once take the bread from their mouths. A tumultuous meeting was held on the Place des Terreaux, when it was determined to destroy the machines. This was however prevented by the military. But Jacquard was denounced and hanged in effigy. The 'Conseil des prud'hommes' in vain endeavoured to allay the excitement, and they were themselves denounced. At length, carried away by the popular impulse, the prud'hommes, most of whom had been workmen and sympathised with the class, had one of Jacquard's looms carried off and publicly broken in pieces. Riots followed, in one of which Jacquard was dragged along the quay by an infuriated mob intending to drown him, but he was rescued.

The great value of the Jacquard loom, however, could not be denied, and its success was only a question of time. Jacquard was urged by some English silk manufacturers to pass over into England and settle there. But notwithstanding the harsh and cruel treatment he had received at the hands of his townspeople, his patriotism was too strong to permit him to accept their offer. The English manufacturers, however, adopted his loom. Then it was, and only then, that Lyons, threatened to be beaten out of the field, adopted it with eagerness; and before long the Jacquard machine was employed in nearly all kinds of weaving. The result proved that the fears of the workpeople had been entirely unfounded. Instead of diminishing employment, the Jacquard loom increased it at least tenfold. The number of persons occupied in the manufacture of figured goods in Lyons, was stated by M. Leon Faucher to have been 60,000 in 1833; and that number has since been considerably increased.

As for Jacquard himself, the rest of his life passed peacefully, excepting that the workpeople who dragged him along the quay to drown him were shortly after found eager to bear him in triumph along the same route in celebration of his birthday. But his modesty would not permit him to take part in such a demonstration. The Municipal Council of Lyons proposed to him that he should devote himself to improving his machine for the benefit of the local industry, to which Jacquard agreed in consideration of a moderate pension, the amount of which was fixed by himself. After perfecting his invention accordingly, he retired at sixty to end his days at Oullins, his father's native place. It was there that he received, in 1820, the decoration of the Legion of Honour; and it was there that he died and was buried in 1834. A statue was erected to his memory, but his relatives remained in poverty; and twenty years after his death, his two nieces were under the necessity of selling for a few hundred francs the gold medal bestowed upon their uncle by Louis XVIII. "Such," says a French writer, "was the gratitude of the manufacturing interests of Lyons to the man to whom it owes so large a portion of its splendour."

It would be easy to extend the martyrology of inventors, and to cite the names of other equally distinguished men who have, without any corresponding advantage to themselves, contributed to the industrial progress of the age,— for it has too often happened that genius has planted the tree, of which patient dulness has gathered the fruit; but we will confine ourselves for the present to a brief account of an inventor of comparatively recent date, by way of illustration of the difficulties and privations which it is so frequently the lot of mechanical genius to surmount. We allude to Joshua Heilmann, the inventor of the Combing Machine.

Heilmann was born in 1796 at Mulhouse, the principal seat of the Alsace cotton manufacture. His father was engaged in that business; and Joshua entered his office at fifteen. He remained there for two years, employing his spare time in mechanical drawing. He afterwards spent two years in his uncle's banking-house in Paris, prosecuting the study of mathematics in the evenings. Some of his relatives having established a small cotton-spinning factory at Mulhouse, young Heilmann was placed with Messrs. Tissot and Rey, at Paris, to learn the practice of that firm. At the same time he became a student at the Conservatoire des Arts et Métiers, where he attended the lectures, and studied the machines in the museum. He also took practical lessons in turning from a toymaker. After some time, thus diligently occupied, he returned to Alsace, to superintend the construction of the machinery for the new factory at Vieux-Thann, which was shortly finished and set to work. The operations of the manufactory were, however, seriously affected by a commercial crisis which occurred, and it passed into other hands, on which Heilmann returned to his family at Mulhouse.

He had in the mean time been occupying much of his leisure with inventions, more particularly in connection with the weaving of cotton and the preparation of the staple for spinning. One of his earliest contrivances was an embroidering-machine, in which twenty needles were employed, working simultaneously; and he succeeded in accomplishing his object after about six months' labour. For this invention, which he exhibited at the Exposition of 1834, he received a gold medal, and was decorated with the Legion of Honour. Other inventions quickly followed—an improved loom, a machine for measuring and folding fabrics, an improvement of the "bobbin and fly frames" of the English spinners, and a weft winding-machine, with various improvements in the machinery for preparing, spinning, and weaving silk and cotton. One of his most ingenious contrivances was his loom for weaving simultaneously two pieces of velvet or other piled fabric, united by the pile common to both, with a knife and traversing apparatus for separating the two fabrics when woven. But by far the most beautiful and ingenious of his inventions was the combing-machine, the history of which we now proceed shortly to describe.

Heilmann had for some years been diligently studying the contrivance of a machine for combing long-stapled cotton, the ordinary carding-machine being found ineffective in pre· paring the raw material for spinning, especially the finer sorts of yarn, besides causing considerable waste. To avoid these imperfections, the cotton-spinners of Alsace offered a prize of 5000 francs for an improved combing-machine, and Heilmann immediately proceeded to compete for the reward. He was not stimulated by the desire of gain, for he was comparatively rich, having acquired a considerable fortune by his wife. It was a saying of his that " one will never accomplish great things who is constantly asking himself, how much gain will this bring me?" What mainly impelled him was the irrepressible instinct of the inventor, who no sooner has a mechanical problem set before him than he feels impelled to undertake its solution. The problem in this case was, however, much more difficult than he had anticipated. The close study of the subject occupied him for several years, and the expenses in which he became involved in connection with it were so great, that his wife's fortune was shortly swallowed up, and he was reduced to poverty, without being able to bring his machine to perfection. From that time he was under the necessity of relying mainly on the help of his friends to enable him to prosecute the invention.

While still struggling with poverty and difficulties, Heilmann's wife died, believing her husband ruined; and shortly after he proceeded to England and settled for a time at Manchester, still labouring at his machine. He had a model made for him by the eminent machine-makers, Sharpe, Roberts, and Company; but still he could not make it work satisfactorily, and he was at length brought almost to the verge of despair. He returned to France to visit his family, still pursuing his idea, which had obtained complete possession of his mind. While sitting by his hearth one evening, meditating upon the hard fate of inventors and the misfortunes in which their families so often become involved, he found himself almost unconsciously watching his daughters combing their long hair and drawing it out at full length between their fingers. The thought suddenly struck him that if he could successfully imitate in a machine the process of combing out the longest hair and forcing back the short by reversing the action of the comb, it might serve to extricate him from his difficulty. It may be remembered that this incident in the life of Heilmann has been made the subject of a beautiful picture by Mr. Elmore, R.A., which was exhibited at the Royal Academy Exhibition of 1862.

Upon this idea he proceeded, introduced the apparently simple but really most intricate process of machine-combing, and after great labour he succeeded in perfecting the invention. The singular beauty of the process can only be appreciated by those who have witnessed the machine at work, when the similarity of its movements to that of combing the hair, which suggested the invention, is at once apparent. The machine has been described as " acting with almost the delicacy of touch of the human fingers." It combs the lock of cotton *at both ends*, places the fibres exactly parallel with each other, separates the long from the short, and unites the long fibres in one sliver and the short ones in another. In fine, the machine not only acts with the delicate accuracy of the human fingers, but apparently with the delicate intelligence of the human mind.

The chief commercial value of the invention consisted in its rendering the commoner sorts of cotton available for fine spinning. The manufacturers were thereby enabled to select the most suitable fibres for high-priced fabrics, and to produce the finer sorts of yarn in much larger quantities. It became possible by its means to make thread so fine that a length of 334 miles might be spun from a single pound weight of the prepared cotton, and, worked up into the finer sorts of lace, the original shilling's worth of cotton-wool, before it passed into the hands of the consumer, might thus be increased to the value of between 300*l.* and 400*l.* sterling.

The beauty and utility of Heilmann's invention were at once appreciated by the English cotton-spinners. Six Lancashire firms united and purchased the patent for cotton-spinning for England for the sum of 30,000*l.*; the wool-spinners paid the same sum for the privilege of applying the process to wool; and the Messrs. Marshall, of Leeds, 20,000*l.* for the privilege of applying it to flax. Thus wealth suddenly flowed in upon poor Heilmann at last. But he did not live to enjoy it. Scarcely had his long labours been crowned by success than he died, and his son, who had shared in his privations, shortly followed him.

It is at the price of lives such as these that the wonders of civilisation are achieved.

CHAPTER III.

"Patience is the finest and worthiest part of fortitude, and the rarest too. . . Patience lies at the root of all pleasures, as well as of all powers. Hope herself ceases to be happiness when Impatience companions her."—*John Ruskin.*

"Il y a vingt et cinq ans passez qu'il ne me fut monstré une coupe de terre, tournée et esmaillée d'une telle beauté que . . . dèslors, sans avoir esgard que je n'avois nulle connoissance des terres argileuses, je me mis a chercher les émaux, comme un homme qui taste en ténèbres."—*Bernard Palissy.*

IT so happens that the history of Pottery furnishes some of the most remarkable instances of patient perseverance to be found in the whole range of biography. Of these we select three of the most striking, as exhibited in the lives of Bernard Palissy, the Frenchman; Johann Friedrich Böttgher, the German; and Josiah Wedgwood, the Englishman.

Though the art of making common vessels of clay was known to most of the ancient nations, that of manufacturing enamelled earthenware was much less common. It was, however, practised by the ancient Etruscans, specimens of whose ware are still to be found in antiquarian collections. But it became a lost art, and was only recovered at a comparatively recent date. The Etruscan ware was very valuable in ancient times, a vase being worth its weight in gold in the time of Augustus. The Moors seem to have preserved amongst them a knowledge of the art, which they were found practising in the island of Majorca when it was taken by the Pisans in 1115. Among the spoil carried away were many plates of Moorish earthenware, which, in token of triumph, were embedded in the walls of several of the ancient churches of Pisa, where they are to be seen to this day. About two centuries later the Italians began to make an imitation enamelled ware, which they named Majolica, after the Moorish place of manufacture.

The reviver or re-discoverer of the art of enamelling in Italy was Luca della Robbia, a Florentine sculptor. Vasari describes him as a man of indefatigable perseverance, working with his chisel all day and practising drawing during the greater part of the night. He pursued the latter art with so much assiduity, that when working late, to prevent his feet from freezing with the cold, he was accustomed to provide himself with a basket of shavings, in which he placed them to keep himself warm and enable him to proceed with his drawings. "Nor," says Vasari, "am I in the least astonished at this, since no man ever becomes distinguished in any art whatsoever who does not early begin to acquire the power of supporting heat, cold, hunger, thirst, and other discomforts; whereas those persons deceive themselves altogether who suppose that when taking their ease and surrounded by all the enjoyments of the world they may still attain to honourable distinction,—for it is not by sleeping, but by waking, watching, and labouring continually, that proficiency is attained and reputation acquired."

But Luca, notwithstanding all his application and industry, did not succeed in earning enough money by sculpture to enable him to live by the art, and the idea occurred to him that he might nevertheless be able to pursue his modelling in some material more facile and less dear than marble. Hence it was that he began to make his models in clay, and to endeavour by experiment so to coat and bake the clay as to render those models durable. After many trials he at length discovered a method of covering the clay with a material, which, when exposed to the intense heat of a furnace, became converted into an almost imperishable enamel. He afterwards made the further discovery of a method of imparting colour to the enamel, thus greatly adding to its beauty.

The fame of Luca's work extended throughout Europe, and specimens of his art became widely diffused. Many of them were sent into France and Spain, where they were greatly prized. At that time coarse brown jars and pipkins were almost the only articles of earthenware produced in France ; and this continued to be the case, with comparatively small improvement, until the time of Palissy—a man who toiled and fought against stupendous difficulties with a heroism that sheds a glow almost of romance over the events of his chequered life.

Bernard Palissy is supposed to have been born in the south of France, in the diocese of Agen, about the year 1510. His father was probably a worker in glass, to which trade Bernard was brought up. His parents were poor people—too poor to give him the benefit of any school education. "I had no other books," said he afterwards, " than heaven and earth, which are open to all." He learnt, however, the art of glass-painting, to which he added that of drawing, and afterwards reading and writing.

When about eighteen years old, the glass trade becoming decayed, Palissy left his father's house, with his wallet on his back, and went out into the world to search whether there was any place in it for him. He first travelled towards Gascony, working at his trade where he could find employment, and occasionally occupying part of his time in land-measuring. Then he travelled northwards, sojourning for various periods at different places in France, Flanders, and Lower Germany.

Thus Palissy occupied about ten more years of his life, after which he married, and ceased from his wanderings. settling down to practise glass-painting and land-measuring at the small town of Saintes, in the Lower Charente. There children were born to him; and not only his responsibilities but his expenses increased, while, do what he could, his earnings remained too small for his nèeds. It was therefore necessary for him to bestir himself. Probably he felt capable of better things than drudging in an employment so precarious as glass-painting; and hence he was induced to turn his attention to the kindred art of painting and enamelling earthenware. Yet on this subject he was wholly ignorant; for he had never seen earth baked before he began his operations. He had therefore everything to learn by himself, without any helper. But he was full of hope, eager to learn, of unbounded perseverance and inexhaustible patience.

It was the sight of an elegant cup of Italian manufacture—most probably one of Luca della Robbia's make—which first set Palissy a-thinking about the new art. A circumstance so apparently insignificant would have produced no effect upon an ordinary mind, or even upon Palissy himself at an ordinary time; but occurring as it did when he was meditating a change of calling, he at once became inflamed with the desire of imitating it. The sight of this cup disturbed his whole existence; and the determination to discover the enamel with which it was glazed thenceforward possessed him like a passion. Had he been a single man he might have travelled into Italy in search of the secret; but he was bound to his wife and his children, and could not leave them; so he remained by their side groping in the dark in the hope of finding out the process of making and enamelling earthenware.

At first he could merely guess the materials of which the enamel was composed; and he proceeded to try all manner of experiments to ascertain what they really were. He pounded all the substances which he supposed were likely to produce it. Then he bought common earthen pots.

broke them into pieces, and, spreading his compounds over them, subjected them to the heat of a furnace which he erected for the purpose of baking them. His experiments failed; and the results were broken pots and a waste of fuel, drugs, time, and labour. Women do not readily sympathise with experiments whose only tangible effect is to dissipate the means of buying clothes and food for their children; and Palissy's wife, however dutiful in other respects, could not be reconciled to the purchase of more earthen pots, which seemed to her to be bought only to be broken. Yet she must needs submit; for Palissy had become thoroughly possessed by the determination to master the secret of the enamel, and would not leave it alone.

For many successive months and years Palissy pursued his experiments. The first furnace having proved a failure, he proceeded to erect another out of doors. There he burnt more wood, spoiled more drugs and pots, and lost more time, until poverty stared him and his family in the face. "Thus," said he, "I fooled away several years, with sorrow and sighs, because I could not at all arrive at my intention." In the intervals of his experiments he occasionally worked at his former callings, painting on glass, drawing portraits, and measuring land; but his earnings from these sources were very small. At length he was no longer able to carry on his experiments in his own furnace because of the heavy cost of fuel; but he bought more potsherds, broke them up as before into three or four hundred pieces, and, covering them with chemicals, carried them to a tile-work a league and a half distant from Saintes, there to be baked in an ordinary furnace. After the operation he went to see the pieces taken out; and, to his dismay, the whole of the experiments were failures. But though disappointed, he was not yet defeated; for he determined on the very spot to " begin afresh."

His business as a land-measurer called him away for a brief season from the pursuit of his experiments. In conformity with an edict of the State, it became necessary to survey the salt-marshes in the neighbourhood of Saintes for the purpose of levying the land-tax. Palissy was employed to make this survey, and prepare the requisite map. The work occupied him some time, and he was doubtless well paid for it; but no sooner was it completed than he proceeded, with redoubled zeal, to follow up his old investigations "in the track of the enamels." He began by breaking three dozen new earthen pots, the pieces of which he covered with different materials which he had compounded, and then took them to a neighbouring glass-furnace to be baked. The results gave him a glimmer of hope. The greater heat of the glass-furnace had melted some of the compounds; but though Palissy searched diligently for the white enamel he could find none.

For two more years he went on experimenting without any satisfactory result, until the proceeds of his survey of the salt-marshes having become nearly spent, he was reduced to poverty again. But he resolved to make a last great effort; and he began by breaking more pots than ever. More than three hundred pieces of pottery covered with his compounds were sent to the glass-furnace; and thither he himself went to watch the results of the baking. Four hours passed, during which he watched; and then the furnace was opened. The material on *one* only of the three hundred pieces of potsherd had melted, and it was taken out to cool. As it hardened, it grew white—white and polished! The piece of potsherd was covered with white enamel, described by Palissy as "singularly beautiful!" And beautiful it must no doubt have been in his eyes after all his weary waiting. He ran home with it to his wife, feeling himself, as he expressed it, quite a new creature. But the prize was not yet won—far from it. The partial success of this intended last effort merely had the effect of luring him on to a succession of further experiments and failures.

In order that he might complete the invention, which he now believed to be at hand, he resolved to build for himself a glass-furnace near his dwelling, where he might carry on his operations in secret. He proceeded to build the furnace with his own hands, carrying the bricks from the brick-field upon his back. He was bricklayer, labourer, and all. From seven to eight more months passed. At last the furnace was built and ready for use. Palissy had in the mean time fashioned a number of vessels of clay in readiness for the laying on of the enamel. After being subjected to a preliminary process of baking, they were covered with the enamel compound, and again placed in the furnace for the grand crucial experiment. Although his means were nearly exhausted, Palissy had been for some time accumulating a great store of fuel for the final effort ; and he thought it was enough. At last the fire was lit, and the operation proceeded. All day he sat by the furnace, feeding it with fuel. He sat there watching and feeding all through the long night. But the enamel did not melt. The sun rose upon his labours. His wife brought him a portion of the scanty morning meal,—for he would not stir from the furnace, into which he continued from time to time to heave more fuel. The second day passed, and still the enamel did not melt. The sun set, and another night passed. The pale, haggard, unshorn, baffled yet not beaten Palissy sat by his furnace eagerly looking for the melting of the enamel. A third day and night passed—a fourth, a fifth, and even a sixth,—yes, for six long days and nights did the unconquerable Palissy watch and toil, fighting against hope ; and still the enamel would not melt.

It then occurred to him that there might be some defect in the materials for the enamel—perhaps something wanting in the flux ; so he set to work to pound and compound fresh materials for a new experiment. Thus two or three more weeks passed. But how to buy more pots?—for those

which he had made with his own hands for the purposes
of the first experiment were by long baking irretrievably
spoilt for the purposes of a second. His money was now
all spent; but he could borrow. His character was still
good, though his wife and the neighbours thought him
foolishly wasting his means in futile experiments. Nevertheless he succeeded. He borrowed sufficient from a friend
to enable him to buy more fuel and more pots, and he was
again ready for a further experiment. The pots were covered
with the new compound, placed in the furnace, and the fire
was again lit.

It was the last and most desperate experiment of the
whole. The fire blazed up; the heat became intense; but
still the enamel did not melt. The fuel began to run
short! How to keep up the fire? There were the garden
palings: these would burn. They must be sacrificed rather
than that the great experiment should fail. The garden
palings were pulled up and cast into the furnace. They
were burnt in vain! The enamel had not yet melted.
Ten minutes more heat might do it. Fuel must be had
at whatever cost. There remained the household furniture and shelving. A crashing noise was heard in the
house; and amidst the screams of his wife and children,
who now feared Palissy's reason was giving way, the tables
were seized, broken up, and heaved into the furnace. The
enamel had not melted yet! There remained the shelving.
Another noise of the wrenching of timber was heard within
the house; and the shelves were torn down and hurled after
the furniture into the fire. Wife and children then rushed
from the house, and went frantically through the town, calling out that poor Palissy had gone mad, and was breaking
up his very furniture for firewood !*

* Palissy's own words are :—" Le bois m'ayant failli, je fus contraint
brusler les estapes (étaies) qui soustenoyent les tailles de mon jardin,
lesquelles estant bruslées, je fus contraint brusler les tables et plancber

For an entire month his shirt had not been off his back, and he was utterly worn out—wasted with toil, anxiety, watching, and want of food. He was in debt, and seemed on the verge of ruin. But he had at length mastered the secret; for the last great burst of heat had melted the enamel. The common brown household jars, when taken out of the furnace after it had become cool, were found covered with a white glaze! For this he could endure reproach, contumely, and scorn, and wait patiently for the opportunity of putting his discovery into practice as better days came round.

Palissy next hired a potter to make some earthen vessels after designs which he furnished; while he himself proceeded to model some medallions in clay for the purpose of enamelling them. But how to maintain himself and his family until the wares were made and ready for sale? Fortunately there remained one man in Saintes who still believed in the integrity, if not in the judgment, of Palissy—an innkeeper, who agreed to feed and lodge him for six months, while he went on with his manufacture. As for the working potter whom he had hired, Palissy soon found that he could not pay him the stipulated wages. Having already stripped his dwelling, he could but strip himself; and he

de la maison, afin de faire fondre la seconde composition. J'estois en une telle angoisse que je ne sçaurois dire : car j'estois tout tari et deseché à cause du labeur et de la chaleur du fourneau ; il y avoit plus d'un mois que ma chemise n'avoit seiché sur moy, encores pour me consoler on se moquoit de moy, et mesme ceux qui me devoient secourir alloient crier par la ville que je faisois brusler le plancher : et par tel moyen l'on me faisoit perdre mon credit et m'estimoit-on estre fol. Les autres disoient que je cherchois à faire la fausse monnoye, qui estoit un mal qui me faisoit seicher sur les pieds ; et m'en allois par les ruës tout baissé comme un homme honteux : . . . . personne ne me secouroit : Mais au contraire ils se mocquoyent de moy, en disant : Il luy appartient bien de mourir de faim, par ce qu'il delaisse son mestier. Toutes ces nouvelles venoyent a mes aureilles quand je passois par la ruë."—' Œuvres Complètes de Palissy, Paris, 1844 ;' De l'Art de Terre, p. 315.

accordingly parted with some of his clothes to the potter, in part payment of the wages which he owed him.

Palissy next erected an improved furnace, but he was so unfortunate as to build part of the inside with flints. When it was heated, these flints cracked and burst, and the spiculæ were scattered over the pieces of pottery, sticking to them. Though the enamel came out right, the work was irretrievably spoilt, and thus six more months' labour was lost. Persons were found willing to buy the articles at a low price, notwithstanding the injury they had sustained; but Palissy would not sell them, considering that to have done so would be to " decry and abase his honour;" and so he broke in pieces the entire batch. " Nevertheless," says he, " hope continued to inspire me, and I held on manfully; sometimes, when visitors called, I entertained them with pleasantry, while I was really sad at heart. . . . Worst of all the sufferings I had to endure, were the mockeries and persecutions of those of my own household, who were so unreasonable as to expect me to execute work without the means of doing so. For years my furnaces were without any covering or protection, and while attending them I have been for nights at the mercy of the wind and the rain, without help or consolation, save it might be the wailing of cats on the one side and the howling of dogs on the other. Sometimes the tempest would beat so furiously against the furnaces that I was compelled to leave them and seek shelter within doors. Drenched by rain, and in no better plight than if I had been dragged through mire, I have gone to lie down at midnight or at daybreak, stumbling into the house without a light, and reeling from one side to another as if I had been drunken, but really weary with watching and filled with sorrow at the loss of my labour after such long toiling. But alas! my home proved no refuge; for, drenched and besmeared as I was, I found in my chamber a second persecution worse than the first, which makes me even now marvel that I was not utterly consumed by my many sorrows."

At this stage of his affairs, Palissy became melancholy and almost hopeless, and seems to have all but broken down. He wandered gloomily about the fields near Saintes, his clothes hanging in tatters, and himself worn to a skeleton. In a curious passage in his writings he describes how that the calves of his legs had disappeared and were no longer able with the help of garters to hold up his stockings, which fell about his heels when he walked.* The family continued to reproach him for his recklessness, and his neighbours cried shame upon him for his obstinate folly. So he returned for a time to his former calling; and after about a year's diligent labour, during which he earned bread for his household and somewhat recovered his character among his neighbours, he again resumed his darling enterprise. But though he had already spent about ten years in the search for the enamel, it cost him nearly eight more years of experimental plodding before he perfected his invention. He gradually learnt dexterity and certainty of result by experience, gathering practical knowledge out of many failures. Every mishap was a fresh lesson to him, teaching him something new about the nature of enamels, the qualities of argillaceous earths, the tempering of clays, and the construction and management of furnaces.

At last, after about sixteen years' labour, Palissy took heart and called himself Potter. These sixteen years had

---

* "Toutes ces fautes m'ont causé un tel lasseur et tristesse d'esprit, qu'auparavant que j'aye rendu mes émaux fusible à un mesme degré de feu, j'ay cuidé entrer jusques à la porte du sepulchre : aussi en me travaillant à tels affaires je me suis trouvé l'espace de plus se dix ans si fort escoulé en ma personne, qu'il n'y avoit aucune forme ny apparence de bosse aux bras ny aux jambes : ains estoyent mes dites jambes toutes d'une venue : de sorte que les liens de quoy j'attachois mes bas de chausses estoyent, soudain que je cheminois, sur les talons avec le residu de mes chausses."—Œuvres, 319-20.

been his term of apprenticeship to the art ; during which he had wholly to teach himself, beginning at the very beginning. He was now able to sell his wares and thereby maintain his family in comfort. But he never rested satisfied with what he had accomplished. He proceeded from one step of improvement to another; always aiming at the greatest perfection possible. He studied natural objects for patterns, and with such success that the great Buffon spoke of him as "so great a naturalist as Nature only can produce." His ornamental pieces are now regarded as rare gems in the cabinets of virtuosi, and sell at almost fabulous prices.* The ornaments on them are for the most part accurate models from life, of wild animals, lizards, and plants, found in the fields about Saintes, and tastefully combined as ornaments into the texture of a plate or vase. When Palissy had reached the height of his art he styled himself "Ouvrier de Terre et Inventeur des Rustics Figulines."

We have not, however, come to an end of the sufferings of Palissy, respecting which a few words remain to be said. Being a Protestant, at a time when religious persecution waxed hot in the south of France, and expressing his views without fear, he was regarded as a dangerous heretic. His enemies having informed against him, his house at Saintes was entered by the officers of "justice," and his workshop was thrown open to the rabble, who entered and smashed his pottery, while he himself was hurried off by night and cast into a dungeon at Bordeaux, to wait his turn at the stake or the scaffold. He was condemned to be burnt; but a powerful noble, the Constable de Montmorency, interposed to save his life—not because he had any special regard for Palissy or his religion, but because no other artist could be found capable of executing the enamelled pave-

---

* At the sale of Mr. Bernal's articles of vertu in London a few years since, one of Palissy's small dishes, 12 inches in diameter, with a lizard in the centre, sold for 162*l.*

ment for his magnificent château then in course of erection at Ecouen, about four leagues from Paris. By his influence an edict was issued appointing Palissy Inventor of Rustic Figulines to the King and to the Constable, which had the effect of immediately removing him from the jurisdiction of Bourdeaux. He was accordingly liberated, and returned to his home at Saintes only to find it devastated and broken up. His workshop was open to the sky, and his works lay in ruins. Shaking the dust of Saintes from his feet he left the place never to return to it, and removed to Paris to carry on the works ordered of him by the Constable and the Queen Mother, being lodged in the Tuileries * while so occupied.

Besides carrying on the manufacture of pottery, with the aid of his two sons, Palissy, during the latter part of his life, wrote and published several books on the potter's art, with a view to the instruction of his countrymen, and in order that they might avoid the many mistakes which he himself had made. He also wrote on agriculture, on fortification, and natural history, on which latter subject he even delivered lectures to a limited number of persons. He waged war against astrology, alchemy, witchcraft, and like impostures. This stirred up against him many enemies, who pointed the finger at him as a heretic, and he was again arrested for his religion and imprisoned in the Bastille. He was now an old man of seventy-eight, trembling on the verge of the grave, but his spirit was as brave as ever. He was threatened with death unless he recanted; but he was as obstinate in holding to his religion as he had been in hunt-

---

* Within the last few months, Mr. Charles Read, a gentleman curious in matters of Protestant antiquarianism in France, has discovered one of the ovens in which Palissy baked his chefs-d'œuvre. Several moulds of faces, plants, animals, &c., were dug up in a good state of preservation, bearing his well-known stamp. It is situated under the gallery of the Louvre, in the Place du Carrousel.

ing out the secret of the enamel. The king, Henry III.,
even went to see him in prison to induce him to abjure his
faith. "My good man," said the King, "you have now
served my mother and myself for forty-five years. We have
put up with your adhering to your religion amidst fires and
massacres : now I am so pressed by the Guise party as well
as by my own people, that I am constrained to leave you
in the hands of your enemies, and to-morrow you will be
burnt unless you become converted." "Sire," answered the
unconquerable old man, "I am ready to give my life for
the glory of God. You have said many times that you have
pity on me; and now I have pity on you, who have pronounced the words *I am constrained!* It is not spoken like
a king, sire; it is what you, and those who constrain you,
the Guisards and all your people, can never effect upon me,.
for I know how to die."* Palissy did indeed die shortly
after, a martyr, though not at the stake. He died in the
Bastille, after enduring about a year's imprisonment,—there
peacefully terminating a life distinguished for heroic labour,
extraordinary endurance, inflexible rectitude, and the exhibition of many rare and noble virtues.†

The life of John Frederick Böttgher, the inventor of hard
porcelain, presents a remarkable contrast to that of Palissy ;
though it also contains many points of singular and almost
romantic interest. Böttgher was born at Schleiz, in the Voight-
land, in 1685, and at twelve years of age was placed apprentice with an apothecary at Berlin. He seems to have been early
fascinated by chemistry, and occupied most of his leisure
in making experiments. These for the most part tended in

---

* D'Aubigné, ' Histoire Universelle.' The historian adds, " Voyez
l'impudence de ce bilistre ! vous diriez qu'il auroit lu ce vers de Sénèque :
' On ne peut contraindre celui qui sait mourir : *Qui mori scit,* cogi nescit.' "

† The subject of Palissy's life and labours has been ably and elaborately treated by Professor Morley in his well-known work. In the
above brief narrative we have for the most part followed Palissy's own
account of his experiments as given in his 'Art de Terre.'

one direction—the art of converting common metals into gold. At the end of several years, Böttgher pretended to have discovered the universal solvent of the alchemists, and professed that he had made gold by its means. He exhibited its powers before his master, the apothecary Zörn, and by some trick or other succeeded in making him and several other witnesses believe that he had actually converted copper into gold.

The news spread abroad that the apothecary's apprentice had discovered the grand secret, and crowds collected about the shop to get a sight of the wonderful young "gold-cook." The king himself expressed a wish to see and converse with him, and when Frederick I. was presented with a piece of the gold pretended to have been converted from copper, he was so dazzled with the prospect of securing an infinite quantity of it—Prussia being then in great straits for money—that he determined to secure Böttgher and employ him to make gold for him within the strong fortress of Spandau. But the young apothecary, suspecting the king's intention, and probably fearing detection, at once resolved on flight, and he succeeded in getting across the frontier into Saxony.

A reward of a thousand thalers was offered for Böttgher's apprehension, but in vain. He arrived at Wittenberg, and appealed for protection to the Elector of Saxony, Frederick Augustus I. (King of Poland), surnamed " the Strong." Frederick was himself very much in want of money at the time, and he was overjoyed at the prospect of obtaining gold in any quantity by the aid of the young alchemist. Böttgher was accordingly conveyed in secret to Dresden, accompanied by a royal escort. He had scarcely left Wittenberg when a battalion of Prussian grenadiers appeared before the gates demanding the gold-maker's extradition. But it was too late : Böttgher had already arrived in Dresden, where he was lodged in the Golden House, and treated with every consideration, though strictly watched and kept under guard.

G

The Elector, however, must needs leave him there for a time, having to depart forthwith to Poland, then almost in a state of anarchy. But, impatient for gold, he wrote Böttgner from Warsaw, urging him to communicate the secret, so that he himself might practise the art of commutation. The young " gold-cook," thus pressed, forwarded to Frederick a small phial containing " a reddish fluid," which, it was asserted, changed all metals, when in a molten state, into gold. This important phial was taken in charge by the Prince Fürst von Fürstenburg, who, accompanied by a regiment of Guards, hurried with it to Warsaw. Arrived there, it was determined to make immediate trial of the process. The King and the Prince locked themselves up in a secret chamber of the palace, girt themselves about with leather aprons, and like true " gold-cooks " set to work melting copper in a crucible and afterwards applying to it the red fluid of Böttgher. But the result was unsatisfactory; for notwithstanding all that they could do, the copper obstinately remained copper. On referring to the alchemist's instructions, however, the King found that, to succeed with the process, it was necessary that the fluid should be used " in great purity of heart;" and as his Majesty was conscious of having spent the evening in very bad company he attributed the failure of the experiment to that cause. A second trial was followed by no better results, and then the King became furious; for he had confessed and received absolution before beginning the second experiment.

Frederick Augustus now resolved on forcing Böttgher to disclose the golden secret, as the only means of relief from his urgent pecuniary difficulties. The alchemist, hearing of the royal intention, again determined to fly. He succeeded in escaping his guard, and, after three days' travel, arrived at Ens in Austria, where he thought himself safe. The agents of the Elector were, however, at his heels; they had tracked him to the " Golden Stag," which they surrounded, and seizing him in his bed, notwithstanding his resistance and appeals to the Austrian authorities for help, they carried him by force to Dresden. From this time he was more strictly watched than ever, and he was shortly after transferred to the strong fortress of Köningstein. It was communicated to him that the royal exchequer was completely empty, and that ten regiments of Poles in arrears of pay were waiting for his gold. The King himself visited him, and told him in a severe tone that if he did not at once proceed to make gold, he would be hung! (" *Thu mir zurecht, Böttgher, sonst lass ich dich hangen* ").

Years passed, and still Böttgher made no gold; but he was not hung. It was reserved for him to make a far more important discovery than the conversion of copper into gold, namely, the conversion of clay into porcelain. Some rare specimens of this ware had been brought by the Portuguese from China, which were sold for more than their weight in gold. Böttgher was first induced to turn his attention to the subject by Walter von Tschirnhaus, a maker of optical instruments, also an alchemist. Tschirnhaus was a man of education and distinction, and was held in much esteem by Prince Fürstenburg as well as by the Elector. He very sensibly said to Böttgher, still in fear of the gallows—" If you can't make gold, try and do something else; make porcelain."

The alchemist acted on the hint, and began his experiments, working night and day. He prosecuted his investigations for a long time with great assiduity, but without success. At length some red clay, brought to him for the purpose of making his crucibles, set him on the right track. He found that this clay, when submitted to a high temperature, became vitrified and retained its shape; and that its texture resembled that of porcelain, excepting in colour and opacity. He had in fact accidentally discovered red porcelain; and he proceeded to manufacture it and sell it as porcelain.

Böttgher was, however, well aware that the white colour was an essential property of true porcelain ; and he therefore prosecuted his experiments in the hope of discovering the secret. Several years thus passed, but without success ; until again accident stood his friend, and helped him to a knowledge of the art of making white porcelain. One day, in the year 1707, he found his perruque unusually heavy, and asked of his valet the reason. The answer was, that it was owing to the powder with which the wig was dressed, which consisted of a kind of earth then much used for hair powder. Böttgher's quick imagination immediately seized upon the idea. This white earthy powder might possibly be the very earth of which he was in search—at all events the opportunity must not be let slip of ascertaining what it really was. He was rewarded for his painstaking care and watchfulness ; for he found, on experiment, that the principal ingredient of the hair-powder consisted of *kaolin*, the want of which had so long formed an insuperable difficulty in the way of his inquiries.

The discovery, in Böttgher's intelligent hands, led to great results, and proved of far greater importance than the discovery of the philosopher's stone would have been. In October, 1707, he presented his first piece of porcelain to the Elector, who was greatly pleased with it ; and it was resolved that Böttgher should be furnished with the means necessary for perfecting his invention. Having obtained a skilled workman from Delft, he began to *turn* porcelain with great success. He now entirely abandoned alchemy for pottery, and inscribed over the door of his workshop this distich :—

" Es machte Gott, der grosse Schöpfer,
Aus einem Goldmacher einen Töpfer." *

---

* "Almighty God, the great Creator,
Has changed a goldmaker to a potter."

Böttgher, however, was still under strict surveillance, for fear lest he should communicate his secret to others or escape the Elector's control. The new workshops and furnaces which were erected for him, were guarded by troops night and day, and six superior officers were made responsible for the personal security of the potter.

Böttgher's further experiments with his new furnaces proving very successful, and the porcelain which he manufactured being found to fetch large prices, it was next determined to establish a Royal Manufactory of porcelain. The manufacture of delft ware was known to have greatly enriched Holland. Why should not the manufacture of porcelain equally enrich the Elector? Accordingly, a decree went forth, dated the 23rd of January, 1710, for the establishment of "a large manufactory of porcelain" at the Albrechtsburg in Meissen. In this decree, which was translated into Latin, French, and Dutch, and distributed by the Ambassadors of the Elector at all the European Courts, Frederick Augustus set forth that to promote the welfare of Saxony, which had suffered much through the Swedish invasion, he had " directed his attention to the subterranean treasures (*unterirdischen Schätze*) " of the country, and having employed some able persons in the investigation, they had succeeded in manufacturing " a sort of red vessels (*eine Art rother Gefässe*) far superior to the Indian terra sigillata ; " * as also " coloured ware and plates (*buntes Geschirr und Tafeln*) which may be cut, ground, and polished, and are quite equal to Indian vessels," and finally that " specimens of white porcelain (*Proben von weissem Porzellan*) " had already been obtained, and it was hoped that this quality, too, would soon be manufactured in considerable quantities.

---

* The whole of the Chinese and Japanese porcelain was formerly known as Indian porcelain—probably because it was first brought by the Portuguese from India to Europe, after the discovery of the Cape of Good Hope by Vasco da Gama.

The royal decree concluded by inviting " foreign artists and handicraftmen " to come to Saxony and engage as assistants in the new factory, at high wages, and under the patronage of the King. This royal edict probably gives the best account of the actual state of Böttgher's invention at the time.

It has been stated in German publications that Böttgher, for the great services rendered by him to the Elector and to Saxony, was made Manager of the Royal Porcelain Works, and further promoted to the dignity of Baron. Doubtless he deserved these honours ; but his treatment was of an altogether different character, for it was shabby, cruel, and inhuman. Two royal officials, named Matthieu and Nehmitz, were put over his head as directors of the factory, while he himself only held the position of foreman of potters, and at the same time was detained the King's prisoner. During the erection of the factory at Meissen, while his assistance was still indispensable, he was conducted by soldiers to and from Dresden ; and even after the works were finished, he was locked up nightly in his room. All this preyed upon his mind, and in repeated letters to the King he sought to obtain mitigation of his fate. Some of these letters are very touching. " I will devote my whole soul to the art of making porcelain," he writes on one occasion, "I will do more than any inventor ever did before ; only give me liberty, liberty !"

To these appeals, the King turned a deaf ear. He was ready to spend money and grant favours ; but liberty he would not give. He regarded Böttgher as his slave. In this position, the persecuted man kept on working for some time, till, at the end of a year or two, he grew negligent. Disgusted with the world and with himself, he took to drinking. Such is the force of example, that it no sooner became known that Böttgher had betaken himself to this vice, than the greater number of the workmen at the Meissen factory became drunkards too. Quarrels and fightings

without end were the consequence, so that the troops were
frequently called upon to interfere and keep peace among
the " Porzellanern," as they were nicknamed. After a while,
the whole of them, more than three hundred, were shut up
in the Albrechtsburg, and treated as prisoners of state.

Böttgher at last fell seriously ill, and in May, 1713, his
dissolution was hourly expected. The King, alarmed at
losing so valuable a slave, now gave him permission to take
carriage exercise under a guard ; and, having somewhat recovered, he was allowed occasionally to go to Dresden. In
a letter written by the King in April, 1714, Böttgher was
promised his full liberty; but the offer came too late.
Broken in body and mind, alternately working and drinking,
though with occasional gleams of nobler intention, and
suffering under constant ill-health, the result of his enforced
confinement, Böttgher lingered on for a few years more,
until death freed him from his sufferings on the 13th March,
1719, in the thirty-fifth year of his age. He was buried *at
night*—as if he had been a dog—in the Johannis Cemetery
of Meissen. Such was the treatment and such the unhappy
end, of one of Saxony's greatest benefactors.

The porcelain manufacture immediately opened up an
important source of public revenue, and it became so productive to the Elector of Saxony, that his example was shortly
after followed by most European monarchs. Although soft
porcelain had been made at St. Cloud fourteen years before
Böttgher's discovery, the superiority of the hard porcelain
soon became generally recognised. Its manufacture was
begun at Sèvres in 1770, and it has since almost entirely
superseded the softer material. This is now one of the most
thriving branches of French industry, of which the high
quality of the articles produced is certainly indisputable.

The career of Josiah Wedgwood, the English potter, was
less chequered and more prosperous than that of either
Palissy or Böttgher, and his lot was cast in happier times.

Down to the middle of last century England was behind most other nations of the first order in Europe in respect of skilled industry. Although there were many potters in Staffordshire—and Wedgwood himself belonged to a numerous clan of potters of the same name—their productions were of the rudest kind, for the most part only plain brown ware, with the patterns scratched in while the clay was wet. The principal supply of the better articles of earthenware came from Delft in Holland, and of drinking stone pots from Cologne. Two foreign potters, the brothers Elers from Nuremberg, settled for a time in Staffordshire, and introduced an improved manufacture, but they shortly after removed to Chelsea, where they confined themselves to the manufacture of ornamental pieces. No porcelain capable of resisting a scratch with a hard point had yet been made in England; and for a long time the " white ware " made in Staffordshire was not white, but of a dirty cream colour. Such, in a few words, was the condition of the pottery manufacture when Josiah Wedgwood was born at Burslem in 1730. By the time that he died, sixty-four years later, it had become completely changed. By his energy, skill, and genius, he established the trade upon a new and solid foundation ; and, in the words of his epitaph, " converted a rude and inconsiderable manufacture into an elegant art and an important branch of national commerce."

Josiah Wedgwood was one of those indefatigable men who from time to time spring from the ranks of the common people, and by their energetic character not only practically educate the working population in habits of industry, but by the example of diligence and perseverance which they set before them, largely influence the public activity in all directions, and contribute in a great degree to form the national character. He was, like Arkwright, the youngest of a family of thirteen children. His grandfather and granduncle were both potters, as was also his father, who died when he was a mere boy, leaving him a patrimony of twenty pounds. He had learned to read and write at the village school ; but on the death of his father he was taken from it and set to work as a "thrower" in a small pottery carried on by his elder brother. There he began life, his working life, to use his own words, "at the lowest round of the ladder," when only eleven years old. He was shortly after seized by an attack of virulent smallpox, from the effects of which he suffered during the rest of his life, for it was followed by a disease in the right knee, which recurred at frequent intervals, and was only got rid of by the amputation of the limb many years later. Mr. Gladstone, in his eloquent Éloge on Wedgwood recently delivered at Burslem, well observed that the disease from which he suffered was not improbably the occasion of his subsequent excellence. "It prevented him from growing up to be the active, vigorous English workman, possessed of all his limbs, and knowing right well the use of them ; but it put him upon considering whether, as he could not be that, he might not be something else, and something greater. It sent his mind inwards ; it drove him to meditate upon the laws and secrets of his art. The result was, that he arrived at a perception and a grasp of them which might, perhaps, have been envied, certainly have been owned, by an Athenian potter."*

When he had completed his apprenticeship with his brother, Josiah joined partnership with another workman, and carried on a small business in making knife-hafts, boxes, and sundry articles for domestic use. Another partnership followed, when he proceeded to make melon table plates, green pickle leaves, candlesticks, snuffboxes, and such like articles ; but he made comparatively little progress until he began business on his own account at Burslem in the year 1759. There he diligently pursued his calling, introducing

* 'Wedgwood: an Address delivered at Burslem, Oct. 26th, 1863.' By the Right Hon. W. E. Gladstone, M.P.

new articles to the trade, and gradually extending his business. What he chiefly aimed at was to manufacture cream-coloured ware of a better quality than was then produced in Staffordshire as regarded shape, colour, glaze, and durability. To understand the subject thoroughly, he devoted his leisure to the study of chemistry; and he made numerous experiments on fluxes, glazes, and various sorts of clay. Being a close inquirer and accurate observer, he noticed that a certain earth containing silica, which was black before calcination, became white after exposure to the heat of a furnace. This fact, observed and pondered on, led to the idea of mixing silica with the red powder of the potteries, and to the discovery that the mixture becomes white when calcined. He had but to cover this material with a vitrification of transparent glaze, to obtain one of the most important products of fictile art—that which, under the name of English earthenware, was to attain the greatest commercial value and become of the most extensive utility.

Wedgwood was for some time much troubled by his furnaces, though nothing like to the same extent that Palissy was; and he overcame his difficulties in the same way—by repeated experiments and unfaltering perseverance. His first attempts at making porcelain for table use was a succession of disastrous failures,—the labours of months being often destroyed in a day. It was only after a long series of trials, in the course of which he lost time, money, and labour, that he arrived at the proper sort of glaze to be used; but he would not be denied, and at last he conquered success through patience. The improvement of pottery became his passion, and was never lost sight of for a moment. Even when he had mastered his difficulties, and become a prosperous man — manufacturing white stone ware and cream-coloured ware in large quantities for home and foreign use—he went forward perfecting his manufactures, until, his example extending in all directions, the action of the entire district was stimulated, and a great branch of British industry was eventually established on firm foundations. He aimed throughout at the highest excellence, declaring his determination " to give over manufacturing any article, whatsoever it might be, rather than to degrade it." Wedgwood was cordially helped by many persons of rank and influence; for, working in the truest spirit, he readily commanded the help and encouragement of other true workers. He made for Queen Charlotte the first royal table-service of English manufacture, of the kind afterwards called " Queen's-ware," and was appointed Royal Potter; a title which he prized more than if he had been made a baron. Valuable sets of porcelain were entrusted to him for imitation, in which he succeeded to admiration. Sir William Hamilton lent him specimens of ancient art from Herculaneum, of which he produced accurate and beautiful copies. The Duchess of Portland outbid him for the Barberini Vase when that article was offered for sale. He bid as high as seventeen hundred guineas for it : her grace secured it for eighteen hundred ; but when she learnt Wedgwood's object she at once generously lent him the vase to copy. He produced fifty copies at a cost of about 2500*l.*, and his expenses were not covered by their sale; but he gained his object, which was to show that whatever had been done, that English skill and energy could and would accomplish.

Wedgwood called to his aid the crucible of the chemist, the knowledge of the antiquary, and the skill of the artist. He found out Flaxman when a youth, and while he liberally nurtured his genius drew from him a large number of beautiful designs for his pottery and porcelain ; converting them by his manufacture into objects of taste and excellence, and thus making them instrumental in the diffusion of classical art amongst the people. By careful experiment and study he was even enabled to rediscover the art of painting on porcelain or earthenware vases and similar articles—an art practised by the ancient Etruscans, but which had been lost since the time of Pliny. He distinguished himself by his own contributions to science, and his name is still identified with the Pyrometer which he invented. He was an indefatigable supporter of all measures of public utility; and the construction of the Trent and Mersey Canal, which completed the navigable communication between the eastern and western sides of the island, was mainly due to his public-spirited exertions, allied to the engineering skill of Brindley. The road accommodation of the district being of an execrable character, he planned and executed a turnpike-road through the Potteries, ten miles in length. The reputation he achieved was such that his works at Burslem, and subsequently those at Etruria, which he founded and built, became a point of attraction to distinguished visitors from all parts of Europe.

The result of Wedgwood's labours was, that the manufacture of pottery, which he found in the very lowest condition, became one of the staples of England; and instead of importing what we needed for home use from abroad, we became large exporters to other countries, supplying them with earthenware even in the face of enormous prohibitory duties on articles of British produce. Wedgwood gave evidence as to his manufactures before Parliament in 1785, only some thirty years after he had begun his operations; from which it appeared, that instead of providing only casual employment to a small number of inefficient and badly remunerated workmen, about 20,000 persons then derived their bread directly from the manufacture of earthenware, without taking into account the increased numbers to which it gave employment in coal-mines, and in the carrying trade by land and sea, and the stimulus which it gave to employment in many ways in various parts of the country. Yet, important as had been the advances made in his time, Mr. Wedgwood was of opinion that the manufacture was but in its infancy, and that the improvements which he had effected were of but small amount compared with those to which the art was capable of attaining, through the continued industry and growing intelligence of the manufacturers, and the natural facilities and political advantages enjoyed by Great Britain ; an opinion which has been fully borne out by the progress which has since been effected in this important branch of industry.   In 1852 not fewer than 84,000,000 pieces of pottery were exported from England to other countries, besides what were made for home use. But it is not merely the quantity and value of the produce that is entitled to consideration, but the improvement of the condition of the population by whom this great branch of industry is conducted.   When Wedgwood began his labours, the Staffordshire district was only in a half-civilized state. The people were poor, uncultivated, and few in number. When Wedgwood's manufacture was firmly established, there was found ample employment at good wages for three times the number of population ; while their moral advancement had kept pace with their material improvement.

Men such as these are fairly entitled to take rank as the Industrial Heroes of the civilized world.   Their patient self-reliance amidst trials and difficulties, their courage and perseverance in the pursuit of worthy objects, are not less heroic of their kind than the bravery and devotion of the soldier and the sailor, whose duty and pride it is heroically to defend what these valiant leaders of industry have so heroically achieved.

CHAPTER IV.

APPLICATION AND PERSEVERANCE.

" Rich are the diligent, who can command
  Time, nature's stock! and could his hour-glass fall,
Would, as for seed of stars, stoop for the sand,
  And, by incessant labour, gather all."—*D'Avenant.*
" Allez en avant, et la foi vous viendra ! "—*D'Alembert.*

T H E greatest results in life are usually attained by simple means, and the exercise of ordinary quali-ties. The common life of every day, with its cares, necessities, and duties, affords ample oppor-tunity for acquiring experience of the best kind; and its most beaten paths provide the true worker with abundant scope for effort and room for self-improvement. The road of human welfare lies along the old highway of steadfast well-doing; and they who are the most persistent, and work in the truest spirit, will usually be the most successful.

Fortune has often been blamed for her blindness; but fortune is not so blind as men are. Those who look into practical life will find that fortune is usually on the side of the industrious, as the winds and waves are on the side of the best navigators. In the pursuit of even the highest branches of human inquiry, the commoner qualities are found the most useful—such as common sense, attention, application, and perseverance. Genius may not be necessary, though even genius of the highest sort does not disdain the use of these ordinary qualities. The very greatest men have been

among the least believers in the power of genius, and as
worldly wise and persevering as successful men of the com·
moner sort. Some have even defined genius to be only
common sense intensified. A distinguished teacher and
president of a college spoke of it as the power of making
efforts. John Foster held it to be the power of lighting
one's own fire. Buffon said of genius " it is patience."

Newton's was unquestionably a mind of the very highest
order, and yet, when asked by what means he had worked
out his extraordinary discoveries, he modestly answered,
" By always thinking unto them." At another time he thus
expressed his method of study : "I keep the subject continually before me, and wait till the first dawnings open
slowly by little and little into a full and clear light." It
was in Newton's case, as in every other, only by diligent
application and perseverance that his great reputation was
achieved. Even his recreation consisted in change of study,
laying down one subject to take up another. To Dr.
Bentley he said : "If I have done the public any service, it
is due to nothing but industry and patient thought." So
Kepler, another great philosopher, speaking of his studies
and his progress, said : "As in Virgil, ' Fama mobilitate
viget, vires acquirit eundo,' so it was with me, that the
diligent thought on these things was the occasion of still
further thinking ; until at last I brooded with the whole
energy of my mind upon the subject."

The extraordinary results effected by dint of sheer industry and perseverance, have led many distinguished men
to doubt whether the gift of genius be so exceptional
an endowment as it is usually supposed to be. Thus
Voltaire held that it is only a very slight line of separation
that divides the man of genius from the man of ordinary
mould. Beccaria was even of opinion that all men might
be poets and orators, and Reynolds that they might be
painters and sculptors. If this were really so, that stolid

Englishman might not have been so very far wrong after all, who, on Canova's death, inquired of his brother whether it was "his intention to carry on the business!" Locke, Helvetius, and Diderot believed that all men have an equal aptitude for genius, and that what some are able to effect, under the laws which regulate the operations of the intellect, must also be within the reach of others who, under like circumstances, apply themselves to like pursuits. But while admitting to the fullest extent the wonderful achievements of labour, and recognising the fact that men of the most distinguished genius have invariably been found the most indefatigible workers, it must nevertheless be sufficiently obvious that, without the original endowment of heart and brain, no amount of labour, however well applied, could have produced a Shakespeare, a Newton, a Beethoven, or a Michael Angelo.

Dalton, the chemist, repudiated the notion of his being "a genius," attributing everything which he had accomplished to simple industry and accumulation. John Hunter said of himself, "My mind is like a beehive; but full as it is of buzz and apparent confusion, it is yet full of order and regularity, and food collected with incessant industry from the choicest stores of nature." We have, indeed, but to glance at the biographies of great men to find that the most distinguished inventors, artists, thinkers, and workers of all kinds, owe their success, in a great measure, to their indefatigable industry and application. They were men who turned all things to gold—even time itself. Disraeli the elder held that the secret of success consisted in being master of your subject, such mastery being attainable only through continuous application and study. Hence it happens that the men who have most moved the world, have not been so much men of genius, strictly so called, as men of intense mediocre abilities, and untiring perseverance; not so often the gifted, of naturally bright and shining qualities, as those who have applied themselves diligently to their work, in whatsoever line that might lie. "Alas!" said a widow, speaking of her brilliant but careless son, "he has not the gift of continuance." Wanting in perseverance, such volatile natures are outstripped in the race of life by the diligent and even the dull. "Che va piano, va longano, e va lontano," says the Italian proverb: Who goes slowly, goes long, and goes far.

Hence, a great point to be aimed at is to get the working quality well trained. When that is done, the race will be found comparatively easy. We must repeat and again repeat; facility will come with labour. Not even the simplest art can be accomplished without it; and what difficulties it is found capable of achieving! It was by early discipline and repetition that the late Sir Robert Peel cultivated those remarkable, though still mediocre powers, which rendered him so illustrious an ornament of the British Senate. When a boy at Drayton Manor, his father was accustomed to set him up at table to practise speaking extempore; and he early accustomed him to repeat as much of the Sunday's sermon as he could remember. Little progress was made at first, but by steady perseverance the habit of attention became powerful, and the sermon was at length repeated almost verbatim. When afterwards replying in succession to the arguments of his parliamentary opponents—an art in which he was perhaps unrivalled—it was little surmised that the extraordinary power of accurate remembrance which he displayed on such occasions had been originally trained under the discipline of his father in the parish church of Drayton.

It is indeed marvellous what continuous application will effect in the commonest of things. It may seem a simple affair to play upon a violin; yet what a long and laborious practice it requires! Giardini said to a youth who asked him how long it would take to learn it, "Twelve hours

H

a day for twenty years together.·' Industry, it is said, *fait l'ours danser.* The poor figurante must devote years of incessant toil to her profitless task before she can shine in it. When Taglioni was preparing herself for her evening exhibition, she would, after a severe two hours' lesson from her father, fall down exhausted, and had to be undressed, sponged, and resuscitated, totally unconscious. The agility and bounds of the evening were insured only at a price like this.

Progress, however, of the best kind, is comparatively slow. Great results cannot be achieved at once; and we must be satisfied to advance in life as we walk, step by step. De Maistre says that "to know *how to wait* is the great secret of success." We must sow before we can reap, and often have to wait long, content meanwhile to look patiently forward in hope; the fruit best worth waiting for often ripening the slowest. But "time and patience," says the Eastern proverb, "change the mulberry leaf to satin."

To wait patiently, however, men must work cheerfully. Cheerfulness is an excellent working quality, imparting great elasticity to the character. As a bishop has said, "Temper is nine-tenths of Christianity;" so are cheerfulness and diligence nine-tenths of practical wisdom. They are the life and soul of success, as well as of happiness; perhaps the very highest pleasure in life consisting in clear, brisk, conscious working; energy, confidence, and every other good quality mainly depending upon it. Sydney Smith, when labouring as a parish priest at Foston-le-Clay, in Yorkshire, —though he did not feel himself to be in his proper element,—went cheerfully to work in the firm determination to do his best. "I am resolved," he said, "to like it, and reconcile myself to it, which is more manly than to feign myself above it, and to send up complaints by the post of being thrown away, and being desolate, and such like trash." So Dr. Hook, when leaving Leeds for a new sphere of labour

said, "Wherever I may be, I shall, by God's blessing, do
with my might what my hand findeth to do; and if I do
not find work, I shall make it."

Labourers for the public good especially, have to work
long and patiently, often uncheered by the prospect of
immediate recompense or result. The seeds they sow sometimes lie hidden under the winter's snow, and before the
spring comes the husbandman may have gone to his rest.
It is not every public worker who, like Rowland Hill, sees
his great idea bring forth fruit in his life-time. Adam Smith
sowed the seeds of a great social amelioration in that dingy
old University of Glasgow where he so long laboured, and
laid the foundations of his 'Wealth of Nations;' but
seventy years passed before his work bore substantial fruits,
nor indeed are they all gathered in yet.

Nothing can compensate for the loss of hope in a man:
it entirely changes the character. " How can I work— how
can I be happy," said a great but miserable thinker, "when
I have lost all hope?" One of the most cheerful and
courageous, because one of the most hopeful of workers,
was Carey, the missionary. When in India, it was no un-
common thing for him to weary out three pundits, who
officiated as his clerks, in one day, he himself taking rest
only in change of employment. Carey, the son of a shoemaker, was supported in his labours by Ward, the son of a
carpenter, and Marsham, the son of a weaver. By their
labours, a magnificent college was erected at Serampore;
sixteen flourishing stations were established; the Bible was
translated into sixteen languages, and the seeds were sown
of a beneficent moral revolution in British India. Carey was
never ashamed of the humbleness of his origin. On one
occasion, when at the Governor-General's table he overheard an officer opposite him asking another, loud enough
to be heard, whether Carey had not once been a shoemaker:
" No, sir," exclaimed Carey immediately; " only a cobbler."

An eminently characteristic anecdote has been told of his perseverance as a boy. When climbing a tree one day, his foot slipped, and he fell to the ground, breaking his leg by the fall. He was confined to his bed for weeks, but when he recovered and was able to walk without support, the very first thing he did was to go and climb that tree. Carey had need of this sort of dauntless courage for the great missionary work of his life, and nobly and resolutely he did it.

It was a maxim of Dr. Young, the philosopher, that "Any man can do what any other man has done ;" and it is unquestionable that he himself never recoiled from any trials to which he determined to subject himself. It is related of him, that the first time he mounted a horse, he was in company with the grandson of Mr. Barclay of Ury, the well-known sportsman; when the horseman who preceded them leapt a high fence. Young wished to imitate him, but fell off his horse in the attempt. Without saying a word, he remounted, made a second effort, and was again unsuccessful, but this time he was not thrown further than on to the horse's neck, to which he clung. At the third trial, he succeeded, and cleared the fence.

The story of Timour the Tartar learning a lesson of perseverance under adversity from the spider is well known. Not less interesting is the anecdote of Audubon, the American ornithologist, as related by himself: "An accident," he says, "which happened to two hundred of my original drawings, nearly put a stop to my researches in ornithology. I shall relate it, merely to show how far enthusiasm—for by no other name can I call my perseverance—may enable the preserver of nature to surmount the most disheartening difficulties. I left the village of Henderson, in Kentucky, situated on the banks of the Ohio, where I resided for several years, to proceed to Philadelphia on business. I looked to my drawings before my departure, placed them carefully in a wooden box, and gave them in charge of a relative, with injunctions to see that no injury should happen to them. My absence was of several months; and when I returned, after having enjoyed the pleasures of home for a few days, I inquired after my box, and what I was pleased to call my treasure. The box was produced and opened; but reader, feel for me—a pair of Norway rats had taken possession of the whole, and reared a young family among the gnawed bits of paper, which, but a month previous, represented nearly a thousand inhabitants of air! The burning heat which instantly rushed through my brain was too great to be endured without affecting my whole nervous system. I slept for several nights, and the days passed like days of oblivion—until the animal powers being recalled into action through the strength of my constitution, I took up my gun, my notebook, and my pencils, and went forth to the woods as gaily as if nothing had happened. I felt pleased that I might now make better drawings than before; and, ere a period not exceeding three years had elapsed, my portfolio was again filled."

The accidental destruction of Sir Isaac Newton's papers, by his little dog 'Diamond' upsetting a lighted taper upon his desk, by which the elaborate calculations of many years were in a moment destroyed, is a well-known anecdote, and need not be repeated: it is said that the loss caused the philosopher such profound grief that it seriously injured his health, and impaired his understanding. An accident of a somewhat similiar kind happened to the MS. of Mr. Carlyle's first volume of his 'French Revolution.' He had lent the MS. to a literary neighbour to peruse. By some mischance, it had been left lying on the parlour floor, and become forgotten. Weeks ran on, and the historian sent for his work, the printers being loud for "copy." Inquiries were made, and it was found that the maid-of-all-work, finding what she conceived to be a bundle of waste paper on the floor, had used it to light the kitchen and parlour fires with ! Such was the answer returned to Mr. Carlyle ; and his feelings may be imagined. There was, however, no help for him but to set resolutely to work to re-write the book ; and he turned to and did it. He had no draft, and was compelled to rake up from his memory facts, ideas, and expressions, which had been long since dismissed. The composition of the book in the first instance had been a work of pleasure ; the re-writing of it a second time was one of pain and anguish almost beyond belief. That he persevered and finished the volume under such circumstances, affords an instance of determination of purpose which has seldom been surpassed.

The lives of eminent inventors are eminently illustrative of the same quality of perseverance. George Stephenson, when addressing young men, was accustomed to sum up his best advice to them in the words, "Do as I have done —persevere." He had worked at the improvement of his locomotive for some fifteen years before achieving his decisive victory at Rainhill ; and Watt was engaged for some thirty years upon the condensing-engine before he brought it to perfection. But there are equally striking illustrations of perseverance to be found in every other branch of science, art, and industry. Perhaps one of the most interesting is that connected with the disentombment of the Nineveh marbles, and the discovery of the long-lost cuneiform or arrow-headed character in which the inscriptions on them are written—a kind of writing which had been lost to the world since the period of the Macedonian conquest of Persia.

An intelligent cadet of the East India Company, stationed at Kermanshah, in Persia, had observed the curious cunei- form inscriptions on the old monuments in the neighbour- hood—so old that all historical traces of them had been lost,—and amongst the inscriptions which he copied was that on the celebrated rock of Behistun—a perpendicular rock rising abruptly some 1700 feet from the plain, the lower part bearing inscriptions for the space of about 300 feet in three languages—Persian, Scythian, and Assyrian. Comparison of the known with the unknown, of the language which survived with the language that had been lost, enabled this cadet to acquire some knowledge of the cuneiform character, and even to form an alphabet. Mr. (afterwards Sir Henry) Rawlinson sent his tracings home for examination. No professors in colleges as yet knew anything of the cuneiform character ; but there was a ci-devant clerk of the East India House—a modest unknown man of the name of Norris —who had made this little-understood subject his study, to whom the tracings were submitted ; and so accurate was his knowledge, that, though he had never seen the Behistun rock, he pronounced that the cadet had not copied the puzzling inscription with proper exactness. Rawlinson, who was still in the neighbourhood of the rock, compared his copy with the original, and found that Norris was right ; and by further comparison and careful study the knowledge of the cuneiform writing was thus greatly advanced.

But to make the learning of these two self-taught men of avail, a third labourer was necessary in order to supply them with material for the exercise of their skill. Such a labourer presented himself in the person of Austen Layard, originally an articled clerk in the office of a London solicitor. One would scarcely have expected to find in these three men, a cadet, an India-House clerk, and a lawyer's clerk, the discoverers of a forgotten language, and of the buried history of Babylon ; yet it was so. Layard was a youth of only twenty-two, travelling in the East, when he was possessed with a desire to penetrate the regions beyond the Euphrates. Accompanied by a single companion, trusting to his arms for protection, and, what was better, to his cheerfulness, politeness, and chivalrous bearing, he passed safely amidst tribes at deadly war with each other; and, after the lapse of many years, with comparatively slender means at his command, but aided by application and perseverance, resolute will and purpose, and almost sublime patience,—borne up throughout by his passionate enthusiasm for discovery and research,—he succeeded in laying bare and digging up an amount of historical treasures, the like of which has probably never before been collected by the industry of any one man. Not less than two miles of bas-reliefs were thus brought to light by Mr. Layard. The selection of these valuable antiquities, now placed in the British Museum, was found so curiously corroborative of the scriptural records of events which occurred some three thousand years ago, that they burst upon the world almost like a new revelation. And the story of the disentombment of these remarkable works, as told by Mr. Layard himself in his 'Monuments of Nineveh,' will always be regarded as one of the most charming and unaffected records which we possess of individual enterprise, industry, and energy.

The career of the Comte de Buffon presents another remarkable illustration of the power of patient industry, as well as of his own saying, that "Genius is patience." Notwithstanding the great results achieved by him in natural history, Buffon, when a youth, was regarded as of mediocre talents. His mind was slow in forming itself, and slow in reproducing what it had acquired. He was also constitutionally indolent; and being born to good estate, it might be supposed that he would indulge his liking for ease and luxury. Instead of which, he early formed the resolution of denying himself pleasure, and devoting himself to study and self-culture. Regarding time as a treasure that was limited, and finding that he was losing many hours by lying a-bed in the mornings, he determined to break himself of the habit. He struggled hard against it for some time, but failed in being able to rise at the hour he had fixed. He then called his servant, Joseph, to his help, and promised him the reward of a crown every time that he succeeded in getting him up before six. At first, when called, Buffon declined to rise—pleaded that he was ill, or pretended anger at being disturbed; and on the Count at length getting up, Joseph found that he had earned nothing but reproaches for having permitted his master to lie a-bed contrary to his express orders. At length the valet determined to earn his crown; and again and again he forced Buffon to rise, notwithstanding his entreaties, expostulations, and threats of immediate discharge from his service. One morning Buffon was unusually obstinate, and Joseph found it necessary to resort to the extreme measure of dashing a basin of ice-cold water under the bed-clothes, the effect of which was instantaneous. By the persistent use of such means, Buffon at length conquered his habit; and he was accustomed to say that he owed to Joseph three or four volumes of his Natural History.

For forty years of his life, Buffon worked every morning at his desk from nine till two, and again in the evening from five till nine. His diligence was so continuous and so regular that it became habitual. His biographer has said of him, "Work was his necessity; his studies were the charm of his life; and towards the last term of his glorious career he frequently said that he still hoped to be able to consecrate to them a few more years." He was a most conscientious worker, always studying to give the reader his best thoughts, expressed in the very best manner. He was never wearied with touching and retouching his compositions, so that his style may be pronounced almost perfect. He wrote the 'Époques de la Nature' not fewer than eleven times before he was satisfied with it; although he had thought over the work about fifty years. He was a thorough man of business, most orderly in everything; and he was accustomed to say that genius without order lost three-fourths of its power.

His great success as a writer was the result mainly of his painstaking labour and diligent application. "Buffon" observed Madame Necker, "strongly persuaded that genius is the result of a profound attention directed to a particular subject, said that he was thoroughly wearied out when composing his first writings, but compelled himself to return to them and go over them carefully again, even when he thought he had already brought them to a certain degree of perfection; and that at length he found pleasure instead of weariness in this long and elaborate correction." It ought also to be added that Buffon wrote and published all his great works while afflicted by one of the most painful diseases to which the human frame is subject.

Literary life affords abundant illustrations of the same power of perseverance; and perhaps no career is more instructive, viewed in this light, than that of Sir Walter Scott. His admirable working qualities were trained in a lawyer's office, where he pursued for many years a sort of drudgery scarcely above that of a copying clerk. His daily dull routine made his evenings, which were his own, all the more sweet; and he generally devoted them to reading and study. He himself attributed to his prosaic office discipline that habit of steady, sober diligence, in which mere literary men are so often found wanting. As a copying clerk he was allowed 3*d.* for every page containing a certain number of words; and he sometimes, by extra work, was able to copy as many as 120 pages in twenty-four hours, thus earning some 30*s.*; out of which he would occasionally purchase an odd volume, otherwise beyond his means.

During his after-life Scott was wont to pride himself upon being a man of business, and he averred, in contradiction to what he called the cant of sonnetteers, that there was no necessary connection between genius and an aversion or contempt for the common duties of life. On the contrary, he was of opinion that to spend some fair portion of every day in any matter-of-fact occupation was good for the higher faculties themselves in the upshot. While afterwards acting as clerk to the Court of Session in Edinburgh, he performed his literary work chiefly before breakfast, attending the court during the day, where he authenticated registered deeds and writings of various kinds. On the whole, says Lockhart, "it forms one of the most remarkable features in his history, that throughout the most active period of his literary career, he must have devoted a large proportion of his hours, during half at least of every year, to the conscientious discharge of professional duties." It was a principle of action which he laid down for himself, that he must earn his living by business, and not by literature. On one occasion he said, "I determined that literature should be my staff, not my crutch, and that the profits of my literary labour, however convenient otherwise, should not, if I could help it, become necessary to my ordinary expenses."

His punctuality was one of the most carefully cultivated of his habits, otherwise it had not been possible for him to get through so enormous an amount of literary labour. He made it a rule to answer every letter received by him on the same day, except where inquiry and deliberation were requisite. Nothing else could have enabled him to keep abreast with the flood of communications that poured in upon him and sometimes put his good nature to the severest test. It was his practice to rise by five o'clock, and light his own fire. He shaved and dressed with deliberation, and was seated at his desk by six o'clock, with his papers arranged before him in the most accurate order, his works of reference marshalled round him on the floor, while at least one favourite dog lay watching his eye, outside the line of books. Thus by the time the family assembled for breakfast, between nine and ten, he had done enough—to use his own words—to break the neck of the day's work. But with all his diligent and indefatigable industry, and his immense knowledge, the result of many years' patient labour, Scott always spoke with the greatest diffidence of his own powers. On one occasion he said, "Throughout every part of my career I have felt pinched and hampered by my own ignorance."

Such is true wisdom and humility; for the more a man really knows, the less conceited he will be. The student at Trinity College who went up to his professor to take leave of him because he had "finished his education," was wisely rebuked by the professor's reply, "Indeed! I am only beginning mine." The superficial person who has obtained a smattering of many things, but knows nothing well, may pride himself upon his gifts; but the sage humbly confesses that "all he knows is, that he knows nothing," or like Newton, that he has been only engaged in picking shells by the sea shore, while the great ocean of truth lies all unexplored before him.

The lives of second-rate literary men furnish equally remarkable illustrations of the power of perseverance. The late John Britton, author of 'The Beauties of England and Wales,' and of many valuable architectural works, was born in a miserable cot in Kingston, Wiltshire. His father had been a baker and maltster, but was ruined in trade and became insane while Britton was yet a child. The boy received very little schooling, but a great deal of bad example, which happily did not corrupt him. He was early in life set to labour with an uncle, a tavern-keeper in Clerkenwell, under whom he bottled, corked, and binned wine for more than five years. His health failing him, his uncle turned him adrift in the world, with only two guineas, the fruits of his five years' service, in his pocket. During the next seven years of his life he endured many vicissitudes and hardships. Yet he says, in his autobiography, "in my poor and obscure lodgings, at eighteenpence a week, I indulged in study, and often read in bed during the winter evenings,

because I could not afford a fire." Travelling on foot to
Bath, he there obtained an engagement as a cellarman, but
shortly after we find him back in the metropolis again,
almost penniless, shoeless, and shirtless. He succeeded,
however, in obtaining employment as a cellarman at the
London Tavern, where it was his duty to be in the cellar from
seven in the morning until eleven at night. His health
broke down under this confinement in the dark, added to
the heavy work; and he then engaged himself, at fifteen
shillings a week, to an attorney,—for he had been diligently
cultivating the art of writing during the few spare minutes
that he could call his own. While in this employment, he
devoted his leisure principally to perambulating the book-
stalls, where he read books by snatches which he could not
buy, and thus picked up a good deal of odd knowledge.
Then he shifted to another office, at the advanced wages of
twenty shillings a week, still reading and studying. At
twenty-eight he was able to write a book, which he published
under the title of ' The Enterprising Adventures of Pizarro ; '
and from that time until his death, during a period of about
fifty-five years, Britton was occupied in laborious literary
occupation. The number of his published works is not
fewer than eighty-seven ; the most important being ' The
Cathedral Antiquities of England,' in fourteen volumes, a
truly magnificent work ; itself the best monument of John
Britton's indefatigable industry.

Loudon, the landscape gardener, was a man of somewhat
similar character, possessed of an extraordinary working
power. The son of a farmer near Edinburgh, he was early
inured to work. His skill in drawing plans and making
sketches of scenery induced his father to train him for a
landscape gardener. During his apprenticeship he sat up
two whole nights every week to study ; yet he worked harder
during the day than any labourer. In the course of his
night studies he learnt French, and before he was eighteen

he translated a life of Abelard for an Encyclopædia. He was so eager to make progress in life, that when only twenty, while working as a gardener in England, he wrote down in his note-book, "I am now twenty years of age, and perhaps a third part of my life has passed away, and yet what have I done to benefit my fellow men?" an unusual reflection for a youth of only twenty. From French he proceeded to learn German, and rapidly mastered that language. Having taken a large farm, for the purpose of introducing Scotch improvements in the art of agriculture, he shortly succeeded in realising a considerable income. The continent being thrown open at the end of the war, he travelled abroad for the purpose of inquiring into the system of gardening and agriculture in other countries. He twice repeated his journeys, and the results were published in his Encyclopædias, which are among the most remarkable works of their kind,—distinguished for the immense mass of useful matter which they contain, collected by an amount of industry and labour which has rarely been equalled.

The career of Samuel Drew is not less remarkable than any of those which we have cited. His father was a hardworking labourer of the parish of St. Austell, in Cornwall. Though poor, he contrived to send his two sons to a penny-a-week school in the neighbourhood. Jabez, the elder, took delight in learning, and made great progress in his lessons ; but Samuel, the younger, was a dunce, notoriously given to mischief and playing truant. When about eight years old he was put to manual labour, earning three-halfpence a day as a buddle-boy at a tin mine. At ten he was apprenticed to a shoemaker, and while in this employment he endured much hardship,—living, as he used to say, "like a toad under a harrow." He often thought of running away and becoming a pirate, or something of the sort, and he seems to have grown in recklessness as he grew in years. In robbing orchards he was usually a leader ; and, as he grew older, he delighted to take part in any poaching or smuggling adventure. When about seventeen, before his apprenticeship was out, he ran away, intending to enter on board a man-of-war ; but, sleeping in a hay-field at night cooled him a little, and he returned to his trade.

Drew next removed to the neighbourhood of Plymouth to work at his shoemaking business, and while at Cawsand he won a prize for cudgel-playing, in which he seems to have been an adept. While living there, he had nearly lost his life in a smuggling exploit which he had joined, partly induced by the love of adventure, and partly by the love of gain, for his regular wages were not more than eight shillings a-week. One night, notice was given throughout Crafthole, that a smuggler was off the coast, ready to land her cargo ; on which the male population of the place—nearly all smugglers—made for the shore. One party remained on the rocks to make signals and dispose of the goods as they were landed ; and another manned the boats, Drew being of the latter party. The night was intensely dark, and very little of the cargo had been landed, when the wind rose, with a heavy sea. The men in the boats, however, determined to persevere, and several trips were made between the smuggler, now standing farther out to sea, and the shore. One of the men in the boat in which Drew was, had his hat blown off by the wind, and in attempting to recover it, the boat was upset. Three of the men were immediately drowned ; the others clung to the boat for a time, but finding it drifting out to sea, they took to swimming. They were two miles from land, and the night was intensely dark. After being about three hours in the water, Drew reached a rock near the shore, with one or two others, where he remained benumbed with cold till morning, when he and his companions were discovered and taken off, more dead than alive. A keg of brandy from the cargo just landed was brought, the head knocked in with a hatchet, and a bowlfull of the liquid presented to the survivors; and, shortly after, Drew was able to walk two miles through deep snow, to his lodgings.

This was a very unpromising beginning of a life; and yet this same Drew, scapegrace, orchard-robber, shoemaker, cudgel-player, and smuggler, outlived the recklessness of his youth, and became distinguished as a minister of the Gospel and a writer of good books. Happily, before it was too late, the energy which characterised him was turned into a more healthy direction, and rendered him as eminent in usefulness as he had before been in wickedness. His father again took him back to St. Austell, and found employment for him as a journeyman shoemaker. Perhaps his recent escape from death had tended to make the young man serious, as we shortly find him, attracted by the forcible preaching of Dr. Adam Clarke, a minister of the Wesleyan Methodists. His brother having died about the same time, the impression of seriousness was deepened; and thenceforward he was an altered man. He began anew the work of education, for he had almost forgotten how to read and write; and even after several years' practice, a friend compared his writing to the traces of a spider dipped in ink set to crawl upon paper. Speaking of himself, about that time, Drew afterwards said, "The more I read, the more I felt my own ignorance; and the more I felt my ignorance, the more invincible became my energy to surmount it. Every leisure moment was now employed in reading one thing or another. Having to support myself by manual labour, my time for reading was but little, and to overcome this disadvantage, my usual method was to place a book before me while at meat, and at every repast I read five or six pages." The perusal of Locke's 'Essay on the Understanding' gave the first metaphysical turn to his mind. "It awakened me from my stupor," said he, "and induced me to form a resolution to abandon the grovelling views which I had been accustomed to entertain."

Drew began business on his own account, with a capital of a few shillings; but his character for steadiness was such that a neighbouring miller offered him a loan, which was accepted, and, success attending his industry, the debt was repaid at the end of a year. He started with a determination to "owe no man anything," and he held to it in the midst of many privations. Often he went to bed supperless, to avoid rising in debt. His ambition was to achieve independence by industry and economy, and in this he gradually succeeded. In the midst of incessant labour, he sedulously strove to improve his mind, studying astronomy, history, and metaphysics. He was induced to pursue the latter study chiefly because it required fewer books to consult than either of the others. "It appeared to be a thorny path," he said, "but I determined, nevertheless, to enter, and accordingly began to tread it."

Added to his labours in shoemaking and metaphysics, Drew became a local preacher and a class leader. He took an eager interest in politics, and his shop became a favourite resort with the village politicians. And when they did not come to him, he went to them to talk over public affairs. This so encroached upon his time that he found it necessary sometimes to work until midnight to make up for the hours lost during the day. His political fervour became the talk of the village. While busy one night hammering away at a shoe-sole, a little boy, seeing a light in the shop, put his mouth to the keyhole of the door, and called out in a shrill pipe, "Shoemaker! shoemaker! work by night and run about by day!" A friend, to whom Drew afterwards told the story, asked, "And did not you run after the boy, and strap him?" "No, no," was the reply; "had a pistol been fired off at my ear, I could not have been more dismayed or confounded. I dropped my work, and said to myself, 'True, true! but you shall never have that to say of me again.' To me that

I

cry was as the voice of God, and it has been a word in season throughout my life. I learnt from it not to leave till to-morrow the work of to-day, or to idle when I ought to be working."

From that moment Drew dropped politics, and stuck to his work, reading and studying in his spare hours : but he never allowed the latter pursuit to interfere with his business, though it frequently broke in upon his rest. He married, and thought of emigrating to America ; but he remained working on. His literary taste first took the direction of poetical composition ; and from some of the fragments which have been preserved, it appears that his speculations as to the immaterialty and immortality of the soul had their origin in these poetical musings. His study was the kitchen, where his wife's bellows served him for a desk ; and he wrote amidst the cries and cradlings of his children. Paine's 'Age of Reason' having appeared about this time and excited much interest, he composed a pamphlet in refutation of its arguments, which was published. He used afterwards to say that it was the 'Age of Reason' that made him an author. Various pamphlets from his pen shortly appeared in rapid succession, and a few years later, while still working at shoemaking, he wrote and published his admirable 'Essay on the Immaterialty and Immortality of the Human Soul,' which he sold for twenty pounds, a great sum in his estimation at the time. The book went through many editions, and is still prized.

Drew was in no wise puffed up by his success, as many young authors are, but, long after he had become celebrated as a writer, used to be seen sweeping the street before his door, or helping his apprentices to carry in the winter's coals. Nor could he, for some time, bring himself to regard literature as a profession to live by. His first care was to secure an honest livelihood by his business, and to put into the "lottery of literary success," as he termed it, only the surplus of his time. At length, however, he devoted himself wholly to literature, more particularly in connection with the Wesleyan body ; editing one of their magazines, and superintending the publication of several of their denominational works. He also wrote in the ' Eclectic Review,' and compiled and published a valuable history of his native county, Cornwall, with numerous other works. Towards the close of his career, he said of himself,—" Raised from one of the lowest stations in society, I have endeavoured through life to bring my family into a state of respectability, by honest industry, frugality, and a high regard for my moral character. Divine providence has smiled on my exertions, and crowned my wishes with success."

The late Joseph Hume pursued a very different career, but worked in an equally persevering spirit. He was a man of moderate parts, but of great industry and unimpeachable honesty of purpose. The motto of his life was "Perseverance," and well he acted up to it. His father dying while he was a mere child, his mother opened a small shop in Montrose, and toiled hard to maintain her family and bring them up respectably. Joseph she put apprentice to a surgeon, and educated for the medical profession. Having got his diploma, he made several voyages to India as ship's surgeon,* and afterwards obtained a cadetship in the

* It was characteristic of Mr. Hume, that, during his professional voyages between England and India, he should diligently apply his spare time to the study of navigation and seamanship ; and many years after, it proved of use to him in a remarkable manner. In 1825, when on his passage from London to Leith by a sailing smack, the vessel had scarcely cleared the mouth of the Thames when a sudden storm came on, she was driven out of her course, and, in the darkness of the night, she struck on the Goodwin Sands. The captain, losing his presence of mind, seemed incapable of giving coherent orders, and it is probable that the vessel would have become a total wreck, had not one of the passengers suddenly taken the command and directed the working of the ship, himself taking the helm while the danger lasted. The vessel was saved, and the stranger was Mr. Hume.

Company's service. None worked harder, or lived more temperately, than he did; and, securing the confidence of his superiors, who found him a capable man in the performance of his duty, they gradually promoted him to higher offices. In 1803 he was with the division of the army under General Powell, in the Mahratta war; and the interpreter having died, Hume, who had meanwhile studied and mastered the native languages, was appointed in his stead. He was next made chief of the medical staff. But as if this were not enough to occupy his full working power, he undertook in addition the offices of paymaster and postmaster, and filled them satisfactorily. He also contracted to supply the commissariat, which he did with advantage to the army and profit to himself. After about ten years' unremitting labour, he returned to England with a competency; and one of his first acts was to make provision for the poorer members of his family.

But Joseph Hume was not a man to enjoy the fruits of his industry in idleness. Work and occupation had become necessary for his comfort and happiness. To make himself fully acquainted with the actual state of his own country, and the condition of the people, he visited every town in the kingdom which then enjoyed any degree of manufacturing celebrity. He afterwards travelled abroad for the purpose of obtaining a knowledge of foreign states. Returned to England, he entered Parliament in 1812, and continued a member of that assembly, with a short interruption, for a period of about thirty-four years. His first recorded speech was on the subject of public education, and throughout his long and honourable career he took an active and earnest interest in that and all other questions calculated to elevate and improve the condition of the people—criminal reform, savings-banks, free trade, economy and retrenchment, extended representation, and such like measures, all of which he indefatigably promoted. Whatever subject he undertook,

he worked at with all his might.   He was not a good
speaker, but what he said was believed to proceed from the
lips of an honest, single-minded, accurate man.   If ridicule,
as Shaftesbury says, be the test of truth, Joseph Hume stood
the test well.   No man was more laughed at, but there he
stood perpetually, and literally, "at his post."   He was
usually beaten on a division, but the influence which he
exercised was nevertheless felt, and many important financial
improvements were effected by him even with the vote
directly against him.   The amount of hard work which he
contrived to get through was something extraordinary.   He
rose at six, wrote letters and arranged his papers for parliament; then, after breakfast, he received persons on business,
sometimes as many as twenty in a morning.   The House
rarely assembled without him, and though the debate might
be prolonged to two or three o'clock in the morning, his
name was seldom found absent from the division.   In short,
to perform the work which he did, extending over so long a
period, in the face of so many Administrations, week after
week, year after year,—to be outvoted, beaten, laughed at,
standing on many occasions almost alone,—to persevere in
the face of every discouragement, preserving his temper
unruffled, never relaxing in his energy or his hope, and
living to see the greater number of his measures adopted
with acclamation, must be regarded as one of the most
remarkable illustrations of the power of human perseverance
that biography can exhibit.

CHAPTER V.

HELPS AND OPPORTUNITIES — SCIENTIFIC PURSUITS.

" Neither the naked hand, nor the understanding, left to itself, can do much ; the work is accomplished by instruments and helps, of which the need is not less for the understanding than the hand."—*Bacon.*

" Opportunity has hair in front, behind she is bald; if you seize her by the forelock you may hold her, but, if suffered to escape, not Jupiter himself can catch her again."—*From the Latin.*

ACCIDENT does very little towards the production of any great result in life. Though sometimes what is called "a happy hit" may be made by a bold venture, the common highway of steady industry and application is the only safe road to travel. It is said of the landscape painter Wilson, that when he had nearly finished a picture in a tame, correct manner, he would step back from it, his pencil fixed at the end of a long stick, and after gazing earnestly on the work, he would suddenly walk up and by a few bold touches give a brilliant finish to the painting. But it will not do for every one who would produce an effect, to throw his brush at the canvas in the hope of producing a picture. The capability of putting in these last vital touches is acquired only by the labour of a life; and the probability is, that the artist who has not carefully trained himself beforehand, in attempting to produce a brilliant effect at a dash, will only produce a blotch.

Sedulous attention and painstaking industry always mark the true worker. The greatest men are not those who "despise the day of small things," but those who improve them the most carefully. Michael Angelo was one day explaining to a visitor at his studio, what he had been doing at a statue since his previous visit. "I have retouched this part—polished that—softened this feature—brought out that muscle—given some expression to this lip, and more energy to that limb." "But these are trifles," remarked the visitor. "It may be so," replied the sculptor, "but recollect that trifles make perfection, and perfection is no trifle." So it was said of Nicholas Poussin, the painter, that the rule of his conduct was, that "whatever was worth doing at all was worth doing well;" and when asked, late in life, by his friend Vigneul de Marville, by what means he had gained so high a reputation among the painters of Italy, Poussin emphatically answered, "Because I have neglected nothing."

Although there are discoveries which are said to have been made by accident, if carefully inquired into, it will be found that there has really been very little that was accidental about them. For the most part, these so-called accidents have only been opportunities, carefully improved by genius. The fall of the apple at Newton's feet has often been quoted in proof of the accidental character of some discoveries. But Newton's whole mind had already been devoted for years to the laborious and patient investigation of the subject of gravitation ; and the circumstance of the apple falling before his eyes was suddenly apprehended only as genius could apprehend it, and served to flash upon him the brilliant discovery then opening to his sight. In like manner, the brilliantly-coloured soap-bubbles blown from a common tobacco pipe—though "trifles light as air" in most eyes—suggested to Dr. Young his beautiful theory of "interferences," and led to his discovery relating to the diffraction of light. Although great men are popularly supposed only to deal with great things, men such as Newton and Young were ready to detect the significance of the most familiar and simple facts; their greatness consisting mainly in their wise interpretation of them.

The difference between men consists, in a great measure, in the intelligence of their observation. The Russian proverb says of the non-observant man, " He goes through the forest and sees no firewood." " The wise man's eyes are in his head," says Solomon, " but the fool walketh in darkness." " Sir," said Johnson, on one occasion, to a fine gentleman just returned from Italy, " some men will learn more in the Hampstead stage than others in the tour of Europe." It is the mind that sees as well as the eye. Where unthinking gazers observe nothing, men of intelligent vision penetrate into the very fibre of the phenomena presented to them, attentively noting differences, making comparisons, and recognizing their underlying idea. Many before Galileo had seen a suspended weight swing before their eyes with a measured beat; but he was the first to detect the value of the fact. One of the vergers in the cathedral at Pisa, after replenishing with oil a lamp which hung from the roof, left it swinging to and fro; and Galileo, then a youth of only eighteen, noting it attentively, conceived the idea of applying it to the measurement of time. Fifty years of study and labour, however, elapsed, before he completed the invention of his Pendulum,—the importance of which, in the measurement of time and in astronomical calculations, can scarcely be overrated. In like manner, Galileo, having casually heard that one Lippershey, a Dutch spectacle-maker, had presented to Count Maurice of Nassau an instrument by means of which distant objects appeared nearer to the beholder, addressed himself to the cause of such a phenomenon, which led to the invention of the telescope, and proved the beginning of the modern science of astronomy. Discoveries such as these could never have been made by a negligent observer, or by a mere passive listener.

While Captain (afterwards Sir Samuel) Brown was occupied in studying the construction of bridges, with the view of contriving one of a cheap description to be thrown across the Tweed, near which he lived, he was walking in his garden one dewy autumn morning, when he saw a tiny spider's net suspended across his path. The idea immediately occurred to him, that a bridge of iron ropes or chains might be constructed in like manner, and the result was the invention of his Suspension Bridge. So James Watt, when consulted about the mode of carrying water by pipes under the Clyde, along the unequal bed of the river, turned his attention one day to the shell of a lobster presented at table; and from that model he invented an iron tube, which, when laid down, was found effectually to answer the purpose. Sir Isambert Brunel took his first lessons in forming the Thames Tunnel from the tiny shipworm : he saw how the little creature per- forated the wood with its well-armed head, first in one direction and then in another, till the archway was complete, and then daubed over the roof and sides with a kind of varnish ; and by copying this work exactly on a large scale, Brunel was at length enabled to construct his shield and accomplish his great engineering work.

It is the intelligent eye of the careful observer which gives these apparently trivial phenomena their value. So trifling a matter as the sight of seaweed floating past his ship, enabled Columbus to quell the mutiny which arose amongst his sailors at not discovering land, and to assure them that the eagerly sought New World was not far off. There is nothing so small that it should remain forgotten ; and no fact, however trivial, but may prove useful in some way or other if carefully interpreted. Who could have imagined that the famous " chalk cliffs of Albion " had been built up by tiny insects—detected only by the help of the microscope—of the same order of creatures that have gemmed the sea with islands of coral ! And who that contemplates such extraordinary results, arising from infinitely minute operations, will venture to question the power of little things?

It is the close observation of little things which is the secret of success in business, in art, in science, and in every pursuit in life. Human knowledge is but an accumulation of small facts, made by successive generations of men, the little bits of knowledge and experience carefully treasured up by them growing at length into a mighty pyramid. Though many of these facts and observations seemed in the first instance to have but slight significance, they are all found to have their eventual uses, and to fit into their proper places. Even many speculations seemingly remote, turn out to be the basis of results the most obviously practical. In the case of the conic sections discovered by Apollonius Pergæus, twenty centuries elapsed before they were made the basis of astronomy—a science which enables the modern navigator to steer his way through unknown seas and traces for him in the heavens an unerring path to his appointed haven. And had not mathematicians toiled for so long, and, to uninstructed observers, apparently so fruitlessly, over the abstract relations of lines and surfaces, it is probable that but few of our mechanical inventions would have seen the light.

When Franklin made his discovery of the identity of lightning and electricity, it was sneered at, and people asked, " Of what use is it?" To which his reply was, "What is the use of a child? It may become a man!" When Galvani discovered that a frog's leg twitched when placed in contact with different metals, it could scarcely have been imagined that so apparently insignificant a fact could have led to important results. Yet therein lay the germ of the Electric Telegraph, which binds the intelligence of continents together, and, probably before many years have elapsed will "put a girdle round the globe." So too, little bits of stone and fossil, dug out of the earth, intelligently interpreted, have issued in the science of geology and the practical operations of mining, in which large capitals are invested and vast numbers of persons profitably employed.

The gigantic machinery employed in pumping our mines, working our mills and manufactures, and driving our steamships and locomotives, in like manner depends for its supply of power upon so slight an agency as little drops of water expanded by heat,—that familiar agency called steam, which we see issuing from that common tea-kettle spout, but which, when pent up within an ingeniously contrived mechanism, displays a force equal to that of millions of horses, and contains a power to rebuke the waves and set even the hurricane at defiance. The same power at work within the bowels of the earth has been the cause of those volcanoes and earthquakes which have played so mighty a part in the history or the globe.

It is said that the Marquis of Worcester's attention was first accidentally directed to the subject of steam power, by the tight cover of a vessel containing hot water having been blown off before his eyes, when confined a prisoner in the Tower. He published the result of his observations in his 'Century of Inventions,' which formed a sort of text-book for inquirers into the powers of steam for a time, until Savary, Newcomen, and others, applying it to practical purposes, brought the steam-engine to the state in which Watt found it when called upon to repair a model of Newcomen's engine, which belonged to the University of Glasgow. This accidental circumstance was an opportunity for Watt, which he was not slow to improve; and it was the labour of his life to bring the steam-engine to perfection.

This art of seizing opportunities and turning even accidents to account, bending them to some purpose, is a great secret of success. Dr. Johnson has defined genius to be "a mind of large general powers accidentally determined in some particular direction." Men who are resolved to find a way for themselves, will always find opportunities enough ; and if they do not lie ready to their hand, they will make them. It is not those who have enjoyed the advantages of colleges, museums, and public galleries, that have accomplished the most for science and art; nor have the greatest mechanics and inventors been trained in mechanics' institutes. Necessity, oftener than facility, has been the mother of invention ; and the most prolific school of all has been the school of difficulty. Some of the very best workmen have had the most indifferent tools to work with. But it is not tools that make the workman, but the trained skill and perseverance of the man himself. Indeed it is proverbial that the bad workman never yet had a good tool. Some one asked Opie by what wonderful process he mixed his colours. "I mix them with my brains, sir," was his reply. It is the same with every workman who would excel. Ferguson made marvellous things—such as his wooden clock, that accurately measured the hours—by means of a common penknife, a tool in everybody's hand; but then everybody is not a Ferguson. A pan of water and two thermometers were the tools by which Dr. Black discovered latent heat; and a prism, a lens, and a sheet of pastebord enabled Newton to unfold the composition of light and the origin of colours. An eminent foreign *savant* once called upon Dr. Wollaston, and requested to be shown over his laboratories in which science had been enriched by so many important discoveries, when the doctor took him into a little study, and, pointing to an old tea-tray on the table, containing a few watch-glasses, test papers, a small balance, and a blowpipe, said, "There is all the laboratory that I have!"

Stothard learnt the art of combining colours by closely studying butterflies' wings : he would often say that no one knew what he owed to these tiny insects. A burnt stick and a barn door served Wilkie in lieu of pencil and canvas.

Bewick first practised drawing on the cottage walls of his native village, which he covered with his sketches in chalk; and Benjamin West made his first brushes out of the cat's tail. Ferguson laid himself down in the fields at night in a blanket, and made a map of the heavenly bodies by means of a thread with small beads on it stretched between his eye and the stars. Franklin first robbed the thundercloud of its lightning by means of a kite made with two cross sticks and a silk handkerchief. Watt made his first model of the condensing steam-engine out of an old anatomist's syringe, used to inject the arteries previous to dissection. Gifford worked his first problems in mathematics, when a cobbler's apprentice, upon small scraps of leather, which he beat smooth for the purpose; whilst Rittenhouse, the astronomer, first calculated eclipses on his plough handle.

The most ordinary occasions will furnish a man with opportunities or suggestions for improvement, if he be but prompt to take advantage of them. Professor Lee was attracted to the study of Hebrew by finding a Bible in that tongue in a synagogue, while working as a common carpenter at the repairs of the benches. He became possessed with a desire to read the book in the original, and, buying a cheap second-hand copy of a Hebrew grammar, he set to work and learnt the language for himself. As Edmund Stone said to the Duke of Argyle, in answer to his grace's inquiry how he, a poor gardener's boy, had contrived to be able to read Newton's Principia in Latin, " One needs only to know the twenty-four letters of the alphabet in order to learn everything else that one wishes." Application and perseverance, and the diligent improvement of opportunities, will do the rest.

Sir Walter Scott found opportunities for self-improvement in every pursuit, and turned even accidents to account. Thus it was in the discharge of his functions as a writer's apprentice that he first visited the Highlands, and formed those friendships among the surviving heroes of 1745 which served to lay the foundation of a large class of his works. Later in life, when employed as quartermaster of the Edinburgh Light Cavalry, he was accidentally disabled by the kick of a horse, and confined for some time to his house ; but Scott was a sworn enemy to idleness, and he forthwith set his mind to work. In three days he had composed the first canto of ' The Lay of the Last Minstrel,' which he shortly after finished,—his first great original work.

The attention of Dr. Priestley, the discoverer of so many gases, was accidentally drawn to the subject of chemistry through his living in the neighbourhood of a brewery. When visiting the place one day, he noted the peculiar appearances attending the extinction of lighted chips in the gas floating over the fermented liquor. He was forty years old at the time, and knew nothing of chemistry. He consulted books to ascertain the cause, but they told him little, for as yet nothing was known on the subject. Then he began to experiment, with some rude apparatus of his own contrivance. The curious results of his first experiments led to others, which in his hands shortly became the science of pneumatic chemistry. About the same time, Scheele was obscurely working in the same direction in a remote Swedish village; and he discovered several new gases, with no more effective apparatus at his command than a few apothecaries' phials and pigs' bladders.

Sir Humphry Davy, when an apothecary's apprentice, performed his first experiments with instruments of the rudest description. He extemporised the greater part of them himself, out of the motley materials which chance threw in his way,—the pots and pans of the kitchen, and the phials and vessels of his master's surgery. It happened that a French ship was wrecked off the Land's End, and the surgeon escaped, bearing with him his case of instruments, amongst which was an old-fashioned glyster apparatus ; this article he presented to Davy, with whom he had become acquainted. The apo-thecary's apprentice received it with great exultation, and forthwith employed it as a part of a pneumatic apparatus which he contrived, afterwards using it to perform the duties of an air-pump in one of his experiments on the nature and sources of heat.

In like manner Professor Faraday, Sir Humphry Davy's scientific successor, made his first experiments in electricity by means of an old bottle, while he was still a working bookbinder. And it is a curious fact that Faraday was first attracted to the study of chemistry by hearing one of Sir Humphry Davy's lectures on the subject at the Royal Institution. A gentleman, who was a member, calling one day at the shop where Faraday was employed in binding books, found him poring over the article "Electricity" in an Encyclopædia placed in his hands to bind. The gentleman, having made inquiries, found that the young bookbinder was curious about such subjects, and gave him an order of admission to the Royal Institution, where he attended a course of four lectures delivered by Sir Humphry. He took notes of them, which he showed to the lecturer, who acknowledged their scientific accuracy, and was surprised when informed of the humble position of the reporter. Faraday then expressed his desire to devote himself to the prosecution of chemical studies, from which Sir Humphry at first endeavoured to dissuade him : but the young man persisting, he was at length taken into the Royal Institution as an assistant ; and eventually the mantle of the brilliant apothecary's boy fell upon the worthy shoulders of the equally brilliant bookbinder's apprentice.

The words which Davy entered in his note-book, when about twenty years of age, working in Dr. Beddoes' laboratory at Bristol, were eminently characteristic of him : " I have neither riches, nor power, nor birth to recommend me ; yet if I live, I trust I shall not be of less service to mankind and my friends, than if I had been born with all these advantages." Davy possessed the capability, as Faraday does, of devoting the whole power of his mind to the practical and experimental investigation of a subject in all its bearings; and such a mind will rarely fail, by dint of mere industry and patient thinking, in producing results of the highest order. Coleridge said of Davy, " There is an energy and elasticity in his mind, which enables him to seize on and analyze all questions, pushing them to their legitimate consequences. Every subject in Davy's mind has the principle of vitality. Living thoughts spring up like turf under his feet." Davy, on his part, said of Coleridge, whose abilities he greatly admired, "With the most exalted genius, enlarged views, sensitive heart, and enlightened mind, he will be the victim of a want of order, precision, and regularity."

The great Cuvier was a singularly accurate, careful, and industrious observer. When a boy, he was attracted to the subject of natural history by the sight of a volume of Buffon which accidentally fell in his way. He at once proceeded to copy the drawings, and to colour them after the descriptions given in the text. While still at school, one of his teachers made him a present of ' Linnæus's System of Nature ;' and for more than ten years this constituted his library of natural history. At eighteen he was offered the situation of tutor in a family residing near Fécamp, in Normandy. Living close to the sea-shore, he was brought face to face with the wonders of marine life. Strolling along the sands one day, he observed a stranded cuttle-fish. He was attracted by the curious objcet, took it home to dissect, and thus began the study of the molluscæ, in the pursuit of which he achieved so distinguished a reputation. He had no books to refer to, excepting only the great book of Nature which lay open before him. The study of the novel and interesting objects which it daily presented to his eyes made a much deeper impression on his mind than any written or engraved descriptions could possibly have done. Three years thus passed, during which he compared the living species of marine animals with the fossil remains found in the neighbourhood, dissected the specimens of marine life that came under his notice, and, by careful observation, prepared the way for a complete reform in the classification of the animal kingdom. About this time Cuvier became known to the learned Abbé Teissier, who wrote to Jussieu and other friends in Paris on the subject of the young naturalist's inquiries, in terms of such high commendation, that Cuvier was requested to send some of his papers to the Society of Natural History ; and he was shortly after appointed assistant-superintendent at the Jardin des Plantes. In the letter written by Teissier to Jussieu, introducing the young naturalist to his notice, he said, " You remember that it was I who gave Delambre to the Academy in another branch of science : this also will be a Delambre." We need scarcely add that the prediction of Teissier was more than fulfilled.

It is not accident, then, that helps a man in the world so much as purpose and persistent industry. To the feeble, the sluggish and purposeless, the happiest accidents avail nothing,—they pass them by, seeing no meaning in them. But it is astonishing how much can be accomplished if we are prompt to seize and improve the opportunities for action and effort which are constantly presenting themselves. Watt taught himself chemistry and mechanics while working at his trade of a mathematical-instrument maker, at the same time that he was learning German from a Swiss dyer. Stephenson taught himself arithmetic and mensuration while working as an engineman during the night shifts; and when he could snatch a few moments in the intervals allowed for meals during the day, he worked his sums with a bit of chalk upon the sides of the colliery waggons. Dalton's industry was the habit of his life. He began from his boyhood, for he taught a little village-school when he was only about

K

twelve years old,—keeping the school in winter, and working upon his father's farm in summer. He would sometimes urge himself and companions to study by the stimulus of a bet, though bred a Quaker; and on one occasion, by his satisfactory solution of a problem, he won as much as enabled him to buy a winter's store of candles. He continued his meteorological observations until a day or two before he died,—having made and recorded upwards of 200,000 in the course of his life.

With perseverance, the very odds and ends of time may be worked up into results of the greatest value. An hour in every day withdrawn from frivolous pursuits would, if profitably employed, enable a person of ordinary capacity to go far towards mastering a science. It would make an ignorant man a well-informed one in less than ten years. Time should not be allowed to pass without yielding fruits, in the form of something learnt worthy of being known, some good principle cultivated, or some good habit strengthened. Dr. Mason Good translated Lucretius while riding in his carriage in the streets of London, going the round of his patients. Dr. Darwin composed nearly all his works in the same way while driving about in his "sulky" from house to house in the country,—writing down his thoughts on little scraps of paper, which he carried about with him for the purpose. Hale wrote his 'Contemplations' while travelling on circuit. Dr. Burney learnt French and Italian while travelling on horseback from one musical pupil to another in the course of his profession. Kirke White learnt Greek while walking to and from a lawyer's office; and we personally know a man of eminent position who learnt Latin and French while going messages as an errand-boy in the streets of Manchester.

Daguesseau, one of the great Chancellors of France, by carefully working up his odd bits of time, wrote a bulky and able volume in the successive intervals of waiting for dinner, and Madame de Genlis composed several of her charming volumes while waiting for the princess to whom she gave her daily lessons. Elihu Burritt attributed his first success in self-improvement, not to genius, which he disclaimed, but simply to the careful employment of those invaluable fragments of time, called "odd moments." While working and earning his living as a blacksmith, he mastered some eighteen ancient and modern languages, and twenty-two European dialects.

What a solemn and striking admonition to youth is that inscribed on the dial at All Souls, Oxford—"Pereunt et imputantur"—the hours perish, and are laid to our charge. Time is the only little fragment of Eternity that belongs to man; and, like life, it can never be recalled. "In the dissipation of worldly treasure," says Jackson of Exeter, "the frugality of the future may balance the extravagance of the past; but who can say, 'I will take from minutes to-morrow to compensate for those I have lost to-day?'" Melancthon noted down the time lost by him, that he might thereby reanimate his industry, and not lose an hour. An Italian scholar put over his door an inscription intimating that whosoever remained there should join in his labours. "We are afraid," said some visitors to Baxter, "that we break in upon your time." "To be sure you do," replied the disturbed and blunt divine. Time was the estate out of which these great workers, and all other workers, formed that rich treasury of thoughts and deeds which they have left to their successors.

The mere drudgery undergone by some men in carrying on their undertakings has been something extraordinary, but the drudgery they regarded as the price of success. Addison amassed as much as three folios of manuscript materials before he began his 'Spectator.' Newton wrote his 'Chronology' fifteen times over before he was satisfied with it; and Gibbon wrote out his 'Memoir' nine times.

Hale studied for many years at the rate of sixteen hours a day, and when wearied with the study of the law, he would recreate himself with philosophy and the study of the mathematics. Hume wrote thirteen hours a day while preparing his ' History of England.' Montesquieu, speaking of one part of his writings, said to a friend, "You will read it in a few hours; but I assure you it has cost me so much labour that it has whitened my hair."

The practice of writing down thoughts and facts for the purpose of holding them fast and preventing their escape into the dim region of forgetfulness, has been much resorted to by thoughtful and studious men. Lord Bacon left behind him many manuscripts entitled "Sudden thoughts set down for use." Erskine made great extracts from Burke; and Eldon copied Coke upon Littleton twice over with his own hand, so that the book became, as it were, part of his own mind. The late Dr. Pye Smith, when apprenticed to his father as a bookbinder, was accustomed to make copious memoranda of all the books he read, with extracts and criticisms. This indomitable industry in collecting materials distinguished him through life, his biographer describing him as "always at work, always in advance, always accumulating." These note-books afterwards proved, like Richter's "quarries," the great storehouse from which he drew his illustrations.

The same practice characterized the eminent John Hunter, who adopted it for the purpose of supplying the defects of memory; and he was accustomed thus to illustrate the advantages which one derives from putting one's thoughts in writing: "It resembles," he said, "a tradesman taking stock, without which he never knows either what he possesses or in what he is deficient." John Hunter—whose observation was so keen that Abernethy was accustomed to speak of him as "the Argus-eyed"—furnished an illustrious example of the power of patient industry. He received little or no education till he was about twenty years of age, and it was with difficulty that he acquired the arts of reading and writing. He worked for some years as a common carpenter at Glasgow, after which he joined his brother William, who had settled in London as a lecturer and anatomical demonstrator. John entered his dissecting-room as an assistant, but soon shot ahead of his brother, partly by virtue of his great natural ability, but mainly by reason of his patient application and indefatigable industry. He was one of the first in this country to devote himself assiduously to the study of comparative anatomy, and the objects he dissected and collected took the eminent Professor Owen no less than ten years to arrange. The collection contains some twenty thousand specimens, and is the most precious treasure of the kind that has ever been accumulated by the industry of one man. Hunter used to spend every morning from sunrise until eight o'clock in his museum ; and throughout the day he carried on his extensive private practice, performed his laborious duties as surgeon to St. George's Hospital and deputy surgeon-general to the army; delivered lectures to students, and superintended a school of practical anatomy at his own house; finding leisure, amidst all, for elaborate experiments on the animal economy, and the composition of various works of great scientific importance. To find time for this gigantic amount of work, he allowed himself only four hours of sleep at night, and an hour after dinner. When once asked what method he nad adopted to insure success in his undertakings, he replied " My rule is, deliberately to consider, before I commence, whether the thing be practicable. If it be not practicable, I do not attempt it. If it be practicable, I can accomplish it if I give sufficient pains to it ; and having begun, I never stop till the thing is done. To this rule I owe all my success."

Hunter occupied a great deal of his time in collecting

definite facts respecting matters which, before his day, were regarded as exceedingly trivial. Thus it was supposed by many of his contemporaries that he was only wasting his time and thought in studying so carefully as he did the growth of a deer's horn. But Hunter was impressed with the conviction that no accurate knowledge of scientific facts is without its value. By the study referred to, he learnt how arteries accommodate themselves to circumstances, and enlarge as occasion requires; and the knowledge thus acquired emboldened him, in a case of aneurism in a branch artery, to tie the main trunk where no surgeon before him had dared to tie it, and the life of his patient was saved. Like many original men, he worked for a long time as it were underground, digging and laying foundations. He was a solitary and self-reliant genius, holding on his course without the solace of sympathy or approbation,—for but few of his contemporaries perceived the ultimate object of his pursuits. But like all true workers, he did not fail in securing his best reward—that which depends less upon others than upon one's self—the approval of conscience, which in a right-minded man invariably follows the honest and energetic performance of duty.

Ambrose Paré, the great French surgeon, was another illustrious instance of close observation, patient application, and indefatigable perseverance. He was the son of a barber at Laval, in Maine, where he was born in 1509. His parents were too poor to send him to school, but they placed him as foot-boy with the curé of the village, hoping that under that learned man he might pick up an education for himself. But the curé kept him so busily employed in grooming his mule and in other menial offices that the boy found no time for learning. While in his service, it happened that the celebrated lithotomist, Cotot, came to Laval to operate on one of the curé's ecclesiastical brethren. Paré was present at the operation, and was so much interested by it that he is said to have from that time formed the determination of devoting himself to the art of surgery.

Leaving the curé's household service, Paré apprenticed himself to a barber-surgeon named Vialot, under whom he learnt to let blood, draw teeth, and perform the minor operations. After four years' experience of this kind, he went to Paris to study at the school of anatomy and surgery, meanwhile maintaining himself by his trade of a barber. He afterwards succeeded in obtaining an appointment as assistant at the Hôtel Dieu, where his conduct was so exemplary, and his progress so marked, that the chief surgeon, Goupil, entrusted him with the charge of the patients whom he could not himself attend to. After the usual course of instruction, Paré was admitted a master barber-surgeon, and shortly after was appointed to a charge with the French army under Montmorenci in Piedmont. Paré was not a man to follow in the ordinary ruts of his profession, but brought the resources of an ardent and original mind to bear upon his daily work, diligently thinking out for himself the *rationale* of diseases and their befitting remedies. Before his time the wounded suffered much more at the hands of their surgeons than they did at those of their enemies. To stop bleeding from gunshot wounds, the barbarous expedient was resorted to of dressing them with boiling oil. Hæmorrhage was also stopped by searing the wounds with a red-hot iron; and when amputation was necessary, it was performed with a red-hot knife. At first Paré treated wounds according to the approved methods; but, fortunately, on one occasion, running short of boiling oil, he substituted a mild and emollient application. He was in great fear all night lest he should have done wrong in adopting this treatment; but was greatly relieved next morning on finding his patients comparatively comfortable, while those whose wounds had been treated in the usual way were writhing in torment. Such was the casual origin of

one of Paré's greatest improvements in the treatment of gunshot wounds; and he proceeded to adopt the emollient
treatment in all future cases. Another still more important
improvement was his employment of the ligature in tying
arteries to stop hæmorrhage, instead of the actual cautery.
Paré, however, met with the usual fate of innovators and
reformers. His practice was denounced by his surgical
brethren as dangerous, unprofessional, and empirical; and
the older surgeons banded themselves together to resist
its adoption. They reproached him for his want of education, more especially for his ignorance of Latin and Greek;
and they assailed him with quotations from ancient writers,
which he was unable either to verify or refute. But the
best answer to his assailants was the success of his practice.
The wounded soldiers called out everywhere for Paré, and
he was always at their service : he tended them carefully
and affectionately; and he usually took leave of them with
the words, "I have dressed you; may God cure you."

After three years' active service as army-surgeon, Paré
returned to Paris with such a reputation that he was at once
appointed surgeon in ordinary to the King. When Metz
was besieged by the Spanish army, under Charles V., the
garrison suffered heavy loss, and the number of wounded
was very great. The surgeons were few and incompetent,
and probably slew more by their bad treatment than the
Spaniards did by the sword. The Duke of Guise, who
commanded the garrison, wrote to the King imploring him
to send Paré to his help. The courageous surgeon at once
set out, and, after braving many dangers (to use his own
words, "d'estre pendu, estranglé ou mis en pièces"), he
succeeded in passing the enemy's lines, and entered Metz
in safety. The Duke, the generals, and the captains gave
him an affectionate welcome; while the soldiers, when they
heard of his arrival, cried, "We no longer fear dying of our
wounds; our friend is among us." In the following year

Paré was in like manner with the besieged in the town of Hesdin, which shortly fell before the Duke of Savoy, and he was taken prisoner.   But having succeeded in curing one of the enemy's chief officers of a serious wound, he was discharged without ransom, and returned in safety to Paris.

The rest of his life was occupied in study, in self-improvement, in piety, and in good deeds.   Urged by some of the most learned among his contemporaries, he placed on record the results of his surgical experience in twenty-eight books, which were published by him at different times.   His writings are valuable and remarkable chiefly on account of the great number of facts and cases contained in them, and the care with which he avoids giving any directions resting merely upon theory unsupported by observation.   Paré continued, though a Protestant, to hold the office of surgeon in ordinary to the King; and during the Massacre of St. Bartholomew he owed his life to the personal friendship of Charles IX., whom he had on one occasion saved from the dangerous effects of a wound inflicted by a clumsy surgeon in performing the operation of venesection.   Brantôme, in his 'Mémoires,' thus speaks of the King's rescue of Paré on the night of Saint Bartholomew—"He sent to fetch him, and to remain during the night in his chamber and wardrobe-room, commanding him not to stir, and saying that it was not reasonable that a man who had preserved the lives of so many people should himself be massacred."   Thus Paré escaped the horrors of that fearful night, which he survived for many years, and was permitted to die in peace, full of age and honours.

Harvey was as indefatigable a labourer as any we have named.   He spent not less than eight long years of investigation and research before he published his views of the circulation of the blood.   He repeated and verified his experiments again and again, probably anticipating the opposition he would have to encounter from the profession on making

known his discovery. The tract in which he at length announced his views, was a most modest one,—but simple,
perspicuous, and conclusive. It was nevertheless received
with ridicule, as the utterance of a crack-brained impostor.
For some time, he did not make a single convert, and gained
nothing but contumely and abuse. He had called in question
the revered authority of the ancients; and it was even averred
that his views were calculated to subvert the authority of the
Scriptures and undermine the very foundations of morality
and religion. His little practice fell away, and he was left
almost without a friend. This lasted for some years, until
the great truth, held fast by Harvey amidst all his adversity,
and which had dropped into many thoughtful minds, gradually
ripened by further observation, and after a period of about
twenty-five years, it became generally recognised as an established scientific truth.

The difficulties encountered by Dr. Jenner in promul-
gating and establishing his discovery of vaccination as a
preventive of small-pox, were even greater than those of
Harvey. Many, before him, had witnessed the cow-pox,
and had heard of the report current among the milkmaids in
Gloucestershire, that whoever had taken that disease was
secure against small-pox. It was a trifling, vulgar rumour,
supposed to have no significance whatever; and no one had
thought it worthy of investigation, until it was accidentally
brought under the notice of Jenner. He was a youth,
pursuing his studies at Sodbury, when his attention was
arrested by the casual observation made by a country girl
who came to his master's shop for advice. The small-pox
was mentioned, when the girl said, " I can't take that disease,
for I have had cow-pox." The observation immediately
riveted Jenner's attention, and he forthwith set about inquiring
and making observations on the subject. His professional
friends, to whom he mentioned his views as to the prophy-
lactic virtues of cow-pox, laughed at him, and even threatened

to expel him from their society, if he persisted in harassing them with the subject.   In London he was so fortunate as to study under John Hunter, to whom he communicated his views.   The advice of the great anatomist was thoroughly characteristic: " Don't think, but *try;* be patient, be accurate."   Jenner's courage was supported by the advice, which conveyed to him the true art of philosophical investigation. He went back to the country to practise his profession and make observations and experiments, which he continued to pursue for a period of twenty years.   His faith in his discovery was so implicit that he vaccinated his own son on three several occasions.   At length he published his views in a quarto of about seventy pages, in which he gave the details of twenty-three cases of successful vaccination of individuals, to whom it was found afterwards impossible to communicate the small-pox either by contagion or inoculation. It was in 1798 that this treatise was published ; though he had been working out his ideas since the year 1775, when they had begun to assume a definite form.

How was the discovery received?   First with indifference, then with active hostility.   Jenner proceeded to London to exhibit to the profession the process of vaccination and its results ; but not a single medical man could be induced to make trial of it, and after fruitlessly waiting for nearly three months, he returned to his native village.   He was even caricatured and abused for his attempt to " bestialize " his species by the introduction into their systems of diseased matter from the cow's udder.   Vaccination was denounced from the pulpit as " diabolical."   It was averred that vaccinated children became " ox-faced," that abscesses broke out to " indicate sprouting horns," and that the countenance was gradually " transmuted into the visage of a cow, the voice into the bellowing of bulls."   Vaccination, however, was a truth, and notwithstanding the violence of the opposition, belief in it spread slowly.   In one village, where a gentleman tried to introduce the practice, the first persons who permitted themselves to be vaccinated were absolutely pelted and driven into their houses if they appeared out of doors. Two ladies of title—Lady Ducie and the Countess of Berkeley—to their honour be it remembered—had the courage to vaccinate their children ; and the prejudices of the day were at once broken through. The medical profession gradually came round, and there were several who even sought to rob Dr. Jenner of the merit of the discovery, when its importance came to be recognised. Jenner's cause at last triumphed, and he was publicly honoured and rewarded. In his prosperity he was as modest as he had been in his obscurity. He was invited to settle in London, and told that he might command a practice of 10,000*l.* a year. But his answer was, " No ! In the morning of my days I have sought the sequestered and lowly paths of life—the valley, and not the mountain,—and now, in the evening of my days, it is not meet for me to hold myself up as an object for fortune and for fame." During Jenner's own life-time the practice of vaccination became adopted all over the civilized world ; and when he died, his title as a Benefactor of his kind was recognised far and wide. Cuvier has said, " If vaccine were the only discovery of the epoch, it would serve to render it illustrious for ever ; yet it knocked twenty times in vain at the doors of the Academies."

Not less patient, resolute, and persevering was Sir Charles Bell in the prosecution of his discoveries relating to the nervous system. Previous to his time, the most confused notions prevailed as to the functions of the nerves, and this branch of study was little more advanced than it had been in the times of Democritus and Anaxagoras three thousand years before. Sir Charles Bell, in the valuable series of papers the publication of which was commenced in 1821, took an entirely original view of the subject, based upon a long series of careful, accurate, and oft-repeated experiments. Elaborately tracing the development of the nervous system up from the lowest order of animated being, to man —the lord of the animal kingdom,—he displayed it, to use his own words, "as plainly as if it were written in our mother-tongue." His discovery consisted in the fact, that the spinal nerves are double in their function, and arise by double roots from the spinal marrow,—volition being conveyed by that part of the nerves springing from the one root, and sensation by the other. The subject occupied the mind of Sir Charles Bell for a period of forty years, when, in 1840, he laid his last paper before the Royal Society. As in the cases of Harvey and Jenner, when he had lived down the ridicule and opposition with which his views were first received, and their truth came to be recognised, numerous claims for priority in making the discovery were set up at home and abroad. Like them, too, he lost practice by the publication of his papers; and he left it on record that, after every step in his discovery, he was obliged to work harder than ever to preserve his reputation as a practitioner. The great merits of Sir Charles Bell were, however, at length fully recognised; and Cuvier himself, when on his death-bed, finding his face distorted and drawn to one side, pointed out the symptom to his attendants as a proof of the correctness of Sir Charles Bell's theory.

An equally devoted pursuer of the same branch of science was the late Dr. Marshall Hall, whose name posterity will rank with those of Harvey, Hunter, Jenner, and Bell. During the whole course of his long and useful life he was a most careful and minute observer; and no fact, however apparently insignificant, escaped his attention. His important discovery of the diastaltic nervous system, by which his name will long be known amongst scientific men, originated in an exceedingly simple circumstance. When investigating the pneumonic circulation in the Triton, the decapitated object lay upon the table; and on separating the tail and accidentally pricking the external integument, he observed that it moved with energy, and became contorted into various forms.   He had not touched a muscle or a muscular nerve ; what then was the nature of these movements ?   The same phenomena had probably been often observed before, but Dr. Hall was the first to apply himself perseveringly to the investigation of their causes ; and he exclaimed on the occa-sion, " I will never rest satisfied until I have found all this out, and made it clear."   His attention to the subject was almost incessant ; and it is estimated that in the course of his life he devoted not less than 25,000 hours to its experi-mental and chemical investigation.   He was at the same time carrying on an extensive private practice, and officiating as lecturer at St. Thomas's Hospital and other Medical Schools.   It will scarcely be credited that the paper in which he embodied his discovery was rejected by the Royal Society, and was only accepted after the lapse of seventeen years, when the truth of his views had become acknowledged by scientific men both at home and abroad.

The life of Sir William Herschel affords another remark-able illustration of the force of perseverance in another branch of science.   His father was a poor German musician, who brought up his four sons to the same calling.   William came over to England to seek his fortune, and he joined the band of the Durham Militia, in which he played the oboe. The regiment was lying at Doncaster, where Dr. Miller first became acquainted with Herschel, having heard him per-form a solo on the violin in a surprising manner.   The Doctor entered into conversation with the youth, and was so pleased with him, that he urged him to leave the militia and take up his residence at his house for a time.   Herschel did so, and while at Doncaster was principally occupied in violin-playing at concerts, availing himself of the advantages of Dr. Miller's library to study at his leisure hours.   A new organ having been built for the parish church of Halifax, an organist was advertised for, on which Herschel applied for the office, and was selected.   Leading the wandering life of an artist, he was next attracted to Bath, where he played in the Pump-room band, and also officiated as organist in the Octagon chapel.   Some recent discoveries in astronomy having arrested his mind, and awakened in him a powerful spirit of curiosity, he sought and obtained from a friend the loan of a two-foot Gregorian telescope.   So fascinated was the poor musician by the science, that he even thought of purchasing a telescope, but the price asked by the London optician was so alarming, that he determined to make one.   Those who know what a reflecting telescope is, and the skill which is required to prepare the concave metallic speculum which forms the most important part of the apparatus, will be able to form some idea of the difficulty of this undertaking. ' Nevertheless, Herschel succeeded, after long and painful labour, in completing a five-foot reflector, with which he had the gratification of observing the ring and satellites of Saturn.   Not satisfied with his triumph, he proceeded to make other instruments in succession, of seven, ten, and even twenty feet.   In constructing the seven-foot reflector, he finished no fewer than two hundred specula before he produced one that would bear any power that was applied to it,—a striking instance of the persevering laboriousness of the man.   While gauging the heavens with his instruments, he continued patiently to earn his bread by piping to the fashionable frequenters of the Pump-room.   So eager was he in his astronomical observations, that he would steal away from the room during an interval of the performance, give a little turn at his telescope, and contentedly return to his oboe.   Thus working away, Herschel discovered the Georgium Sidus, the orbit and rate of motion of which he carefully calculated, and sent the result to the Royal Society ; when the humble oboe player found himself at once elevated from obscurity to fame.   He was shortly after appointed Astronomer Royal, and by the kind-

ness of George III. was placed in a position of honourable
competency for life. He bore his honours with the same
meekness and humility which had distinguished him in the
days of his obscurity.   So gentle and patient, and withal
so distinguished and successful a follower of science under
difficulties, perhaps cannot be found in the entire history of
biography.

The career of William Smith, the father of English geology, though perhaps less known, is not less interesting and
instructive as an example of patient and laborious effort, and
the diligent cultivation of opportunities. He was born in
1769, the son of a yeoman farmer at Churchill, in Oxfordshire. His father dying when he was but a child, he received a very sparing education at the village school, and
even that was to a considerable extent interfered with by his
wandering and somewhat idle habits as a boy. His mother
having married a second time, he was taken in charge by
an uncle, also a farmer, by whom he was brought up. Though
the uncle was by no means pleased with the boy's love of
wandering about, collecting "poundstones," "pundips," and
other stony curiosities which lay scattered about the adjoining land, he yet enabled him to purchase a few of the necessary books wherewith to instruct himself in the rudiments of
geometry and surveying ; for the boy was already destined
for the business of a land-surveyor. One of his marked characteristics, even as a youth, was the accuracy and keenness
of his observation ; and what he once clearly saw he never
forgot. He began to draw, attempted to colour, and practised the arts of mensuration and surveying, all without
regular instruction ; and by his efforts in self-culture, he
shortly became so proficient, that he was taken on as
assistant to a local surveyor of ability in the neighbourhood.
In carrying on his business he was constantly under the
necessity of traversing Oxfordshire and the adjoining counties. One of the first things he seriously pondered over,

was the position of the various soils and strata that came under his notice on the lands which he surveyed or travelled over; more especially the position of the red earth in regard to the lias and superincumbent rocks. The surveys of numerous collieries which he was called upon to make, gave him further experience; and already, when only twenty-three years of age, he contemplated making a model of the strata of the earth.

While engaged in levelling for a proposed canal in Gloucestershire, the idea of a general law occurred to him relating to the strata of that district. He conceived that the strata lying above the coal were not laid horizontally, but inclined, and in one direction, towards the east; resembling, on a large scale, "the ordinary appearance of superposed slices of bread and butter." The correctness of this theory he shortly after confirmed by observations of the strata in two parallel valleys, the "red ground," "lias," and "freestone" or "oolite," being found to come down in an eastern direction, and to sink below the level, yielding place to the next in succession. He was shortly enabled to verify the truth of his views on a larger scale, having been appointed to examine personally into the management of canals in England and Wales. During his journeys, which extended from Bath to Newcastle-on-Tyne, returning by Shropshire and Wales, his keen eyes were never idle for a moment. He rapidly noted the aspect and structure of the country through which he passed with his companions, treasuring up his observations for future use. His geologic vision was so acute, that though the road along which he passed from York to Newcastle in the post chaise was from five to fifteen miles distant from the hills of chalk and oolite on the east, he was satisfied as to their nature, by their contours and relative position, and their ranges on the surface in relation to the lias and "red ground" occasionally seen on the road.

L

The general results of his observation seem to have been these. He noted that the rocky masses of country in the western parts of England generally inclined to the east and south-east; that the red sandstones and marls above the coal measures passed beneath the lias, clay, and lime-stone, that these again passed beneath the sands, yellow limestones and clays, forming the table-land of the Cotswold Hills, while these in turn passed beneath the great chalk deposits occupying the eastern parts of England. He further observed, that each layer of clay, sand, and limestone held its own peculiar classes of fossils ; and pondering much on these things, he at length came to the then unheard-of conclusion, that each distinct deposit of marine animals, in these several strata, indicated a distinct sea-bottom, and that each layer of clay, sand, chalk, and stone, marked a distinct epoch of time in the history of the earth.

This idea took firm possession of his mind, and he could talk and think of nothing else. At canal boards, at sheep-shearings, at county meetings, and at agricultural associations, ' Strata Smith,' as he came to be called, was always running over with the subject that possessed him. He had indeed made a great discovery, though he was as yet a man utterly unknown in the scientific world. He proceeded to pro-ject a map of the stratification of England ; but was for some time deterred from proceeding .with it, being fully occupied in carrying out the works of the Somersetshire coal canal, which engaged him for a period of about six years. He continued, nevertheless, to be unremitting in his observation of facts ; and he became so expert in appre-hending the internal structure of a district and detecting the lie of the strata from its external configuration, that he was often consulted respecting the drainage of extensive tracts of land, in which, guided by his geological knowledge, he proved remarkably successful, and acquired an extensive reputation.

One day, when looking over the cabinet collection of
fossils belonging to the Rev. Samuel Richardson, at Bath,
Smith astonished his friend by suddenly disarranging his
classification, and re-arranging the fossils in their strati-
graphical, order, saying—" These came from the blue lias,
these from the over-lying sand and freestone, these from the
fuller's earth, and these from the Bath building stone."
A new light flashed upon Mr. Richardson's mind, and he
shortly became a convert to and believer in William Smith's
doctrine.   The geologists of the day were not, however, so
easily convinced;   and it was scarcely to be tolerated
that an unknown land-surveyor should pretend to teach
them the science of geology.   But William Smith had an
eye and mind to penetrate deep beneath the skin of the
earth ; he saw its very fibre and skeleton, and, as it were,
divined its organization.   His knowledge of the strata in
the neighbourhood of Bath was so accurate, that one evening,
when dining at the house of the Rev. Joseph Townsend, he
dictated to Mr. Richardson the different strata according to
their order of succession in descending order, twenty-three
in number, commencing with the chalk and descending in
continuous series down to the coal, below which the strata
were not then sufficiently determined.   To this was added a
list of the more remarkable fossils which had been gathered
in the several layers of rock.   This was printed and extensively circulated in 1801.

He next determined to trace out the strata through districts as remote from Bath as his means would enable him to
reach.   For years he journeyed to and fro, sometimes on
foot, sometimes on horseback, riding on the tops of stage
coaches, often making up by night-travelling the time he
had lost by day, so as not to fail in his ordinary business
engagements.   When he was professionally called away to
any distance from home—as, for instance, when travelling
from Bath to Holkham, in Norfolk, to direct the irrigation

and drainage of Mr. Coke's land in that county—he rode on horseback, making frequent detours from the road to note the geological features of the country which he traversed.

For several years he was thus engaged in his journeys to distant quarters in England and Ireland, to the extent of upwards of ten thousand miles yearly ; and it was amidst this incessant and laborious travelling, that he contrived to commit to paper his fast-growing generalizations on what he rightly regarded as a new science. No observation, howsoever trivial it might appear, was neglected, and no opportunity of collecting fresh facts was overlooked. Whenever he could, he possessed himself of records of borings, natural and artificial sections, drew them to a constant scale of eight yards to the inch, and coloured them up. Of his keenness of observation take the following illustration. When making one of his geological excursions about the country near Woburn, as he was drawing near to the foot of the Dunstable chalk hills, he observed to his companion, " If there be any broken ground about the foot of these hills, we may find *shark's teeth ;*" and they had not proceeded far, before they picked up six from the white bank of a new fence-ditch. As he afterwards said of himself, " The habit of observation crept on me, gained a settlement in my mind, became a constant associate of my life, and started up in activity at the first thought of a journey ; so that I generally went off well prepared with maps, and sometimes with contemplations on its objects, or on those on the road, reduced to writing before it commenced. My mind was, therefore, like the canvas of a painter, well prepared for the first and best impressions."

Notwithstanding his courageous and indefatigable industry, many circumstances contributed to prevent the promised publication of William Smith's ' Map of the Strata of England and Wales,' and it was not until 1814 that he was enabled, by the assistance of some friends, to give to the world the fruits of his twenty years' incessant labour. To prosecute his inquiries, and collect the extensive series of facts and observations requisite for his purpose, he had to expend the whole of the profits of his professional labours during that period; and he even sold off his small property to provide the means of visiting remoter parts of the island. Meanwhile he had entered on a quarrying speculation near Bath, which proved unsuccessful, and he was under the necessity of selling his geological collection (which was purchased by the British Museum), his furniture and library, reserving only his papers, maps, and sections, which were useless save to himself. He bore his losses and misfortunes with exemplary fortitude; and amidst all, he went on working with cheerful courage and untiring patience. He died at Northampton, in August, 1839, while on his way to attend the meeting of the British Association at Birmingham.

It is difficult to speak in terms of too high praise of the first geological map of England, which we owe to the industry of this courageous man of science. An accomplished writer says of it, " It was a work so masterly in conception and so correct in general outline, that in principle it served as a basis not only for the production of later maps of the British Islands, but for geological maps of all other parts of the world, wherever they have been undertaken. In the apartments of the Geological Society Smith's map may yet be seen—a great historical document, old and worn, calling for renewal of its faded tints. Let any one conversant with the subject compare it with later works on a similar scale, and he will find that in all essential features it will not suffer by the comparison—the intricate anatomy of the Silurian rocks of Wales and the north of England by Murchison and Sedgwick being the chief additions made to his great generalizations." * The genius of the Oxfordshire surveyor

* 'Saturday Review,' July 3rd, 1858.

did not fail to be duly recognised and honoured by men of science during his lifetime. In 1831 the Geological Society of London awarded to him the Wollaston medal, "in consideration of his being a great original discoverer in English geology, and especially for his being the first in this country to discover and to teach the identification of strata, and to determine their succession by means of their imbedded fossils." William Smith, in his simple, earnest way, gained for himself a name as lasting as the science he loved so well. To use the words of the writer above quoted, "Till the manner as well as the fact of the first appearance of successive forms of life shall be solved, it is not easy to surmise how any discovery can be made in geology equal in value to that which we owe to the genius of William Smith."

Hugh Miller was a man of like observant faculties, who studied literature as well as science with zeal and success. The book in which he has told the story of his life, ('My Schools and Schoolmasters'), is extremely interesting, and calculated to be eminently useful. It is the history of the formation of a truly noble character in the humblest condition of life; and inculcates most powerfully the lessons of self-help, self-respect, and self-dependence. While Hugh was but a child, his father, who was a sailor, was drowned at sea, and he was brought up by his widowed mother. He had a school training after a sort, but his best teachers were the boys with whom he played, the men amongst whom he worked, the friends and relatives with whom he lived. He read much and miscellaneously, and picked up odd sorts of knowledge from many quarters,—from workmen, carpenters, fishermen and sailors, and above all, from the old boulders strewed along the shores of the Cromarty Frith. With a big hammer which had belonged to his great-grandfather, an old buccaneer, the boy went about chipping the stones, and accumulating specimens of mica, porphyry, garnet, and such like. Sometimes he had a day in the woods, and there, too, the boy's attention was excited by the peculiar geological curiosities which came in his way. While searching among the rocks on the beach, he was sometimes asked, in irony, by the farm servants who came to load their carts with sea-weed, whether he "was gettin' siller in the stanes," but was so unlucky as never to be able to answer in the affirmative. When of a suitable age he was apprenticed to the trade of his choice—that of a working stonemason; and he began his labouring career in a quarry looking out upon the Cromarty Frith. This quarry proved one of his best schools. The remarkable geological formations which it displayed awakened his curiosity. The bar of deep-red stone beneath, and the bar of pale-red clay above, were noted by the young quarryman, who even in such unpromising subjects found matter for observation and reflection. Where other men saw nothing, he detected analogies, differences, and peculiarities, which set him a-thinking. He simply kept his eyes and his mind open; was sober, diligent, and persevering; and this was the secret of his intellectual growth.

His curiosity was excited and kept alive by the curious organic remains, principally of old and extinct species of fishes, ferns, and ammonites, which were revealed along the coast by the washings of the waves, or were exposed by the stroke of his mason's hammer. He never lost sight of the subject; but went on accumulating observations and comparing formations, until at length, many years afterwards, when no longer a working mason, he gave to the world his highly interesting work on the Old Red Sandstone, which at once established his reputation as a scientific geologist. But this work was the fruit of long years of patient observation and research. As he modestly states in his autobiography, "the only merit to which I lay claim in the case is that of patient research—a merit in which whoever wills may rival or surpass

me; and this humble faculty of patience, when rightly
developed, may lead to more extraordinary developments
of idea than even genius itself."

The late John Brown, the eminent English geologist,
was, like Miller, a stonemason in his early life, serving an
apprenticeship to the trade at Colchester, and afterwards
working as a journeyman mason at Norwich. He began
business as a builder on his own account at Colchester,
where by frugality and industry he secured a competency.
It was while working at his trade that his attention was first
drawn to the study of fossils and shells; and he proceeded
to make a collection of them, which afterwards grew into
one of the finest in England. His researches along the
coasts of Essex, Kent, and Sussex brought to light some
magnificent remains of the elephant and rhinoceros, the
most valuable of which were presented by him to the British
Museum. During the last few years of his life he devoted
considerable attention to the study of the Foraminifera in
chalk, respecting which he made several interesting discoveries. His life was useful, happy, and honoured; and
he died at Stanway, in Essex, in November 1859, at the
ripe age of eighty years.

Not long ago, Sir Roderick Murchison discovered at
Thurso, in the far north of Scotland, a profound geologist, in
the person of a baker there, named Robert Dick. When Sir
Roderick called upon him at the bakehouse in which he
baked and earned his bread, Robert Dick delineated to him,
by means of flour upon the board, the geographical features
and geological phenomena of his native county, pointing out
the imperfections in the existing maps, which he had ascertained by travelling over the country in his leisure hours.
On further inquiry, Sir Roderick ascertained that the humble
individual before him was not only a capital baker and geologist, but a first-rate botanist. " I found," said the President
of the Geographical Society, " to my great humiliation that

the baker knew infinitely more of botanical science, ay, ten times more, than I did; and that there were only some twenty or thirty specimens of flowers which he had not collected. Some he had obtained as presents, some he had purchased, but the greater portion had been accumulated by his industry, in his native county of Caithness; and the specimens were all arranged in the most beautiful order, with their scientific names affixed."

Sir Roderick Murchison himself is an illustrious follower of these and kindred branches of science. A writer in the 'Quarterly Review' cites him as a "singular instance of a man who, having passed the early part of his life as a soldier, never having had the advantage, or disadvantage as the case might have been, of a scientific training, instead of remaining a fox-hunting country gentleman, has succeeded by his own native vigour and sagacity, untiring industry and zeal, in making for himself a scientific reputation that is as wide as it is likely to be lasting. He took first of all an unexplored and difficult district at home, and, by the labour of many years, examined its rock-formations, classed them in natural groups, assigned to each its characteristic assemblage of fossils, and was the first to decipher two great chapters in the world's geological history, which must always henceforth carry his name on their title-page. Not only so, but he applied the knowledge thus acquired to the dissection of large districts, both at home and abroad, so as to become the geological discoverer of great countries which had formerly been 'terræ incognitæ.'" But Sir Roderick Murchison is not merely a geologist. His indefatigable labours in many branches of knowledge have contributed to render him among the most accomplished and complete of scientific men.

CHAPTER VI.

WORKERS IN ART.

"If what shone afar so grand,
Turn to nothing in thy hand,
On again ; the virtue lies
In the struggle, not the prize."—*R. M. Milnes.*
" Excelle, et tu vivras."—*Joubert.*

XCELLENCE in art, as in everything else, can only be achieved by dint of painstaking labour. There is nothing less accidental than the painting of a fine picture or the chiselling of a noble statue. Every skilled touch of the artist's brush or chisel, though guided by genius, is the product of unremitting study.

Sir Joshua Reynolds was such a believer in the force of industry, that he held that artistic excellence, "however expressed by genius, taste, or the gift of heaven, may be acquired." Writing to Barry he said, " Whoever is resolved to excel in painting, or indeed any other art, must bring all his mind to bear upon that one object from the moment that he rises till he goes to bed." And on another occasion he said, " Those who are resolved to excel must go to their work, willing or unwilling, morning, noon, and night : they will find it no play, but very hard labour." But although diligent application is no doubt absolutely necessary for the achievement of the highest distinction in art, it is equally true that without the inborn genius, no amount of mere industry, however well applied, will make an artist. The gift comes by nature, but is perfected by self-culture, which is of more avail than all the imparted education of the schools.

Some of the greatest artists have had to force their way upward in the face of poverty and manifold obstructions. Illustrious instances will at once flash upon the reader's mind. Claude Lorraine, the pastrycook ; Tintoretto, the dyer ; the two Caravaggios, the one a colour-grinder, the other a mortar-carrier at the Vatican ; Salvator Rosa, the associate of bandits ; Giotto, the peasant boy ; Zingaro, the gipsy ; Cavedone, turned out of doors to beg by his father ; Canova, the stone-cutter ; these, and many other well-known artists, succeeded in achieving distinction by severe study and labour, under circumstances the most adverse.

Nor have the most distinguished artists of our own country been born in a position of life more than ordinarily favourable to the culture of artistic genius. Gainsborough and Bacon were the sons of cloth-workers ; Barry was an Irish sailor boy, and Maclise a banker's apprentice at Cork ; Opie and Romney, like Inigo Jones, were carpenters ; West was the son of a small Quaker farmer in Pennsylvania ; Northcote was a watchmaker, Jackson a tailor, and Etty a printer ; Reynolds, Wilson, and Wilkie, were the sons of clergymen ; Lawrence was the son of a publican, and Turner of a barber. Several of our painters, it is true, originally had some connection with art, though in a very humble way,—such as Flaxman, whose father sold plaster casts ; Bird, who ornamented tea-trays ; Martin, who was a coach-painter ; Wright and Gilpin, who were ship-painters ; Chantrey, who was a carver and gilder ; and David Cox, Stanfield, and Roberts, who were scene-painters.

It was not by luck or accident that these men achieved distinction, but by sheer industry and hard work. Though some achieved wealth, yet this was rarely, if ever, their ruling motive. Indeed, no mere love of money could sustain the efforts of the artist in his early career of self-denial and application. The pleasure of the pursuit has always been its best reward ; the wealth which followed but an accident. Many noble-minded artists have preferred following the bent of their genius, to chaffering with the public for terms. Spagnoletto verified in his life the beautiful fiction of Xenophon, and after he had acquired the means of luxury, preferred withdrawing himself from their influence, and voluntarily returned to poverty and labour. When Michael Angelo was asked his opinion respecting a work which a painter had taken great pains to exhibit for profit, he said, " I think that he will be a poor fellow so long as he shows such an extreme eagerness to become rich."

Like Sir Joshua Reynolds, Michael Angelo was a great believer in the force of labour ; and he held that there was nothing which the imagination conceived, that could not be embodied in marble, if the hand were made vigorously to obey the mind. He was himself one of the most indefatigable of workers ; and he attributed his power of studying for a greater number of hours than most of his contemporaries, to his spare habits of living. A little bread and wine was all he required for the chief part of the day when employed at his work ; and very frequently he rose in the middle of the night to resume his labours. On these occasions, it was his practice to fix the candle, by the light of which he chiselled, on the summit of a pasteboard cap which he wore. Sometimes he was too wearied to undress, and he slept in his clothes, ready to spring to his work so soon as refreshed by sleep. He had a favourite device of an old man in a go-cart, with an hour-glass upon it bearing the inscription, *Ancora imparo!* Still I am learning.

Titian, also, was an indefatigable worker. His celebrated " Pietro Martire " was eight years in hand, and his " Last

Supper" seven. In his letter to Charles V. he said, "I
send your Majesty the 'Last Supper' after working at it
almost daily for seven years—*dopo sette anni lavorandovi
quasi continuamente.*" Few think of the patient labour and
long training involved in the greatest works of the artist.
They seem easy and quickly accomplished, yet with how
great difficulty has this ease been acquired. "You charge
me fifty sequins," said the Venetian nobleman to the
sculptor, "for a bust that cost you only ten days' labour."
"You forget," said the artist, "that I have been thirty
years learning to make that bust in ten days." Once
when Domenichino was blamed for his slowness in finishing a picture which was bespoken, he made answer, "I am
continually painting it within myself." It was eminently
characteristic of the industry of the late Sir Augustus
Callcott, that he made not fewer than forty separate
sketches in the composition of his famous picture of
"Rochester." This constant repetition is one of the main
conditions of success in art, as in life itself.

No matter how generous nature has been in bestowing
the gift of genius, the pursuit of art is nevertheless a long
and continuous labour. Many artists have been precocious,
but without diligence their precocity would have come to
nothing. The anecdote related of West is well known.
When only seven years old, struck with the beauty of the
sleeping infant of his eldest sister whilst watching by its
cradle, he ran to seek some paper and forthwith drew its
portrait in red and black ink. The little incident revealed
the artist in him, and it was found impossible to draw him
from his bent. West might have been a greater painter,
had he not been injured by too early success: his fame,
though great, was not purchased by study, trials, and difficulties, and it has not been enduring.

Richard Wilson, when a mere child, indulged himself
with tracing figures of men and animals on the walls of his

father's house, with a burnt stick. He first directed his attention to portrait painting; but when in Italy, calling one day at the house of Zucarelli, and growing weary with waiting, he began painting the scene on which his friend's chamber window looked. When Zucarelli arrived, he was so charmed with the picture, that he asked if Wilson had not studied landscape, to which he replied that he had not. "Then, I advise you," said the other, "to try; for you are sure of great success." Wilson adopted the advice, studied and worked hard, and became our first great English landscape painter.

Sir Joshua Reynolds, when a boy, forgot his lessons, and took pleasure only in drawing, for which his father was accustomed to rebuke him. The boy was destined for the profession of physic, but his strong instinct for art could not be repressed, and he became a painter. Gainsborough went sketching, when a schoolboy, in the woods of Sudbury; and at twelve he was a confirmed artist : he was a keen observer and a hard worker,—no picturesque feature of any scene he had once looked upon, escaping his diligent pencil. William Blake, a hosier's son, employed himself in drawing designs on the backs of his father's shop-bills, and making sketches on the counter. Edward Bird, when a child only three or four years old, would mount a chair and draw figures on the walls, which he called French and English soldiers. A box of colours was purchased for him, and his father, desirous of turning his love of art to account, put him apprentice to a maker of tea-trays! Out of this trade he gradually raised himself, by study and labour, to the rank of a Royal Academician.

Hogarth, though a very dull boy at his lessons, took pleasure in making drawings of the letters of the alphabet, and his school exercises were more remarkable for the ornaments with which he embellished them, than for the matter of the exercises themselves. In the latter respect he was beaten by all the blockheads of the school, but in his adornments he stood alone.   His father put him apprentice to a silversmith, where he learnt to draw, and also to engrave spoons and forks with crests and ciphers. From silver-chasing, he went on to teach himself engraving on copper, principally griffins and monsters of heraldry, in the course of which practice he became ambitious to delineate the varieties of human character.   The singular excellence which he reached in this art, was mainly the result of careful observation and study.   He had the gift, which he sedulously cultivated, of committing to memory the precise features of any remarkable face, and afterwards reproducing them on paper ;   but if any singularly fantastic form or *outré* face came in his way, he would make a sketch of it on the spot, upon his thumb-nail, and carry it home to expand at his leisure.   Everything fantastical and original had a powerful attraction for him, and he wandered into many out-of-the-way places for the purpose of meeting with character.   By this careful storing of his mind, he was afterwards enabled to crowd an immense amount of thought and treasured observation into his works.   Hence it is that Hogarth's pictures are so truthful a memorial of the character, the manners, and even the very thoughts of the times in which he lived.   True painting, he himself observed, can only be learnt in one school, and that is kept by Nature.   But he was not a highly cultivated man, except in his own walk.   His school education had been of the slenderest kind, scarcely even perfecting him in the art of spelling ; his self-culture did the rest.   For a long time he was in very straitened circumstances, but nevertheless worked on with a cheerful heart.   Poor though he was, he contrived to live within his small means, and he boasted, with becoming pride, that he was "a punctual paymaster." When he had conquered all his difficulties and become a famous and thriving man, he loved to dwell upon his early labours and privations, and to fight over again the battle which ended so honourably to him as a man and so gloriously as an artist. "I remember the time," said he on one occasion, "when I have gone moping into the city with scarce a shilling, but as soon as I have received ten guineas there for a plate, I have returned home, put on my sword, and sallied out with all the confidence of a man who had thousands in his pockets."

"Industry and perseverance" was the motto of the sculptor Banks, which he acted on himself, and strongly recommended to others. His well-known kindness induced many aspiring youths to call upon him and ask for his advice and assistance; and it is related that one day a boy called at his door to see him with this object, but the servant, angry at the loud knock he had given, scolded him, and was about sending him away, when Banks overhearing her, himself went out. The little boy stood at the door with some drawings in his hand. "What do you want with me?" asked the sculptor. "I want, sir, if you please, to be admitted to draw at the Academy." Banks explained that he himself could not procure his admission, but he asked to look at the boy's drawings. Examining them, he said, "Time enough for the Academy, my little man! go home—mind your schooling—try to make a better drawing of the Apollo—and in a month come again and let me see it." The boy went home—sketched and worked with redoubled diligence—and, at the end of the month, called again on the sculptor. The drawing was better; but again Banks sent him back, with good advice, to work and study. In a week the boy was again at his door, his drawing much improved; and Banks bid him be of good cheer, for if spared he would distinguish himself. The boy was Mulready; and the sculptor's augury was amply fulfilled.

The fame of Claude Lorraine is partly explained by his

indefatigable industry. Born at Champagne, in Lorraine, of poor parents, he was first apprenticed to a pastrycook. His brother, who was a wood-carver, afterwards took him into his shop to learn that trade. Having there shown indications of artistic skill, a travelling dealer persuaded the brother to allow Claude to accompany him to Italy. He assented, and the young man reached Rome, where he was shortly after engaged by Agostino Tassi, the landscape painter, as his house-servant. In that capacity Claude first learnt landscape painting, and in course of time he began to produce pictures. We next find him making the tour of Italy, France, and Germany, occasionally resting by the way to paint landscapes, and thereby replenish his purse. On returning to Rome he found an increasing demand for his works, and his reputation at length became European. He was unwearied in the study of nature in her various aspects. It was his practice to spend a great part of his time in closely copying buildings, bits of ground, trees, leaves, and such like, which he finished in detail, keeping the drawings by him in store for the purpose of introducing them in his studied landscapes. He also gave close attention to the sky, watching it for whole days from morning till night, and noting the various changes occasioned by the passing clouds and the increasing and waning light. By this constant practice he acquired, although it is said very slowly, such a mastery of hand and eye as eventually secured for him the first rank among landscape painters.

Turner, who has been styled "the English Claude," pursued a career of like laborious industry. He was destined by his father for his own trade of a barber, which he carried on in London, until one day the sketch which the boy had made of a coat of arms on a silver salver having attracted the notice of a customer whom his father was shaving, the latter was urged to allow his son to follow his bias, and he was eventually permitted to follow art as a pro-

fession. Like all young artists, Turner had many difficulties to encounter, and they were all the greater that
his circumstances were so straitened. But he was always
willing to work, and to take pains with his work, no matter
how humble it might be. He was glad to hire himself
out at half-a-crown a night to wash in skies in Indian ink
upon other people's drawings, getting his supper into the
bargain. Thus he earned money and acquired expertness.
Then he took to illustrating guide-books, almanacs, and
any sort of books that wanted cheap frontispieces. "What
could I have done better?" said he afterwards; "it was
first-rate practice." He did everything carefully and conscientiously, never slurring over his work because he was
ill-remunerated for it. He aimed at learning as well as
living; always doing his best, and never leaving a drawing
without having made a step in advance upon his previous
work. A man who thus laboured was sure to do much;
and his growth in power and grasp of thought was, to use
Ruskin's words, "as steady as the increasing light of sunrise." But Turner's genius needs no panegyric; his best
monument is the noble gallery of pictures bequeathed by
him to the nation, which will ever be the most lasting
memorial of his fame.

To reach Rome, the capital of the fine arts, is usually the
highest ambition of the art student. But the journey to
Rome is costly, and the student is often poor. With a will
resolute to overcome difficulties, Rome may however at last
be reached. Thus François Perrier, an early French painter,
in his eager desire to visit the Eternal City, consented
to act as guide to a blind vagrant. After long wanderings
he reached the Vatican, studied and became famous. Not
less enthusiasm was displayed by Jacques Callot in his
determination to visit Rome. Though opposed by his
father in his wish to be an artist, the boy would not be
baulked, but fled from home to make his way to Italy

Having set out without means, he was soon reduced to great straits; but falling in with a band of gipsies, he joined their company, and wandered about with them from one fair to another, sharing in their numerous adventures. During this remarkable journey Callot picked up much of that extraordinary knowledge of figure, feature, and character which he afterwards reproduced, sometimes in such exaggerated forms, in his wonderful engravings.

When Callot at length reached Florence, a gentleman, pleased with his ingenious ardour, placed him with an artist to study; but he was not satisfied to stop short of Rome, and we find him shortly on his way thither. At Rome he made the acquaintance of Porigi and Thomassin, who, on seeing his crayon sketches, predicted for him a brilliant career as an artist. But a friend of Callot's family having accidentally encountered him, took steps to compel the fugitive to return home. By this time he had acquired such a love of wandering that he could not rest; so he ran away a second time, and a second time he was brought back by his elder brother, who caught him at Turin. At last the father, seeing resistance was in vain, gave his reluctant consent to Callot's prosecuting his studies at Rome. Thither he went accordingly; and this time he remained, diligently studying design and engraving for several years, under competent masters. On his way back to France, he was encouraged by Cosmo II. to remain at Florence, where he studied and worked for several years more. On the death of his patron he returned to his family at Nancy, where, by the use of his burin and needle, he shortly acquired both wealth and fame. When Nancy was taken by siege during the civil wars, Callot was requested by Richelieu to make a design and engraving of the event, but the artist would not commemorate the disaster which had befallen his native place, and he refused point-blank. Richelieu could not shake his resolution, and threw him into prison. There Callot

met with some of his old friends the gipsies, who had
relieved his wants on his first journey to Rome. When
Louis XIII. heard of his imprisonment, he not only released
him, but offered to grant him any favour he might ask.
Callot immediately requested that his old companions, the
gipsies, might be set free and permitted to beg in Paris
without molestation. This odd request was granted on
condition that Callot should engrave their portraits, and
hence his curious book of engravings entitled " The
Beggars." Louis is said to have offered Callot a pension
of 3000 livres provided he would not leave Paris ; but the
artist was now too much of a Bohemian, and prized his
liberty too highly to permit him to accept it ; and he returned
to Nancy, where he worked till his death. His industry
may be inferred from the number of his engravings and
etchings, of which he left not fewer than 1600. He was
especially fond of grotesque subjects, which he treated
with great skill ; his free etchings, touched with the graver,
being executed with especial delicacy and wonderful minute-
ness.

Still more romantic and adventurous was the career of
Benvenuto Cellini, the marvellous gold worker, painter,
sculptor, engraver, engineer, and author. His life, as told
by himself, is one of the most extraordinary autobiographies
ever written. Giovanni Cellini, his father, was one of the
Court musicians to Lorenzo de Medici at Florence ; and
his highest ambition concerning his son Benvenuto was that
he should become an expert player on the flute. But
Giovanni having lost his appointment, found it necessary to
send his son to learn some trade, and he was apprenticed
to a goldsmith. The boy had already displayed a love
of drawing and of art ; and, applying himself to his business,
he soon became a dexterous workman. Having got mixed
up in a quarrel with some of the townspeople, he was
banished for six months, during which period he worked

with a goldsmith at Sienna, gaining further experience in jewellery and gold-working.

His father still insisting on his becoming a flute-player, Benvenuto continued to practise on the instrument, though he detested it. His chief pleasure was in art, which he pursued with enthusiasm. Returning to Florence, he carefully studied the designs of Leonardo da Vinci and Michael Angelo; and, still further to improve himself in gold-working, he went on foot to Rome, where he met with a variety of adventures. He returned to Florence with the reputation of being a most expert worker in the precious metals, and his skill was soon in great request. But being of an irascible temper, he was constantly getting into scrapes, and was frequently under the necessity of flying for his life. Thus he fled from Florence in the disguise of a friar, again taking refuge at Sienna, and afterwards at Rome.

During his second residence in Rome, Cellini met with extensive patronage, and he was taken into the Pope's service in the double capacity of goldsmith and musician. He was constantly studying and improving himself by acquaintance with the works of the best masters. He mounted jewels, finished enamels, engraved seals, and designed and executed works in gold, silver, and bronze, in such a style as to excel all other artists. Whenever he heard of a goldsmith who was famous in any particular branch, he immediately determined to surpass him. Thus it was that he rivalled the medals of one, the enamels of another, and the jewellery of a third; in fact, there was not a branch of his business that he did not feel impelled to excel in.

Working in this spirit, it is not so wonderful that Cellini should have been able to accomplish so much. He was a man of indefatigable activity, and was constantly on the move. At one time we find him at Florence, at another at Rome; then he is at Mantua, at Rome, at Naples, and back to Florence again; then at Venice, and in Paris, making all his long journeys on horseback. He could not carry much luggage with him; so, wherever he went, he usually began by making his own tools. He not only designed his works, but executed them himself,—hammered and carved, and cast and shaped them with his own hands. Indeed, his works have the impress of genius so clearly stamped upon them, that they could never have been designed by one person, and executed by another. The humblest article—a buckle for a lady's girdle, a seal, a locket, a brooch, a ring, or a button—became in his hands a beautiful work of art.

Cellini was remarkable for his readiness and dexterity in handicraft. One day a surgeon entered the shop of Raffaello del Moro, the goldsmith, to perform an operation on his daughter's hand. On looking at the surgeon's instruments, Cellini, who was present, found them rude and clumsy, as they usually were in those days, and he asked the surgeon to proceed no further with the operation for a quarter of an hour. He then ran to his shop, and taking a piece of the finest steel, wrought out of it a beautifully finished knife, with which the operation was successfully performed.

Among the statues executed by Cellini, the most important are the silver figure of Jupiter, executed at Paris for Francis I., and the Perseus, executed in bronze for the Grand Duke Cosmo of Florence. He also executed statues in marble of Apollo, Hyacinthus, Narcissus, and Neptune. The extraordinary incidents connected with the casting of the Perseus were peculiarly illustrative of the remarkable character of the man.

The Grand Duke having expressed a decided opinion that the model, when shown to him in wax, could not possibly be cast in bronze, Cellini was immediately stimulated by the predicted impossibility, not only to attempt, but to do it. He first made the clay model, baked it, and covered it with wax, which he shaped into the perfect form of a statue. Then coating the wax with a sort of earth, he baked the second covering, during which the wax dissolved and escaped, leaving the space between the two layers for the reception of the metal. To avoid disturbance, the latter process was conducted in a pit dug immediately under the furnace, from which the liquid metal was to be introduced by pipes and apertures into the mould prepared for it.

Cellini had purchased and laid in several loads of pine-wood, in anticipation of the process of casting, which now began. The furnace was filled with pieces of brass and bronze, and the fire was lit. The resinous pine-wood was soon in such a furious blaze, that the shop took fire, and part of the roof was burnt; while at the same time the wind blowing and the rain falling on the furnace, kept down the heat, and prevented the metals from melting. For hours Cellini struggled to keep up the heat, continually throwing in more wood, until at length he became so exhausted and ill, that he feared he should die before the statue could be cast. He was forced to leave to his assistants the pouring in of the metal when melted, and betook himself to his bed. While those about him were condoling with him in his distress, a workman suddenly entered the room, lamenting that " poor Benvenuto's work was irretrievably spoiled !" On hearing this, Cellini immediately sprang from his bed and rushed to the workshop, where he found the fire so much gone down that the metal had again become hard.

Sending across to a neighbour for a load of young oak which had been more than a year in drying, he soon had the fire blazing again and the metal melting and glittering. The wind was, however, still blowing with fury, and the rain falling heavily ; so, to protect himself, Cellini had some tables with pieces of tapestry and old clothes brought to him, behind which he went on hurling the wood into the furnace. A mass of pewter was thrown in upon the other metal, and by stirring, sometimes with iron and sometimes with long poles, the whole soon became completely melted. At this juncture, when the trying moment was close at hand, a terrible noise as of a thunderbolt was heard, and a glittering of fire flashed before Cellini's eyes. The cover of the furnace had burst, and the metal began to flow! Finding that it did not run with the proper velocity, Cellini rushed into the kitchen, bore away every piece of copper and pewter that it contained—some two hundred porringers, dishes, and kettles of different kinds—and threw them into the furnace. Then at length the metal flowed freely, and thus the splendid statue of Perseus was cast.

The divine fury of genius in which Cellini rushed to his kitchen and stripped it of its utensils for the purposes of his furnace, will remind the reader of the like act of Pallissy in breaking up his furniture for the purpose of baking his earthenware. Excepting, however, in their enthusiasm, no two men could be less alike in character. Cellini was an Ishmael against whom, according to his own account, every man's hand was turned. But about his extraordinary skill as a workman, and his genius as an artist, there cannot be two opinions.

Much less turbulent was the career of Nicolas Poussin, a man as pure and elevated in his ideas of art as he was in his daily life, and distinguished alike for his vigour of intellect, his rectitude of character, and his noble simplicity. He was born in a very humble station, at Andeleys, near Rouen, where his father kept a small school. The boy had the benefit of his parent's instruction, such as it was, but of that he is said to have been somewhat negligent, preferring to spend his time in covering his lesson-books and his slate with drawings. A country painter, much pleased with his sketches, besought his parents not to thwart him in his tastes. The painter agreed to give Poussin lessons, and he soon made such progress that his master had nothing more to teach him. Becoming restless, and desirous of further improving himself, Poussin, at the age of 18, set out for Paris, painting signboards on his way for a maintenance.

At Paris a new world of art opened before him, exciting his wonder and stimulating his emulation. He worked diligently in many studios, drawing, copying, and painting pictures. After a time, he resolved, if possible, to visit Rome, and set out on his journey; but he only succeeded in getting as far as Florence, and again returned to Paris. A second attempt which he made to reach Rome was even less successful; for this time he only got as far as Lyons. He was, nevertheless, careful to take advantage of all opportunities for improvement which came in his way, and continued as sedulous as before in studying and working.

Thus twelve years passed, years of obscurity and toil, of failures and disappointments, and probably of privations. At length Poussin succeeded in reaching Rome. There he diligently studied the old masters, and especially the ancient statues, with whose perfection he was greatly impressed. For some time he lived with the sculptor Duquesnoi, as poor as himself, and assisted him in modelling figures after the antique. With him he carefully measured some of the most celebrated statues in Rome, more particularly the 'Antinous:' and it is supposed that this practice exercised considerable influence on the formation of his future style. At the same time he studied anatomy, practised drawing from the life, and made a great store of sketches of postures and attitudes of people whom he met, carefully reading at his leisure such standard books on art as he could borrow from his friends.

During all this time he remained very poor, satisfied to be continually improving himself. He was glad to sell his pictures for whatever they would bring. One, of a prophet, he sold for eight livres; and another, the 'Plague of the Philistines,' he sold for 60 crowns—a picture afterwards bought by Cardinal de Richelieu for a thousand. To add to his troubles, he was stricken by a cruel malady, during the help-lessness occasioned by which the Chevalier del Posso assisted him with money. For this gentleman Poussin afterwards painted the ' Rest in the Desert,' a fine picture, which far more than repaid the advances made during his illness.

The brave man went on toiling and learning through suffering. Still aiming at higher things, he went to Florence and Venice, enlarging the range of his studies. The fruits of his conscientious labour at length appeared in the series of great pictures which he now began to produce,—his ' Death of Germanicus,' followed by ' Extreme Unction,' the ' Testa-ment of Eudamidas,' the ' Manna,' and the 'Abduction of the Sabines.'

The reputation of Poussin, however, grew but slowly. He was of a retiring disposition and shunned society. People gave him credit for being a thinker much more than a painter. When not actually employed in painting, he took long solitary walks in the country, meditating the designs of future pictures. One of his few friends while at Rome was Claude Lorraine, with whom he spent many hours at a time on the terrace of La Trinité-du-Mont, conversing about art and antiquarianism. The monotony and the quiet of Rome were suited to his taste, and, provided he could earn a moderate living by his brush, he had no wish to leave it.

But his fame now extended beyond Rome, and repeated invitations were sent him to return to Paris. He was offered the appointment of principal painter to the King. At first he hesitated ; quoted the Italian proverb, *Chi sta bene non si muove;* said he had lived fifteen years in Rome, married a wife there, and looked forward to dying and being buried there. Urged again, he consented, and returned to Paris. But his appearance there awakened much professional jealousy, and he soon wished himself back in Rome again.

While in Paris he painted some of his greatest works—his 'Saint Xavier,' the 'Baptism,' and the 'Last Supper.' He was kept constantly at work. At first he did whatever he was asked to do, such as designing frontispieces for the royal books, more particularly a Bible and a Virgil, cartoons for the Louvre, and designs for tapestry; but at length he expostulated :—" It is impossible for me," he said to M. de Chanteloup, "to work at the same time at frontispieces for books, at a Virgin, at a picture of the Congregation of St. Louis, at the various designs for the gallery, and, finally, at designs for the royal tapestry. I have only one pair of hands and a feeble head, and can neither be helped nor can my labours be lightened by another."

Annoyed by the enemies his success had provoked and whom he was unable to conciliate, he determined, at the end of less than two years' labour in Paris, to return to Rome. Again settled there in his humble dwelling on Mont Pincio, he employed himself diligently in the practice of his art during the remaining years of his life, living in great simplicity and privacy. Though suffering much from the disease which afflicted him, he solaced himself by study, always striving after excellence. "In growing old," he said, "I feel myself becoming more and more inflamed with the desire of surpassing myself and reaching the highest degree of perfection." Thus toiling, struggling, and suffering, Poussin spent his later years. He had no children; his wife died before him; all his friends were gone : so that in his old age he was left absolutely alone in Rome, so full of tombs, and died there in 1665, bequeathing to his relatives at Andeleys the savings of his life, amounting to about 1000 crowns; and leaving behind him, as a legacy to his race, the great works of his genius.

The career of Ary Scheffer furnishes one of the best examples in modern times of a like high-minded devotion to art. Born at Dordrecht, the son of a German artist, he early manifested an aptitude for drawing and painting, which his parents encouraged. His father dying while he was still young, his mother resolved, though her means were but small, to remove the family to Paris, in order that her son might obtain the best opportunities for instruction. There young Scheffer was placed with Guérin the painter. But his mother's means were too limited to permit him to devote himself exclusively to study. She had sold the few jewels she possessed, and refused herself every indulgence, in order to forward the instruction of her other children. Under such circumstances, it was natural that Ary should wish to help her ; and by the time he was eighteen years of age he began to paint small pictures of simple subjects, which met with a ready sale at moderate prices. He also practised portrait painting, at the same time gathering experience and earning honest money. He gradually improved in drawing, colouring, and composition. The 'Baptism' marked a new epoch in his career, and from that point he went on advancing, until his fame culminated in his pictures illustrative of 'Faust,' his 'Francisca de Rimini,' 'Christ the Consoler,' the 'Holy Women,' 'St. Monica and St. Augustin,' and many other noble works.

"The amount of labour, thought, and attention," says Mr. Grote, "which Scheffer brought to the production of the 'Francisca,' must have been enormous. In truth, his technical education having been so imperfect, he was forced to climb the steep of art by drawing upon his own resources, and thus, whilst his hand was at work, his mind was engaged in meditation. He had to try various processes of handling, and experiments in colouring; to paint and repaint, with tedious and unremitting assiduity. But Nature had endowed him with that which proved in some sort an equivalent for shortcomings of a professional kind. His own elevation of character, and his profound sensibility, aided him in acting upon the feelings of others through the medium of the pencil." *

One of the artists whom Scheffer most admired was Flaxman ; and he once said to a friend, " If I have unconsciously borrowed from any one in the design of the ' Francisca,' it must have been from something I had seen among Flaxman's drawings." John Flaxman was the son of a humble seller of plaster casts in New Street, Covent Garden. When a child, he was such an invalid that it was his custom to sit behind his father's shop counter propped by pillows, amusing himself with drawing and reading. A benevolent clergyman, the Rev. Mr. Matthews, calling at the shop one day, saw the boy trying to read a book, and on inquiring what it was, found it to be a Cornelius Nepos, which his father had picked up for a few pence at a bookstall. The gentleman, after some conversation with the boy, said that was not the proper book for him to read, but that he would bring him one. The next day he called with translations of Homer and ' Don Quixote,' which the boy proceeded to read with great avidity. His mind was soon filled with the heroism which breathed through the pages of the former, and, with the stucco Ajaxes and Achilleses about him, ranged along the shop shelves, the ambition took possession of him, that he too would design and embody in poetic forms those majestic heroes.

Like all youthful efforts, his first designs were crude. The proud father one day showed some of them to Roubilliac the sculptor, who turned from them with a contemptuous " pshaw !" But the boy had the right stuff in him ; he had industry and patience ; and he continued to labour incessantly at his books and drawings. He then tried his young powers in modelling figures in plaster of Paris, wax, and

* Mr. Grote's ' Memoir of the Life of Ary Scheffer,' p. 67.

clay. Some of these early works are still preserved, not because of their merit, but because they are curious as the first healthy efforts of patient genius. It was long before the boy could walk, and he only learnt to do so by hobbling along upon crutches. At length he became strong enough to walk without them.

The kind Mr. Matthews invited him to his house, where his wife explained Homer and Milton to him. They helped him also in his self-culture—giving him lessons in Greek and Latin, the study of which he prosecuted at home. By dint of patience and perseverance, his drawing improved so much that he obtained a commission from a lady, to execute six original drawings in black chalk of subjects in Homer. His first commission! What an event in the artist's life! A surgeon's first fee, a lawyer's first retainer, a legislator's first speech, a singer's first appearance behind the foot-lights, an author's first book, are not any of them more full of interest to the aspirant for fame than the artist's first commission. The boy at once proceeded to execute the order, and he was both well praised and well paid for his work.

At fifteen Flaxman entered a pupil at the Royal Academy. Notwithstanding his retiring disposition, he soon became known among the students, and great things were expected of him. Nor were their expectations disappointed: in his fifteenth year he gained the silver prize, and next year he became a candidate for the gold one. Everybody prophesied that he would carry off the medal, for there was none who surpassed him in ability and industry. Yet he lost it, and the gold medal was adjudged to a pupil who was not afterwards heard of. This failure on the part of the youth was really of service to him; for defeats do not long cast down the resolute-hearted, but only serve to call forth their real powers. "Give me time," said he to his father, "and I will yet produce works that the Academy will be proud to recognise." He redoubled his efforts, spared no pains, designed and modelled incessantly, and made steady if not rapid progress. But meanwhile poverty threatened his father's household; the plaster-cast trade yielded a very bare living; and young Flaxman, with resolute self-denial, curtailed his hours of study, and devoted himself to helping his father in the humble details of his business. He laid aside his Homer to take up the plaster-trowel. He was willing to work in the humblest department of the trade so that his father's family might be supported, and the wolf kept from the door. To this drudgery of his art he served a long apprenticeship; but it did him good. It familiarised him with steady work, and cultivated in him the spirit of patience. The discipline may have been hard, but it was wholesome.

Happily, young Flaxman's skill in design had reached the knowledge of Josiah Wedgwood, who sought him out for the purpose of employing him to design improved patterns of china and earthenware. It may seem a humble department of art for such a genius as Flaxman to work in; but it really was not so. An artist may be labouring truly in his vocation while designing a common teapot or water-jug. Articles in daily use amongst the people, which are before their eyes at every meal, may be made the vehicles of education to all, and minister to their highest culture. The most ambitious artist may thus confer a greater practical benefit on his countrymen than by executing an elaborate work which he may sell for thousands of pounds to be placed in some wealthy man's gallery, where it is hidden away from public sight. Before Wedgwood's time the designs which figured upon our china and stoneware were hideous both in drawing and execution, and he determined to improve both. Flaxman did his best to carry out the manufacturer's views. He supplied him from time to time with models and designs of various pieces of earthenware, the subjects of which were principally from ancient verse and history. Many of them are still in existence, and some are equal in beauty and simplicity to his after designs for marble. The celebrated Etruscan vases, specimens of which were to be found in public museums and in the cabinets of the curious, furnished him with the best examples of form, and these he embellished with his own elegant devices. ' Stuart's Athens,' then recently published, furnished him with specimens of the purest-shaped Greek utensils ; of these he adopted the best, and worked them into new shapes of elegance and beauty. Flaxman then saw that he was labouring in a great work—no less than the promotion of popular education ; and he was proud, in after life, to allude to his early labours in this walk, by which he was enabled at the same time to cultivate his love of the beautiful, to diffuse a taste for art among the people, and to replenish his own purse, while he promoted the prosperity of his friend and benefactor.

At length, in the year 1782, when twenty-seven years of age, he quitted his father's roof and rented a small house and studio in Wardour Street, Soho ; and what was more, he married—Ann Denman was the name of his wife—and a cheerful, bright-souled, noble woman she was. He believed that in marrying her he should be able to work with an intenser spirit ; for, like him, she had a taste for poetry and art ; and besides was an enthusiastic admirer of her husband's genius. Yet when Sir Joshua Reynolds—himself a bachelor —met Flaxman shortly after his marriage, he said to him, " So, Flaxman, I am told you are married ; if so, sir, I tell you you are ruined for an artist." Flaxman went straight home, sat down beside his wife, took her hand in his, and said, "Ann, I am ruined for an artist." " How so, John ? How has it happened ? and who has done it ? " " It happened," he replied, " in the church, and Ann Denman has done it." He then told her of Sir Joshua's remark—whose opinion was well known, and had often been expressed, that if students would excel they must bring the whole powers of their mind to bear upon their art, from the moment they rose until they went to bed; and also, that no man could be a *great* artist unless he studied the grand works of Raffaelle, Michael Angelo, and others, at Rome and Florence. "And I," said Flaxman, drawing up his little figure to its full height, "*I* would be a great artist." "And a great artist you shall be," said his wife, "and visit Rome too, if that be really necessary to make you great." "But how?" asked Flaxman. "*Work and economise,*" rejoined the brave wife; "I will never have it said that Ann Denman ruined John Flaxman for an artist." And so it was determined by the pair that the journey to Rome was to be made when their means would admit. "I will go to Rome," said Flaxman, "and show the President that wedlock is for a man's good rather than his harm; and you, Ann, shall accompany me."

Patiently and happily the affectionate couple plodded on during five years in their humble little home in Wardour Street, always with the long journey to Rome before them. It was never lost sight of for a moment, and not a penny was uselessly spent that could be saved towards the necessary expenses. They said no word to any one about their project; solicited no aid from the Academy; but trusted only to their own patient labour and love to pursue and achieve their object. During this time Flaxman exhibited very few works. He could not afford marble to experiment in original designs; but he obtained frequent commissions for monuments, by the profits of which he maintained himself. He still worked for Wedgwood, who was a prompt paymaster; and, on the whole, he was thriving, happy, and hopeful. His local respectability was even such as to bring local honours and local work upon him; for he was elected by the ratepayers to collect the watch-rate for the Parish of St. Anne, when he might be seen going about with an ink-bottle suspended from his button-hole, collecting the money.

At length Flaxman and his wife having accumulated a

N

sufficient store of savings, set out for Rome. Arrived there, he applied himself diligently to study; maintaining himself, like other poor artists, by making copies from the antique. English visitors sought his studio, and gave him commissions; and it was then that he composed his beautiful designs illustrative of Homer, Æschylus, and Dante. The price paid for them was moderate—only fifteen shillings a-piece; but Flaxman worked for art as well as money; and the beauty of the designs brought him other friends and patrons. He executed Cupid and Aurora for the munificent Thomas Hope, and the Fury of Athamas for the Earl of Bristol. He then prepared to return to England, his taste improved and cultivated by careful study; but before he left Italy, the Academies of Florence and Carrara recognised his merit by electing him a member.

His fame had preceded him to London, where he soon found abundant employment. While at Rome he had been commissioned to execute his famous monument in memory of Lord Mansfield, and it was erected in the north transept of Westminster Abbey shortly after his return. It stands there in majestic grandeur, a monument to the genius of Flaxman himself—calm, simple, and severe. No wonder that Banks, the sculptor, then in the heyday of his fame, exclaimed when he saw it, " This little man cuts us all out ! "

When the members of the Royal Academy heard of Flaxman's return, and especially when they had an opportunity of seeing and admiring his portrait-statue of Mansfield, they were eager to have him enrolled among their number. He allowed his name to be proposed in the candidates' list of associates, and was immediately elected. Shortly after, he appeared in an entirely new character. The little boy who had begun his studies behind the plaster-cast-seller's shop-counter in New Street, Covent Garden, was now, a man of high intellect and recognised supremacy in art, to instruct students, in the character of Professor of Sculpture to the Royal Academy ! And no man better deserved to fill that distinguished office; for none is so able to instruct others as he who, for himself and by his own efforts, has learnt to grapple with and overcome difficulties.

After a long, peaceful, and happy life, Flaxman found himself growing old. The loss which he sustained by the death of his affectionate wife Ann, was a severe shock to him; but he survived her several years, during which he executed his celebrated "Shield of Achilles," and his noble "Archangel Michael vanquishing Satan,"—perhaps his two greatest works.

Chantrey was a more robust man;—somewhat rough, but hearty in his demeanour; proud of his successful struggle with the difficulties which beset him in early life; and, above all, proud of his independence. He was born a poor man's child, at Norton, near Sheffield. His father dying when he was a mere boy, his mother married again. Young Chantrey used to drive an ass laden with milk-cans across its back into the neighbouring town of Sheffield, and there serve his mother's customers with milk. Such was the humble beginning of his industrial career; and it was by his own strength that he rose from that position, and achieved the highest eminence as an artist. Not taking kindly to his step-father, the boy was sent to trade, and was first placed with a grocer in Sheffield. The business was very distasteful to him; but, passing a carver's shop window one day, his eye was attracted by the glittering articles it contained, and, charmed with the idea of being a carver, he begged to be released from the grocery business with that object. His friends consented, and he was bound apprentice to the carver and gilder for seven years. His new master, besides being a carver in wood, was also a dealer in prints and plaster models; and Chantrey at once set about imitating both, studying with great industry and energy. All his spare hours were devoted to drawing, modelling, and self-improvement, and he often carried his labours far into the night. Before his apprenticeship was out—at the age of twenty-one —he paid over to his master the whole wealth which he was able to muster—a sum of 50*l.*—to cancel his indentures, determined to devote himself to the career of an artist. He then made the best of his way to London, and with characteristic good sense, sought employment as an assistant carver, studying painting and modelling at his bye-hours. Among the jobs on which he was first employed as a journeyman carver, was the decoration of the dining-room of Mr. Rogers, the poet—a room in which he was in after years a welcome visitor; and he usually took pleasure in pointing out his early handywork to the guests whom he met at his friend's table.

Returning to Sheffield on a professional visit, he advertised himself in the local papers as a painter of portraits in crayons and miniatures, and also in oil. For his first crayon portrait he was paid a guinea by a cutler; and for a portrait in oil, a confectioner paid him as much as 5*l.* and a pair of top boots! Chantrey was soon in London again to study at the Royal Academy; and next time he returned to Sheffield he advertised himself as ready to model plaster busts of his townsmen, as well as paint portraits of them. He was even selected to design a monument to a deceased vicar of the town, and executed it to the general satisfaction. When in London he used a room over a stable as a studio, and there he modelled his first original work for exhibition. It was a gigantic head of Satan. Towards the close of Chantrey's life, a friend passing through his studio was struck by this model lying in a corner. "That head," said the sculptor, "was the first thing that I did after I came to London. I worked at it in a garret with a paper cap on my head; and as I could then afford only one candle, I stuck that one in my cap that it might move along with me, and give me light whichever way I turned." Flaxman saw and admired this head at the Academy Exhibition, and recommended Chantrey for the execution of the busts of four admirals, required for the Naval Asylum at Greenwich. This commission led to others, and painting was given up. But for eight years before, he had not earned 5*l.* by his modelling. His famous head of Horne Tooke was such a success that, according to his own account, it brought him commissions amounting to 12,000*l.*

Chantrey had now succeeded, but he had worked hard, and fairly earned his good fortune. He was selected from amongst sixteen competitors to execute the statue of George III. for the city of London. A few years later, he produced the exquisite monument of the Sleeping Children, now in Lichfield Cathedral,—a work of great tenderness and beauty; and thenceforward his career was one of increasing honour, fame, and prosperity. His patience, industry, and steady perseverance were the means by which he achieved his greatness. Nature endowed him with genius, and his sound sense enabled him to employ the precious gift as a blessing. He was prudent and shrewd, like the men amongst whom he was born; the pocket-book which accompanied him on his Italian tour containing mingled notes on art, records of daily expenses, and the current prices of marble. His tastes were simple, and he made his finest subjects great by the mere force of simplicity. His statue of Watt, in Handsworth church, seems to us the very consummation of art; yet it is perfectly artless and simple. His generosity to brother artists in need was splendid, but quiet and unostentatious. He left the principal part of his fortune to the Royal Academy for the promotion of British art.

The same honest and persistent industry was throughout distinctive of the career of David Wilkie. The son of a

Scotch minister, he gave early indications of an artistic turn; and though he was a negligent and inapt scholar, he was a sedulous drawer of faces and figures. A silent boy, he already displayed that quiet concentrated energy of character which distinguished him through life. He was always on the look-out for an opportunity to draw,— and the walls of the manse, or the smooth sand by the river side, were alike convenient for his purpose. Any sort of tool would serve him; like Giotto, he found a pencil in a burnt stick, a prepared canvas in any smooth stone, and the subject for a picture in every ragged mendicant he met. When he visited a house, he generally left his mark on the walls as an indication of his presence, sometimes to the disgust of cleanly housewives. In short, notwithstanding the aversion of his father, the minister, to the "sinful" profession of painting, Wilkie's strong propensity was not to be thwarted, and he became an artist; working his way manfully up the steep of difficulty. Though rejected on his first application as a candidate for admission to the Scottish Academy, at Edinburgh, on account of the rudeness and inaccuracy of his introductory specimens, he persevered in producing better, until he was admitted. But his progress was slow. He applied himself diligently to the drawing of the human figure, and held on with the determination to succeed, as if with a resolute confidence in the result. He displayed none of the eccentric humour and fitful application of many youths who conceive themselves geniuses, but kept up the routine of steady application to such an extent that he himself was afterwards accustomed to attribute his success to his dogged perseverance rather than to any higher innate power. "The single element," he said, "in all the progressive movements of my pencil was persevering industry." At Edinburgh he gained a few premiums, thought of turning his attention to portrait painting, with a view to its higher and more certain remuneration,

but eventually went boldly into the line in which he earned
his fame,—and painted his Pitlessie Fair. What was bolder
still, he determined to proceed to London, on account of its
presenting so much wider a field for study and work; and
the poor Scotch lad arrived in town, and painted his Village
Politicians while living in a humble lodging on eighteen
shillings a week.

Notwithstanding the success of this picture, and the commissions which followed it, Wilkie long continued poor.
The prices which his works realized were not great, for he
bestowed upon them so much time and labour, that his
earnings continued comparatively small for many years.
Every picture was carefully studied and elaborated beforehand; nothing was struck off at a heat; many occupied
him for years—touching, retouching, and improving them
until they finally passed out of his hands. As with Reynolds, his motto was "Work! work! work!" and, like him,
he expressed great dislike for talking artists. Talkers may
sow, but the silent reap. "Let us be *doing* something,"
was his oblique mode of rebuking the loquacious and
admonishing the idle. He once related to his friend
Constable that when he studied at the Scottish Academy,
Graham, the master of it, was accustomed to say to the
students, in the words of Reynolds, "If you have genius,
industry will improve it; if you have none, industry will
supply its place." "So," said Wilkie, "I was determined
to be very industrious, for I knew I had no genius." He
also told Constable that when Linnell and Burnett, his
fellow-students in London, were talking about art, he
always contrived to get as close to them as he could to
hear all they said, "for," said he, "they know a great
deal, and I know very little." This was said with perfect
sincerity, for Wilkie was habitually modest. One of the
first things that he did with the sum of thirty pounds
which he obtained from Lord Mansfield for his Village

Politicians, was to buy a present—of bonnets, shawls, and dresses—for his mother and sister at home ; though but little able to afford it at the time. Wilkie's early poverty had trained him in habits of strict economy, which were, however, consistent with a noble liberality, as appears from sundry passages in the Autobiography of Abraham Raimbach the engraver.

William Etty was another notable instance of unflagging industry and indomitable perseverance in art. His father was a ginger-bread and spicemaker at York, and his mother —a woman of considerable force and originality of character—was the daughter of a ropemaker. The boy early displayed a love of drawing, covering walls, floors, and tables with specimens of his skill ; his first crayon being a farthing's worth of chalk, and this giving place to a piece of coal or a bit of charred stick. His mother, knowing nothing of art, put the boy apprentice to a trade—that of a printer. But in his leisure hours he went on with the practice of drawing ; and when his time was out he determined to follow his bent—he would be a painter and nothing else. Fortunately his uncle and elder brother were able and willing to help him on in his new career, and they provided him with the means of entering as pupil at the Royal Academy. We observe, from Leslie's Autobiography, that Etty was looked upon by his fellow students as a worthy but dull, plodding person, who would never distinguish himself. But he had in him the divine faculty of work, and diligently plodded his way upward to eminence in the highest walks of art.

Many artists have had to encounter privations which have tried their courage and endurance to the utmost before they succeeded. What number may have sunk under them we can never know. Martin encountered difficulties in the course of his career such as perhaps fall to the lot of few. More than once he found himself on the verge of starvation while engaged on his first great picture. It is related of him that on one occasion he found himself reduced to his last shilling—a *bright* shilling—which he had kept because of its very brightness, but at length he found it necessary to exchange it for bread. He went to a baker's shop, bought a loaf, and was taking it away, when the baker snatched it from him, and tossed back the shilling to the starving painter. The bright shilling had failed him in his hour of need—it was a bad one! Returning to his lodgings, he rummaged his trunk for some remaining crust to satisfy his hunger. Upheld throughout by the victorious power of enthusiasm, he pursued his design with unsubdued energy. He had the courage to work on and to wait; and when, a few days after, he found an opportunity to exhibit his picture, he was from that time famous. Like many other great artists, his life proves that, in despite of outward circumstances, genius, aided by industry, will be its own protector, and that fame, though she comes late, will never ultimately refuse her favours to real merit.

The most careful discipline and training after academic methods will fail in making an artist, unless he himself take an active part in the work. Like every highly cultivated man, he must be mainly self-educated. When Pugin, who was brought up in his father's office, had learnt all that he could learn of architecture according to the usual formulas, he still found that he had learned but little; and that he must begin at the beginning, and pass through the discipline of labour. Young Pugin accordingly hired himself out as a common carpenter at Covent Garden Theatre— first working under the stage, then behind the flys, then upon the stage itself. He thus acquired a familiarity with work, and cultivated an architectural taste, to which the diversity of the mechanical employment about a large operatic establishment is peculiarly favourable. When the

theatre closed for the season, he worked a sailing-ship between London and some of the French ports, carrying on
at the same time a profitable trade.   At every opportunity
he would land and make drawings of any old building, and
especially of any ecclesiastical structure which fell in his
way.   Afterwards he would make special journeys to the
Continent for the same purpose, and returned home laden
with drawings.   Thus he plodded and laboured on, making
sure of the excellence and distinction which he eventually
achieved.

A similar illustration of plodding industry in the same
walk is presented in the career of George Kemp, the architect of the beautiful Scott Monument at Edinbugh.   He
was the son of a poor shepherd, who pursued his calling on
the southern slope of the Pentland Hills.   Amidst that
pastoral solitude the boy had no opportunity of enjoying
the contemplation of works of art.   It happened, however,
that in his tenth year he was sent on a message to Roslin,
by the farmer for whom his father herded sheep, and the
sight of the beautiful castle and chapel there seems to
have made a vivid and enduring impression on his mind.
Probably to enable him to indulge his love of architectural
construction, the boy besought his father to let him be a
joiner; and he was accordingly put apprentice to a neighbouring village carpenter.   Having served his time, he went
to Galashiels to seek work.   As he was plodding along the
valley of the Tweed with his tools upon his back, a carriage
overtook him near Elibank Tower; and the coachman,
doubtless at the suggestion of his master, who was seated
inside, having asked the youth how far he had to walk, and
learning that he was on his way to Galashiels, invited him
to mount the box beside him, and thus to ride thither.   It
turned out that the kindly gentleman inside was no other
than Sir Walter Scott, then travelling on his official duty as
Sheriff of Selkirkshire.   Whilst working at Galashiels, Kemp

had frequent opportunities of visiting Melrose, Dryburgh, and Jedburgh Abbeys, which he studied carefully. Inspired by his love of architecture, he worked his way as a carpenter over the greater part of the north of England, never omitting an opportunity of inspecting and making sketches of any fine Gothic building. On one occasion, when working in Lancashire, he walked fifty miles to York, spent a week in carefully examining the Minster, and returned in like manner on foot. We next find him in Glasgow, where he remained four years, studying the fine cathedral there during his spare time. He returned to England again, this time working his way further south ; studying Canterbury, Winchester, Tintern, and other well-known structures. In 1824 he formed the design of travelling over Europe with the same object, supporting himself by his trade. Reaching Boulogne, he proceeded by Abbeville and Beauvais to Paris, spending a few weeks making drawings and studies at each place. His skill as a mechanic, and especially his knowledge of mill-work, readily secured him employment wherever he went ; and he usually chose the site of his employment in the neighbourhood of some fine old Gothic structure, in studying which he occupied his leisure. After a year's working, travel, and study abroad, he returned to Scotland. He continued his studies, and became a proficient in drawing and perspective : Melrose was his favourite ruin ; and he produced several elaborate drawings of the building, one of which, exhibiting it in a "restored" state, was afterwards engraved. He also obtained employment as a modeller of architectural designs ; and made drawings for a work begun by an Edinburgh engraver, after the plan of Britton's 'Cathedral Antiquities.' This was a task congenial to his tastes, and he laboured at it with an enthusiasm which ensured its rapid advance ; walking on foot for the purpose over half Scotland, and living as an ordinary mechanic, whilst executing drawings which would have done credit

to the best masters in the art. The projector of the work
having died suddenly, the publication was however stopped,
and Kemp sought other employment. Few knew of the
genius of this man—for he was exceedingly taciturn and
habitually modest—when the Committee of the Scott Monument offered a prize for the best design. The competitors
were numerous—including some of the greatest names in
classical architecture; but the design unanimously selected
was that of George Kemp, who was working at Kilwinning
Abbey in Ayrshire, many miles off, when the letter reached
him intimating the decision of the committee. Poor Kemp!
Shortly after this event he met an untimely death, and did
not live to see the first result of his indefatigable industry
and self-culture embodied in stone,—one of the most beautiful and appropriate memorials ever erected to literary
genius.

John Gibson was another artist full of a genuine enthusiasm and love for his art, which placed him high above
those sordid temptations which urge meaner natures to make
time the measure of profit. He was born at Gyffn, near
Conway, in North Wales—the son of a gardener. He early
showed indications of his talent by the carvings in wood
which he made by means of a common pocket knife; and
his father, noting the direction of his talent, sent him to
Liverpool and bound him apprentice to a cabinet-maker
and wood-carver. He rapidly improved at his trade, and
some of his carvings were much admired. He was thus
naturally led to sculpture, and when eighteen years old he
modelled a small figure of Time in wax, which attracted
considerable notice. The Messrs. Franceys, sculptors, of
Liverpool, having purchased the boy's indentures, took him
as their apprentice for six years, during which his genius
displayed itself in many original works. From thence he
proceeded to London, and afterwards to Rome; and his
fame became European.

Robert Thorburn, the Royal Academician, like John Gibson, was born of poor parents. His father was a shoemaker at Dumfries. Besides Robert there were two other sons; one of whom is a skilful carver in wood. One day a lady called at the shoemaker's, and found Robert, then a mere boy, engaged in drawing upon a stool which served him for a table. She examined his work, and observing his abilities, interested herself in obtaining for him some employment in drawing, and enlisted in his behalf the services of others who could assist him in prosecuting the study of art. The boy was diligent, pains-taking, staid, and silent, mixing little with his companions, and forming but few intimacies. About the year 1830, some gentlemen of the town provided him with the means of proceeding to Edinburgh, where he was admitted a student at the Scottish Academy. There he had the advantage of studying under competent masters, and the progress which he made was rapid. From Edinburgh he removed to London, where, we understand, he had the advantage of being introduced to notice under the patronage of the Duke of Buccleuch. We need scarcely say, however, that of whatever use patronage may have been to Thorburn in giving him an introduction to the best circles, patronage of no kind could have made him the great artist that he unquestionably is, without native genius and diligent application.

Noel Paton, the well-known painter, began his artistic career at Dunfermline and Paisley, as a drawer of patterns for table-cloths and muslin embroidered by hand; meanwhile working diligently at higher subjects, including the drawing of the human figure. He was, like Turner, ready to turn his hand to any kind of work, and in 1840, when a mere youth, we find him engaged, among his other labours, in illustrating the 'Renfrewshire Annual.' He worked his way step by step, slowly yet surely; but he remained unknown until the exhibition of the prize cartoons painted for the houses of Parliament, when his picture of the Spirit of Religion (for which he obtained one of the first prizes) revealed him to the world as a genuine artist ; and the works which he has since exhibited — such as the ' Reconciliation of Oberon and Titania,' ' Home,' and ' The bluidy Tryste'—have shown a steady advance in artistic power and culture.

Another striking exemplification of perseverance and industry in the cultivation of art in humble life is presented in the career of James Sharples, a working blacksmith at Blackburn. He was born at Wakefield in Yorkshire, in 1825, one of a family of thirteen children. His father was a working ironfounder, and removed to Bury to follow his business. The boys received no school education, but were all sent to work as soon as they were able; and at about ten James was placed in a foundry, where he was employed for about two years as smithy-boy. After that he was sent into the engine-shop where his father worked as engine-smith. The boy's employment was to heat and carry rivets for the boiler-makers. Though his hours of labour were very long —often from six in the morning until eight at night—his father contrived to give him some little teaching after working hours ; and it was thus that he partially learned his letters. An incident occurred in the course of his employment among the boiler-makers, which first awakened in him the desire to learn drawing. He had occasionally been employed by the foreman to hold the chalked line with which he made the designs of boilers upon the floor of the workshop ; and on such occasions the foreman was accustomed to hold the line, and direct the boy to make the necessary dimensions. James soon became so expert at this as to be of considerable service to the foreman ; and at his leisure hours at home his great delight was to practise drawing designs of boilers upon his mother's floor. On one occasion, when a female relative was expected from Manchester to pay the family a visit, and

the house had been made as decent as possible for her reception, the boy, on coming in from the foundry in the evening,
began his usual operations upon the floor. He had proceeded some way with his design of a large boiler in chalk,
when his mother arrived with the visitor, and to her dismay
found the boy unwashed and the floor chalked all over.
The relative, however, professed to be pleased with the boy's
industry, praised his design, and recommended his mother
to provide " the little sweep," as she called him, with paper
and pencils.   •

Encouraged by his elder brother, he began to practise
figure and landscape drawing, making copies of lithographs,
but as yet without any knowledge of the rules of perspective
and the principles of light and shade. He worked on,
however, and gradually acquired expertness in copying.
At sixteen, he entered the Bury Mechanic's Institution in
order to attend the drawing class, taught by an amateur
who followed the trade of a barber. There he had a lesson
a week during three months. The teacher recommended
him to obtain from the library Burnet's ' Practical Treatise
on Painting ;' but as he could not yet read with ease, he
was under the necessity of getting his mother, and sometimes
his elder brother, to read passages from the book for him
while he sat by and listened. Feeling hampered by his
ignorance of the art of reading, and eager to master the
contents of Burnet's book, he ceased attending the drawing
class at the Institute after the first quarter, and devoted
himself to learning reading and writing at home. In this
he soon succeeded ; and when he again entered the Institute
and took out ' Burnet' a second time, he was not only able
to read it, but to make written extracts for future use. So
ardently did he study the volume, that he used to rise at
four o'clock in the morning to read it and copy out
passages ; after which he went to the foundry at six, worked
until six and sometimes eight in the evening ; and returned

home to enter with fresh zest upon the study of Burnet, which he continued often until a late hour. Parts of his nights were also occupied in drawing and making copies of drawings. On one of these—a copy of Leonardo da Vinci's " Last Supper "—he spent an entire night. He went to bed indeed, but his mind was so engrossed with the subject that he could not sleep, and rose again to resume his pencil.

He next proceeded to try his hand at painting in oil, for which purpose he procured some canvas from a draper, stretched it on a frame, coated it over with white lead, and began painting on it with colours bought from a house-painter. But his work proved a total failure ; for the canvas was rough and knotty, and the paint would not dry. In his extremity he applied to his old teacher, the barber, from whom he first learnt that prepared canvas was to be had, and that there were colours and varnishes made for the special purpose of oil-painting. As soon therefore, as his means would allow, he bought a small stock of the necessary articles and began afresh,—his amateur master showing him how to paint; and the pupil succeeded so well that he excelled the master's copy. His first picture was a copy from an engraving called " Sheep-shearing," and was after-wards sold by him for half-a-crown. Aided by a shilling Guide to Oil-painting, he went on working at his leisure hours, and gradually acquired a better knowledge of his materials. He made his own easel and palette, palette-knife, and paint-chest; he bought his paint, brushes, and canvas, as he could raise the money by working over-time. This was the slender fund which his parents consented to allow him for the purpose ; the burden of supporting a very large family precluding them from doing more. Often he would walk to Manchester and back in the evenings to buy two or three shillings' worth of paint and canvas, returning almost at midnight, after his eighteen miles' walk, sometimes wet through and completely exhausted, but borne up throughout

by his inexhaustible hope and invincible determination.
The further progress of the self-taught artist is best narrated
in his own words, as communicated by him in a letter to the
author :—

"The next pictures I painted," he says, "were a Landscape by Moonlight, a Fruitpiece, and one or two others;
after which I conceived the idea of painting 'The Forge.'
I had for some time thought about it, but had not attempted
to embody the conception in a drawing. I now, however,
made a sketch of the subject upon paper, and then proceeded
to paint it on canvas. The picture simply represents the
interior of a large workshop such as I have been accustomed
to work in, although not of any particular shop. It is, therefore,
to this extent, an original conception. Having made an
outline of the subject, I found that, before I could proceed
with it successfully, a knowledge of anatomy was indispensable to enable me accurately to delineate the muscles
of the figures. My brother Peter came to my assistance
at this juncture, and kindly purchased for me Flaxman's
'Anatomical studies,—a work altogether beyond my means
at the time, for it cost twenty-four shillings. This book I
looked upon as a great treasure, and I studied it laboriously,
rising at three o'clock in the morning to draw after it, and
occasionally getting my brother Peter to stand for me as
a model at that untimely hour. Although I gradually
improved myself by this practice, it was some time before
I felt sufficient confidence to go on with my picture. I
also felt hampered by my want of knowledge of perspective,
which I endeavoured to remedy by carefully studying Brook
Taylor's 'Principles;' and shortly after I resumed my painting. While engaged in the study of perspective at home, I
used to apply for and obtain leave to work at the heavier
kinds of smith work at the foundry, and for this reason—the
time required for heating the heaviest iron work is so much
longer than that required for heating the lighter, that it

enabled me to secure a number of spare minutes in the
course of the day, which I carefully employed in making
diagrams in perspective upon the sheet iron casing in front
of the hearth at which I worked."

Thus assiduously working and studying, James Sharples
steadily advanced in his knowledge of the principles of art,
and acquired greater facility in its practice. Some eighteen
months after the expiry of his apprenticeship he painted a
portrait of his father, which attracted considerable notice
in the town; as also did the picture of "The Forge," which
he finished soon after. His success in portrait-painting
obtained for him a commission from the foreman of the
shop to paint a family group, and Sharples executed it so
well that the foreman not only paid him the agreed price
of eighteen pounds, but thirty shillings to boot. While
engaged on this group he ceased to work at the foundry,
and he had thoughts of giving up his trade altogether and
devoting himself exclusively to painting. He proceeded
to paint several pictures, amongst others a head of Christ,
an original conception, life-size, and a view of Bury; but
not obtaining sufficient employment at portraits to occupy
his time, or give him the prospect of a steady income, he
had the good sense to resume his leather apron, and go on
working at his honest trade of a blacksmith; employing
his leisure hours in engraving his picture of "The Forge,"
since published. He was induced to commence the engraving by the following circumstance. A Manchester
picture-dealer, to whom he showed the painting, let drop
the observation, that in the hands of a skilful engraver it
would make a very good print. Sharples immediately
conceived the idea of engraving it himself, though altogether
ignorant of the art. The difficulties which he encountered
and successfully overcame in carrying out his project are
thus described by himself :—

"I had seen an advertisement of a Sheffield steel-plate

maker, giving a list of the prices at which he supplied plates of various sizes, and, fixing upon one of suitable dimensions, I remitted the amount, together with a small additional sum for which I requested him to send me a few engraving tools. I could not specify the articles wanted, for I did not then know anything about the process of engraving. However, there duly arrived with the plate three or four gravers and an etching needle; the latter I spoiled before I knew its use. While working at the plate, the Amalgamated Society of Engineers offered a premium for the best design for an emblematical picture, for which I determined to compete, and I was so fortunate as to win the prize. Shortly after this I removed to Blackburn, where I obtained employment at Messrs. Yates', engineers, as an engine-smith; and continued to employ my leisure time in drawing, painting, and engraving, as before. With the engraving I made but very slow progress, owing to the difficulties I experienced from not possessing proper tools. I then determined to try to make some that would suit my purpose, and after several failures I succeeded in making many that I have used in the course of my engraving. I was also greatly at a loss for want of a proper magnifying glass, and part of the plate was executed with no other assistance of this sort than what my father's spectacles afforded, though I afterwards succeeded in obtaining a proper magnifier, which was of the utmost use to me. An incident occurred while I was engraving the plate, which had almost caused me to abandon it altogether. It sometimes happened that I was obliged to lay it aside for a considerable time, when other work pressed; and in order to guard it against rust, I was accustomed to rub over the graven parts with oil. But on examining the plate after one of such intervals, I found that the oil had become a dark sticky substance extremely difficult to get out. I tried to pick it out with a needle, but found that it would almost take as much time as to engrave the parts afresh. I was in great despair at this, but at length hit upon the expedient of boiling it in water containing soda, and afterwards rubbing the engraved parts with a tooth-brush; and to my delight found the plan succeeded perfectly. My greatest difficulties now over, patience and perseverance were all that were needed to bring my labours to a successful issue. I had neither advice nor assistance from any one in finishing the plate. If, therefore, the work possess any merit, I can claim it as my own; and if in its accomplishment I have contributed to show what can be done by persevering industry and determination, it is all the honour I wish to lay claim to."

It would be beside our purpose to enter upon any criticism of " The Forge " as an engraving; its merits having been already fully recognised by the art journals. The execution of the work occupied Sharples's leisure evening hours during a period of five years; and it was only when he took the plate to the printer that he for the first time saw an engraved plate produced by any other man. To this unvarnished picture of industry and genius, we add one other trait, and it is a domestic one. " I have been married seven years," says he, " and during that time my greatest pleasure, after I have finished my daily labour at the foundry, has been to resume my pencil or graver, frequently until a late hour of the evening, my wife meanwhile sitting by my side and reading to me from some interesting book," —a simple but beautiful testimony to the thorough common sense as well as the genuine right-heartedness of this most interesting and deserving workman.

The same industry and application which we have found to be necessary in order to acquire excellence in painting and sculpture, are equally required in the sister art of music —the one being the poetry of form and colour, the other of the sounds of nature. Handel was an indefatigable and constant worker; he was never cast down by defeat, but his energy seemed to increase the more that adversity struck him. When a prey to his mortifications as an insolvent debtor, he did not give way for a moment, but in one year produced his 'Saul,' 'Israel,' the music for Dryden's 'Ode,' his 'Twelve Grand Concertos,' and the opera of 'Jupiter in Argos,' among the finest of his works. As his biographer says of him, " He braved everything, and, by his unaided self, accomplished the work of twelve men."

Haydn, speaking of his art, said, " It consists in taking up a subject and pursuing it." "Work," said Mozart, "is my chief pleasure." Beethoven's favourite maxim was, " The barriers are not erected which can say to aspiring talents and industry, ' Thus far and no farther.'" When Moscheles submitted his score of ' Fidelio' for the pianoforte to Beethoven, the latter found written at the bottom of the last page, " Finis, with God's help." Beethoven immediately wrote underneath, " O man ! help thyself !" This was the motto of his artistic life. John Sebastian Bach said of himself, " I was industrious ; whoever is equally sedulous, will be equally successful." But there is no doubt that Bach was born with a passion for music, which formed the mainspring of his industry, and was the true secret of his success. When a mere youth, his elder brother, wishing to turn his abilities in another direction, destroyed a collection of studies which the young Sebastian, being denied candles, had copied by moonlight ; proving the strong natural bent of the boy's genius. Of Meyerbeer, Bayle thus wrote from Milan in 1820 :—" He is a man of some talent, but no genius ; he lives solitary, working fifteen hours a day at music." Years passed, and Meyerbeer's hard work fully brought out his genius, as displayed in his ' Roberto,' ' Huguenots,' ' Prophète,' and other works, confessedly amongst the greatest operas which have been produced in modern times.

Although musical composition is not an art in which Englishmen have as yet greatly distinguished themselves, their energies having for the most part taken other and more practical directions, we are not without native illustrations of the power of perseverance in this special pursuit. Arne was an upholsterer's son, intended by his father for the legal profession; but his love of music was so great, that he could not be withheld from pursuing it. While engaged in an attorney's office, his means were very limited, but, to gratify his tastes, he was accustomed to borrow a livery and go into the gallery of the Opera, then appropriated to domestics. Unknown to his father he made great progress with the violin, and the first knowledge his father had of the circumstance was when accidentally calling at the house of a neighbouring gentleman, to his surprise and consternation he found his son playing the leading instrument with a party of musicians. This incident decided the fate of Arne. His father offered no further opposition to his wishes ; and the world thereby lost a lawyer, but gained a musician of much taste and delicacy of feeling, who added many valuable works to our stores of English music.

The career of the late William Jackson, author of ' The Deliverance of Israel,' an oratorio which has been successfully performed in the principal towns of his native county of York, furnishes an interesting illustration of the triumph of perseverance over difficulties in the pursuit of musical science. He was the son of a miller at Masham, a little town situated in the valley of the Yore, in the northwest corner of Yorkshire. Musical taste seems to have been hereditary in the family, for his father played the fife in the band of the Masham Volunteers, and was a singer in the parish choir. His grandfather also was leading singer and ringer at Masham Church ; and one of the boy's earliest musical treats was to be present at the bell-pealing on

Sunday mornings. During the service, his wonder was still more excited by the organist's performance on the barrel-organ, the doors of which were thrown open behind to let the sound fully into the church, by which the stops, pipes, barrels, staples, keyboard, and jacks, were fully exposed, to the wonderment of the little boys sitting in the gallery behind, and to none more than our young musician. At eight years of age he began to play upon his father's old fife, which, however, would not sound D ; but his mother remedied the difficulty by buying for him a one-keyed flute ; and shortly after, a gentleman of the neighbourhood presented him with a flute with four silver keys. As the boy made no progress with his "book learning," being fonder of cricket, fives, and boxing, than of his school lessons—the village schoolmaster giving him up as "a bad job"—his parents sent him off to a school at Pateley Bridge. While there he found congenial society in a club of village choral singers at Brighouse Gate, and with them he learnt the sol-fa-ing gamut on the old English plan. He was thus well drilled in the reading of music, in which he soon became a proficient. His progress astonished the club, and he returned home full of musical ambition. He now learnt to play upon his father's old piano, but with little melodious result ; and he became eager to possess a finger-organ, but had no means of procuring one. About this time, a neighbouring parish clerk had purchased, for an insignificant sum, a small disabled barrel-organ, which had gone the circuit of the northern counties with a show. The clerk tried to revive the tones of the instrument, but failed ; at last he bethought him that he would try the skill of young Jackson, who had succeeded in making some alterations and improvements in the hand-organ of the parish church. He accordingly brought it to the lad's house in a donkey cart, and in a short time the instrument was repaired, and played over its old tunes again, greatly to the owner's satisfaction.

The thought now haunted the youth that he could make a barrel-organ, and he determined to do so. His father and he set to work, and though without practice in carpentering, yet, by dint of hard labour and after many failures, they at last succeeded ; and an organ was constructed which played ten tunes very decently, and the instrument was generally regarded as a marvel in the neighbourhood. Young Jackson was now frequently sent for to repair old church organs, and to put new music upon the barrels which he added to them. All this he accomplished to the satisfaction of his employers, after which he proceeded with the construction of a four-stop finger-organ, adapting to it the keys of an old harpsichord. This he learnt to play upon,— studying 'Callcott's Thorough Bass' in the evening, and working at his trade of a miller during the day ; occasionally also tramping about the country as a "cadger," with an ass and a cart. During summer he worked in the fields, at turnip-time, hay-time, and harvest, but was never without the solace of music in his leisure evening hours. He next tried his hand at musical composition, and twelve of his anthems were shown to the late Mr. Camidge, of York, as "the production of a miller's lad of fourteen." Mr. Camidge was pleased with them, marked the objectionable passages, and returned them with the encouraging remark, that they did the youth great credit, and that he must "go on writing."

A village band having been set on foot at Masham, young Jackson joined it, and was ultimately appointed leader. He played all the instruments by turns, and thus acquired a considerable practical knowledge of his art : he also composed numerous tunes for the band. A new finger-organ having been presented to the parish church, he was appointed the organist. He now gave up his employment as a journeyman miller, and commenced tallow-chandling, still employing his spare hours in the study of music. In 1839 he published his first anthem—'For joy let fertile valleys sing;' and in the following year he gained the first prize from the Huddersfield Glee Club, for his 'Sisters of the Lea.' His other anthem, 'God be merciful to us,' and the 103rd Psalm, written for a double chorus and orchestra, are well known. In the midst of these minor works, Jackson proceeded with the composition of his oratorio,—'The Deliverance of Israel from Babylon.' His practice was, to jot down a sketch of the ideas as they presented themselves to his mind, and to write them out in score in the evenings, after he had left his work in the candle-shop. His oratorio was published in parts, in the course of 1844-5, and he published the last chorus on his twenty-ninth birthday. The work was exceedingly well received, and has been frequently performed with much success in the northern towns. Mr. Jackson eventually settled as a professor of music at Bradford, where he contributed in no small degree to the cultivation of the musical taste of that town and its neighbourhood. Some years since he had the honour of leading his fine company of Bradford choral singers before Her Majesty at Buckingham Palace; on which occasion, as well as at the Crystal Palace, some choral pieces of his composition, were performed with great effect.*

Such is a brief outline of the career of a self-taught musician, whose life affords but another illustration of the power of self-help, and the force of courage and industry in enabling a man to surmount and overcome early difficulties and obstructions of no ordinary kind.

* While the sheets of this revised edition are passing through the press, the announcement appears in the local papers of the death of Mr. Jackson at the age of fifty. His last work, completed shortly before his death, was a cantata, entitled 'The Praise of Music.' The above particulars of his early life were communicated by himself to the author several years since, while he was still carrying on his business of a tallow-chandler at Masham.

CHAPTER VII.

INDUSTRY AND THE PEERAGE.

" He either fears his fate too much,
Or his deserts are small,
That dares not put it to the touch,
To gain or lose it all."—*Marquis of Montrose.*

" He hath put down the mighty from their seats; and exalted them of low degree."—
St. Luke.

WE have already referred to some illustrious Commoners raised from humble to elevated positions by the power of application and industry; and we might point to even the Peerage itself as affording equally instructive examples. One reason why the Peerage of England has succeeded so well in holding its own, arises from the fact that, unlike the peerages of other countries, it has been fed, from time to time, by the best industrial blood of the country—the very "liver, heart, and brain of Britain." Like the fabled Antæus, it has been invigorated and refreshed by touching its mother earth, and mingling with that most ancient order of nobility—the working order.

The blood of all men flows from equally remote sources; and though some are unable to trace their line directly beyond their grandfathers, all are nevertheless justified in placing at the head of their pedigree the great progenitors of the race, as Lord Chesterfield did when he wrote, " ADAM *de Stanhope*—EVE *de Stanhope.*" No class is ever long stationary. The mighty fall, and the humble are exalted. New families take the place of the old, who disappear among the ranks of the common people. Burke's 'Vicissitudes or Families' strikingly exhibit this rise and fall of families, and show that the misfortunes which overtake the rich and noble are greater in proportion than those which overwhelm the poor. This author points out that of the twenty-five barons selected to enforce the observance of Magna Charta, there is not now in the House of Peers a single male descendant. Civil wars and rebellions ruined many of the old nobility and dispersed their families. Yet their descendants in many cases survive, and are to be found among the ranks of the people. Fuller wrote in his 'Worthies,' that "some who justly hold the surnames of Bohuns, Mortimers, and Plantagenets, are hid in the heap of common men." Thus Burke shows that two of the lineal descendants of the Earl of Kent, sixth son of Edward I., were discovered in a butcher and a toll-gatherer ; that the great grandson of Margaret Plantagenet, daughter of the Duke of Clarence, sank to the condition of a cobbler at Newport, in Shropshire ; and that among the lineal descendants of the Duke of Gloucester, son of Edward III., was the late sexton of St. George's, Hanover Square. It is understood that the lineal descendant of Simon de Montfort, England's premier baron, is a saddler in Tooley Street. One of the descendants of the "Proud Percys," a claimant of the title of Duke of Northumberland, was a Dublin trunk-maker ; and not many years since one of the claimants for the title of Earl of Perth presented himself in the person of a labourer in a Northumberland coal-pit. Hugh Miller, when working as a stone-mason near Edinburgh, was served by a hodman, who was one of the numerous claimants for the earldom of Crauford—all that was wanted to establish his claim being a missing marriage certificate ; and while the work was going on, the cry resounded from the walls many times in the day, of—" John, Yearl Crauford, bring us

anither hod o' lime." One of Oliver Cromwell's great grand-
sons was a grocer on Snow Hill, and others of his descendants
died in great poverty. Many barons of proud names and
titles have perished, like the sloth, upon their family tree, after
eating up all the leaves; while others have been overtaken
by adversities which they have been unable to retrieve, and
sunk at last into poverty and obscurity. Such are the muta-
bilities of rank and fortune.

The great bulk of our peerage is comparatively modern,
so far as the titles go; but it is not the less noble that it has
been recruited to so large an extent from the ranks of
honourable industry. In olden times, the wealth and commerce of London, conducted as it was by energetic and
enterprising men, was a prolific source of peerages. Thus,
the earldom of Cornwallis was founded by Thomas Cornwallis, the Cheapside merchant; that of Essex by William
Capel, the draper; and that of Craven by William Craven,
the merchant tailor. The modern Earl of Warwick is not
descended from the " King-maker," but from William
Greville, the woolstapler; whilst the modern dukes of
Northumberland find their head, not in the Percies, but in
Hugh Smithson, a respectable London apothecary. The
founders of the families of Dartmouth, Radnor, Ducie, and
Pomfret, were respectively a skinner, a silk manufacturer, a
merchant tailor, and a Calais merchant; whilst the founders
of the peerages of Tankerville, Dormer, and Coventry, were
mercers. The ancestors of Earl Romney, and Lord Dudley
and Ward, were goldsmiths and jewellers; and Lord Dacres
was a banker in the reign of Charles I., as Lord Overstone
is in that of Queen Victoria. Edward Osborne, the founder
of the Dukedom of Leeds, was apprentice to William
Hewet, a rich clothworker on London Bridge, whose only
daughter he courageously rescued from drowning, by leaping
into the Thames after her, and eventually married. Among
other peerages founded by trade are those of Fitzwilliam,

Leigh, Petre, Cowper, Darnley, Hill, and Carrington. The founders of the houses of Foley and Normanby were remarkable men in many respects, and, as furnishing striking examples of energy of character, the story of their lives is worthy of preservation.

The father of Richard Foley, the founder of the family, was a small yeoman living in the neighbourhood of Stourbridge in the time of Charles I. That place was then the centre of the iron manufacture of the midland districts, and Richard was brought up to work at one of the branches of the trade—that of nail-making. He was thus a daily observer of the great labour and loss of time caused by the clumsy process then adopted for dividing the rods of iron in the manufacture of nails. It appeared that the Stourbridge nailers were gradually losing their trade in consequence of the importation of nails from Sweden, by which they were undersold in the market. It became known that the Swedes were enabled to make their nails so much cheaper, by the use of splitting mills and machinery, which had completely superseded the laborious process of preparing the rods for nail-making then practised in England.

Richard Foley, having ascertained this much, determined to make himself master of the new process. He suddenly disappeared from the neighbourhood of Stourbridge, and was not heard of for several years. No one knew whither he had gone, not even his own family; for he had not informed them of his intention, lest he should fail. He had little or no money in his pocket, but contrived to get to Hull, where he engaged himself on board a ship bound for a Swedish port, and worked his passage there. The only article of property which he possessed was his fiddle, and on landing in Sweden he begged and fiddled his way to the Dannemora mines, near Upsala. He was a capital musician, as well as a pleasant fellow, and soon ingratiated himself with the iron-workers. He was received into the

works, to every part of which he had access; and he seized
the opportunity thus afforded him of storing his mind with
observations, and mastering, as he thought, the mechanism
of iron splitting. After a continued stay for this purpose,
he suddenly disappeared from amongst his kind friends the
miners—no one knew whither.

Returned to England, he communicated the results of his
voyage to Mr. Knight and another person at Stourbridge,
who had sufficient confidence in him to advance the requisite funds for the purpose of erecting buildings and
machinery for splitting iron by the new process. But when
set to work, to the great vexation and disappointment of
all, and especially of Richard Foley, it was found that the
machinery would not act—at all events it would not split
the bars of iron. Again Foley disappeared. It was thought
that shame and mortification at his failure had driven him
away for ever. Not so! Foley had determined to master
this secret of iron-splitting, and he would yet do it. He
had again set out for Sweden, accompanied by his fiddle as
before, and found his way to the iron works, where he was
joyfully welcomed by the miners; and, to make sure of
their fiddler, they this time lodged him in the very splitting-
mill itself. There was such an apparent absence of intelligence about the man, except in fiddle-playing, that the
miners entertained no suspicions as to the object of their
minstrel, whom they thus enabled to attain the very end
and aim of his life. He now carefully examined the works,
and soon discovered the cause of his failure. He made
drawings or tracings of the machinery as well as he could,
though this was a branch of art quite new to him ; and after
remaining at the place long enough to enable him to verify
his observations, and to impress the mechanical arrangements clearly and vividly on his mind, he again left the
miners, reached a Swedish port, and took ship for England.
A man of such purpose could not but succeed. Arrived

amongst his surprised friends, he now completed his arrangements, and the results were entirely successful. By his skill and his industry he soon laid the foundations of a large fortune, at the same time that he restored the business of an extensive district. He himself continued, during his life, to carry on his trade, aiding and encouraging all works of benevolence in his neighbourhood. He founded and endowed a school at Stourbridge ; and his son Thomas (a great benefactor of Kidderminster), who was High Sheriff of Worcestershire in the time of " The Rump," founded and endowed an hospital, still in existence, for the free education of children at Old Swinford. All the early Foleys were Puritans. Richard Baxter seems to have been on familiar and intimate terms with various members of the family, and makes frequent mention of them in his ' Life and Times.' Thomas Foley, when appointed high sheriff of the county, requested Baxter to preach the customary sermon before him ; and Baxter in his ' Life' speaks of him as " of so just and blameless dealing, that all men he ever had to do with magnified his great integrity and honesty, which were questioned by none." The family was ennobled in the reign of Charles the Second.

William Phipps, the founder of the Mulgrave or Normanby family, was a man quite as remarkable in his way as Richard Foley. His father was a gunsmith—a robust Englishman settled at Woolwich, in Maine, then forming part of our English colonies in America. He was born in 1651, one of a family of not fewer than twenty-six children (of whom twenty-one were sons), whose only fortune lay in their stout hearts and strong arms. William seems to have had a dash of the Danish-sea blood in his veins, and did not take kindly to the quiet life of a shepherd in which he spent his early years. By nature bold and adventurous, he longed to become a sailor and roam through the world. He sought to join some ship ; but not being able to find one, he apprenticed himself to a shipbuilder, with whom he thoroughly learnt his trade, acquiring the arts of reading and writing during his leisure hours. Having completed his apprenticeship and removed to Boston, he wooed and married a widow of some means, after which he set up a little shipbuilding yard of his own, built a ship, and, putting to sea in her, he engaged in the lumber trade, which he carried on in a plodding and laborious way for the space of about ten years.

It happened that one day, whilst passing through the crooked streets of old Boston, he overheard some sailors talking to each other of a wreck which had just taken place off the Bahamas; that of a Spanish ship, supposed to have much money on board. His adventurous spirit was at once kindled, and getting together a likely crew without loss of time, he set sail for the Bahamas. The wreck being well in-shore, he easily found it, and succeeded in recovering a great deal of its cargo, but very little money; and the result was, that he barely defrayed his expenses. His success had been such, however, as to stimulate his enterprising spirit; and when he was told of another and far more richly laden vessel which had been wrecked near Port de la Plata more than half a century before, he forthwith formed the resolution of raising the wreck, or at all events of fishing up the treasure.

Being too poor, however, to undertake such an enterprise without powerful help, he set sail for England in the hope that he might there obtain it. The fame of his success in raising the wreck off the Bahamas had already preceded him. He applied direct to the Government. By his urgent enthusiasm, he succeeded in overcoming the usual inertia of official minds; and Charles II. eventually placed at his disposal the " Rose Algier," a ship of eighteen guns and ninety-five men, appointing him to the chief command.

Phipps then set sail to find the Spanish ship and fish up

the treasure. He reached the coast of Hispaniola in safety; but how to find the sunken ship was the great difficulty. The fact of the wreck was more than fifty years old ; and Phipps had only the traditionary rumours of the event to work upon. There was a wide coast to explore, and an outspread ocean without any trace whatever of the argosy which lay somewhere at its bottom. But the man was stout in heart, and full of hope. He set his seamen to work to drag along the coast, and for weeks they went on fishing up sea-weed, shingle, and bits of rock. No occupation could be more trying to seamen, and they began to grumble one to another, and to whisper that the man in command had brought them on a fool's errand.

At length the murmurers gained head, and the men broke into open mutiny. A body of them rushed one day on to the quarter-deck, and demanded that the voyage should be relinquished. Phipps, however, was not a man to be intimidated ; he seized the ringleaders, and sent the others back to their duty. It became necessary to bring the ship to anchor close to a small island for the purpose of repairs ; and, to lighten her, the chief part of the stores was landed. Discontent still increasing amongst the crew, a new plot was laid amongst the men on shore to seize the ship, throw Phipps overboard, and start on a piratical cruize against the Spaniards in the South Seas. But it was necessary to secure the services of the chief ship carpenter, who was consequently made privy to the plot. This man proved faithful, and at once told the captain of his danger. Summoning about him those whom he knew to be loyal, Phipps had the ship's guns loaded which commanded the shore, and ordered the bridge communicating with the vessel to be drawn up. When the mutineers made their appearance, the captain hailed them, and told the men he would fire upon them if they approached the stores (still on land),—when they drew back ; on which Phipps had the stores reshipped under cover of his guns. The mutineers, fearful of being left upon the barren island, threw down their arms and implored to be permitted to return to their duty. The request was granted, and suitable precautions were taken against future mischief. Phipps, however, took the first opportunity of landing the mutinous part of the crew, and engaging other men in their places; but, by the time that he could again proceed actively with his explorations, he found it absolutely necessary to proceed to England for the purpose of repairing the ship. He had now, however, gained more precise information as to the spot where the Spanish treasure ship had sunk; and, though as yet baffled, he was more confident than ever of the eventual success of his enterprise.

Returned to London, Phipps reported the result of his voyage to the Admiralty, who professed to be pleased with his exertions; but he had been unsuccessful, and they would not entrust him with another king's ship. James II. was now on the throne, and the Government was in trouble; so Phipps and his golden project appealed to them in vain. He next tried to raise the requisite means by a public subscription. At first he was laughed at; but his ceaseless importunity at length prevailed, and after four years' dinning of his project into the ears of the great and influential— during which time he lived in poverty—he at length succeeded. A company was formed in twenty shares, the Duke of Albemarle, son of General Monk, taking the chief interest in it, and subscribing the principal part of the necessary fund for the prosecution of the enterprise.

Like Foley, Phipps proved more fortunate in his second voyage than in his first. The ship arrived without accident at Port de la Plata, in the neighbourhood of the reef of rocks supposed to have been the scene of the wreck. His first object was to build a stout boat capable of carrying eight or ten oars, in constructing which Phipps used · the adze himself. It is also said that he constructed a machine for the purpose of exploring the bottom of the sea similar to what is now known as the Diving Bell. Such a machine was found referred to in books, but Phipps knew little of books, and may be said to have re-invented the apparatus for his own use. He also engaged Indian divers, whose feats of diving for pearls, and in submarine operations, were very remarkable. The tender and boat having been taken to the reef, the men were set to work, the diving bell was sunk, and the various modes of dragging the bottom of the sea were employed continuously for many weeks, but without any prospect of success. Phipps, however, held on valiantly, hoping almost against hope. At length, one day, a sailor, looking over the boat's side down into the clear water, observed a curious sea-plant growing in what appeared to be a crevice of the rock ; and he called upon an Indian diver to go down and fetch it for him. On the red man coming up with the weed, he reported that a number of ship's guns were lying in the same place. The intelligence was at first received with incredulity, but on further investigation it proved to be correct. Search was made, and presently a diver came up with a solid bar of silver in his arms. When Phipps was shown it, he exclaimed, "Thanks be to God! we are all made men." Diving bell and divers now went to work with a will, and in a few days, treasure was brought up to the value of about £300,000, with which Phipps set sail for England. On his arrival, it was urged upon the king that he should seize the ship and its cargo, under the pretence that Phipps, when soliciting his Majesty's permission, had not given accurate information respecting the business. But the king replied, that he knew Phipps to be an honest man, and that he and his friends should divide the whole treasure amongst them, even though he had returned with double the value. Phipps's share was about £20,000, and the king, to show his approval of his energy and honesty in conducting the enterprise, conferred upon him the honour of knighthood. He was also made High Sheriff of New England ; and during the time he held the office, he did valiant service for the mother country and the colonists against the French, by expeditions against Port Royal and Quebec. He also held the post of Governor of Massachusetts, from which he returned to England, and died in London, in 1695.

Phipps throughout the latter part of his career, was not ashamed to allude to the lowness of his origin, and it was matter of honest pride to him that he had risen from the condition of a common ship carpenter to the honours of knighthood and the government of a province. When perplexed with public business, he would often declare that it would be easier for him to go back to his broad axe again. He left behind him a character for probity, honesty, patriotism, and courage, which is certainly not the least noble inheritance of the house of Normanby.

William Petty, the founder of the house of Lansdowne, was a man of like energy and public usefulness in his day. He was the son of a clothier in humble circumstances, at Romsey, in Hampshire, where he was born in 1623. In his boyhood he obtained a tolerable education at the grammar school of his native town ; after which he determined to improve himself by study at the University of Caen, in Normandy. Whilst there he contrived to support himself unassisted by his father, carrying on a sort of small pedler's trade with "a little stock of merchandize." Returning to England, he had himself bound apprentice to a sea captain, who " drubbed him with a rope's end " for the badness of his sight. He left the navy in disgust, taking to the study of medicine. When at Paris he engaged in dissection, during which time he also drew diagrams for Hobbes, who was then writing his treatise on Optics. He was reduced to such poverty that he subsisted for two or three weeks entirely on walnuts. But again he began to trade in a small way, turning an honest penny, and he was enabled shortly to return to England with money in his pocket. Being of an ingenious mechanical turn, we find him taking out a patent for a letter-copying machine. He began to write upon the arts and sciences, and practised chemistry and physic with such success that his reputation shortly became considerable. Associating with men of science, the project of forming a Society for its prosecution was discussed, and the first meetings of the infant Royal Society were held at his lodgings. At Oxford he acted for a time as deputy to the anatomical professor there, who had a great repugnance to dissection. In 1652 his industry was rewarded by the appointment of physician to the army in Ireland, whither he went; and whilst there he was the medical attendant of three successive lords-lieu-tenant, Lambert, Fleetwood, and Henry Cromwell. Large grants of forfeited land having been awarded to the Puritan soldiery, Petty observed that the lands were very inaccu-rately measured; and in the midst of his many avocations he undertook to do the work himself. His appointments became so numerous and lucrative that he was charged by the envious with corruption, and removed from them all; but he was again taken into favour at the Restoration.

Petty was a most indefatigable contriver, inventor, and organizer of industry. One of his inventions was a double-bottomed ship, to sail against wind and tide. He published treatises on dyeing, on naval philosophy, on woollen cloth manufacture, on political arithmetic, and many other sub-jects. He founded iron works, opened lead mines, and commenced a pilchard fishery and a timber trade; in the midst of which he found time to take part in the discussions of the Royal Society, to which he largely contributed. He left an ample fortune to his sons, the eldest of whom was created Baron Shelburne. His will was a curious document, singularly illustrative of his character; containing a detail of the principal events of his life, and the gradual advancement of his fortune. His sentiments on pauperism are characteristic : "As for legacies for the poor," said he, " I am at a stand; as for beggars by trade and election, I give them nothing; as for impotents by the hand of God, the public ought to maintain them ; as for those who have been bred to no calling nor estate, they should be put upon their kindred;" . . . "wherefore I am contented that I have assisted all my poor relations, and put many into a way or getting their own bread ; have laboured in public works ; and by inventions have sought out real objects of charity; and I do hereby conjure all who partake of my estate, from time to time, to do the same at their peril. Nevertheless to answer custom, and to take the surer side, I give 20*l.* to the most wanting of the parish wherein I die." He was interred in the fine old Norman church of Romsey—the town wherein he was born a poor man's son—and on the south side of the choir is still to be seen a plain slab, with the inscription, cut by an illiterate workman, "Here Layes Sir William Petty."

Another family, ennobled by invention and trade in our own day, is that of Strutt of Belper. Their patent of nobility was virtually secured by Jedediah Strutt in 1758, when he invented his machine for making ribbed stockings, and thereby laid the foundations of a fortune which the subsequent bearers of the name have largely increased and nobly employed. The father of Jedediah was a farmer and maltster, who did but little for the education of his children; yet they all prospered. Jedediah was the second son, and when a boy assisted his father in the work of the farm. At an early age he exhibited a taste for mechanics, and introduced several improvements in the rude agricultural implements of the period. On the death of his uncle he succeeded to a farm at Blackwall, near Normanton, long in the tenancy of the family, and shortly after he married Miss Wollatt, the daughter of a Derby hosier. Having learned from his wife's brother that various unsuccessful attempts had been made to manufacture ribbed-stockings, he proceeded to study the subject with a view to effect what others had failed in accomplishing. He accordingly obtained a stocking-frame, and after mastering its construction and mode of action, he proceeded to introduce new combinations, by means of which he succeeded in effecting a variation in the plain looped-work of the frame, and was thereby enabled to turn out "ribbed" hosiery. Having secured a patent for the improved machine, he removed to Derby, and there entered largely on the manufacture of ribbed-stockings, in which he was very successful. He afterwards joined Arkwright, of the merits of whose invention he fully satisfied himself, and found the means of securing his patent, as well as erecting a large cotton-mill at Cranford, in Derbyshire. After the expiry of the partnership with Arkwright, the Strutts erected extensive cotton-mills at Milford, near Belper, which worthily gives its title to the present head of the family. The sons of the founder were, like their father, distinguished for their mechanical ability. Thus William Strutt, the eldest, is said to have invented a self-acting mule, the success of which was only prevented by the mechanical skill of that day being unequal to its manufacture. Edward, the son of William, was a man of eminent mechanical genius, having early discovered the principle of suspension-wheels for carriages : he had a wheelbarrow and two carts made on the principle, which were used on his farm near Belper. It may be added that the Strutts have throughout been distinguished for their noble employment of the wealth which their industry and skill have brought them; that they have sought in all ways to improve the moral and social condition of the work-people in their employment; and that they have been liberal donors in every good cause—of which the presentation, by Mr. Joseph Strutt, of the beautiful park or Arboretum at

Derby, as a gift to the townspeople for ever, affords only one of many illustrations. The concluding words of the short address which he delivered on presenting this valuable gift are worthy of being quoted and remembered :—" As the sun has shone brightly on me through life, it would be ungrateful in me not to employ a portion of the fortune I possess in promoting the welfare of those amongst whom I live, and by whose industry I have been aided in its organisation."

No less industry and energy have been displayed by the many brave men, both in present and past times, who have earned the peerage by their valour on land and at sea. Not to mention the older feudal lords, whose tenure depended upon·military service, and who so often led the van of the English armies in great national encounters, we may point to Nelson, St. Vincent, and Lyons—to Wellington, Hill, Hardinge, Clyde, and many more in recent times, who have nobly earned their rank by their distinguished services. But plodding industry has far oftener worked its way to the peerage by the honourable pursuit of the legal profession, than by any other. No fewer than seventy British peerages, including two dukedoms, have been founded by successful lawyers. Mansfield and Erskine were, it is true, of noble family ; but the latter used to thank God that out of his own family he did not know a lord.* The others were, for the most part, the sons of attorneys, grocers, clergymen, merchants, and hardworking members of the middle class.

---

* Mansfield owed nothing to his noble relations, who were poor and uninfluential. His success was the legitimate and logical result of the means which he sedulously employed to secure it. When a boy he rode up from Scotland to London on a pony—taking two months to make the journey. After a course of school and college, he entered upon the profession of the law, and he closed a career of patient and ceaseless labour as Lord Chief Justice of England—the functions of which he is universally admitted to have performed with unsurpassed ability, justice, and honour.

Out of this profession have sprung the peerages of Howard and Cavendish, the first peers of both families having been judges ; those of Aylesford, Ellenborough, Guildford, Shaftesbury, Hardwicke, Cardigan, Clarendon, Camden, Ellesmere, Rosslyn; and others nearer our own day, such as Tenterden, Eldon, Brougham, Denman, Truro, Lyndhurst, St. Leonards, Cranworth, Campbell, and Chelmsford.

Lord Lyndhurst's father was a portrait painter, and that of St. Leonards a perfumer and hairdresser in Burlington Street. Young Edward Sugden was originally an errand-boy in the office of the late Mr. Groom, of Henrietta Street, Cavendish Square, a certificated conveyancer; and it was there that the future Lord Chancellor of Ireland obtained his first notions of law. The origin of the late Lord Tenterden was perhaps the humblest of all, nor was he ashamed of it ; for he felt that the industry, study, and application, by means of which he achieved his eminent position, were entirely due to himself. It is related of him, that on one occasion he took his son Charles to a little shed, then standing opposite the western front of Canterbury Cathedral, and pointing it out to him, said, "Charles, you see this little shop ; I have brought you here on purpose to show it you. In that shop your grandfather used to shave for a penny : that is the proudest reflection of my life." When a boy, Lord Tenterden was a singer in the Cathedral, and it is a curious circumstance that his destination in life was changed by a disappointment. When he and Mr. Justice Richards were going the Home Circuit together, they went to service in the cathedral ; and on Richards commending the voice of a singing man in the choir, Lord Tenterden said, "Ah! that is the only man I ever envied ! When at school in this town, we were candidates for a chorister's place, and he obtained it."

Not less remarkable was the rise to the same distinguished office of Lord Chief Justice, of the rugged Kenyon and the robust Ellenborough; nor was he a less notable man who recently held the same office—the astute Lord Campbell, late Lord Chancellor of England, son of a parish minister in Fifeshire. For many years he worked hard as a reporter for the press, while diligently preparing himself for the practice of his profession. It is said of him, that at the beginning of his career, he was accustomed to walk from county town to county town when on circuit, being as yet too poor to afford the luxury of posting. But step by step he rose slowly but surely to that eminence and distinction which ever follow a career of industry honourably and energetically pursued, in the legal, as in every other profession.

There have been other illustrious instances of Lords Chancellors who have plodded up the steep of fame and honour with equal energy and success. The career of the late Lord Eldon is perhaps one of the most remarkable examples. He was the son of a Newcastle coal-fitter; a mischievous rather than a studious boy; a great scapegrace at school, and the subject of many terrible thrashings,—for orchard-robbing was one of the favourite exploits of the future Lord Chancellor. His father first thought of putting him apprentice to a grocer, and afterwards had almost made up his mind to bring him up to his own trade of a coal-fitter. But by this time his eldest son William (afterwards Lord Stowell) who had gained a scholarship at Oxford, wrote to his father, "Send Jack up to me, I can do better for him." John was sent up to Oxford accordingly, where, by his brother's influence and his own application, he succeeded in obtaining a fellowship. But when at home during the vacation, he was so unfortunate—or rather so fortunate, as the issue proved—as to fall in love; and running across the Border with his eloped bride, he married, and as his friends thought, ruined himself for life. He had neither house nor home when he married, and had not yet earned a penny. He lost his fellowship, and at the same time shut himself out from preferment in the Church, for which he had been destined. He accordingly turned his attention to the study of the law. To a friend he wrote, "I have married rashly; but it is my determination to work hard to provide for the woman I love."

John Scott came up to London, and took a small house in Cursitor Lane, where he settled down to the study of the law. He worked with great diligence and resolution; rising at four every morning and studying till late at night, binding a wet towel round his head to keep himself awake. Too poor to study under a special pleader, he copied out three folio volumes from a manuscript collection of precedents. Long after, when Lord Chancellor, passing down Cursitor Lane one day, he said to his secretary, "Here was my first perch: many a time do I recollect coming down this street with sixpence in my hand to buy sprats for supper." When at length called to the bar, he waited long for employment. His first year's earnings amounted to only nine shillings. For four years he assiduously attended the London Courts and the Northern Circuit, with little better success. Even in his native town, he seldom had other than pauper cases to defend. The results were indeed so discouraging, that he had almost determined to relinquish his chance of London business, and settle down in some provincial town as a country barrister. His brother William wrote home, "Business is dull with poor Jack, very dull indeed!" But as he had escaped being a grocer, a coal-fitter, and a country parson, so did he also escape being a country lawyer.

An opportunity at length occurred which enabled John Scott to exhibit the large legal knowledge which he had so laboriously acquired. In a case in which he was engaged, he urged a legal point against the wishes both of the attorney and client who employed him. The Master of the Rolls decided against him, but on an appeal to the House of Lords, Lord Thurlow reversed the decision on the very point that Scott had urged. On leaving the House that day, a solicitor tapped him on the shoulder and said, " Young man, your bread and butter's cut for life." And the prophecy proved a true one. Lord Mansfield used to say that he knew no interval between no business and 3000*l* a-year, and Scott might have told the same story; for so rapid was his progress, that in 1783, when only thirty-two, he was appointed King's Counsel, was at the head of the Northern Circuit, and sat in Parliament for the borough of Weobley. It was in the dull but unflinching drudgery of the early part of his career that he laid the foundation of his future success. He won his spurs by perseverance, knowledge, and ability, diligently cultivated. He was successively appointed to the offices of solicitor and attorney-general, and rose steadily upwards to the highest office that the Crown had to bestow—that of Lord Chancellor of England, which he held for a quarter of a century.

Henry Bickersteth was the son of a surgeon at Kirkby Lonsdale, in Westmoreland, and was himself educated to that profession. As a student at Edinburgh, he distinguished himself by the steadiness with which he worked, and the application which he devoted to the science of medicine. Returned to Kirkby Lonsdale, he took an active part in his father's practice; but he had no liking for the profession, and grew discontented with the obscurity of a country town. He went on, nevertheless, diligently improving himself, and engaged on speculations in the higher branches of physiology. In conformity with his own wish, his father consented to send him to Cambridge, where it was his intention to take a medical degree with the view of practising in the metropolis. Close application to his studies, however, threw him out of health, and with a view to re-establishing his strength he accepted the appointment of travelling physician to Lord Oxford. While abroad he mastered Italian, and acquired a great admiration for Italian literature, but no greater liking for medicine than before. On the contrary, he determined to abandon it; but returning to Cambridge, he took his degree; and that he worked hard may be inferred from the fact that he was senior wrangler of his year. Disappointed in his desire to enter the army, he turned to the bar, and entered a student of the Inner Temple. He worked as hard at law as he had done at medicine. Writing to his father, he said, " Everybody says to me, ' You are certain of success in the end— only persevere ;' and though I don't well understand how this is to happen, I try to believe it as much as I can, and I shall not fail to do everything in my power." At twenty-eight he was called to the bar, and had every step in life yet to make. His means were straitened, and he lived upon the contributions of his friends. For years he studied and waited. Still no business came. He stinted himself in recreation, in clothes, and even in the necessaries of life ; struggling on indefatigably through all. Writing home, he " confessed that he hardly knew how he should be able to struggle on till he had fair time and opportunity to establish himself." After three years waiting, still without success, he wrote to his friends that rather than be a burden upon them longer, he was willing to give the matter up and return to Cambridge, "where he was sure of support and some profit." The friends at home sent him another small remittance, and he persevered. Business gradually came in. Acquitting himself creditably in small matters, he was at length entrusted with cases of greater importance. He was a man who never missed an opportunity, nor allowed a legitimate chance of improvement to escape him. His unflinching industry soon began to tell upon his fortunes ; a few more years and he was not only enabled to do without assistance from home, but he was in a position to pay back with interest the debts which he had incurred. The clouds had dispersed, and the after career of Henry Bickersteth was one of honour, of emolument, and of distinguished fame. He ended his career as Master of the Rolls, sitting in the House of Peers as Baron Langdale. His life affords only another illustration of the power of patience, perseverance, and conscientious working, in elevating the character of the individual, and crowning his labours with the most complete success.

Such are a few of the distinguished men who have honourably worked their way to the highest position, and won the richest rewards of their profession, by the diligent exercise of qualities in many respects of an ordinary character, but made potent by the force of application and industry.

CHAPTER VIII.

Energy and Courage.

"A cœur vaillant rien d'impossible."—*Jacques Cœur.*

"Den Muthigen gehört die Welt.—*German Proverb.*

In every work that he began . . . . he did it with all his heart, and prospered."—
II. Chron. xxxi. 21.

HERE is a famous speech recorded of an old Norseman, thoroughly characteristic of the Teuton. "I believe neither in idols nor demons," said he, "I put my sole trust in my own strength of body and soul." The ancient crest of a pickaxe with the motto of "Either I will find a way or make one," was an expression of the same sturdy independence which to this day distinguishes the descendants of the Northmen. Indeed nothing could be more characteristic of the Scandinavian mythology, than that it had a god with a hammer. A man's character is seen in small matters; and from even so slight a test as the mode in which a man wields a hammer, his energy may in some measure be inferred. Thus an eminent Frenchman hit off in a single phrase the characteristic quality of the inhabitants of a particular district, in which a friend of his proposed to settle and buy land. "Beware," said he, "of making a purchase there; I know the men of that department; the pupils who come from it to our veterinary school at Paris *do not strike hard upon the anvil;* they want energy; and you will not get

a satisfactory return on any capital you may invest there."
A fine and just appreciation of character, indicating the
thoughtful observer; and strikingly illustrative of the fact
that it is the energy of the individual men that gives strength
to a State, and confers a value even upon the very soil
which they cultivate. As the French proverb has it: "Tant
vaut l'homme, tant vaut sa terre."

The cultivation of this quality is of the greatest importance; resolute determination in the pursuit of worthy
objects being the foundation of all true greatness of cha·
racter. Energy enables a man to force his way through
irksome drudgery and dry details, and carries him onward
and upward in every station in life. It accomplishes more
than genius, with not one-half the disappointment and peril.
It is not eminent talent that is required to ensure success in any pursuit, so much as purpose,—not merely the
power to achieve, but the will to labour energetically and
perseveringly. Hence energy of will may be defined to be
the very central power of character in a man—in a word, it
is the Man himself. It gives impulse to his every action,
and soul to every effort. True hope is based on it,—and
it is hope that gives the real perfume to life. There is a
fine heraldic motto on a broken helmet in Battle Abbey,
"L'espoir est ma force," which might be the motto of every
man's life. "Woe unto him that is faint-hearted," says the
son of Sirach. There is, indeed, no blessing equal to
the possession of a stout heart. Even if a man fail
in his efforts, it will be a satisfaction to him to enjoy the
consciousness of having done his best. In humble life
nothing can be more cheering and beautiful than to see a
man combating suffering by patience, triumphing in his
integrity, and who, when his feet are bleeding and his
limbs failing him, still walks upon his courage.

Mere wishes and desires but engender a sort of green
sickness in young minds, unless they are promptly em-

bodied in act and deed. It will not avail merely to wait, as so many do, "until Blucher comes up," but they must struggle on and persevere in the mean time, as Wellington did. The good purpose once formed must be carried out with alacrity and without swerving. In most conditions of life, drudgery and toil are to be cheerfully endured as the best and most wholesome discipline. "In life," said Ary Scheffer, "nothing bears fruit except by labour of mind or body. To strive and still strive—such is life; and in this respect mine is fulfilled; but I dare to say, with just pride, that nothing has ever shaken my courage. With a strong soul, and a noble aim, one can do what one wills, morally speaking."

Hugh Miller said the only school in which he was properly taught was "that world-wide school in which toil and hardship are the severe but noble teachers." He who allows his application to falter, or shirks his work on frivolous pretexts, is on the sure road to ultimate failure. Let any task be undertaken as a thing not possible to be evaded, and it will soon come to be performed with alacrity and cheerfulness. Charles IX. of Sweden was a firm believer in the power of will, even in youth. Laying his hand on the head of his youngest son when engaged on a difficult task, he exclaimed, "He *shall* do it! he *shall* do it!" The habit of application becomes easy in time, like every other habit. Thus persons with comparatively moderate powers will accomplish much, if they apply themselves wholly and indefatigably to one thing at a time. Fowell Buxton placed his confidence in ordinary means and extraordinary application; realizing the scriptural injunction, "Whatsoever thy hand findeth to do, do it with all thy might;" and he attributed his own success in life to his practice of "being a whole man to one thing at a time."

Nothing that is of real worth can be achieved without courageous working. Man owes his growth chiefly to that active striving of the will, that encounter with difficulty

Q

which we call effort; and it is astonishing to find how often results apparently impracticable are thus made possible. An intense anticipation itself transforms possibility into reality; our desires being often but the precursors of the things which we are capable of performing. On the contrary, the timid and hesitating find everything impossible, chiefly because it seems so. It is related of a young French officer, that he used to walk about his apartment exclaiming, "I *will* be Marshal of France and a great general." His ardent desire was the presentiment of his success; for the young officer did become a distinguished commander, and he died a Marshal of France.

Mr. Walker, author of the 'Original,' had so great a faith in the power of will, that he says on one occasion he *determined* to be well, and he was so. This may answer once; but, though safer to follow than many prescriptions, it will not always succeed. The power of mind over body is no doubt great, but it may be strained until the physical power breaks down altogether. It is related of Muley Moluc, the Moorish leader, that, when lying ill, almost worn out by an incurable disease, a battle took place between his troops and the Portuguese; when, starting from his litter at the great crisis of the fight, he rallied his army, led them to victory, and instantly afterwards sank exhausted and expired.

It is *will*,—force of purpose,—that enables a man to do or be whatever he sets his mind on being or doing. A holy man was accustomed to say, "Whatever you wish, that you are : for such is the force of our will, joined to the Divine, that whatever we wish to be, seriously, and with a true intention, that we become. No one ardently wishes to be submissive, patient, modest, or liberal, who does not become what he wishes." The story is told of a working carpenter, who was observed one day planing a magistrate's bench which he was repairing, with more than usual carefulness; and when asked the reason, he replied, "Because

I wish to make it easy against the time when I come to sit upon it myself." And singularly enough, the man actually lived to sit upon that very bench as a magistrate.

Whatever theoretical conclusions logicians may have formed as to the freedom of the will, each individual feels that practically he is free to choose between good and evil— that he is not as a mere straw thrown upon the water to mark the direction of the current, but that he has within him the power of a strong swimmer, and is capable of striking out for himself, of buffeting with the waves, and directing to a great extent his own independent course. There is no absolute constraint upon our volitions, and we feel and know that we are not bound, as by a spell, with reference to our actions. It would paralyze all desire of excellence were we to think otherwise. The entire business and conduct of life, with its domestic rules, its social arrangements, and its public institutions, proceed upon the practical conviction that the will is free. Without this where would be responsibility?—and what the advantage of teaching, advising, preaching, reproof, and correction? What were the use of laws, were it not the universal belief, as it is the universal fact, that men obey them or not, very much as they individually determine? In every moment of our life, conscience is proclaiming that our will is free. It is the only thing that is wholly ours, and it rests solely with ourselves individually, whether we give it the right or the wrong direction. Our habits or our temptations are not our masters, but we of them. Even in yielding, conscience tells us we might resist; and that were we determined to master them, there would not be required for that purpose a stronger resolution than we know ourselves to be capable of exercising.

"You are now at the age," said Lamennais once, addressing a gay youth, "at which a decision must be formed by you; a little later, and you may have to groan within the tomb which you yourself have dug, without the power of rolling away the stone. That which the easiest becomes a habit in us is the will. Learn then to will strongly and decisively; thus fix your floating life, and leave it no longer to be carried hither and thither, like a withered leaf, by every wind that blows."

Buxton held the conviction that a young man might be very much what he pleased, provided he formed a strong resolution and held to it. Writing to one of his sons, he said to him, "You are now at that period of life, in which you must make a turn to the right or the left. You must now give proofs of principle, determination, and strength of mind; or you must sink into idleness, and acquire the habits and character of a desultory, ineffective young man; and if once you fall to that point, you will find it no easy matter to rise again. I am sure that a young man may be very much what he pleases. In my own case it was so. . . . Much of my happiness, and all my prosperity in life, have resulted from the change I made at your age. If you seriously resolve to be energetic and industrious, depend upon it that you will for your whole life have reason to rejoice that you were wise enough to form and to act upon that determination." As will, considered without regard to direction, is simply constancy, firmness, perseverance, it will be obvious that everything depends upon right direction and motives. Directed towards the enjoyment of the senses, the strong will may be a demon, and the intellect merely its debased slave; but directed towards good, the strong will is a king, and the intellect the minister of man's highest well-being.

"Where there is a will there is a way," is an old and true saying. He who resolves upon doing a thing, by that very resolution often scales the barriers to it, and secures its achievement. To think we are able, is almost to be so—to determine upon attainment is frequently attainment itself. Thus, earnest resolution has often seemed to have about it almost a savour of omnipotence. The strength of Suwarrow's character lay in his power of willing, and, like most resolute persons, he preached it up as a system. "You can only half will," he would say to people who failed. Like Richelieu and Napoleon, he would have the word "impossible" banished from the dictionary. " I don't know," "I can't," and "impossible," were words which he detested above all others. "Learn ! Do ! Try !" he would exclaim. His biographer has said of him, that he furnished a remarkable illustration of what may be effected by the energetic development and exercise of faculties, the germs of which at least are in every human heart.

One of Napoleon's favourite maxims was, "The truest wisdom is a resolute determination." His life, beyond most others, vividly showed what a powerful and un-scrupulous will could accomplish. He threw his whole force of body and mind direct upon his work. Imbecile rulers and the nations they governed went down before him in succession. He was told that the Alps stood in the way of his armies—"There shall be no Alps," he said, and the road across the Simplon was constructed, through a district formerly almost inaccessible. "Impossible," said he, "is a word only to be found in the dictionary of fools." He was a man who toiled terribly ; sometimes employing and exhausting four secretaries at a time. He spared no one, not even himself. His influence inspired other men, and put a new life into them. "I made my generals out of mud," he said. But all was of no avail ; for Napoleon's intense selfishness was his ruin, and the ruin of France, which he left a prey to anarchy. His life taught the lesson that power, however energetically wielded, without benefi-cence, is fatal to its possessor and its subjects ; and that knowledge, or knowingness, without goodness, is but the incarnate principle of Evil.

Our own Wellington was a far greater man. Not less resolute, firm, and persistent, but more self-denying, conscientious, and truly patriotic. Napoleon's aim was "Glory;" Wellington's watchword, like Nelson's, was "Duty." The former word, it is said, does not once occur in his despatches; the latter often, but never accompanied by any high-sounding professions. The greatest difficulties could neither embarrass nor intimidate Wellington; his energy invariably rising in proportion to the obstacles to be surmounted. The patience, the firmness, the resolution, with which he bore through the maddening vexations and gigantic difficulties of the Peninsular campaigns, is, perhaps, one of the sublimest things to be found in history. In Spain, Wellington not only exhibited the genius of the general, but the comprehensive wisdom of the statesman. Though his natural temper was irritable in the extreme, his high sense of duty enabled him to restrain it; and to those about him his patience seemed absolutely inexhaustible. His great character stands untarnished by ambition, by avarice, or any low passion. Though a man of powerful individuality, he yet displayed a great variety of endowment. The equal of Napoleon in generalship, he was as prompt, vigorous, and daring as Clive; as wise a statesman as Cromwell; and as pure and high-minded as Washington. The great Wellington left behind him an enduring reputation, founded on toilsome campaigns won by skilful combination, by fortitude which nothing could exhaust, by sublime daring, and perhaps by still sublimer patience.

Energy usually displays itself in promptitude and decision. When Ledyard the traveller was asked by the African Association when he would be ready to set out for Africa, he immediately answered, "To-morrow morning." Blucher's promptitude obtained for him the cognomen of "Marshal Forwards" throughout the Prussian army. When John Jervis, afterwards Earl St. Vincent, was asked when he would be ready to join his ship, he replied, "Directly." And when

Sir Colin Campbell, appointed to the command of the Indian army, was asked when he could set out, his answer was, "To-morrow,"—an earnest of his subsequent success. For it is rapid decision, and a similar promptitude in action, such as taking instant advantage of an enemy's mistakes, that so often wins battles. "At Arcola," said Napoleon, "I won the battle with twenty-five horsemen. I seized a moment of lassitude, gave every man a trumpet, and gained the day with this handful. Two armies are two bodies which meet and endeavour to frighten each other : a moment of panic occurs, and *that moment* must be turned to advantage." "Every moment lost," said he at another time, "gives an opportunity for misfortune ;" and he declared that he beat the Austrians because they never knew the value of time : while they dawdled, he overthrew them.

India has, during the last century, been a great field for the display of British energy. From Clive to Havelock and Clyde there is a long and honourable roll of distinguished names in Indian legislation and warfare,—such as Wellesley, Metcalfe, Outram, Edwardes, and the Lawrences. Another great but sullied name is that of Warren Hastings—a man of dauntless will and indefatigable industry. His family was ancient and illustrious ; but their vicissitudes of fortune and ill-requited loyalty in the cause of the Stuarts, brought them to poverty, and the family estate at Daylesford, of which they had been lords of the manor for hundreds of years, at length passed from their hands. The last Hastings of Daylesford had, however, presented the parish living to his second son ; and it was in his house, many years later, that Warren Hastings, his grandson, was born. The boy learnt his letters at the village school, on the same bench with the children of the peasantry. He played in the fields which his fathers had owned ; and what the loyal and brave Hastings of Daylesford *had* been, was ever in the boy's thoughts. His young ambition was fired, and it is said that one summer's day, when only seven years old, as he laid him down on the bank of the stream which flowed through the domain, he formed in his mind the resolution that he would yet recover possession of the family lands. It was the romantic vision of a boy; yet he lived to realise it. The dream became a passion, rooted in his very life; and he pursued his determination through youth up to manhood, with that calm but indomitable force of will which was the most striking peculiarity of his character. The orphan boy became one of the most powerful men of his time; he retrieved the fortunes of his line; bought back the old estate, and rebuilt the family mansion. "When, under a tropical sun," says Macaulay, "he ruled fifty millions of Asiatics, his hopes, amidst all the cares of war, finance, and legislation, still pointed to Daylesford. And when his long public life, so singularly chequered with good and evil, with glory and obloquy, had at length closed for ever, it was to Daylesford that he retired to die."

Sir Charles Napier was another Indian leader of extraordinary courage and determination. He once said of the difficulties with which he was surrounded in one of his campaigns, "They only make my feet go deeper into the ground." His battle of Meeanee was one of the most extraordinary feats in history. With 2000 men, of whom only 400 were Europeans, he encountered an army of 35,000 hardy and well-armed Beloochees. It was an act, apparently, of the most daring temerity, but the general had faith in himself and in his men. He charged the Belooch centre up a high bank which formed their rampart in front, and for three mortal hours the battle raged. Each man of that small force, inspired by the chief, became for the time a hero. The Beloochees, though twenty to one, were driven back, but with their faces to the foe. It is this sort of pluck, tenacity, and determined perseverance which wins soldiers' battles, and, indeed, every battle. It is the one neck nearer that wins the race and shows the blood; it is the one march more that wins the campaign; the five minutes' more persistent courage that wins the fight. Though your force be less than another's, you equal and outmaster your opponent if you continue it longer and concentrate it more. The reply of the Spartan father, who said to his son, when complaining that his sword was too short, "Add a step to it," is applicable to everything in life.

Napier took the right method of inspiring his men with his own heroic spirit. He worked as hard as any private in the ranks. "The great art of commanding," he said, "is to take a fair share of the work. The man who leads an army cannot succeed unless his whole mind is thrown into his work. The more trouble, the more labour must be given; the more danger, the more pluck must be shown, till all is overpowered." A young officer who accompanied him in his campaign in the Cutchee Hills, once said, "When I see that old man incessantly on his horse, how can I be idle who am young and strong? I would go into a loaded cannon's mouth if he ordered me." This remark, when repeated to Napier, he said was ample reward for his toils. The anecdote of his interview with the Indian juggler strikingly illustrates his cool courage as well as his remarkable simplicity and honesty of character. On one occasion, after the Indian battles, a famous juggler visited the camp and performed his feats before the General, his family, and staff. Among other performances, this man cut in two with a stroke of his sword a lime or lemon placed in the hand of his assistant. Napier thought there was some collusion between the juggler and his retainer. To divide by a sweep of the sword on a man's hand so small an object without touching the flesh he believed to be impossible, though a similar incident is related by Scott in his romance of the 'Talisman.' To determine the point, the General offered his own hand for the experiment, and he stretched out his right arm. The juggler looked attentively at the hand, and said he would not make the trial. " I thought I would find you out!" exclaimed Napier. " But stop," added the other, " let me see your left hand." The left hand was submitted, and the man then said firmly, " If you will hold your arm steady I will perform the feat." " But why the left hand and not the right ?" " Because the right hand is hollow in the centre, and there is a risk of cutting off the thumb; the left is high, and the danger will be less." Napier was startled. " I got frightened," he said; " I saw it was an actual feat of delicate swordsmanship, and if I had not abused the man as I did before my staff, and challenged him to the trial, I honestly acknowledge I would have retired from the encounter. However, I put the lime on my hand, and held out my arm steadily. The juggler balanced himself, and, with a swift stroke cut the lime in two pieces. I felt the edge of the sword on my hand as if a cold thread had been drawn across it. So much (he added) for the brave swordsmen of India, whom our fine fellows defeated at Meeanee."

The recent terrible struggle in India has served to bring out, perhaps more prominently than any previous event in our history, the determined energy and self-reliance of the national character. Although English officialism may often drift stupidly into gigantic blunders, the men of the nation generally contrive to work their way out of them with a heroism almost approaching the sublime. In May, 1857, when the revolt burst upon India like a thunder-clap, the British forces had been allowed to dwindle to their extreme minimum, and were scattered over a wide extent of country, many of them in remote cantonments. The Bengal regiments, one after another, rose against their officers, broke away, and rushed to Delhi. Province after province was lapped in mutiny and rebellion; and the cry for help rose from east to west. Everywhere the English stood at bay in small detachments, beleaguered and surrounded, apparently incapable of resistance. Their discomfiture seemed so complete, and the utter ruin of the British cause in India so certain, that it might be said of them then, as it had been said before, " These English never know when they are beaten." According to rule, they ought then and there to have succumbed to inevitable fate.

While the issue of the mutiny still appeared uncertain, Holkar, one of the native princes, consulted his astrologer for information. The reply was, " If all the Europeans save one are slain, that one will remain to fight and reconquer." In their very darkest moment—even where, as at Lucknow, a mere handful of British soldiers, civilians, and women, held out amidst a city and province in arms against them—there was no word of despair, no thought of surrender. Though cut off from all communication with their friends for months, and not knowing whether India was lost or held, they never ceased to have perfect faith in the courage and devotedness of their countrymen. They knew that while a body of men of English race held together in India, they would not be left unheeded to perish. They never dreamt of any other issue but retrieval of their misfortune and ultimate triumph ; and if the worst came to the worst, they could but fall at their post, and die in the performance of their duty. Need we remind the reader of the names of Havelock, Inglis, Neill, and Outram—men of truly heroic mould—of each of whom it might with truth be said that he had the heart of a chevalier, the soul of a believer, and the temperament of a martyr. Montalembert has said of them that " they do honour to the human race." But throughout that terrible trial almost all proved equally great—women, civilians and soldiers—from the general down through all grades to the private and bugleman. The men were not picked : they belonged to the same ordinary people whom we daily meet at home—in the streets, in workshops, in the fields, at clubs ; yet when sudden disaster fell upon them, each and all displayed a wealth or personal resources and energy, and became as it were indi-

vidually heroic. " Not one of them," says Montalembert,
" shrank or trembled—all, military and civilians, young and
old, generals and soldiers, resisted, fought, and perished with
a coolness and intrepidity which never faltered. It is in this
circumstance that shines out the immense value of public
education, which invites the Englishman from his youth to
make use of his strength and his liberty, to associate, resist,
fear nothing, to be astonished at nothing, and to save himself,
by his own sole exertions, from every sore strait in life."

It has been said that Delhi was taken and India saved by
the personal character of Sir John Lawrence. The very
name of " Lawrence " represented power in the North-West
Provinces. His standard of duty, zeal, and personal effort,
was of the highest ; and every man who served under him
seemed to be inspired by his spirit. It was declared of
him that his character alone was worth an army. The same
might be said of his brother Sir Henry, who organised the
Punjaub force that took so prominent a part in the capture
of Delhi. Both brothers inspired those who were about
them with perfect love and confidence. Both possessed that
quality of tenderness, which is one of the true elements of the
heroic character. Both lived amongst the people, and powerfully influenced them for good. Above all, as Col. Edwardes
says, " they drew models on young fellows' minds, which they
went forth and copied in their several administrations : they
sketched a *faith*, and begot a *school*, which are both living
things at this day." Sir John Lawrence had by his side such
men as Montgomery, Nicholson, Cotton, and Edwardes, as
prompt, decisive, and high-souled as himself. John Nicholson
was one of the finest, manliest, and noblest of men—" every
inch a hakim," the natives said of him — " a tower of
strength," as he was characterised by Lord Dalhousie. In
whatever capacity he acted he was great, because he acted
with his whole strength and soul. A brotherhood of fakeers
—borne away by their enthusiastic admiration of the man—

even began the worship of Nikkil Seyn : he had some of them punished for their folly, but they continued their worship nevertheless. Of his sustained energy and persistency an illustration may be cited in his pursuit of the 55th Sepoy mutineers, when he was in the saddle for twenty consecutive hours, and travelled more than seventy miles. When the enemy set up their standard at Delhi, Lawrence and Montgomery, relying on the support of the people of the Punjaub, and compelling their admiration and confidence, strained every nerve to keep their own province in perfect order, whilst they hurled every available soldier, European and Sikh, against that city. Sir John wrote to the commander-in-chief to "hang on to the rebels' noses before Delhi," while the troops pressed on by forced marches under Nicholson, "the tramp of whose war-horse might be heard miles off," as was afterwards said of him by a rough Sikh who wept over his grave.

The siege and storming of Delhi was the most illustrious event which occurred in the course of that gigantic struggle, although the leaguer of Lucknow, during which the merest skeleton of a British regiment—the 32nd—held out, under the heroic Inglis, for six months against two hundred thousand armed enemies, has perhaps excited more intense interest. At Delhi, too, the British were really the besieged, though ostensibly the besiegers ; they were a mere handful of men "in the open "—not more than 3,700 bayonets, European and native—and they were assailed from day to day by an army of rebels numbering at one time as many as 75,000 men, trained to European discipline by English officers, and supplied with all but exhaustless munitions of war. The heroic little band sat down before the city under the burning rays of a tropical sun. Death, wounds, and fever failed to turn them from their purpose. Thirty times they were attacked by overwhelming numbers, and thirty times did they drive back the enemy behind their defences. As Captain Hodson—

himself one of the bravest there—has said, "I venture to aver that no other nation in the world would have remained here, or avoided defeat if they had attempted to do so." Never for an instant did these heroes falter at their work ; with sublime endurance they held on, fought on, and never relaxed until, dashing through the "imminent deadly breach," the place was won, and the British flag was again unfurled on the walls of Delhi. All were great—privates, officers, and generals. Common soldiers who had been inured to a life of hardship, and young officers who had been nursed in luxurious homes, alike proved their manhood, and emerged from that terrible trial with equal honour. The native strength and soundness of the English race, and of manly English training and discipline, were never more powerfully exhibited ; and it was there emphatically proved that the Men of England are, after all, its greatest products. A terrible price was paid for this great chapter in our history, but if those who survive, and those who come after, profit by the lesson and example, it may not have been purchased at too great a cost.

But not less energy and courage have been displayed in India and the East by men of various nations, in other lines of action more peaceful and beneficent than that of war. And while the heroes of the sword are remembered, the heroes of the gospel ought not to be forgotten. From Xavier to Martyn and Williams, there has been a succession of illustrious missionary labourers, working in a spirit of sublime self-sacrifice, without any thought of worldly honour, inspired solely by the hope of seeking out and rescuing the lost and fallen of their race. Borne up by invincible courage and never-failing patience, these men have endured privations, braved dangers, walked through pestilence, and borne all toils, fatigues, and sufferings, yet held on their way rejoicing, glorying even in martyrdom itself. Of these one of the first and most illustrious was Francis Xavier. Born of noble lineage, and with pleasure, power, and honour within his reach, he proved by his life that there are higher objects in the world than rank, and nobler aspirations than the accumulation of wealth. He was a true gentleman in manners and sentiment; brave, honourable, generous; easily led, yet capable of leading; easily persuaded, yet himself persuasive; a most patient, resolute and energetic man. At the age of twenty-two he was earning his living as a public teacher of philosophy at the University of Paris. There Xavier became the intimate friend and associate of Loyola, and shortly afterwards he conducted the pilgrimage of the first little band of proselytes to Rome.

When John III. of Portugal resolved to plant Christianity in the Indian territories subject to his influence, Bobadilla was first selected as his missionary; but being disabled by illness, it was found necessary to make another selection, and Xavier was chosen. Repairing his tattered cassock, and with no other baggage than his breviary, he at once started for Lisbon and embarked for the East. The ship in which he set sail for Goa had the Governor on board, with a rein-forcement of a thousand men for the garrison of the place. Though a cabin was placed at his disposal, Xavier slept on deck throughout the voyage with his head on a coil of ropes, messing with the sailors. By ministering to their wants, inventing innocent sports for their amusement, and attend-ing them in their sickness, he wholly won their hearts, and they regarded him with veneration.

Arrived at Goa, Xavier was shocked at the depravity of the people, settlers as well as natives; for the former had imported the vices without the restraints of civilization, and the latter had only been too apt to imitate their bad example. Passing along the streets of the city, sounding his handbell as he went, he implored the people to send him their children to be instructed. He shortly succeeded in collecting a large number of scholars, whom he carefully taught day by day, at the same time visiting the sick, the lepers, and the wretched of all classes, with the object of assuaging their miseries, and bringing them to the Truth. No cry of human suffering which reached him was disregarded. Hearing of the degradation and misery of the pearl fishers of Manaar, he set out to visit them, and his bell again rang out the invitation of mercy. He baptized and he taught, but the latter he could only do through interpreters. His most eloquent teaching was his ministration to the wants and the sufferings of the wretched.

On he went, his hand-bell sounding along the coast of Comorin, among the towns and villages, the temples and the bazaars, summoning the natives to gather about him and be instructed. He had translations made of the Catechism, the Apostles' Creed, the Commandments, the Lord's Prayer, and some of the devotional offices of the Church. Committing these to memory in their own tongue he recited them to the children, until they had them by heart; after which he sent them forth to teach the words to their parents and neighbours. At Cape Comorin, he appointed thirty teachers, who under himself presided over thirty Christian Churches, though the Churches were but humble, in most cases consisting only of a cottage surmounted by a cross. Thence he passed to Travancore, sounding his way from village to village, baptizing until his hands dropped with weariness, and repeating his formulas until his voice became almost inaudible. According to his own account, the success of his mission surpassed his highest expectations. His pure, earnest, and beautiful life, and the irresistible eloquence of his deeds, made converts wherever he went; and by sheer force of sympathy, those who saw him and listened to him insensibly caught a portion of his ardour.

Burdened with the thought that "the harvest is great and the labourers are few," Xavier next sailed to Malacca and Japan, where he found himself amongst entirely new races, speaking other tongues. The most that he could do here was to weep and pray, to smooth the pillow and watch by the sick-bed, sometimes soaking the sleeve of his surplice in water, from which to squeeze out a few drops and baptize the dying. Hoping all things, and fearing nothing, this valiant soldier of the truth was borne onward throughout by faith and energy. "Whatever form of death or torture," said he, "awaits me, I am ready to suffer it ten thousand times for the salvation of a single soul." He battled with hunger, thirst, privations and dangers of all kinds, still pursuing his mission of love, unresting and unwearying. At length, after eleven years labour, this great good man, while striving to find a way into China, was stricken with fever in the Island of Sanchian, and there received his crown of glory. A hero of nobler mould, more pure, self-denying, and courageous, has probably never trod this earth.

Other missionaries have followed Xavier in the same field of work, such as Schwartz, Carey, and Marshman in India ; Gutzlaff and Morrison in China ; Williams in the South Seas ; Campbell, Moffatt and Livingstone in Africa. John Williams, the martyr of Erromanga, was originally apprenticed to a furnishing ironmonger. Though considered a dull boy, he was handy at his trade, in which he acquired so much skill that his master usually entrusted him with any blacksmith's work that required the exercise of more than ordinary care. He was also fond of bell-hanging and other employments which took him away from the shop. A casual sermon which he heard gave his mind a serious bias, and he became a Sunday-school teacher. The cause of missions having been brought under his notice at some of his society's meetings, he determined to devote himself to this work. His services were accepted by the London Missionary Society ; and his master allowed him to leave the ironmonger's shop before the expiry of his indentures. The islands of the Pacific Ocean were the principal scene of his

R

labours—more particularly Huahine in Tahiti, Raiatea, and Rarotonga. Like the Apostles he worked with his hands,— at blacksmith work, gardening, shipbuilding ; and he endeavoured to teach the islanders the arts of civilised life, at the same time that he instructed them in the truths of religion. It was in the course of his indefatigable labours that he was massacred by savages on the shore of Erromanga—none worthier than he to wear the martyr's crown.

The career of Dr. Livingstone is one of the most interesting of all. He has told the story of his life in that modest and unassuming manner which is so characteristic of the man himself. His ancestors were poor but honest Highlanders, and it is related of one of them, renowned in his district for wisdom and prudence, that when on his deathbed he called his children round him and left them these words, the only legacy he had to bequeath—" In my lifetime," said he, " I have searched most carefully through all the traditions I could find of our family, and I never could discover that there was a dishonest man among our forefathers : if, therefore, any of you or any of your children should take to dishonest ways, it will not be because it runs in our blood ; it does not belong to you : I leave this precept with you—Be honest." At the age of ten Livingstone was sent to work in a cotton factory near Glasgow as a " piecer." With part of his first week's wages he bought a Latin grammar, and began to learn that language, pursuing the study for years at a night school. He would sit up conning his lessons till twelve or later, when not sent to bed by his mother, for he had to be up and at work in the factory every morning by six. In this way he plodded through Virgil and Horace, also reading extensively all books, excepting novels, that came in his way, but more especially scientific works and books of travels. He occupied his spare hours, which were but few, in the pursuit of botany, scouring the neighbourhood to collect plants. He even carried on his reading

amidst the roar of the factory machinery, so placing the
book upon the spinning jenny which he worked that he
could catch sentence after sentence as he passed it. In
this way the persevering youth acquired much useful knowledge ; and as he grew older, the desire possessed him of
becoming a missionary to the heathen. With this object he
set himself to obtain a medical education, in order the better
to be qualified for the work. He accordingly economised
his earnings, and saved as much money as enabled him to
support himself while attending the Medical and Greek
classes, as well as the Divinity Lectures, at Glasgow, for
several winters, working as a cotton spinner during the
remainder of each year. He thus supported himself, during
his college career, entirely by his own earnings as a factory
workman, never having received a farthing of help from any
other source. "Looking back now," he honestly says, "at
that life of toil, I cannot but feel thankful that it formed
such a material part of my early education ; and, were it
possible, I should like to begin life over again in the same
lowly style, and to pass through the same hardy training."
At length he finished his medical curriculum, wrote his
Latin thesis, passed his examinations, and was admitted a
licentiate of the Faculty of Physicians and Surgeons. At
first he thought of going to China, but the war then waging
with that country prevented his following out the idea ; and
having offered his services to the London Missionary Society,
he was by them sent out to Africa, which he reached in 1840.
He had intended to proceed to China by his own efforts ;
and he says the only pang he had in going to Africa at the
charge of the London Missionary Society was, because "it
was not quite agreeable to one accustomed to work his own
way to become, in a manner, dependent upon others."
Arrived in Africa he set to work with great zeal. He could
not brook the idea of merely entering upon the labours of
others, but cut out a large sphere of independent work, pre-

paring himself for it by undertaking manual labour in building and other handicraft employment, in addition to teaching, which, he says, "made me generally as much exhausted and unfit for study in the evenings as ever I had been when a cotton-spinner." Whilst labouring amongst the Bechuanas, he dug canals, built houses, cultivated fields, reared cattle, and taught the natives to work as well as worship. When he first started with a party of them on foot upon a long journey, he overheard their observations upon his appearance and powers—" He is not strong," said they; " he is quite slim, and only appears stout because he puts himself into those bags (trowsers) : he will soon knock up." This caused the missionary's Highland blood to rise, and made him despise the fatigue of keeping them all at the top of their speed for days together, until he heard them express-ing proper opinions of his pedestrian powers. What he did in Africa, and how he worked, may be learnt from his own ' Missionary Travels,' one of the most fascinating books of its kind that has ever been given to the public. One of his last known acts is thoroughly characteristic of the man. The ' Birkenhead' steam launch, which he took out with him to Africa, having proved a failure, he sent home orders for the construction of another vessel at an estimated cost of 2000*l.* This sum he proposed to defray out of the means which he had set aside for his children arising from the profits of his books of travels. " The children must make it up them-selves," was in effect his expression in sending home the order for the appropriation of the money.

The career of John Howard was throughout a striking illustration of the same power of patient purpose. His sub-lime life proved that even physical weakness could remove mountains in the pursuit of an end recommended by duty. The idea of ameliorating the condition of prisoners engrossed his whole thoughts and possessed him like a passion ; and no toil, nor danger, nor bodily suffering could turn him from that great object of his life. Though a man of no genius and but moderate talent, his heart was pure and his will was strong. Even in his own time he achieved a remarkable degree of success; and his influence did not die with him, for it has continued powerfully to affect not only the legislation of England, but of all civilised nations, down to the present hour.

Jonas Hanway was another of the many patient and persevering men who have made England what it is—content simply to do with energy the work they have been appointed to do, and go to their rest thankfully when it is done—

> " Leaving no memorial but a world
> Made better by their lives."

He was born in 1712, at Portsmouth, where his father, a storekeeper in the dockyard, being killed by an accident, he was left an orphan at an early age. His mother removed with her children to London, where she had them put to school, and struggled hard to bring them up respectably. At seventeen Jonas was sent to Lisbon to be apprenticed to a merchant, where his close attention to business, his punctuality, and his strict honour and integrity, gained for him the respect and esteem of all who knew him. Returning to London in 1743, he accepted the offer of a partnership in an English mercantile house at St. Petersburg engaged in the Caspian trade, then in its infancy. Hanway went to Russia for the purpose of extending the business; and shortly after his arrival at the capital he set out for Persia, with a caravan of English bales of cloth making twenty carriage loads. At Astracan he sailed for Astrabad, on the southeastern shore of the Caspian; but he had scarcely landed his bales, when an insurrection broke out, his goods were seized, and though he afterwards recovered the principal part of them, the fruits of his enterprise were in a great measure lost. A plot was set on foot to seize himself and his party;

so he took to sea and, after encountering great perils, reached Ghilan in safety. His escape on this occasion gave him the first idea of the words which he afterwards adopted as the motto of his life—"*Never Despair.*" He afterwards resided in St. Petersburg for five years, carrying on a prosperous business. But a relative having left him some property, and his own means being considerable, he left Russia, and arrived in his native country in 1750. His object in returning to England was, as he himself expressed it, "to consult his own health (which was extremely delicate), and do as much good to himself and others as he was able." The rest of his life was spent in deeds of active benevolence and usefulness to his fellow men. He lived in a quiet style, in order that he might employ a larger share of his income in works of benevolence. One of the first public improvements to which he devoted himself was that of the highways of the metropolis, in which he succeeded to a large extent. The rumour of a French invasion being prevalent in 1755, Mr. Hanway turned his attention to the best mode of keeping up the supply of seamen. He summoned a meeting of merchants and shipowners at the Royal Exchange, and there proposed to them to form themselves into a society for fitting out landsmen volunteers and boys, to serve on board the king's ships. The proposal was received with enthusiasm: a society was formed, and officers were appointed, Mr. Hanway directing its entire operations. The result was the establishment in 1756 of The Marine Society, an institution which has proved of much national advantage, and is to this day of great and substantial utility. Within six years from its formation, 5451 boys and 4787 landsmen volunteers had been trained and fitted out by the society and added to the navy, and to this day it is in active operation, about 600 poor boys, after a careful education, being annually apprenticed as sailors, principally in the merchant service.

Mr. Hanway devoted the other portions of his spare time to improving or establishing important public institutions in the metropolis. From an early period he took an active interest in the Foundling Hospital, which had been started by Thomas Coram many years before, but which, by encouraging parents to abandon their children to the charge of a charity, was threatening to do more harm than good. He determined to take steps to stem the evil, entering upon the work in the face of the fashionable philanthropy of the time ; but by holding to his purpose he eventually succeeded in bringing the charity back to its proper objects ; and time and experience have proved that he was right. The Magdalen Hospital was also established in a great measure through Mr. Hanway's exertions. But his most laborious and persevering efforts were in behalf of the infant parish poor. The misery and neglect amidst which the children of the parish poor then grew up, and the mortality which prevailed amongst them, were frightful; but there was no fashionable movement on foot to abate the suffering, as in the case of the foundlings. So Jonas Hanway summoned his energies to the task. Alone and unassisted he first ascertained by personal inquiry the extent of the evil. He explored the dwellings of the poorest classes in London, and visited the poorhouse sick wards, by which he ascertained the management in detail of every workhouse in and near the metropolis. He next made a journey into France and through Holland, visiting the houses for the reception of the poor, and noting whatever he thought might be adopted at home with advantage. He was thus employed for five years ; and on his return to England he published the results of his observations. The consequence was that many of the workhouses were reformed and improved. In 1761 he obtained an Act obliging every London parish to keep an annual register of all the infants received, discharged, and dead ; and he took care that the Act should work, for he

himself superintended its working with indefatigable watchfulness.   He went about from workhouse to workhouse in
the morning, and from one member of parliament to another
in the afternoon, for day after day, and for year after year,
enduring every rebuff, answering every objection, and ac-
commodating himself to every humour.   At length, after a
perseverance hardly to be equalled, and after nearly ten
years' labour, he obtained another Act, at his sole expense
(7 Geo. III. c. 39), directing that all parish infants belonging
to the parishes within the bills of mortality should not be
nursed in the workhouses, but be sent to nurse a certain
number of miles out of town, until they were six years old,
under the care of guardians to be elected triennially.   The
poor people called this " the Act for keeping children alive ;"
and the registers for the years which followed its passing,
as compared with those which preceded it, showed that
thousands of lives had been preserved through the judicious
interference of this good and sensible man.

Wherever a philanthropic work was to be done in London,
be sure that Jonas Hanway's hand was in it.   One of the
first Acts for the protection of chimney-sweepers' boys was
obtained through his influence.   A destructive fire at Mont-
real, and another at Bridgetown, Barbadoes, afforded him
the opportunity for raising a timely subscription for the
relief of the sufferers.   His name appeared in every list,
and his disinterestedness and sincerity were universally
recognized.   But he was not suffered to waste his little
fortune entirely in the service of others.   Five leading
citizens of London, headed by Mr. Hoare, the banker,
without Mr. Hanway's knowledge, waited on Lord Bute, then
prime minister, in a body, and in the names of their fellow-
citizens requested that some notice might be taken of this
good man's disinterested services to his country.   The result
was, his appointment shortly after, as one of the commis-
sioners for victualling the navy.

Towards the close of his life Mr. Hanway's health became very feeble, and although he found it necessary to
resign his office at the Victualling Board, he could not be
idle ; but laboured at the establishment of Sunday Schools,
—a movement then in its infancy,—or in relieving poor
blacks, many of whom wandered destitute about the streets
of the metropolis,—or, in alleviating the sufferings of some
neglected and destitute class of society.   Notwithstanding his familiarity with misery in all its shapes, he was one
of the most cheerful of beings ; and, but for his cheerfulness he could never, with so delicate a frame, have got
through so vast an amount of self-imposed work.   He
dreaded nothing so much as inactivity.   Though fragile, he
was bold and indefatigable ; and his moral courage was of
the first order.   It may be regarded as a trivial matter to
mention that he was the first who ventured to walk the
streets of London with an umbrella over his head.   But let
any modern London merchant venture to walk along Corn-
hill in a peaked Chinese hat, and he will find it takes some
degree of moral courage to persevere in it.   After carrying
an umbrella for thirty years, Mr. Hanway saw the article at
length come into general use.

Hanway was a man of strict honour, truthfulness, and
integrity ; and every word he said might be relied upon.
He had so great a respect, amounting almost to a reverence,
for the character of the honest merchant, that it was the only
subject upon which he was ever seduced into a eulogium.
He strictly practised what he professed, and both as a
merchant, and afterwards as a commissioner for victualling
the navy, his conduct was without stain.   He would not
accept the slightest favour of any sort from a contractor ;
and when any present was sent to him whilst at the
Victualling Office, he would politely return it, with the in-
timation that "he had made it a rule not to accept anything
from any person engaged with the office."   When he found

his powers failing, he prepared for death with as much cheerfulness as he would have prepared himself for a journey into the country. He sent round and paid all his trades-men, took leave of his friends, arranged his affairs, had his person neatly disposed of, and parted with life serenely and peacefully in his 74th year. The property which he left did not amount to two thousand pounds, and, as he had no relatives who wanted it, he divided it amongst sundry orphans and poor persons whom he had befriended during his lifetime. Such, in brief, was the beautiful life of Jonas Hanway,—as honest, energetic, hard-working, and true-hearted a man as ever lived.

The life of Granville Sharp is another striking example of the same power of individual energy—a power which was afterwards transfused into the noble band of workers in the cause of Slavery Abolition, prominent among whom were Clarkson, Wilberforce, Buxton, and Brougham. But. giants though these men were in this cause, Granville Sharp was the first, and perhaps the greatest of them all, in point of perseverance, energy, and intrepidity. He began life as apprentice to a linen-draper on Tower Hill; but, leaving that business after his apprenticeship was out, he next entered as a clerk in the Ordnance Office; and it was while engaged in that humble occupation that he carried on in his spare hours the work of Negro Emancipation. He was always, even when an apprentice, ready to undertake any amount of volunteer labour where a useful purpose was to be served. Thus, while learning the linen-drapery business, a fellow apprentice who lodged in the same house, and was a Unitarian, led him into frequent discussions on religious subjects. The Unitarian youth insisted that Gran-ville's Trinitarian misconception of certain passages of Scrip-ture arose from his want of acquaintance with the Greek tongue; on which he immediately set to work in his evening hours, and shortly acquired an intimate knowledge of Greek.

A similar controversy with another fellow-apprentice, a Jew, as to the interpretation of the prophecies, led him in like manner to undertake and overcome the difficulties of Hebrew.

But the circumstance which gave the bias and direction to the main labours of his life originated in his generosity and benevolence. His brother William, a surgeon in Mincing Lane, gave gratuitous advice to the poor, and amongst the numerous applicants for relief at his surgery was a poor African named Jonathan Strong. It appeared that the negro had been brutally treated by his master, a Barbadoes lawyer then in London, and became lame, almost blind, and unable to work ; on which his owner, regarding him as of no further value as a chattel, cruelly turned him adrift into the streets to starve. This poor man, a mass of disease, supported himself by begging for a time, until he found his way to William Sharp, who gave him some medicine, and shortly after got him admitted to St. Bartholomew's hospital, where he was cured. On coming out of the hospital, the two brothers supported the negro in order to keep him off the streets, but they had not the least suspicion at the time that any one had a claim upon his person. They even succeeded in obtaining a situation for Strong with an apothecary, in whose service he remained for two years ; and it was while he was attending his mistress behind a hackney coach, that his former owner, the Barbadoes lawyer, recognized him, and determined to recover possession of the slave, again rendered valuable by the restoration of his health. The lawyer employed two of the Lord Mayor's officers to apprehend Strong, and he was lodged in the Compter, until he could be shipped off to the West Indies. The negro, bethinking him in his captivity of the kind services which Granville Sharp had rendered him in his great distress some years before, despatched a letter to him requesting his help. Sharp had forgotten the name of Strong, but he sent a

messenger to make inquiries, who returned saying that the
keepers denied having any such person in their charge.   His
suspicions were roused, and he went forthwith to the prison,
and insisted upon seeing Jonathan Strong.   He was admitted, and recognized the poor negro, now in custody as
a recaptured slave.   Mr. Sharp charged the master of the
prison at his own peril not to deliver up Strong to any
person whatever, until he had been carried before the Lord
Mayor, to whom Sharp immediately went, and obtained a
summons against those persons who had seized and imprisoned Strong without a warrant.   The parties appeared
before the Lord Mayor accordingly, and it appeared from
the proceedings that Strong's former master had already
sold him to a new one, who produced the bill of sale and
claimed the negro as his property.   As no charge of offence
was made against Strong, and as the Lord Mayor was
incompetent to deal with the legal question of Strong's
liberty or otherwise, he discharged him, and the slave
followed his benefactor out of court, no one daring to touch
him.   The man's owner immediately gave Sharp notice ot
an action to recover possession of his negro slave, of whom
he declared he had been robbed.

About that time (1767), the personal liberty of the
Englishman, though cherished as a theory, was subject to
grievous infringements, and was almost daily violated.   The
impressment of men for the sea service was constantly
practised, and, besides the press-gangs, there were regular
bands of kidnappers employed in London and all the large
towns of the kingdom, to seize men for the East India
Company's service.   And when the men were not wanted
for India, they were shipped off to the planters in the
American colonies.   Negro slaves were openly advertised
for sale in the London and Liverpool newspapers.   Rewards
were offered for recovering and securing fugitive slaves, and
conveying them down to certain specified ships in the river.

The position of the reputed slave in England was un-
defined and doubtful. The judgments which had been
given in the courts of law were fluctuating and various,
resting on no settled principle. Although it was a popular
belief that no slave could breathe in England, there were
legal men of eminence who expressed a directly contrary
opinion. The lawyers to whom Mr. Sharp resorted for
advice, in defending himself in the action raised against him
in the case of Jonathan Strong, generally concurred in this
view, and he was further told by Jonathan Strong's owner,
that the eminent Lord Chief Justice Mansfield, and all
the leading counsel, were decidedly of opinion that the
slave, by coming into England, did not become free, but
might legally be compelled to return again to the plantations.
Such information would have caused despair in a mind less
courageous and earnest than that of Granville Sharp ; but
it only served to stimulate his resolution to fight the battle
of the negroes' freedom, at least in England. " Forsaken,"
he said, "by my professional defenders, I was compelled,
through the want of regular legal assistance, to make a
hopeless attempt at self-defence, though I was totally un-
acquainted either with the practice of the law or the foundations of it, having never opened a law book (except the
Bible) in my life, until that time, when I most reluctantly
undertook to search the indexes of a law library, which my
bookseller had lately purchased."

The whole of his time during the day was occupied with
the business of the ordnance department, where he held the
most laborious post in the office ; he was therefore under
the necessity of conducting his new studies late at night or
early in the morning. He confessed that he was himself
becoming a sort of slave. Writing to a clerical friend to
excuse himself for delay in replying to a letter, he said, " I
profess myself entirely incapable of holding a literary correspondence. What little time I have been able to save

from sleep at night, and early in the morning, has been necessarily employed in the examination of some points of law, which admitted of no delay, and yet required the most diligent researches and examination in my study."

Mr. Sharp gave up every leisure moment that he could command during the next two years, to the close study of the laws of England affecting personal liberty,—wading through an immense mass of dry and repulsive literature, and making extracts of all the most important Acts of Parliament, decisions of the courts, and opinions of eminent lawyers, as he went along. In this tedious and protracted inquiry he had no instructor, nor assistant, nor adviser. He could not find a single lawyer whose opinion was favourable to his undertaking. The results of his inquiries were, however, as gratifying to himself, as they were surprising to the gentlemen of the law. "God be thanked," he wrote, "there is nothing in any English law or statute—at least that I am able to find out—that can justify the enslaving of others." He had planted his foot firm, and now he doubted nothing. He drew up the result of his studies in a summary form; it was a plain, clear, and manly statement, entitled, 'On the Injustice of Tolerating Slavery in England;' and numerous copies, made by himself, were circulated by him amongst the most eminent lawyers of the time. Strong's owner, finding the sort of man he had to deal with, invented various pretexts for deferring the suit against Sharp, and at length offered a compromise, which was rejected. Granville went on circulating his manuscript tract among the lawyers, until at length those employed against Jonathan Strong were deterred from proceeding further, and the result was, that the plaintiff was compelled to pay treble costs for not bringing forward his action. The tract was then printed in 1769.

In the mean time other cases occurred of the kidnapping of negroes in London, and their shipment to the West

Indies for sale. Wherever Sharp could lay hold of any such case, he at once took proceedings to rescue the negro. Thus the wife of one Hylas, an African, was seized, and despatched to Barbadoes; on which Sharp, in the name of Hylas, instituted legal proceedings against the aggressor, obtained a verdict with damages, and Hylas's wife was brought back to England free.

Another forcible capture of a negro, attended with great cruelty, having occurred in 1770, he immediately set himself on the track of the aggressors. An African, named Lewis, was seized one dark night by two watermen employed by the person who claimed the negro as his property, dragged into the water, hoisted into a boat, where he was gagged, and his limbs were tied; and then rowing down river, they put him on board a ship bound for Jamaica, where he was to be sold for a slave upon his arrival in the island. The cries of the poor negro had, however, attracted the attention of some neighbours; one of whom proceeded direct to Mr. Granville Sharp, now known as the negro's friend, and informed him of the outrage. Sharp immediately got a warrant to bring back Lewis, and he proceeded to Gravesend, but on arrival there the ship had sailed for the Downs. A writ of Habeas Corpus was obtained, sent down to Spithead, and before the ship could leave the shores of England the writ was served. The slave was found chained to the main-mast bathed in tears, casting mournful looks on the land from which he was about to be torn. He was immediately liberated, brought back to London, and a warrant was issued against the author of the outrage. The promptitude of head, heart, and hand, displayed by Mr. Sharp in this transaction could scarcely have been surpassed, and yet he accused himself of slowness. The case was tried before Lord Mansfield—whose opinion it will be remembered, had already been expressed as decidedly opposed to that entertained by Granville Sharp. The judge, however, avoided bringing the question to an issue, or offering any opinion on the legal question as to the slave's personal liberty or otherwise, but discharged the negro because the defendant could bring no evidence that Lewis was even nominally his property.

The question of the personal liberty of the negro in England was therefore still undecided; but in the mean time Mr. Sharp continued steady in his benevolent course, and by his indefatigable exertions and promptitude of action, many more were added to the list of the rescued. At length the important case of James Somerset occurred; a case which is said to have been selected, at the mutual desire of Lord Mansfield and Mr. Sharp, in order to bring the great question involved to a clear legal issue. Somerset had been brought to England by his master, and left there. Afterwards his master sought to apprehend him and send him off to Jamaica, for sale. Mr. Sharp, as usual, at once took the negro's case in hand, and employed counsel to defend him. Lord Mansfield intimated that the case was of such general concern, that he should take the opinion of all the judges upon it. Mr. Sharp now felt that he would have to contend with all the force that could be brought against him, but his resolution was in no wise shaken. Fortunately for him, in this severe struggle, his exertions had already begun to tell: increasing interest was taken in the question, and many eminent legal gentlemen openly declared themselves to be upon his side.

The cause of personal liberty, now at stake, was fairly tried before Lord Mansfield, assisted by the three justices, —and tried on the broad principle of the essential and constitutional right of every man in England to the liberty of his person, unless forfeited by the law. It is unnecessary here to enter into any account of this great trial; the arguments extended to a great length, the cause being carried over to another term,—when it was adjourned and re-adjourned,—but at length judgment was given by Lord Mansfield, in whose powerful mind so gradual a change had been worked by the arguments of counsel, based mainly on Granville Sharp's tract, that he now declared the court to be so clearly of one opinion, that there was no necessity for referring the case to the twelve judges. He then declared that the claim of slavery never can be supported; that the power claimed never was in use in England, nor acknowledged by the law; therefore the man James Somerset must be discharged. By securing this judgment Granville Sharp effectually abolished the Slave Trade until then carried on openly in the streets of Liverpool and London. But he also firmly established the glorious axiom, that as soon as any slave sets his foot on English ground, that moment he becomes free; and there can be no doubt that this great decision of Lord Mansfield was mainly owing to Mr. Sharp's firm, resolute, and intrepid prosecution of the cause from the beginning to the end.

It is unnecessary further to follow the career of Granville Sharp. He continued to labour indefatigably in all good works. He was instrumental in founding the colony of Sierra Leone as an asylum for rescued negroes. He laboured to ameliorate the condition of the native Indians in the American colonies. He agitated the enlargement and extension of the political rights of the English people; and he endeavoured to effect the abolition of the impressment of seamen. Granville held that the British seaman, as well as the African negro, was entitled to the protection of the law; and that the fact of his choosing a seafaring life did not in any way cancel his rights and privileges as an Englishman— first amongst which he ranked personal freedom. Mr. Sharp also laboured, but ineffectually, to restore amity between England and her colonists in America; and when the fratricidal war of the American Revolution was entered on, his sense of integrity was so scrupulous that, resolving not in

s

any way to be concerned in so unnatural a business, he resigned his situation at the Ordnance Office.

To the last he held to the great object of his life—the abolition of slavery. To carry on this work, and organize the efforts of the growing friends of the cause, the Society for the Abolition of Slavery was founded, and new men, inspired by Sharp's example and zeal, sprang forward to help him. His energy became theirs, and the self-sacrificing zeal in which he had so long laboured single-handed, became at length transfused into the nation itself. His mantle fell upon Clarkson, upon Wilberforce, upon Brougham, and upon Buxton, who laboured as he had done, with like energy and stedfastness of purpose, until at length slavery was abolished throughout the British dominions. But though the names last mentioned may be more frequently identified with the triumph of this great cause, the chief merit unquestionably belongs to Granville Sharp. He was encouraged by none of the world's huzzas when he entered upon his work. He stood alone, opposed to the opinion of the ablest lawyers and the most rooted prejudices of the times ; and alone he fought out, by his single exertions, and at his individual expense, the most memorable battle for the constitution of this country and the liberties of British subjects, of which modern times afford a record. What followed was mainly the consequence of his indefatigable constancy. He lighted the torch which kindled other minds, and it was handed on until the illumination became complete.

Before the death of Granville Sharp, Clarkson had already turned his attention to the question of Negro Slavery. He had even selected it for the subject of a college Essay ; and his mind became so possessed by it that he could not shake it off. The spot is pointed out near Wade's Mill, in Hertfordshire, where, alighting from his horse one day, he sat down disconsolate on the turf by the road side, and after long thinking, determined to devote himself wholly to the

work.   He translated his Essay from Latin into English,
added fresh illustrations, and published it.   Then fellow
labourers gathered round him.   The Society for Abolishing
the Slave Trade, unknown to him, had already been formed,
and when he heard of it he joined it.   He sacrificed all
his prospects in life to prosecute this cause.   Wilberforce
was selected to lead in parliament; but upon Clarkson
chiefly devolved the labour of collecting and arranging the
immense mass of evidence offered in support of the abolition.   A remarkable instance of Clarkson's sleuth-hound
sort of perseverance may be mentioned.   The abettors
of slavery, in the course of their defence of the system,
maintained that only such negroes as were captured in
battle were sold as slaves, and if not so sold, then they
were reserved for a still more frightful doom in their own
country.   Clarkson knew of the slave-hunts conducted
by the slave-traders, but had no witnesses to prove it.
Where was one to be found?   Accidentally, a gentleman
whom he met on one of his journeys informed him of a
young sailor, in whose company he had been about a year
before, who had been actually engaged in one of such
slave-hunting expeditions.   The gentleman did not know
his name, and could but indefinitely describe his person.
He did not know where he was, further than that he
belonged to a ship of war in ordinary, but at what port he
could not tell.   With this mere glimmering of information,
Clarkson determined to produce this man as a witness.
He visited personally all the seaport towns where ships in
ordinary lay; boarded and examined every ship without
success, until he came to the very *last* port, and found the
young man, his prize, in the very *last* ship that remained
to be visited.   The young man proved to be one of his
most valuable and effective witnesses.

During several years Clarkson conducted a correspondence
with upwards of four hundred persons, travelling more than

thirty-five thousand miles during the same time in search of evidence. He was at length disabled and exhausted by illness, brought on by his continuous exertions ; but he was not borne from the field until his zeal had fully awakened the public mind, and excited the ardent sympathies of all good men on behalf of the slave.

After years of protracted struggle, the slave trade was abolished. But still another great achievement remained to be accomplished—the abolition of slavery itself throughout the British dominions. And here again determined energy won the day. Of the leaders in the cause, none was more distinguished than Fowell Buxton, who took the position formerly occupied by Wilberforce in the House of Commons. Buxton was a dull, heavy boy, distinguished for his strong self-will, which first exhibited itself in violent, domineering, and headstrong obstinacy. His father died when he was a child ; but fortunately he had a wise mother, who trained his will with great care, constraining him to obey, but encouraging the habit of deciding and acting for himself in matters which might safely be left to him. His mother believed that a strong will, directed upon worthy objects, was a valuable manly quality if properly guided, and she acted accordingly. When others about her commented on the boy's self-will, she would merely say, " Never mind— he is self-willed now—you will see it will turn out well in the end." Fowell learnt very little at school, and was regarded as a dunce and an idler. He got other boys to do his exercises for him, while he romped and scrambled about. He returned home at fifteen, a great, growing, awkward lad, fond only of boating, shooting, riding, and field sports,—spending his time principally with the gamekeeper, a man possessed of a good heart,—an intelligent observer of life and nature, though he could neither read nor write. Buxton had excellent raw material in him, but he wanted culture, training, and development. At this juncture of his life, when his habits were being formed for good or evil, he was happily thrown into the society of the Gurney family, distinguished for their fine social qualities not less than for their intellectual culture and public-spirited philanthropy. This intercourse with the Gurneys, he used afterwards to say, gave the colouring to his life. They encouraged his efforts at self-culture; and when he went to the University of Dublin and gained high honours there, the animating passion in his mind, he said, "was to carry back to them the prizes which they prompted and enabled me to win." He married one of the daughters of the family, and started in life, commencing as a clerk to his uncles Hanbury, the London brewers. His power of will, which made him so difficult to deal with as a boy, now formed the backbone of his character, and made him most indefatigable and energetic in whatever he undertook. He threw his whole strength and bulk right down upon his work; and the great giant—"Elephant Buxton" they called him, for he stood some six feet four in height—became one of the most vigorous and practical of men. "I could brew," he said, "one hour,—do mathematics the next,—and shoot the next,—and each with my whole soul." There was invincible energy and determination in whatever he did. Admitted a partner, he became the active manager of the concern; and the vast business which he conducted felt his influence through every fibre, and prospered far beyond its previous success. Nor did he allow his mind to lie fallow, for he gave his evenings diligently to self-culture, studying and digesting Blackstone, Montesquieu, and solid commentaries on English law. His maxims in reading were, "never to begin a book without finishing it;" "never to consider a book finished until it is mastered;" and "to study everything with the whole mind."

When only thirty-two, Buxton entered parliament, and at once assumed that position of influence there, of which every honest, earnest, well-informed man is secure, who enters that

assembly of the first gentlemen in the world.   The principal
question to which he devoted himself was the complete
emancipation of the slaves in the British colonies.   He himself used to attribute the interest which he early felt in
this question to the influence of Priscilla Gurney, one of
the Earlham family,—a woman of a fine intellect and warm
heart, abounding in illustrious virtues.   When on her
deathbed, in 1821, she repeatedly sent for Buxton, and
urged him " to make the cause of the slaves the great object
of his life."   Her last act was to attempt to reiterate the
solemn charge, and she expired in the ineffectual effort.
Buxton never forgot her counsel; he named one of his
daughters after her; and on the day on which she was
married from his house, on the 1st of August, 1834,—the
day of Negro emancipation—after his Priscilla had been
manumitted from her filial service, and left her father's
home in the company of her husband, Buxton sat down and
thus wrote to a friend :   " The bride is just gone ; everything
has passed off to admiration; and *there is not a slave in
the British colonies !*"

Buxton was no genius—not a great intellectual leader nor
discoverer, but mainly an earnest, straightforward, resolute,
energetic man.   Indeed, his whole character is most forcibly
expressed in his own words, which every young man might
well stamp upon his soul :   " The longer I live," said he,
" the more I am certain that the great difference between
men, between the feeble and the powerful, the great and the
insignificant, is *energy—invincible determination*—a purpose
once fixed, and then death or victory !   That quality will do
anything that can be done in this world ; and no talents, no
circumstances, no opportunities, will make a two-legged
creature a Man without it."

CHAPTER IX.

MEN OF BUSINESS.

"Seest thou a man diligent in his business? he shall stand before kings."—
Proverbs of Solomon.

"That man is but of the lower part of the world that is not brought up to business and affairs."—*Owen Feltham.*

AZLITT, in one of his clever essays, represents the man of business as a mean sort of person put in a go-cart, yoked to a trade or profession ; alleging that all he has to do is, not to go out of the beaten track, but merely to let his affairs take their own course. "The great requisite," he says, "for the prosperous management of ordinary business is the want of imagination, or of any ideas but those of custom and interest on the narrowest scale."* But nothing could be more one-sided. and in effect untrue, than such a definition. Of course, there are narrow-minded men of business, as there are narrow-minded scientific men, literary men, and legislators ; but there are also business men of large and comprehensive minds, capable of action on the very largest scale. As Burke said in his speech on the India Bill, he knew statesmen who were pedlers, and merchants who acted in the spirit of statesmen.

If we take into account the qualities necessary for the successful conduct of any important undertaking,—that it

* On 'Thought and Action.'

requires special aptitude, promptitude of action on emergencies, capacity for organizing the labours often of large numbers of men, great tact and knowledge of human nature, constant self-culture, and growing experience in the practical affairs of life,—it must, we think, be obvious that the school of business is by no means so narrow as some writers would have us believe. Mr. Helps has gone much nearer the truth when he said that consummate men of business are as rare almost as great poets,—rarer, perhaps, than veritable saints and martyrs. Indeed, of no other pursuit can it so emphatically be said, as of this, that "Business makes men."

It has, however, been a favourite fallacy with dunces in all times, that men of genius are unfitted for business, as well as that business occupations unfit men for the pursuits of genius. The unhappy youth who committed suicide a few years since because he had been "born to be a man and condemned to be a grocer," proved by the act that his soul was not equal even to the dignity of grocery. For it is not the calling that degrades the man, but the man that degrades the calling. All work that brings honest gain is honourable, whether it be of hand or mind. The fingers may be soiled, yet the heart remain pure; for it is not material so much as moral dirt that defiles—greed far more than grime, and vice than verdigris.

The greatest have not disdained to labour honestly and usefully for a living, though at the same time aiming after higher things. Thales, the first of the seven sages, Solon, the second founder of Athens, and Hyperates, the mathematician, were all traders. Plato, called the Divine by reason of the excellence of his wisdom, defrayed his travelling expenses in Egypt by the profits derived from the oil which he sold during his journey. Spinoza maintained himself by polishing glasses while he pursued his philosophical investigations. ⅄Linnæus, the great botanist, prosecuted his studies while hammering leather and making shoes. Shakespeare was a successful manager of a theatre—perhaps priding himself more upon his practical qualities in that capacity than on his writing of plays and poetry. Ϫ Pope was of opinion that Shakespeare's principal object in cultivating literature was to secure an honest independence. Indeed he seems to have been altogether indifferent to literary reputation. It is not known that he superintended the publication of a single play, or even sanctioned the printing of one ; and the chronology of his writings is still a mystery. It is certain, however, that he prospered in his business, and realized sufficient to enable him to retire upon a competency to his native town of Stratford-upon-Avon.

Chaucer was in early life a soldier, and afterwards an effective Commissioner of Customs, and Inspector of Woods and Crown Lands. Spencer was Secretary to the Lord Deputy of Ireland, was afterwards Sheriff of Cork, and is said to have been shrewd and attentive in matters of business. Milton, originally a schoolmaster, was elevated to the post of Secretary to the Council of State during the Commonwealth ; and the extant Order-book of the Council, as well as many of Milton's letters which are preserved, give abundant evidence of his activity and usefulness in that office. Sir Isaac Newton proved himself an efficient Master of the Mint ; the new coinage of 1694 having been carried on under his immediate personal superintendence. Cowper prided himself upon his business punctuality, though he confessed that he "never knew a poet, except himself, who was punctual in anything." But against this we may set the lives of Wordsworth and Scott—the former a distributor of stamps, the latter a clerk to the Court of Session,—both of whom, though great poets, were eminently punctual and practical men of business. ϪDavid Ricardo, amidst the occupations of his daily business as a London stock-jobber, in conducting which he acquired an ample fortune, was able to concentrate his mind upon his favourite subject—on which he was enabled to throw great light—the principles of political economy; for he united in himself the sagacious commercial man and the profound philosopher. Baily, the eminent astronomer, was another stockbroker; and Allen, the chemist, was a silk manufacturer.

We have abundant illustrations, in our own day, of the fact that the highest intellectual power is not incompatible with the active and efficient performance of routine duties. Grote, the great historian of Greece, was a London banker. And it is not long since John Stuart Mill, one of our greatest living thinkers, retired from the Examiner's department of the East India Company, carrying with him the admiration and esteem of his fellow officers, not on account of his high views of philosophy, but because of the high standard of efficiency which he had established in his office, and the thoroughly satisfactory manner in which he had conducted the business of his department.

The path of success in business is usually the path of common sense. Patient labour and application are as necessary here as in the acquisition of knowledge or the pursuit of science. The old Greeks said, "to become an able man in any profession, three things are necessary—nature, study, and practice." In business, practice, wisely and diligently improved, is the great secret of success. Some may make what are called "lucky hits," but like money earned by gambling, such "hits" may only serve to lure one to ruin. Bacon was accustomed to say that it was in business as in ways — the nearest way was commonly the foulest, and that if a man would go the fairest way he must go somewhat about. The journey may occupy a longer time, but the pleasure of the labour involved by it, and the enjoyment of the results produced, will be more genuine and unalloyed. To have a daily appointed task of even common drudgery to do makes the rest of life feel all the sweeter.

The fable of the labours of Hercules is the type of all human doing and success. Every youth should be made to feel that his happiness and well-doing in life must necessarily rely mainly on himself and the exercise of his own energies, rather than upon the help and patronage of others. The late Lord Melbourne embodied a piece of useful advice in a letter which he wrote to Lord John Russell, in reply to an application for a provision for one of Moore the poet's sons: "My dear John," he said, "I return you Moore's letter. I shall be ready to do what you like about it when we have the means. I think whatever is done should be done for Moore himself. This is more distinct, direct, and intelligible. Making a small provision for young men is hardly justifiable; and it is of all things the most prejudicial to themselves. They think what they have much larger than it really is; and they make no exertion. The young should never hear any language but this: ' You have your own way to make, and it depends upon your own exertions whether you starve or not.' Believe me, &c., MELBOURNE."

Practical industry, wisely and vigorously applied, always produces its due effects. It carries a man onward, brings out his individual character, and stimulates the action of others. All may not rise equally, yet each, on the whole, very much according to his deserts. "Though all cannot live on the piazza," as the Tuscan proverb has it, "every one may feel the sun."

On the whole, it is not good that human nature should have the road of life made too easy. Better to be under the necessity of working hard and faring meanly, than to have everything done ready to our hand and a pillow of down to repose upon. Indeed, to start in life with comparatively small means seems so necessary as a stimulus to work,

that it may almost be set down as one of the conditions
essential to success in life. Hence, an eminent judge,
when asked what contributed most to success at the bar,
replied, "Some succeed by great talent, some by high
connexions, some by miracle, but the majority by commencing without a shilling."

We have heard of an architect of considerable accomplishments,—a man who had improved himself by long
study, and travel in the classical lands of the East,—who
came home to commence the practice of his profession.
He determined to begin anywhere, provided he could be
employed ; and he accordingly undertook a business connected with dilapidations,—one of the lowest and least
remunerative departments of the architect's calling. But
he had the good sense not to be above his trade, and he had
the resolution to work his way upward, so that he only got
a fair start. One hot day in July a friend found him
sitting astride of a house roof occupied with his dilapidation
business. Drawing his hand across his perspiring countenance, he exclaimed, "Here's a pretty business for a man
who has been all over Greece !" However, he did his
work, such as it was, thoroughly and well ; he persevered
until he advanced by degrees to more remunerative branches
of employment, and eventually he rose to the highest walks
of his profession.

The necessity of labour may, indeed, be regarded as the
main root and spring of all that we call progress in individuals,
and civilization in nations ; and it is doubtful whether any
heavier curse could be imposed on man than the complete
gratification of all his wishes without effort on his part,
leaving nothing for his hopes, desires or struggles. The
feeling that life is destitute of any motive or necessity for
action, must be of all others the most distressing and
insupportable to a rational being. The Marquis de Spinola
asking Sir Horace Vere what his brother died of, Sir Horace

replied, "He died, Sir, of having nothing to do." "Alas!" said Spinola, "that is enough to kill any general of us all."

Those who fail in life are however very apt to assume a tone of injured innocence, and conclude too hastily that everybody excepting themselves has had a hand in their personal misfortunes. An eminent writer lately published a book, in which he described his numerous failures in business, naively admitting, at the same time that he was ignorant of the multiplication table; and he came to the conclusion that the real cause of his ill-success in life was the money-worshipping spirit of the age. Lamartine also did not hesitate to profess his contempt for arithmetic; but, had it been less, probably we should not have witnessed the unseemly spectacle of the admirers of that distinguished personage engaged in collecting subscriptions for his support in his old age.

Again, some consider themselves born to ill luck, and make up their minds that the world invariably goes against them without any fault on their own part. We have heard of a person of this sort, who went so far as to declare his belief that if he had been a hatter people would have been born without heads! There is however a Russian proverb which says that Misfortune is next door to Stupidity; and it will often be found that men who are constantly lamenting their luck, are in some way or other reaping the consequences of their own neglect, mismanagement, improvidence, or want of application. Dr. Johnson, who came up to London with a single guinea in his pocket, and who once accurately described himself in his signature to a letter addressed to a noble lord, as *Impransus*, or Dinnerless, has honestly said, "All the complaints which are made of the world are unjust; I never knew a man of merit neglected; it was generally by his own fault that he failed of success."

Washington Irving, the American author, held like views.

"As for the talk," said he, "about modest merit being neglected, it is too often a cant, by which indolent and irresolute men seek to lay their want of success at the door of the public. Modest merit is, however, too apt to be inactive, or negligent, or uninstructed merit. Well matured and well disciplined talent is always sure of a market, provided it exerts itself; but it must not cower at home and expect to be sought for. There is a good deal of cant too about the success of forward and impudent men, while men of retiring worth are passed over with neglect. But it usually happens that those forward men have that valuable quality of promptness and activity without which worth is a mere inoperative property. A barking dog is often more useful than a sleeping lion."

Attention, application, accuracy, method, punctuality, and despatch, are the principal qualities required for the efficient conduct of business of any sort. These, at first sight, may appear to be small matters ; and yet they are of essential importance to human happiness, well-being, and usefulness. They are little things, it is true ; but human life is made up of comparative trifles. It is the repetition of little acts which constitute not only the sum of human character, but which determine the character of nations. And where men or nations have broken down, it will almost invariably be found that neglect of little things was the rock on which they split. Every human being has duties to be performed, and, therefore, has need of cultivating the capacity for doing them; whether the sphere of action be the management of a household, the conduct of a trade or profession, or the government of a nation.

The examples we have already given of great workers in various branches of industry, art, and science, render it unnecessary further to enforce the importance of persevering application in any department of life. It is the result of every-day experience, that steady attention to matters of detail lies at the root of human progress; and that diligence, above all, is the mother of good luck. Accuracy is also of much importance, and an invariable mark of good training in a man. Accuracy in observation, accuracy in speech, accuracy in the transaction of affairs. What is done in business must be well done; for it is better to accomplish perfectly a small amount of work, than to half-do ten times as much. A wise man used to say, "Stay a little, that we may make an end the sooner."

Too little attention, however, is paid to this highly important quality of accuracy. As a man eminent in practical science lately observed to us, "It is astonishing how few people I have met with in the course of my experience, who can *define a fact* accurately." Yet in business affairs, it is the manner in which even small matters are transacted, that often decides men for or against you. With virtue, capacity, and good conduct in other respects, the person who is habitually inaccurate cannot be trusted; his work has to be gone over again; and he thus causes an infinity of annoyance, vexation, and trouble.

It was one of the characteristic qualities of Charles James Fox, that he was thoroughly pains-taking in all that he did. When appointed Secretary of State, being piqued at some observation as to his bad writing, he actually took a writing-master, and wrote copies like a schoolboy until he had sufficiently improved himself. Though a corpulent man, he was wonderfully active at picking up cut tennis balls, and when asked how he contrived to do so, he playfully replied, "Because I am a very pains-taking man." The same accuracy in trifling matters was displayed by him in things of greater importance; and he acquired his reputation, like the painter, by "neglecting nothing."

Method is essential, and enables a larger amount of work to be got through with satisfaction. "Method," said the Reverend Richard Cecil, "is like packing things in a box;

a good packer will get in half as much again as a bad
one." Cecil's despatch of business was extraordinary, his
maxim being, "The shortest way to do many things is to
do only one thing at once;" and he never left a thing
undone with a view of recurring to it at a period of more
leisure. When business pressed, he rather chose to en-
croach on his hours of meals and rest than omit any part of
his work. De Witt's maxim was like Cecil's: "One thing
at a time." "If," said he, "I have any necessary despatches
to make, I think of nothing else till they are finished; if any
domestic affairs require my attention, I give myself wholly
up to them till they are set in order."

A French minister, who was alike remarkable for his
despatch of business and his constant attendance at places
of amusement, being asked how he contrived to combine
both objects, replied, "Simply by never postponing till
to-morrow what should be done to-day." Lord Brougham
has said that a certain English statesman reversed the
process, and that his maxim was, never to transact to-day
what could be postponed till to-morrow. Unhappily, such
is the practice of many besides that minister, already almost
forgotten; the practice is that of the indolent and the
unsuccessful. Such men, too, are apt to rely upon agents,
who are not always to be relied upon. Important affairs
must be attended to in person. "If you want your business
done," says the proverb, "go and do it; if you don't want
it done, send some one else."

An indolent country gentleman had a freehold estate
producing about five hundred a-year. Becoming involved
in debt, he sold half the estate, and let the remainder to an
industrious farmer for twenty years. About the end of the
term the farmer called to pay his rent, and asked the owner
whether he would sell the farm. "Will *you* buy it?" asked
the owner, surprised. "Yes, if we can agree about the price.'
"That is exceedingly strange," observed the gentleman;

"pray, tell me how it happens that, while I could not live upon twice as much land for which I paid no rent, you are regularly paying me two hundred a-year for your farm, and are able, in a few years, to purchase it." "The reason is plain," was the reply; "you sat still and said *Go*, I got up and said *Come;* you laid in bed and enjoyed your estate, I rose in the morning and minded my business."

Sir Walter Scott, writing to a youth who had obtained a situation and asked for his advice, gave him in reply this sound counsel: "Beware of stumbling over a propensity which easily besets you from not having your time fully employed—I mean what the women call *dawdling*. Your motto must be, *Hoc age*. Do instantly whatever is to be done, and take the hours of recreation after business, never before it. When a regiment is under march, the rear is often thrown into confusion because the front do not move steadily and without interruption. It is the same with business. If that which is first in hand is not instantly, steadily, and regularly despatched, other things accumulate behind, till affairs begin to press all at once, and no human brain can stand the confusion."

Promptitude in action may be stimulated by a due consideration of the value of time. An Italian philosopher was accustomed to call time his estate: an estate which produces nothing of value without cultivation, but, duly improved, never fails to recompense the labours of the diligent worker. Allowed to lie waste, the product will be only noxious weeds and vicious growths of all kinds. One of the minor uses of steady employment is, that it keeps one out of mischief, for truly an idle brain is the devil's workshop, and a lazy man the devil's bolster. To be occupied is to be possessed as by a tenant, whereas to be idle is to be empty; and when the doors of the imagination are opened, temptation finds a ready access, and evil thoughts come trooping in. It is observed at sea, that

T

men are never so much disposed to grumble and mutiny as when least employed. Hence an old captain, when there was nothing else to do, would issue the order to " scour the anchor ! "

— Men of business are accustomed to quote the maxim that Time is money; but it is more; the proper improvement of it is self-culture, self-improvement, and growth of character. An hour wasted daily on trifles or in indolence, would, if devoted to self-improvement, make an ignorant man wise in a few years, and employed in good works, would make his life fruitful, and death a harvest of worthy deeds. Fifteen minutes a day devoted to self-improvement, will be felt at the end of the year. Good thoughts and carefully gathered experience take up no room, and may be carried about as our companions everywhere, without cost or incumbrance. An economical use of time is the true mode of securing leisure : it enables us to get through business and carry it forward, instead of being driven by it. On the other hand, the miscalculation of time involves us in perpetual hurry, confusion, and difficulties; and life becomes a mere shuffle of expedients, usually followed by disaster. Nelson once said, " I owe all my success in life to having been always a quarter of an hour before my time."

Some take no thought of the value of money until they have come to an end of it, and many do the same with their time. The hours are allowed to flow by unemployed and then, when life is fast waning, they bethink themselves of the duty of making a wiser use of it. But the habit of listlessness and idleness may already have become confirmed, and they are unable to break the bonds with which they have permitted themselves to become bound. Lost wealth may be replaced by industry, lost knowledge by study, lost health by temperance or medicine, but lost time is gone . for ever.

A proper consideration of the value of time, will also

inspire habits of punctuality. " Punctuality," said Louis XIV., " is the politeness of kings." It is also the duty of gentlemen, and the necessity of men of business. Nothing begets confidence in a man sooner than the practice of this virtue, and nothing shakes confidence sooner than the want of it. He who holds to his appointment and does not keep you waiting for him, shows that he has regard for your time as well as for his own. Thus punctuality is one of the modes by which we testify our personal respect for those whom we are called upon to meet in the business of life. It is also conscientiousness in a measure ; for an appointment is a contract, express or implied, and he who does not keep it breaks faith, as well as dishonestly uses other people's time, and thus inevitably loses character. We naturally come to the conclusion that the person who is careless about time will be careless about business, and that he is not the one to be trusted with the transaction of matters of importance. When Washington's secretary excused himself for the lateness of his attendance and laid the blame upon his watch, his master quietly said, " Then you must get another watch, or I another secretary."

The person who is negligent of time and its employment is usually found to be a general disturber of others' peace and serenity. It was wittily said by Lord Chesterfield of the old Duke of Newcastle—" His Grace loses an hour in the morning, and is looking for it all the rest of the day." Everybody with whom the unpunctual man has to do is thrown from time to time into a state of fever : he is systematically late ; regular only in his irregularity. He conducts his dawdling as if upon system ; arrives at his appointment after time ; gets to the railway station after the train has started ; posts his letter when the box has closed. Thus business is thrown into confusion, and everybody concerned is put out of temper. It will generally be found that the men who are thus habitually behind time are as habitually behind success ; and the world generally casts them aside to swell the ranks of the grumblers and the railers against fortune.

In addition to the ordinary working qualities the business man of the highest class requires quick perception and firmness in the execution of his plans. Tact is also important; and though this is partly the gift of nature, it is yet capable of being cultivated and developed by observation and experience. Men of this quality are quick to see the right mode of action, and if they have decision of purpose, are prompt to carry out their undertakings to a successful issue. (¹)These qualities are especially valuable, and indeed indispensable, in those who direct the action of other men on a large scale, as for instance, in the case of the commander of an army in the field. It is not merely necessary that the general should be great as a warrior but also as a man of business. He must possess great tact, much knowledge of character, and ability to organize the movements of a large mass of men, whom he has to feed, clothe, and furnish with whatever may be necessary in order that they may keep the field and win battles. In these respects Napoleon and Wellington were both first-rate men of business. (²)

Though Napoleon had an immense love for details, he had also a vivid power of imagination, which enabled him to look along extended lines of action, and deal with those details on a large scale, with judgment and rapidity. He possessed such knowledge of character as enabled him to select, almost unerringly, the best agents for the execution of his designs. But he trusted as little as possible to agents in matters of great moment, on which important results depended. This feature in his character is illustrated in a remarkable degree by the 'Napoleon Correspondence,' now in course of publication, and particularly by the contents of the 15th volume,* which include the letters, orders, and despatches, written by the Emperor at Finken- stein, a little chateau on the frontier of Poland in the year 1807, shortly after the victory of Eylau.

The French army was then lying encamped along the river Passarge with the Russians before them, the Austrians on their right flank, and the conquered Prussians in their rear. A long line of communications had to be maintained with France, through a hostile country ; but so carefully, and with such foresight was this provided for, that it is said Napoleon never missed a post. The movements of armies, the bringing up of reinforcements from remote points in France, Spain, Italy, and Germany, the opening of canals and the levelling of roads to enable the produce of Poland and Prussia to be readily transported to his encampments, had his unceasing attention, down to the minutest details. We find him directing where horses were to be obtained, making arrangements for an adequate supply of saddles, ordering shoes for the soldiers, and specifying the number of rations of bread, biscuit, and spirits, that were to be brought to camp, or stored in magazines for the use of the troops. At the same time we find him writing to Paris giving directions for the reorganization of the French College, devising a scheme of public education, dictating bulletins and articles for the 'Moniteur,' revising the details of the budgets, giving instructions to architects as to altera- tions to be made at the Tuileries and the Church of the Madelaine, throwing an occasional sarcasm at Madame de Stael and the Parisian journals, interfering to put down a squabble at the Grand Opera, carrying on a correspondence with the Sultan of Turkey and the Schah of Persia, so that while his body was at Finkenstein, his mind seemed to be

* 'Correspondance de Napoléon Ier.,' publiée par ordre de l'Empereur Napoléon III. Paris. 1864.

working at a hundred different places in Paris, in Europe, and throughout the world.

We find him in one letter asking Ney if he has duly received the muskets which have been sent him; in another he gives directions to Prince Jerome as to the shirts, great-coats, clothes, shoes, shakos, and arms, to be served out to the Wurtemburg regiments; again he presses Cambacérès to forward to the army a double stock of corn—"The *ifs* and the *buts*" said he "are at present out of season, and above all it must be done with speed." Then he informs Daru that the army want shirts, and that they don't come to hand. To Massena he writes, "Let me know if your biscuit and bread arrangements are yet completed." To the Grand duc de Berg, he gives directions as to the accoutrements of the cuirassiers—"They complain that the men want sabres; send an officer to obtain them at Posen. It is also said they want helmets; order that they be made at Ebling. . . . It is not by sleeping that one can accomplish anything." Thus no point of detail was neglected, and the energies of all were stimulated into action with extraordinary power. Though many of the Emperor's days were occupied by inspections of his troops,—in the course of which he some-times rode from thirty to· forty leagues a day,—and by reviews, receptions, and affairs of state, leaving but little time ·for business matters, he neglected nothing on that account; but devoted the greater part of his nights, when necessary, to examining budgets, dictating dispatches, and attending to the thousand matters of detail in the organiza-tion and working of the Imperial Government; the ma-chinery of which was for the most part concentrated in his own head.

Like Napoleon, the Duke of Wellington was a first-rate man of business; and it is not perhaps saying too much to aver that it was in no small degree because of his possession of a business faculty amounting to genius, that the Duke never lost a battle.

While a subaltern, he became dissatisfied with the slowness of his promotion, and having passed from the infantry to the cavalry twice, and back again, without advancement, he applied to Lord Camden, then Viceroy of Ireland, for employment in the Revenue or Treasury Board. Had he succeeded, no doubt he would have made a first-rate head of a department, as he would have made a first-rate merchant or manufacturer. But his application failed, and he remained with the army to become the greatest of British generals.

The Duke began his active military career under the Duke of York and General Walmoden, in Flanders and Holland, where he learnt, amidst misfortunes and defeats, how bad business arrangements and bad generalship serve to ruin the *morale* of an army. Ten years after entering the army we find him a colonel in India, reported by his superiors as an officer of indefatigable energy and application. He entered into the minutest details of the service, and sought to raise the discipline of his men to the highest standard. "The regiment of Colonel Wellesley," wrote General Harris in 1799, "is a model regiment; on the score of soldierly bearing, discipline, instruction, and orderly behaviour it is above all praise." Thus qualifying himself for posts of greater confidence, he was shortly after nominated governor of the capital of Mysore. In the war with the Mahrattas he was first called upon to try his hand at generalship; and at thirty-four he won the memorable battle of Assaye, with an army composed of 1500 British and 5000 sepoys, over 20,000 Mahratta infantry and 30,000 cavalry. But so brilliant a victory did not in the least disturb his equanimity, or affect the perfect honesty of his character.

Shortly after this event the opportunity occurred for exhibiting his admirable practical qualities as an adminis-

trator. Placed in command of an important district immediately after the capture of Seringapatam, his first object
was to establish rigid order and discipline among his own
men. Flushed with victory, the troops were found riotous
and disorderly. "Send me the provost marshal," said he,
"and put him under my orders : till some of the marauders
are hung, it is impossible to expect order or safety." This
rigid severity of Wellington in the field, though it was the
dread, proved the salvation of his troops in many campaigns. His next step was to re-establish the markets and
re-open the sources of supply. General Harris wrote to
the Governor-general, strongly commending Colonel Wellesley for the perfect discipline he had established, and for
his "judicious and masterly arrangements in respect to
supplies, which opened an abundant free market, and inspired confidence into dealers of every description." The
same close attention to, and mastery of details, characterized
him throughout his Indian career; and it is remarkable
that one of his ablest despatches to Lord Clive, full of
practical information as to the conduct of the campaign,
was written whilst the column he commanded was crossing
the Toombuddra, in the face of the vastly superior army
of Dhoondiah, posted on the opposite bank, and while a
thousand matters of the deepest interest were pressing upon
the commander's mind. But it was one of his most remarkable characteristics, thus to be able to withdraw himself
temporarily from the business immediately in hand, and to
bend his full powers upon the consideration of matters totally
distinct; even the most difficult circumstances on such
occasions failing to embarrass or intimidate him.

Returned to England with a reputation for generalship,
Sir Arthur Wellesley met with immediate employment. In
1808 a corps of 10,000 men destined to liberate Portugal
was placed under his charge. He landed, fought, and won
two battles, and signed the Convention of Cintra. After

the death of Sir John Moore he was entrusted with the command of a new expedition to Portugal. But Wellington was fearfully overmatched throughout his Peninsular campaigns. From 1809 to 1813 he never had more than 30,000 British troops under his command, at a time when there stood opposed to him in the Peninsula some 350,000 French, mostly veterans, led by some of Napoleon's ablest generals. How was he to contend against such immense forces with any fair prospect of success? His clear discernment and strong common sense soon taught him that he must adopt a different policy from that of the Spanish generals, who were invariably beaten and dispersed whenever they ventured to offer battle in the open plains. He perceived he had yet to create the army that was to contend against the French with any reasonable chance of success. Accordingly, after the battle of Talavera in 1809, when he found himself encompassed on all sides by superior forces of French, he retired into Portugal, there to carry out the settled policy on which he had by this time determined. It was, to organise a Portuguese army under British officers, and teach them to act in combination with his own troops, in the mean time avoiding the peril of a defeat by declining all engagements. He would thus, he conceived, destroy the *morale* of the French, who could not exist without victories; and when his army was ripe for action, and the enemy demoralized, he would then fall upon them with all his might.

The extraordinary qualities displayed by Lord Wellington throughout these immortal campaigns, can only be appreciated after a perusal of his despatches, which contain the unvarnished tale of the manifold ways and means by which he laid the foundations of his success. Never was man more tried by difficulty and opposition, arising not less from the imbecility, falsehoods and intrigues of the British

Government of the day, than from the selfishness, cowardice, and vanity of the people he went to save. It may, indeed, be said of him, that he sustained the war in Spain by his individual firmness and self-reliance, which never failed him even in the midst of his greatest discouragements. He had not only to fight Napoleon's veterans, but also to hold in check the Spanish juntas and the Portuguese regency. He had the utmost difficulty in obtaining provisions and clothing for his troops; and it will scarcely be credited that, while engaged with the enemy in the battle of Talavera, the Spaniards, who ran away, fell upon the baggage of the British army, and the ruffians actually plundered it! These and other vexations the Duke bore with a sublime patience and self-control, and held on his course, in the face of ingratitude, treachery, and opposition, with indomitable firmness. He neglected nothing, and attended to every important detail of business himself. When he found that food for his troops was not to be obtained from England, and that he must rely upon his own resources for feeding them, he forthwith commenced business as a corn merchant on a large scale, in copartnery with the British Minister at Lisbon. Commissariat bills were created, with which grain was bought in the ports of the Mediterranean and in South America. When he had thus filled his magazines, the overplus was sold to the Portuguese, who were greatly in want of provisions. He left nothing whatever to chance, but provided for every contingency. He gave his attention to the minutest details of the service; and was accustomed to concentrate his whole energies, from time to time, on such apparently ignominious matters as soldiers' shoes, camp-kettles, biscuits and horse fodder. His magnificent business qualities were everywhere felt; and there can be no doubt that, by the care with which he provided for every contingency, and the personal attention which he gave to every detail, he laid the foundations of his great success.* By such means he transformed an army of raw levies into the best soldiers in Europe, with whom he declared it to be possible to go anywhere and do anything. We have already referred to his remarkable power of abstracting himself from the work, no matter how engrossing, immediately in hand, and concentrating his energies upon the details of some entirely different business. Thus Napier relates that it was while he was preparing to fight the battle of Salamanca that he had to expose to the Ministers at home the futility of relying upon a loan; it was on the heights of San Christoval, on the field of battle itself, that he demonstrated the absurdity of attempting to establish a Portuguese bank ; it was in the trenches of Burgos that he dissected Funchal's scheme of finance, and exposed the folly of attempting the sale of church property ; and on each occasion, he showed himself as well acquainted with these subjects as with the minutest detail in the mechanism of armies.

Another feature in his character, showing the upright man of business, was his thorough honesty. Whilst Soult ransacked and carried away with him from Spain numerous pictures of great value, Wellington did not appropriate to himself a single farthing's worth of property. Everywhere he paid his way, even when in the enemy's country. When he had crossed the French frontier, followed by 40,000 Spaniards, who sought to "make fortunes" by pillage and plunder, he first rebuked their officers, and then, finding his efforts to restrain them unavailing, he sent them back into their own country. It is a remarkable fact, that, even in France the peasantry fled from their own countrymen, and

---

* The recently published correspondence of Napoleon with his brother Joseph, and the Memoirs of the Duke of Ragusa, abundantly confirm this view. The Duke overthrew Napoleon's generals by the superiority of his routine. He used to say that, if he knew anything at all, he knew how to feed an army.

carried their valuables within the protection of the British lines! At the very same time, Wellington was writing home to the British Ministry, "We are overwhelmed with debts, and I can scarcely stir out of my house on account of public creditors waiting to demand payment of what is due to them." Jules Maurel, in his estimate of the Duke's character, says, "Nothing can be grander or more nobly original than this admission. This old soldier, after thirty years' service, this iron man and victorious general, established in an enemy's country at the head of an immense army, is afraid of his creditors! This is a kind of fear that has seldom troubled the mind of conquerors and invaders; and I doubt if the annals of war could present anything comparable to this sublime simplicity." But the Duke himself, had the matter been put to him, would most probably have disclaimed any intention of acting even grandly or nobly in the matter; merely regarding the punctual payment of his debts as the best and most honourable mode of conducting his business.

The truth of the good old maxim, that "Honesty is the best policy," is upheld by the daily experience of life; uprightness and integrity being found as successful in business as in everything else. As Hugh Miller's worthy uncle used to advise him, "In all your dealings give your neighbour the cast of the bauk—'good measure, heaped up, and running over,'—and you will not lose by it in the end." A well-known brewer of beer attributed his success to the liberality with which he used his malt. Going up to the vat and tasting it, he would say, "Still rather poor, my lads; give it another cast of the malt." The brewer put his character into his beer, and it proved generous accordingly, obtaining a reputation in England, India, and the colonies, which laid the foundation of a large fortune. Integrity of word and deed ought to be the very cornerstone of all business transactions. To the tradesman, the merchant, and manufacturer, it should be what honour is to the soldier, and charity to the Christian. In the humblest calling there will always be found scope for the exercise of this uprightness of character. Hugh Miller speaks of the mason with whom he served his apprenticeship, as one who "*put his conscience into every stone that he laid.*" So the true mechanic will pride himself upon the thoroughness and solidity of his work, and the high-minded contractor upon the honesty of performance of his contract in every particular. The upright manufacturer will find not only honour and reputation, but substantial success, in the genuineness of the article which he produces, and the merchant in the honesty of what he sells, and that it really is what it seems to be. Baron Dupin, speaking of the general probity of Englishmen, which he held to be a principal cause of their success, observed, " We may succeed for a time by fraud, by surprise, by violence ; but we can succeed permanently only by means directly opposite. It is not alone the courage, the intelligence, the activity, of the merchant and manufacturer which maintain the superiority of their productions and the character of their country ; it is far more their wisdom, their economy, and, above all, their probity. If ever in the British Islands the useful citizen should lose these virtues, we may be sure that, for England, as for every other country, the vessels of a degenerate commerce, repulsed from every shore, would speedily disappear from those seas whose surface they now cover with the treasures of the universe, bartered for the treasures of the industry of the three kingdoms."

It must be admitted, that Trade tries character perhaps more severely than any other pursuit in life. It puts to the severest tests honesty, self-denial, justice, and truthfulness ; and men of business who pass through such trials unstained are perhaps worthy of as great honour as soldiers

who prove their courage amidst the fire and perils of battle.
And, to the credit of the multitudes of men engaged in the
various departments of trade, we think it must be admitted
that on the whole they pass through their trials nobly.   If
we reflect but for a moment on the vast amount of wealth
daily entrusted even to subordinate persons, who themselves
probably earn but a bare competency—the loose cash which
is constantly passing through the hands of shopmen, agents,
brokers, and clerks in banking houses,—and note how comparatively few are the breaches of trust which occur amidst
all this temptation, it will probably be admitted that this
steady daily honesty of conduct is most honourable to human
nature, if it do not even tempt us to be proud of it.   The
same trust and confidence reposed by men of business in
each other, as implied by the system of Credit, which is
mainly based upon the principle of honour, would be surprising if it were not so much a matter of ordinary practice
in business transactions.   Dr. Chalmers has well said, that
the implicit trust with which merchants are accustomed to
confide in distant agents, separated from them perhaps by
half the globe—often consigning vast wealth to persons,
recommended only by their character, whom perhaps they
have never seen—is probably the finest act of homage which
men can render to one another.

Although common honesty is still happily in the ascen-
dant amongst common people, and the general business
community of England is still sound at heart, putting their
honest character into their respective callings,—there are
unhappily, as there have been in all times, but too many
instances of flagrant dishonesty and fraud, exhibited by the
unscrupulous, the over-speculative, and the intensely selfish,
in their haste to be rich.   There are tradesmen who adul-
terate, contractors who " scamp," manufacturers who give us
shoddy instead of wool, " dressing " instead of cotton, cast-
iron tools instead of steel, needles without eyes, razors made

only "to sell," and swindled fabrics in many shapes. But these we must hold to be the exceptional cases, of low-minded and grasping men, who, though they may gain wealth which they probably cannot enjoy, will never gain an honest character, nor secure that without which wealth is nothing—a heart at peace. "The rogue cozened not me, but his own conscience," said Bishop Latimer of a cutler who made him pay twopence for a knife not worth a penny. Money, earned by screwing, cheating, and overreaching, may for a time dazzle the eyes of the unthinking; but the bubbles .blown by unscrupulous rogues, when full-blown, usually glitter only to burst. The Sadleirs, Dean Pauls, and Redpaths, for the most part, come to a sad end even in this world; and though the successful swindles of others may not be "found out," and the gains of their roguery may remain with them, it will be as a curse and not as a blessing.

It is possible that the scrupulously honest man may not grow rich so fast as the unscrupulous and dishonest one; but the success will be of a truer kind, earned without fraud or injustice. And even though a man should for a time be unsuccessful, still he must be honest: better lose all and save character. For character is itself a fortune; and if the high-principled man will but hold on his way courageously, success will surely come,—nor will the highest reward of all be withheld from him. Wordsworth well describes the "Happy Warrior," as he

> "Who comprehends his trust, and to the same
> Keeps faithful with a singleness of aim;
> And therefore does not stoop, nor lie in wait
> For wealth, or honour, or for worldly state;
> Whom they must follow, on whose head must fall,
> Like showers of manna, if they come at all."

As an example of the high-minded mercantile man trained in upright habits of business, and distinguished for justice, truthfulness, and honesty of dealing in all things, the career of the well-known David Barclay, grandson of Robert Barclay, of Ury, the author of the celebrated ' Apology for the Quakers,' may be briefly referred to.   For many years he was the head of an extensive house in Cheapside, chiefly engaged in the American trade ; but like Granville Sharp, he entertained so strong an opinion against the war with our American colonies, that he determined to retire altogether from the trade.   Whilst a merchant, he was as much distinguished for his talents, knowledge, integrity, and power, as he afterwards was for his patriotism and munificent philanthropy.   He was a mirror of truthfulness and honesty ; and, as became the good Christian and true gentleman, his word was always held to be as good as his bond.   His position, and his high character, induced the Ministers of the day on many occasions to seek his advice ; and, when examined before the House of Commons on the subject of the American dispute, his views were so clearly expressed, and his advice was so strongly justified by the reasons stated by him, that Lord North publicly acknowledged that he had derived more information from David Barclay than from all others east of Temple Bar.   On retiring from business, it was not to rest in luxurious ease, but to enter upon new labours of usefulness for others.   With ample means, he felt that he still owed to society the duty of a good example.   He founded a house of industry near his residence at Walthamstow, which he supported at a heavy outlay for several years, until at length he succeeded in rendering it a source of comfort as well as independence to the well-disposed families of the poor in that neighbourhood.   When an estate in Jamaica fell to him, he determined, though at a cost of some 10,000*l*., at once to give liberty to the whole of the slaves on the property.   He sent out an agent, who hired a ship, and he had the little slave community trans-

ported to one of the free American states, where they
settled down and prospered.   Mr. Barclay had been assured
that the negroes were too ignorant and too barbarous for
freedom, and it was thus that he determined practically
to demonstrate the fallacy of the assertion.   In dealing with
his accumulated savings, he made himself the executor of
his own will, and instead of leaving a large fortune to be
divided among his relatives at his death, he extended to
them his munificent aid during his life, watched and aided
them in their respective careers, and thus not only laid
the foundation, but lived to see the maturity, of some of
the largest and most prosperous business concerns in the
metropolis.   We believe that to this day some of our most
eminent merchants—such as the Gurneys, Hanburys, and
Buxtons—are proud to acknowledge with gratitude the
obligations they owe to David Barclay for the means of their
first introduction to life, and for the benefits of his counsel
and countenance in the early stages of their career.   Such a
man stands as a mark of the mercantile honesty and integrity
of his country, and is a model and example for men of
business in all time to come.

CHAPTER X.

MONEY—ITS USE AND ABUSE.

" Not for to hide it in a hedge,
Nor for a train attendant,
But for the glorious privilege
Of being independent."—*Burns.*

" Neither a borrower nor a lender be :
For loan oft loses both itself and friend ;
And borrowing dulls the edge of husbandry."—*Shakespeare.*

Never treat money affairs with levity—Money is character.—*Sir E. L. Bulwer Lytton.*

HOW a man uses money—makes it, saves it, and spends it—is perhaps one of the best tests of practical wisdom. Although money ought by no means to be regarded as a chief end of man's life, neither is it a trifling matter, to be held in philosophic contempt, representing as it does to so large an extent, the means of physical comfort and social well-being. Indeed, some of the finest qualities of human nature are intimately related to the right use of money ; such as generosity, honesty, justice, and self-sacrifice ; as well as the practical virtues of economy and providence. On the other hand, there are their counterparts of avarice, fraud, injustice, and selfishness, as displayed by the inordinate lovers of gain ; and the vices of thriftlessness, extravagance, and improvidence, on the part of those who misuse and abuse the means entrusted to them. "So that," as is wisely observed by Henry Taylor in his thoughtful ' Notes from Life,' "a right measure and manner in getting, saving, spending, giving, taking, lending, borrowing, and bequeathing, would almost argue a perfect man."

Comfort in worldly circumstances is a condition which every man is justified in striving to attain by all worthy means. It secures that physical satisfaction, which is necessary for the culture of the better part of his nature; and enables him to provide for those of his own household, without which, says the Apostle, a man is "worse than an infidel." Nor ought the duty to be any the less indifferent to us, that the respect which our fellow-men entertain for us in.no slight degree depends upon the manner in which we exercise the opportunities which present themselves for our honourable advancement in life. The very effort required to be made to succeed in life with this object, is of itself an education; stimulating a man's sense of self-respect, bringing out his practical qualities, and disciplining him in the exercise of patience, perseverance, and such like virtues. The provident and careful man must necessarily be a thoughtful man, for he lives not merely for the present, but with provident forecast makes arrangements for the future. He must also be a temperate man, and exercise the virtue of self-denial, than which nothing is so much calculated to give strength to the character. John Sterling says truly, that "the worst education which teaches self-denial, is better than the best which teaches everything else, and not that." The Romans rightly employed the same word (virtus) to designate courage, which is in a physical sense what the other is in a moral; the highest virtue of all being victory over ourselves.

Hence the lesson of self-denial—the sacrificing of a present gratification for a future good—is one of the last that is learnt. Those classes which work the hardest might naturally be expected to value the most the money which they earn. Yet the readiness with which so many are accustomed to eat up and drink up their earnings as they go, renders them to a great extent helpless and dependent upon the frugal. There are large numbers of persons among us who, though enjoying sufficient means of comfort and independence, are often found to be barely a day's march ahead of actual want when a time of pressure occurs ; and hence a great cause of social helplessness and suffering. On one occasion a deputation waited on Lord John Russell, respecting the taxation levied on the working classes of the country, when the noble lord took the opportunity of remarking, "You may rely upon it that the Government of this country durst not tax the working classes to anything like the extent to which they tax themselves in their expenditure upon intoxicating drinks alone !" Of all great public questions, there is perhaps none more important than this,—no great work of reform calling more loudly for labourers. But it must be admitted that "self-denial and self-help" would make a poor rallying cry for the hustings ; and it is to be feared that the patriotism of this day has but little regard for such common things as individual economy and providence, although it is by the practice of such virtues only that the genuine independence of the industrial classes is to be secured. "Prudence, frugality, and good management," said Samuel Drew, the philosophical shoemaker, "are excellent artists for mending bad times : they occupy but little room in any dwelling, but would furnish a more effectual remedy for the evils of life than any Reform Bill that ever passed the Houses of Parliament." Socrates said, "Let him that would move the world move first himself." Or as the old rhyme runs—

> " If every one would see
>   To his own reformation,
> How very easily
>   You might reform a nation."

It is, however, generally felt to be a far easier thing to reform the Church and the State than to reform the least of our own bad habits; and in such matters it is usually found more agreeable to our tastes, as it certainly is the common practice, to begin with our neighbours rather than with ourselves.

Any class of men that lives from hand to mouth will ever be an inferior class. They will necessarily remain impotent and helpless, hanging on to the skirts of society, the sport of times and seasons. Having no respect for themselves, they will fail in securing the respect of others. In commercial crises, such men must inevitably go to the wall. Wanting that husbanded power which a store of savings, no matter how small, invariably gives them, they will be at every man's mercy, and, if possessed of right feelings, they cannot but regard with fear and trembling the future possible fate of their wives and children. "The world," once said Mr. Cobden to the working men of Huddersfield, "has always been divided into two classes,—those who have saved, and those who have spent—the thrifty and the extravagant. The building of all the houses, the mills, the bridges, and the ships, and the accomplishment of all other great works which have rendered man civilized and happy, has been done by the savers, the thrifty; and those who have wasted their resources have always been their slaves. It has been the law of nature and of Providence that this should be so; and I were an impostor if I promised any class that they would advance themselves if they were improvident, thoughtless, and idle."

Equally sound was the advice given by Mr. Bright to an assembly of working men at Rochdale, in 1847, when, after expressing his belief that, "so far as honesty was concerned, it was to be found in pretty equal amount among all classes," he used the following words:—"There is only one way that is safe for any man, or any number of men, by which they can maintain their present position if it be a good one, or raise themselves above it if it be a bad one,

—that is, by the practice of the virtues of industry, frugality, temperance, and honesty. There is no royal road by which men can raise themselves from a position which they feel to be uncomfortable and unsatisfactory, as regards their mental or physical condition, except by the practice of those virtues by which they find numbers amongst them are continually advancing and bettering themselves. "

There is no reason why the condition of the average workman should not be a useful, honourable, respectable, and happy one. The whole body of the working classes might, (with few exceptions) be as frugal, virtuous, well-informed, and well-conditioned as many individuals of the same class have already made themselves. What some men are, all without difficulty might be. Employ the same means, and the same results will follow. That there should be a class of men who live by their daily labour in every state is the ordinance of God, and doubtless is a wise and righteous one ; but that this class should be otherwise than frugal, contented, intelligent, and happy, is not the design of Providence, but springs solely from the weakness, self-indulgence, and perverseness of man himself. The healthy spirit of self-help created amongst working people would more than any other measure serve to raise them as a class, and this, not by pulling down others, but by levelling them up to a higher and still advancing standard of religion, intelligence, and virtue. "All moral philosophy," says Montaigne, "is as applicable to a common and private life as to the most splendid. Every man carries the entire form of the human condition within him."

When a man casts his glance forward, he will find that the three chief temporal contingencies for which he has to provide are want of employment, sickness, and death. The two first he may escape, but the last is inevitable. It is, however, the duty of the prudent man so to live, and so to arrange, that the pressure of suffering, in event of either contingency occurring, shall be mitigated to as great an extent as possible, not only to himself, but also to those who are dependent upon him for their comfort and subsistence. Viewed in this light the honest earning and the frugal use of money are of the greatest importance. Rightly earned, it is the representative of patient industry and untiring effort, of temptation resisted, and hope rewarded ; and rightly used, it affords indications of prudence, fore-thought and self-denial—the true basis of manly character. Though money represents a crowd of objects without any real worth or utility, it also represents many things of great value ; not only food, clothing, and household satisfaction, but personal self-respect and independence. Thus a store of savings is to the working man as a barricade against want ; it secures him a footing, and enables him to wait, it may be in cheerfulness and hope, until better days come round. The very endeavour to gain a firmer position in the world has a certain dignity in it, and tends to make a man stronger and better. At all events it gives him greater freedom of action, and enables him to husband his strength for future effort.

But the man who is always hovering on the verge of want is in a state not far removed from that of slavery. He is in no sense his own master, but is in constant peril of falling under the bondage of others, and accepting the terms which they dictate to him. He cannot help being in a measure, servile, for he dares not look the world boldly in the face ; and in adverse times he must look either to alms or the poor's rates. If work fails him altogether, he has not the means of moving to another field of employment; he is fixed to his parish like a limpet to its rock, and can neither migrate nor emigrate.

To secure independence, the practice of simple economy is all that is necessary. Economy requires neither superior courage nor eminent virtue ; it is satisfied with ordinary energy, and the capacity of average minds. Economy, at bottom, is but the spirit of order applied in the administration of domestic affairs: it means management, regularity, prudence, and the avoidance of waste. The spirit of economy was expressed by our Divine Master in the words ' Gather up the fragments that remain, so that nothing may be lost.' His omnipotence did not disdain the small things of life ; and even while revealing His infinite power to the multitude, he taught the pregnant lesson of carefulness of which all stand so much in need.

Economy also means the power of resisting present gratification for the purpose of securing a future good, and in this light it represents the ascendancy of reason over the animal instincts. It is altogether different from penuriousness : for it is economy that can always best afford to be generous. It does not make money an idol but regards it as a useful agent. As Dean Swift observes, " we must carry money in the head, not in the heart." Economy may be styled the daughter of Prudence, the sister of Temperance, and the mother of Liberty. It is evidently conservative—conservative of character, of domestic happiness, and social well-being. It is, in short, the exhibition of self-help in one of its best forms.

Francis Horner's father gave him this advice on entering life :—" Whilst I wish you to be comfortable in every respect, I cannot too strongly inculcate economy. It is a necessary virtue to all ; and however the shallow part of mankind may despise it, it certainly leads to independence, which is a grand object to every man of a high spirit." Burns' lines, quoted at the head of this chapter, contain the right idea ; but unhappily his strain of song was higher than his practice ; his ideal better than his habit. When laid on his death-bed he wrote to a friend, " Alas ! Clarke, I begin to feel the worst. Burns' poor widow, and half a dozen of his dear little ones helpless orphans ;—there I am weak as a woman's tear. Enough of this ;—'tis half my disease."

Every man ought so to contrive as to live within his means. This practice is of the very essence of honesty. For if a man do not manage honestly to live within his own means, he must necessarily be living dishonestly upon the means of somebody else. Those who are careless about personal expenditure, and consider merely their own gratification, without regard for the comfort of others, generally find out the real uses of money when it is too late. Though by nature generous, these thriftless persons are often driven in the end to do very shabby things. They waste their money as they do their time ; draw bills upon the future ; anticipate their earnings ; and are thus under the necessity of dragging after them a load of debts and obligations which seriously affect their action as free and independent men.

It was a maxim of Lord Bacon, that when it was necessary to economize, it was better to look after petty savings than to descend to petty gettings. The loose cash which many persons throw away uselessly, and worse, would often form a basis of fortune and independence for life. These wasters are their own worst enemies, though generally found amongst the ranks of those who rail at the injustice of " the world." But if a man will not be his own friend, how can he expect that others will? Orderly men of moderate means have always something left in their pockets to help others ; whereas your prodigal and careless fellows who spend all never find an opportunity for helping anybody. It is poor economy, however, to be a scrub. Narrowmindedness in living and in dealing is generally short-sighted, and leads to failure. The penny soul, it is said, never came to twopence. Generosity and liberality, like honesty, prove the best policy after all. Though Jenkinson, in the 'Vicar of Wakefield,' cheated his kind-hearted neighbour Flamborough in one way or another every year, " Flamborough," said he, " has been regularly growing in riches, while I have come to poverty and a gaol." And practical life abounds in cases of brilliant results from a course of generous and honest policy.

The proverb says that "an empty bag cannot stand upright;" neither can a man who is in debt. It is also difficult for a man who is in debt to be truthful; hence it is said that lying rides on debt's back. The debtor has to frame excuses to his creditor for postponing payment of the money he owes him; and probably also to contrive falsehoods. It is easy enough for a man who will exercise a healthy resolution, to avoid incurring the first obligation; but the facility with which that has been incurred often becomes a temptation to a second; and very soon the unfortunate borrower becomes so entangled that no late exertion of industry can set him free. The first step in debt is like the first step in falsehood; almost involving the necessity of proceeding in the same course, debt following debt, as lie follows lie. Haydon, the painter, dated his decline from the day on which he first borrowed money. He realized the truth of the proverb, "Who goes a-borrowing, goes a-sorrowing." The significant entry in his diary is: "Here began debt and obligation, out of which I have never been and never shall be extricated as long as I live." His Autobiography shows but too painfully how embarrassment in money matters produces poignant distress of mind, utter incapacity for work, and constantly recurring humiliations. The written advice which he gave to a youth when entering the navy was as follows: "Never purchase any enjoyment if it cannot be procured without borrowing of others. Never borrow money: it is degrading. I do not say never lend, but never lend if by lending you render yourself unable to pay what you owe; but under any circumstances never borrow." Fichte, the poor student, refused to accept even presents from his still poorer parents.

Dr. Johnson held that early debt is ruin. His words on the subject are weighty, and worthy of being held in remembrance. "Do not," said he, "accustom yourself to consider debt only as an inconvenience; you will find it a calamity. Poverty takes away so many means of doing good, and produces so much inability to resist evil, both natural and moral, that it is by all virtuous means to be avoided. . . . Let it be your first care, then, not to be in any man's debt. Resolve not to be poor; whatever you have spend less. Poverty is a great enemy to human happiness; it certainly destroys liberty, and it makes some virtues impracticable and others extremely difficult. Frugality is not only the basis of quiet, but of beneficence. No man can help others that wants help himself; we must have enough before we have to spare."

It is the bounden duty of every man to look his affairs in the face, and to keep an account of his incomings and outgoings in money matters. The exercise of a little simple arithmetic in this way will be found of great value. Prudence requires that we shall pitch our scale of living a degree below our means, rather than up to them; but this can only be done by carrying out faithfully a plan of living by which both ends may be made to meet. John Locke strongly advised this course: "Nothing," said he "is likelier to keep a man within compass than having constantly before his eyes the state of his affairs in a regular course of account." The Duke of Wellington kept an accurate detailed account of all the monies received and expended by him. "I make a point," said he to Mr. Gleig, "of paying my own bills, and I advise every one to do the same; formerly I used to trust a confidential servant to pay them, but I was cured of that folly by receiving one morning, to my great surprise, duns of a year or two's standing. The fellow had speculated with my money, and left my bills unpaid." Talking of debt his remark was,

"It makes a slave of a man. I have often known what it was to be in want of money, but I never got into debt." Washington was as particular as Wellington was, in matters of business detail; and it is a remarkable fact, that he did not disdain to scrutinize the smallest outgoings of his household—determined as he was to live honestly within his means—even while holding the high office of President of the American Union.

Admiral Jervis, Earl St. Vincent, has told the story of his early struggles, and, amongst other things, of his determination to keep out of debt. "My father had a very large family," said he, "with limited means. He gave me twenty pounds at starting, and that was all he ever gave me. After I had been a considerable time at the station [at sea], I drew for twenty more, but the bill came back protested. I was mortified at this rebuke, and made a promise, which I have ever kept, that I would never draw another bill without a certainty of its being paid. I immediately changed my mode of living, quitted my mess, lived alone, and took up the ship's allowance, which I found quite sufficient; washed and mended my own clothes; made a pair of trousers out of the ticking of my bed; and having by these means saved as much money as would redeem my honour, I took up my bill, and from that time to this I have taken care to keep within my means." Jervis for six years endured pinching privation, but preserved his integrity, studied his profession with success, and gradually and steadily rose by merit and bravery to the highest rank.

Mr. Hume hit the mark when he once stated in the House of Commons—though his words were followed by "laughter"—that the tone of living in England is altogether too high. Middle-class people are too apt to live up to their incomes, if not beyond them: affecting a degree of "style" which is most unhealthy in its effects upon society at large. There is an ambition to bring up boys as gentlemen, or rather "genteel" men; though the result frequently is, only to make them gents. They acquire a taste for dress, style, luxuries, and amusements, which can never form any solid foundation for manly or gentlemanly character; and the result is, that we have a vast number of gingerbread young gentry thrown upon the world, who remind one of the abandoned hulls sometimes picked up at sea, with only a monkey on board.

There is a dreadful ambition abroad for being "genteel." We keep up appearances, too often at the expense of honesty; and, though we may not be rich, yet we must seem to be so. We must be "respectable," though only in the meanest sense—in mere vulgar outward show. We have not the courage to go patiently onward in the condition of life in which it has pleased God to call us; but must needs live in some fashionable state to which we ridiculously please to call ourselves, and all to gratify the vanity of that unsubstantial genteel world of which we form a part. There is a constant struggle and pressure for front seats in the social amphitheatre; in the midst of which all noble self-denying resolve is trodden down, and many fine natures are inevitably crushed to death. What waste, what misery, what bankruptcy, come from all this ambition to dazzle others with the glare of apparent worldly success, we need not describe. The mischievous results show themselves in a thousand ways—in the rank frauds committed by men who dare to be dishonest, but do not dare to seem poor; and in the desperate dashes at fortune, in which the pity is not so much for those who fail, as for the hundreds of innocent families who are so often involved in their ruin.

The late Sir Charles Napier, in taking leave of his command in India, did a bold and honest thing in publishing his strong protest, embodied in his last General

Order to the officers of the Indian army, against the "fast" life led by so many young officers in that service, involving them in ignominious obligations. Sir Charles strongly urged, in that famous document—what had almost been lost sight of—that "honesty is inseparable from the character of a thorough-bred gentleman ;" and that "to drink unpaid-for champagne and unpaid-for beer, and to ride unpaid-for horses, is to be a cheat, and not a gentleman." Men who lived beyond their means and were summoned, often by their own servants, before Courts of Requests for debts contracted in extravagant living, might be officers by virtue of their commissions, but they were not gentlemen. The habit of being constantly in debt, the Commander-in-chief held, made men grow callous to the proper feelings of a gentleman. It was not enough that an officer should be able to fight: that any bull-dog could do. But did he hold his word inviolate?— did he pay his debts? These were among the points of honour which, he insisted, illuminated the true gentleman's and soldier's career. As Bayard was of old, so would Sir Charles Napier have all British officers to be. He knew them to be "without fear," but he would also have them "without reproach." There are, however, many gallant young fellows, both in India and at home, capable of mounting a breach on an emergency amidst belching fire, and of performing the most desperate deeds of valour, who nevertheless cannot or will not exercise the moral courage necessary to enable them to resist a petty temptation presented to their senses. They cannot utter their valiant " No," or " I can't afford it," to the invitations of pleasure and self-enjoyment ; and they are found ready to brave death rather than the ridicule of their companions.

The young man, as he passes through life, advances through a long line of tempters ranged on either side of him ; and the inevitable effect of yielding, is degradation in a greater or a less degree. Contact with them tends insensibly to draw away from him some portion of the divine electric element with which his nature is charged; and his only mode of resisting them is to utter and to act out his "no" manfully and resolutely. He must decide at once, not waiting to deliberate and balance reasons; for the youth, like "the woman who deliberates, is lost." Many deliberate, without deciding; but "not to resolve, *is* to resolve." A perfect knowledge of man is in the prayer, "Lead us not into temptation." But temptation will come to try the young man's strength; and once yielded to, the power to resist grows weaker and weaker. Yield once, and a portion of virtue has gone. Resist manfully, and the first decision will give strength for life; repeated, it will become a habit. It is in the outworks of the habits formed in early life that the real strength of the defence must lie; for it has been wisely ordained, that the machinery of moral existence should be carried on principally through the medium of the habits, so as to save the wear and tear of the great principles within. It is good habits, which insinuate themselves into the thousand inconsiderable acts of life, that really constitute by far the greater part of man's moral conduct.

Hugh Miller has told how, by an act of youthful decision, he saved himself from one of the strong temptations so peculiar to a life of toil. When employed as a mason, it was usual for his fellow-workmen to have an occasional treat of drink, and one day two glasses of whisky fell to his share, which he swallowed. When he reached home, he found, on opening his favourite book—'Bacon's Essays' —that the letters danced before his eyes, and that he could no longer master the sense. "The condition," he says, "into which I had brought myself was, I felt, one of degradation. I had sunk, by my own act, for the time, to a lower level of intelligence than that on which it was my privilege to be placed; and though the state could have been no very favourable one for forming a resolution, I in that hour determined that I should never again sacrifice my capacity of intellectual enjoyment to a drinking usage; and, with God's help, I was enabled to hold by the determination." It is such decisions as this that often form the turning-points in a man's life, and furnish the foundation of his future character. And this rock, on which Hugh Miller might have been wrecked, if he had not at the right moment put forth his moral strength to strike away from it, is one that youth and manhood alike need to be constantly on their guard against. It is about one of the worst and most deadly, as well as extravagant, temptations which lie in the way of youth. Sir Walter Scott used to say that "of all vices drinking is the most incompatible with greatness." Not only so, but it is incompatible with economy, decency, health, and honest living. When a youth cannot restrain, he must abstain. Dr. Johnson's case is the case of many. He said, referring to his own habits, "Sir, I can abstain; but I can't be moderate."

But to wrestle vigorously and successfully with any vicious habit, we must not merely be satisfied with contending on the low ground of worldly prudence, though that is of use, but take stand upon a higher moral elevation. Mechanical aids, such as pledges, may be of service to some, but the great thing is to set up a high standard of thinking and acting, and endeavour to strengthen and purify the principles as well as to reform the habits. For this purpose a youth must study himself, watch his steps, and compare his thoughts and acts with his rule. The more knowledge of himself he gains, the more humble will he be, and perhaps the less confident in his own strength. But the discipline will be always found most valuable which is acquired by resisting

small present gratifications to secure a prospective greater
and higher one.   It is the noblest work in self-education,
—for

> " Real glory
> Springs from the silent conquest of ourselves,
> And without that the conqueror is nought
> But the first slave."

Many popular books have been written for the purpose
of communicating to the public the grand secret of making
money.   But there is no secret whatever about it, as the
proverbs of every nation abundantly testify.   " Take care
of the pennies and the pounds will take care of themselves."
" Diligence is the mother of good luck."   " No pains no
gains."   " No sweat no sweet."   "Work and thou shalt
have."   " The world is his who has patience and industry."
" Better go to bed supperless than rise in debt."   Such
are specimens of the proverbial philosophy, embodying the
hoarded experience of many generations, as to the best
means of thriving in the world.   They were current in
people's mouths long before books were invented; and like
other popular proverbs they were the first codes of popular
morals.   Moreover they have stood the test of time, and the
experience of every day still bears witness to their accuracy,
force, and soundness.   The proverbs of Solomon are full
of wisdom as to the force of industry, and the use and abuse
of money :—" He that is slothful in work is brother to him
that is a great waster."   " Go to the ant thou sluggard; consider her ways, and be wise."   Poverty, says the preacher,
shall come upon the idler, " as one that travelleth, and want
as an armed man ;" but of the industrious and upright, " the
hand of the diligent maketh rich."   " The drunkard and the
glutton shall come to poverty ; and drowsiness shall clothe
a man with rags."   "Seest thou a man diligent in his
business? he shall stand before kings."   But above all,
" It is better to get wisdom than gold ; for wisdom is better

than rubies, and all the things that may be desired are not to be compared to it."

Simple industry and thrift will go far towards making any person of ordinary working faculty comparatively independent in his means. Even a working man may be so, provided he will carefully husband his resources, and watch the little outlets of useless expenditure. A penny is a very small matter, yet the comfort of thousands of families depends upon the proper spending and saving of pennies. If a man allows the little pennies, the results of his hard work, to slip out of his fingers—some to the beershop, some this way and some that—he will find that his life is little raised above one of mere animal drudgery. On the other hand, if he take care of the pennies—putting some weekly into a benefit society or an insurance fund, others into a savings' bank, and confiding the rest to his wife to be carefully laid out, with a view to the comfortable maintenance and education of his family—he will soon find that this attention to small matters will abundantly repay him, in increasing means, growing comfort at home, and a mind comparatively free from fears as to the future. And if a working man have high ambition and possess richness in spirit,—a kind of wealth which far transcends all mere worldly possessions—he may not only help himself, but be a profitable helper of others in his path through life. That this is no impossible thing even for a common labourer in a workshop, may be illustrated by the remarkable career of Thomas Wright of Manchester, who not only attempted but succeeded in the reclamation of many criminals while working for weekly wages in a foundry.

Accident first directed Thomas Wright's attention to the difficulty encountered by liberated convicts in returning to habits of honest industry. His mind was shortly possessed by the subject ; and to remedy the evil became the purpose of his life. Though he worked from six in the morning till six at night, still there were leisure minutes that he could call his own—more especially his Sundays—and these he employed in the service of convicted criminals; a class then far more neglected than they are now. But a few minutes a day, well employed, can effect a great deal; and it will scarcely be credited, that in ten years this working man, by steadfastly holding to his purpose, succeeded in rescuing not fewer than three hundred felons from continuance in a life of villany! He came to be regarded as the moral physician of the Manchester Old Bailey; and where the Chaplain and all others failed, Thomas Wright often succeeded. Children he thus restored reformed to their parents; sons and daughters otherwise lost, to their homes; and many a returned convict did he contrive to settle down to honest and industrious pursuits. The task was by no means easy. It required money, time, energy, prudence, and above all, character, and the confidence which character invariably inspires. The most remarkable circumstance was that Wright relieved many of these poor outcasts out of the comparatively small wages earned by him at foundry work. He did all this on an income which did not average, during his working career, 100*l.* per annum; and yet, while he was able to bestow substantial aid on criminals, to whom he owed no more than the service of kindness which every human being owes to another, he also maintained his family in comfort, and was, by frugality and carefulness, enabled to lay by a store of savings against his approaching old age. Every week he apportioned his income with deliberate care; so much for the indispensable necessaries of food and clothing, so much for the landlord, so much for the schoolmaster, so much for the poor and needy; and the lines of distribution were resolutely observed. By such means did this humble workman pursue his great work, with the results we have so briefly described. Indeed, his career affords one of the most remarkable and striking illustrations of the force of purpose in a man, of the might of small means carefully and sedulously applied, and, above all, of the power which an energetic and upright character invariably exercises upon the lives and conduct of others.

There is no discredit, but honour, in every right walk of industry, whether it be in tilling the ground, making tools, weaving fabrics, or selling the products behind a counter. A youth may handle a yard-stick, or measure a piece of ribbon ; and there will be no discredit in doing so, unless he allows his mind to have no higher range than the stick and ribbon ; to be as short as the one, and as narrow as the other. "Let not those blush who *have,*" said Fuller, "but those who *have not* a lawful calling." And Bishop Hall said, "Sweet is the destiny of all trades, whether of the brow or of the mind." Men who have raised themselves from a humble calling, need not be ashamed, but rather ought to be proud of the difficulties they have surmounted. An American President, when asked what was his coat-of-arms, remembering that he had been a hewer of wood in his youth, replied, "A pair of shirt sleeves." A French doctor once taunted Flechier, Bishop of Nismes, who had been a tallow-chandler in his youth, with the mean- ness of his origin, to which Flechier replied, "If you had been born in the same condition that I was, you would still have been but a maker of candles."

Nothing is more common than energy in money-making, quite independent of any higher object than its accumulation. A man who devotes himself to this pursuit, body and soul, can scarcely fail to become rich. Very little brains will do spend less than you earn ; add guinea to guinea ; scrape and save; and the pile of gold will gradually rise. Osterwald the Parisian banker, began life a poor man. He was ac- customed every evening to drink a pint of beer for supper at a tavern which he visited, during which he collected and pocketed all the corks that he could lay his hands on. In

eight years he had collected as many corks as sold for eight
louis d'ors. With that sum he laid the foundations of his
fortune—gained mostly by stock-jobbing; leaving at his
death some three millions of francs. John Foster has cited
a striking illustration of what this kind of determination will
do in money-making. A young man who ran through his
patrimony, spending it in profligacy, was at length reduced
to utter want and despair. He rushed out of his house
intending to put an end to his life, and stopped on arriving
at an eminence overlooking what were once his estates.
He sat down, ruminated for a time, and rose with the
determination that he would recover them. He returned
to the streets, saw a load of coals which had been shot out
of a cart on to the pavement before a house, offered to
carry them in, and was employed. He thus earned a few
pence, requested some meat and drink as a gratuity, which
was given him, and the pennies were laid by. Pursuing
this menial labour, he earned and saved more pennies;
accumulated sufficient to enable him to purchase some
cattle, the value of which he understood, and these he sold
to advantage. He proceeded by degrees to undertake
larger transactions, until at length he became rich. The
result was, that he more than recovered his possessions, and
died an inveterate miser. When he was buried, mere earth
went to earth. With a nobler spirit, the same determination
might have enabled such a man to be a benefactor to others
as well as to himself. But the life and its end in this case
were alike sordid.

To provide for others and for our own comfort and independence in old age, is honourable, and greatly to be commended; but to hoard for mere wealth's sake is the
characteristic of the narrow-souled and the miserly. It is
against the growth of this habit of inordinate saving that
the wise man needs most carefully to guard himself: else,
what in youth was simple economy, may in old age grow into

avarice, and what was a duty in the one case, may become
a vice in the other. It is the *love* of money—not money
itself—which is "the root of evil,"—a love which narrows
and contracts the soul, and closes it against generous life
and action. Hence, Sir Walter Scott makes one of his
characters declare that "the penny siller slew more souls
than the naked sword slew bodies." It is one of the defects
of business too exclusively followed, that it insensibly tends
to a mechanism of character. The business man gets into
a rut, and often does not look beyond it. If he lives for
himself only, he becomes apt to regard other human beings
only in so far as they minister to his ends. Take a leaf
from such men's ledger and you have their life.

Worldly success, measured by the accumulation of money,
is no doubt a very dazzling thing; and all men are naturally
more or less the admirers of worldly success. But though
men of persevering, sharp, dexterous, and unscrupulous
habits, ever on the watch to push opportunities, may and do
"get on" in the world, yet it is quite possible that they may
not possess the slightest elevation of character, nor a particle
of real goodness. He who recognizes no higher logic than
that of the shilling, may become a very rich man, and yet
remain all the while an exceedingly poor creature. For
riches are no proof whatever of moral worth; and their
glitter often serves only to draw attention to the worthless-
ness of their possessor, as the light of the glowworm reveals
the grub.

The manner in which many allow themselves to be sacrificed to their love of wealth reminds one of the cupidity of
the monkey—that caricature of our species. In Algiers, the
Kabyle peasant attaches a gourd, well fixed, to a tree, and
places within it some rice. The gourd has an opening
merely sufficient to admit the monkey's paw. The creature
comes to the tree by night, inserts his paw, and grasps his
booty. He tries to draw it back, but it is clenched, and he

has not the wisdom to unclench it. So there he stands till morning, when he is caught, looking as foolish as may be, though with the prize in his grasp. The moral of this little story is capable of a very extensive application in life.

The power of money is on the whole over-estimated. The greatest things which have been done for the world have not been accomplished by rich men, nor by subscription lists, but by men generally of small pecuniary means. Christianity was propagated over half the world by men of the poorest class; and the greatest thinkers, discoverers, inventors, and artists, have been men of moderate wealth, many of them little raised above the condition of manual labourers in point of worldly circumstances. And it will always be so. Riches are oftener an impediment than a stimulus to action; and in many cases they are quite as much a misfortune as a blessing. The youth who inherits wealth is apt to have life made too easy for him, and he soon grows sated with it, because he has nothing left to desire. Having no special object to struggle for, he finds time hang heavy on his hands; he remains morally and spiritually asleep; and his position in society is often no higher than that of a polypus over which the tide floats.

> " His only labour is to kill the time,
> And labour dire it is, and weary woe."

Yet the rich man, inspired by a right spirit, will spurn idleness as unmanly; and if he bethink himself of the responsibilities which attach to the possession of wealth and property he will feel even a higher call to work than men of humbler lot. This, however, must be admitted to be by no means the practice of life. The golden mean of Agur's perfect prayer is, perhaps, the best lot of all, did we but know it: "Give me neither poverty nor riches; feed me with food convenient for me." The late Joseph Brotherton, M.P., left a fine motto to be recorded upon his monument in

the Peel Park at Manchester,—the declaration in his case
being strictly true: "My richness consisted not in the
greatness of my possessions, but in the smallness of my
wants." He rose from the humblest station, that of a factory
boy, to an eminent position of usefulness, by the simple
exercise of homely honesty, industry, punctuality, and self-
denial. Down to the close of his life, when not attending
Parliament, he did duty as minister in a small chapel in
Manchester to which he was attached; and in all things he
made it appear, to those who knew him in private life, that
the glory he sought was *not* " to be seen of men," or to excite
their praise, but to earn the consciousness of discharging the
every-day duties of life, down to the smallest and humblest
of them, in an honest, upright, truthful, and loving spirit.

"Respectability," in its best sense, is good. The respectable man is one worthy of regard, literally worth turning to look at. But the respectability that consists in
merely keeping up appearances is not worth looking at in
any sense. Far better and more respectable is the good
poor man than the bad rich one—better the humble silent
man than the agreeable well-appointed rogue who keeps his
gig. A well balanced and well-stored mind, a life full of
useful purpose, whatever the position occupied in it may be,
is of far greater importance than average worldly respectability. The highest object of life we take to be, to form a
manly character, and to work out the best development
possible, of body and spirit—of mind, conscience, heart, and
soul. This is the end: all else ought to be regarded but as
the means. Accordingly, that is not the most successful life
in which a man gets the most pleasure, the most money, the
most power or place, honour or fame; but that in which a
man gets the most manhood, and performs the greatest
amount of useful work and of human duty. Money is power
after its sort, it is true; but intelligence, public spirit, and
moral virtue, are powers too, and far nobler ones. " Let

others plead for pensions," wrote Lord Collingwood to a
friend; "I can be rich without money, by endeavouring to
be superior to everything poor. I would have my services
to my country unstained by any interested motive; and old
Scott * and I can go on in our cabbage-garden without much
greater expense than formerly." On another occasion he
said, "I have motives for my conduct which I would not
give in exchange for a hundred pensions."

The making of a fortune may no doubt enable some
people to "enter society," as it is called; but to be es-
teemed there, they must possess qualities of mind, manners,
or heart, else they are merely rich people, nothing more.
There are men "in society" now, as rich as Crœsus, who
have no consideration extended towards them, and elicit no
respect.   For why?   They are but as money-bags: their
only power is in their till.   The men of mark in society—
the guides and rulers of opinion—the really successful and
useful men—are not necessarily rich men; but men of
sterling character, of disciplined experience, and of moral
excellence.   Even the poor man, like Thomas Wright, though
he possess but little of this world's goods, may, in the enjoyment of a cultivated nature, of opportunities used and not
abused, of a life spent to the best of his means and ability,
look down, without the slightest feeling of envy, upon the
person of mere worldly success, the man of money-bags and
acres.

* His old gardener.   Collingwood's favourite amusement was gardening.   Shortly after the battle of Trafalgar a brother admiral called
upon him, and, after searching for his lordship all over the garden, he
at last discovered him, with old Scott, in the bottom of a deep trench.
which they were busily employed in digging.

CHAPTER XI.

SELF-CULTURE — FACILITIES AND DIFFICULTIES.

" Every person has two educations, one which he receives from others, and one, more important, which he gives to himself."—*Gibbon.*

"Is there one whom difficulties dishearten—who bends to the storm? He will do little. Is there one who *will* conquer? That kind of man never fails."—*John Hunter.*

" The wise and active conquer difficulties,
By daring to attempt them : sloth and folly
Shiver and shrink at sight of toil and danger,
And *make* the impossibility they fear."—*Rowe.*

" T H E best part of every man's education," said Sir Walter Scott, "is that which he gives to himself." The late Sir Benjamin Brodie delighted to remember this saying, and he used to congratulate himself on the fact that professionally he was self-taught. But this is necessarily the case with all men who have acquired distinction in letters, science, or art. The education received at school or college is but a beginning, and is valuable mainly inasmuch as it trains the mind and habituates it to continuous application and study. That which is put into us by others is always far less ours than that which we acquire by our own diligent and persevering effort. Knowledge conquered by labour becomes a possession—a property entirely our own. A greater vividness and permanency of impression is secured ; and facts thus acquired become registered in the mind in a way that mere imparted information can never effect. This kind of self-culture also calls forth power and cultivates strength. The solution of one problem helps the mastery of another; and thus knowledge is carried into faculty. Our own active effort is the essential thing ; and no facilities, no books, no teachers, no amount of lessons learnt by rote will enable us to dispense with it.

The best teachers have been the readiest to recognise the importance of self-culture, and of stimulating the student to acquire knowledge by the active exercise of his own faculties. They have relied more upon *training* than upon *telling*, and sought to make their pupils themselves active parties to the work in which they were engaged; thus making teaching something far higher than the mere passive reception of the scraps and details of knowledge. This was the spirit in which the great Dr. Arnold worked ; he strove to teach his pupils to rely upon themselves, and develop their powers by their own active efforts, himself merely guiding, directing, stimulating, and encouraging them. " I would far rather," he said, "send a boy to Van Diemen's Land, where he must work for his bread, than send him to Oxford to live in luxury, without any desire in his mind to avail himself of his advantages." " If there be one thing on earth," he observed on another occasion, "which is truly admirable, it is to see God's wisdom blessing an inferiority of natural powers, when they have been honestly, truly, and zealously cultivated." Speaking of a pupil of this character, he said, " I would stand to that man hat in hand." Once at Laleham, when teaching a rather dull boy, Arnold spoke somewhat sharply to him, on which the pupil looked up in his face and said, "Why do you speak angrily, sir? *indeed*, I am doing the best I can." Years afterwards, Arnold used to tell the story to his children, and added, " I never felt so much in my life—that look and that speech I have never forgotten."

From the numerous instances already cited of men of humble station who have risen to distinction in science and

literature, it will be obvious that labour is by no means incompatible with the highest intellectual culture. Work in
moderation is healthy, as well as agreeable to the human
constitution. Work educates the body, as study educates
the mind; and that is the best state of society in which
there is some work for every man's leisure, and some leisure
for every man's work. Even the leisure classes are in a
measure compelled to work, sometimes as a relief from
ennui, but in most cases to gratify an instinct which they
cannot resist. Some go foxhunting in the English counties,
others grouse-shooting on the Scotch hills, while many
wander away every summer to climb mountains in Switzer-
land. Hence the boating, running, cricketting, and athletic
sports of the public schools, in which our young men at the
same time so healthfully cultivate their strength both of mind
and body. It is said that the Duke of Wellington, when
once looking on at the boys engaged in their sports in the
play-ground at Eton, where he had spent many of his own
younger days, made the remark, " It was there that the
battle of Waterloo was won ! "

Daniel Malthus urged his son when at college to be most
diligent in the cultivation of knowledge, but he also enjoined
him to pursue manly sports as the best means of keeping
up the full working power of his mind, as well as of enjoying
the pleasures of intellect. " Every kind of knowledge," said
he, " every acquaintance with nature and art, will amuse
and strengthen your mind, and I am perfectly pleased that
cricket should do the same by your arms and legs; I love
to see you excel in exercises of the body, and I think myself that the better half, and much the most agreeable part,
of the pleasures of the mind is best enjoyed while one is
upon one's legs." But a still more important use of active
employment is that referred to by the great divine, Jeremy
Taylor. " Avoid idleness," he says, " and fill up all the
spaces of thy time with severe and useful employment; for

lust easily creeps in at those emptinesses where the soul is unemployed and the body is at ease; for no easy, healthful, idle person was ever chaste if he could be tempted; but of all employments bodily labour is the most useful, and of the greatest benefit for driving away the devil."

Practical success in life depends more upon physical health than is generally imagined. Hodson, of Hodson's Horse, writing home to a friend in England, said, " I believe, if I get on well in India, it will be owing, physically speaking, to a sound digestion." The capacity for continuous working in any calling must necessarily depend in a great measure upon this; and hence the necessity for attending to health, even as a means of intellectual labour. It is perhaps to the neglect of physical exercise that we find amongst students so frequent a tendency towards discontent, unhappiness, inaction, and reverie,—displaying itself in contempt for real life and disgust at the beaten tracks of men,—a tendency which in England has been called Byronism, and in Germany Wertherism. Dr. Channing noted the same growth in America, which led him to make the remark, that " too many of our young men grow up in a school of despair." The only remedy for this green-sickness in youth is physical exercise—action, work, and bodily occupation.

The use of early labour in self-imposed mechanical employments may be illustrated by the boyhood of Sir Isaac Newton. Though a comparatively dull scholar, he was very assiduous in the use of his saw, hammer, and hatchet— "knocking and hammering in his lodging room"—making models of windmills, carriages, and machines of all sorts; and as he grew older, he took delight in making little tables and cupboards for his friends. Smeaton, Watt, and Stephenson, were equally handy with tools when mere boys; and but for such kind of self-culture in their youth, it is doubtful whether they would have accomplished so much in their manhood. Such was also the early training of the great

inventors and mechanics described in the proceeding pages,
whose contrivance and intelligence were practically trained
by the constant use of their hands in early life. Even
where men belonging to the manual labour class have risen
above it, and become more purely intellectual labourers,
they have found the advantages of their early training in
their later pursuits. Elihu Burritt says he found hard labour
necessary to enable him to study with effect; and more than
once he gave up school-teaching and study, and, taking to
his leather-apron again, went back to his blacksmith's forge
and anvil for his health of body and mind's sake.

The training of young men in the use of tools would, at
the same time that it educated them in " common things,"
teach them the use of their hands and arms, familiarize them
with healthy work, exercise their faculties upon things tangible and actual, give them some practical acquaintance
with mechanics, impart to them the ability of being useful,
and implant in them the habit of persevering physical effort.
This is an advantage which the working classes, strictly so-
called, certainly possess over the leisure classes,—that they
are in early life under the necessity of applying themselves
laboriously to some mechanical pursuit or other,—thus
acquiring manual dexterity and the use of their physical
powers. The chief disadvantage attached to the calling of
the laborious classes is, not that they are employed in
physical work, but that they are too exclusively so employed, often to the neglect of their moral and intellectual
faculties. While the youths of the leisure classes, having
been taught to associate labour with servility, have shunned
it, and been allowed to grow up practically ignorant, the
poorer classes, confining themselves within the circle of
their laborious callings, have been allowed to grow up in
a large proportion of cases absolutely illiterate. It seems
possible, however, to avoid both these evils by combining
physical training or physical work with intellectual culture ;

and there are various signs abroad which seem to mark the gradual adoption of this healthier system of education.

The success of even professional men depends in no slight degree on their physical health ; and a public writer has gone so far as to say that "the greatness of our great men is quite as much a bodily affair as a mental one."* A healthy breathing apparatus is as indispensable to the successful lawyer or politician as a well-cultured intellect. The thorough aëration of the blood by free exposure to a large breathing surface in the lungs, is necessary to maintain that full vital power on which the vigorous working of the brain in so large a measure depends. The lawyer has to climb the heights of his profession through close and heated courts, and the political leader has to bear the fatigue and excitement of long and anxious debates in a crowded House. Hence the lawyer in full practice and the parliamentary leader in full work are called upon to display powers of physical endurance and activity even more extraordinary than those of the intellect,—such powers as have been exhibited in so remarkable a degree by Brougham, Lyndhurst, and Campbell ; by Peel, Grahàm, and Palmerston—all full-chested men.

Though Sir Walter Scott, when at Edinburgh College, went by the name of "The Greek Blockhead," he was, notwithstanding his lameness, a remarkably healthy youth : he could spear a salmon with the best fisher on the Tweed, and ride a wild horse with any hunter in Yarrow. When devoting himself in after life to literary pursuits, Sir Walter never lost his taste for field sports ; but while writing 'Waverley' in the morning, he would in the afternoon course hares. Professor Wilson was a very athlete, as great at throwing the hammer as in his flights of eloquence and poetry ; and Burns, when a youth, was remarkable chiefly for his leaping, putting, and wrestling. Some of our greatest divines were distinguished

* Article in the 'Times.'

in their youth for their physical energies. Isaac Barrow, when at the Charterhouse School, was notorious for his pugilistic encounters, in which he got many a bloody nose ; Andrew Fuller, when working as a farmer's lad at Soham, was chiefly famous for his skill in boxing; and Adam Clarke, when a boy, was only remarkable for the strength displayed by him in " rolling large stones about,"—the secret, possibly, of some of the power which he subsequently displayed in rolling forth large thoughts in his manhood.

While it is necessary, then, in the first place to secure this solid foundation of physical health, it must also be observed that the cultivation of the habit of mental application is quite indispensable for the education of the student. The maxim that "Labour conquers all things" holds especially true in the case of the conquest of knowledge. The road into learning is alike free to all who will give the labour and the study requisite to gather it ; nor are there any difficulties so great that the student of resolute purpose may not surmount and overcome them. It was one of the characteristic expressions of Chatterton, that God had sent his creatures into the world with arms long enough to reach anything if they chose to be at the trouble. In study, as in business, energy is the great thing. There must be the "fervet opus": we must not only strike the iron while it is hot, but strike it till it is made hot. It is astonishing how much may be accomplished in self-culture by the energetic and the persevering, who are careful to avail themselves of opportunities, and use up the fragments of spare time which the idle permit to run to waste. Thus Ferguson learnt astronomy from the heavens, while wrapt in a sheep-skin on the highland hills. Thus Stone learnt mathematics while working as a journeyman gardener; thus Drew studied the highest philosophy in the intervals of cobbling shoes ; and thus Miller taught himself geology while working as a day labourer in a quarry.

Sir Joshua Reynolds, as we have already observed, was
so earnest a believer in the force of industry that he held
that all men might achieve excellence if they would but
exercise the power of assiduous and patient working.   He
held that drudgery lay on the road to genius, and that there
was no limit to the proficiency of an artist except the limit
of his own painstaking.   He would not believe in what is
called inspiration, but only in study and labour.   " Excellence," he said, "is never granted to man but as the reward
of labour."   " If you have great talents, industry will
improve them ; if you have but moderate abilities, industry
will supply their deficiency.   Nothing is denied to well-
directed labour ; nothing is to be obtained without it "   Sir
Fowell Buxton was an equal believer in the power of
study ; and he entertained the modest idea that he could do
as well as other men if he devoted to the pursuit double
the time and labour that they did.   He placed his great
confidence in ordinary means and extraordinary application.

" I have known several men in my life," says Dr. Ross,
" who may be recognized in days to come as men of genius,
and they were all plodders, hard-working, *intent* men.
Genius is known by its works ; genius without works is a
blind faith, a dumb oracle.   But meritorious works are the
result of time and labour, and cannot be accomplished by
intention or by a wish. . . . . Every great work is the result
of vast preparatory training.   Facility comes by labour.
Nothing seems easy, not even walking, that was not difficult
at first.   The orator whose eye flashes instantaneous fire,
and whose lips pour out a flood of noble thoughts, startling
by their unexpectedness, and elevating by their wisdom and
truth, has learned his secret by patient repetition, and after
many bitter disappointments." *

* ' Self-Development: an Address to Students,' by George Ross, M.D.,
pp 1-20, reprinted from the ' Medical Circular.'   This address, to which

Thoroughness and accuracy are two principal points to be aimed at in study. Francis Horner, in laying down rules for the cultivation of his mind, placed great stress upon the habit of continuous application to one subject for the sake of mastering it thoroughly; he confined himself, with this object, to only a few books, and resisted with the greatest firmness "every approach to a habit of desultory reading." The value of knowledge to any man consists not in its quantity, but mainly in the good uses to which he can apply it. Hence a little knowledge, of an exact and perfect character, is always found more valuable for practical purposes than any extent of superficial learning.

One of Ignatius Loyola's maxims was, "He who does well one work at a time, does more than all." By spreading our efforts over too large a surface we inevitably weaken our force, hinder our progress, and acquire a habit of fitfulness and ineffective working. Lord St. Leonards once communicated to Sir Fowell Buxton the mode in which he had conducted his studies, and thus explained the secret of his success. "I resolved," said he, "when beginning to read law, to make everything I acquired perfectly my own, and never to go to a second thing till I had entirely accomplished the first. Many of my competitors read as much in a day as I read in a week; but, at the end of twelve months, my knowledge was as fresh as the day it was acquired, while theirs had glided away from recollection."

It is not the quantity of study that one gets through, or the amount of reading, that makes a wise man; but the appositeness of the study to the purpose for which it is pursued; the concentration of the mind for the time being on the subject under consideration; and the habitual discipline by which the whole system of mental applica-

we acknowledge our obligations, contains many admirable thoughts on self-culture, is thoroughly healthy in its tone, and well deserves republication in an enlarged form.

tion is regulated. Abernethy was even of opinion that there was a point of saturation in his own mind, and that if he took into it something more than it could hold, it only had the effect of pushing something else out. Speaking of the study of medicine, he said, "If a man has a clear idea of what he desires to do, he will seldom fail in selecting the proper means of accomplishing it."

The most profitable study is that which is conducted with a definite aim and object. By thoroughly mastering any given branch of knowledge we render it more available for use at any moment. Hence it is not enough merely to have books, or to know where to read for information as we want it. Practical wisdom, for the purposes of life, must be carried about with us, and be ready for use at call. It is not sufficient that we have a fund laid up at home, but not a farthing in the pocket: we must carry about with us a store of the current coin of knowledge ready for exchange on all occasions, else we are comparatively helpless when the opportunity for using it occurs.

Decision and promptitude are as requisite in self-culture as in business. The growth of these qualities may be encouraged by accustoming young people to rely upon their own resources, leaving them to enjoy as much freedom of action in early life as is practicable. Too much guidance and restraint hinder the formation of habits of self-help. They are like bladders tied under the arms of one who has not taught himself to swim. Want of confidence is perhaps a greater obstacle to improvement than is generally imagined. It has been said that half the failures in life arise from pulling in one's horse while he is leaping. Dr. Johnson was accustomed to attribute his success to confidence in his own powers. True modesty is quite compatible with a due estimate of one's own merits, and does not demand the abnegation of all merit. Though there are those who deceive themselves by putting a false figure before their ciphers, the want of confidence, the want of faith in one's self, and consequently the want of promptitude in action, is a defect of character which is found to stand very much in the way of individual progress; and the reason why so little is done, is generally because so little is attempted.

There is usually no want of desire on the part of most persons to arrive at the results of self-culture, but there is a great aversion to pay the inevitable price for it, of hard work. Dr. Johnson held that "impatience of study was the mental disease of the present generation;" and the remark is still applicable. We may not believe that there is a royal road to learning, but we seem to believe very firmly in a "popular" one. In education, we invent labour-saving processes, seek short cuts to science, learn French and Latin "in twelve lessons," or "without a master." We resemble the lady of fashion, who engaged a master to teach her on condition that he did not plague her with verbs and participles. We get our smattering of science in the same way; we learn chemistry by listening to a short course of lectures enlivened by experiments, and when we have inhaled laughing gas, seen green water turned to red, and phosphorus burnt in oxygen, we have got our smattering, of which the most that can be said is, that though it may be better than nothing, it is yet good for nothing. Thus we often imagine we are being educated while we are only being amused. .

The facility with which young people are thus induced to acquire knowledge, without study and labour, is not education. It occupies but does not enrich the mind. It imparts a stimulus for the time, and produces a sort of intellectual keenness and cleverness; but, without an implanted purpose and a higher object than mere pleasure, it will bring with it no solid advantage. In such cases knowledge produces but a passing impression; a sensation,

but no more; it is, in fact, the merest epicurism of intelligence—sensuous, but certainly not intellectual. Thus the
best qualities of many minds, those which are evoked by
vigorous effort and independent action, sleep a deep sleep,
and are often never called to life, except by the rough
awakening of sudden calamity or suffering, which, in such
cases, comes as a blessing, if it serves to rouse up a
courageous spirit that, but for it, would have slept on.

Accustomed to acquire information under the guise of
amusement, young people will soon reject that which is
presented to them under the aspect of study and labour.
Learning their knowledge and science in sport, they will
be too apt to make sport of both; while the habit of intellectual dissipation, thus engendered, cannot fail, in course of
time, to produce a thoroughly emasculating effect both upon
their mind and character. "Multifarious reading," said
Robertson of Brighton, "weakens the mind like smoking,
and is an excuse for its lying dormant. It is the idlest
of all idlenesses, and leaves more of impotency than any
other."

The evil is a growing one, and operates in various ways.
Its least mischief is shallowness; its greatest, the aversion
to steady labour which it induces, and the low and feeble
tone of mind which it encourages. If we would be really
wise, we must diligently apply ourselves, and confront the
same continuous application which our forefathers did; for
labour is still, and ever will be, the inevitable price set upon
everything which is valuable. We must be satisfied to work
with a purpose, and wait the results with patience. All
progress, of the best kind, is slow; but to him who works
faithfully and zealously the reward will, doubtless, be vouch-
safed in good time. The spirit of industry, embodied in
a man's daily life, will gradually lead him to exercise his
powers on objects outside himself, of greater dignity and
more extended usefulness. And still we must labour on;

for the work of self-culture is never finished. "To be employed," said the poet Gray, "is to be happy." "It is better to wear out than rust out," said Bishop Cumberland. "Have we not all eternity to rest in ?" exclaimed Arnauld. "Repos ailleurs" was the motto of Marnix de St. Aldegonde, the energetic and ever-working friend of William the Silent.

It is the use we make of the powers entrusted to us, which constitutes our only just claim to respect. He who employs his one talent aright is as much to be honoured as he to whom ten talents have been given. There is really no more personal merit attaching to the possession of superior intellectual powers than there is in the succession to a large estate. How are those powers used—how is that estate employed? The mind may accumulate large stores of knowledge without any useful purpose ; but the knowledge must be allied to goodness and wisdom, and embodied in upright character, else it is naught. Pestalozzi even held intellectual training by itself to be pernicious ; insisting that the roots of all knowledge must strike and feed in the soil of the rightly-governed will. The acquisition of know-ledge may, it is true, protect a man against the meaner felonies of life ; but not in any degree against its selfish vices, unless fortified by sound principles and habits. Hence do we find in daily life so many instances of men who are well-informed in intellect, but utterly deformed in character ; filled with the learning of the schools, yet pos-sessing little practical wisdom, and offering examples for warning rather than imitation. An often quoted expression at this day is that " Knowledge is power ;" but so also are fanaticism, despotism, and ambition. Knowledge of itself, unless wisely directed, might merely make bad men more dangerous, and the society in which it was regarded as the highest good, little better than a pandemonium.

It is possible that at this day we may even exaggerate the importance of literary culture. We are apt to imagine that because we possess many libraries, institutes, and museums, we are making great progress. But such facilities may as often be a hindrance as a help to individual self-culture of the highest kind. The possession of a library, or the free use of it, no more constitutes learning, than the possession of wealth constitutes generosity. Though we undoubtedly possess great facilities it is nevertheless true, as of old, that wisdom and understanding can only become the possession of individual men by travelling the old road of observation, attention, perseverance, and industry. The possession of the mere materials of knowledge is something very different from wisdom and understanding, which are reached through a higher kind of discipline than that of reading,—which is often but a mere passive reception of other men's thoughts ; there being little or no active effort of mind in the transaction. Then how much of our reading is but the indulgence of a sort of intellectual dram-drinking, imparting a grateful excitement for the moment, without the slightest effect in improving and enriching the mind or building up the character. Thus many indulge themselves in the conceit that they are cultivating their minds, when they are only employed in the humbler occupation of killing time, of which perhaps the best that can be said is that it keeps them from doing worse things.

It is also to be borne in mind that the experience gathered from books, though often valuable, is but of the nature of *learning;* whereas the experience gained from actual life is of the nature of *wisdom;* and a small store of the latter is worth vastly more than any stock of the former. Lord Bolingbroke truly said that "Whatever study tends neither directly nor indirectly to make us better men and citizens, is at best but a specious and ingenious sort of idleness, and the knowledge we acquire by it, only a creditable kind of ignorance—nothing more."

Useful and instructive though good reading may be, it is

yet only one mode of cultivating the mind ; and is much less influential than practical experience and good example in the formation of character. There were wise, valiant, and true-hearted men bred in England, long before the existence of a reading public. Magna Charta was secured by men who signed the deed with their marks. Though altogether unskilled in the art of deciphering the literary signs by which principles were denominated upon paper, they yet understood and appreciated, and boldly contended for, the things themselves. Thus the foundations of English liberty were laid by men, who, though illiterate, were nevertheless of the very highest stamp of character. And it must be admitted that the chief object of culture is, not merely to fill the mind with other men's thoughts, and to be the passive recipient of their impressions of things, but to enlarge our individual intelligence, and render us more useful and efficient workers in the sphere of life to which we may be called. Many of our most energetic and useful workers have been but sparing readers. Brindley and Stephenson did not learn to read and write until they reached manhood, and yet they did great works and lived manly lives ; John Hunter could barely read or write when he was twenty years old, though he could make tables and chairs with any carpenter in the trade. "I never read," said the great physiologist when lecturing before his class ; "this" —pointing to some part of the subject before him—"this is the work that you must study if you wish to become eminent in your profession." When told that one of his contemporaries had charged him with being ignorant of the dead languages, he said, "I would undertake to teach him that on the dead body which he never knew in any language, dead or living."

It is not then how much a man may know, that is of importance, but the end and purpose for which he knows it. The object of knowledge should be to mature wisdom and improve character, to render us better, happier, and more useful; more benevolent, more energetic, and more efficient in the pursuit of every high purpose in life. "When people once fall into the habit of admiring and encouraging ability as such, without reference to moral character—and religious and political opinions are the concrete form of moral character—they are on the highway to all sorts of degradation." * We must ourselves *be* and *do*, and not rest satisfied merely with reading and meditating over what other men have been and done. Our best light must be made life, and our best thought action. At least we ought to be able to say, as Richter did, "I have made as much out of myself as could be made of the stuff, and no man should require more;" for it is every man's duty to discipline and guide himself, with God's help, according to his responsibilties and the faculties with which he has been endowed.

Self-discipline and self-control are the beginnings of practical wisdom; and these must have their root in self-respect. Hope springs from it—hope, which is the companion of power, and the mother of success; for whoso hopes strongly has within him the gift of miracles. The humblest may say, "To respect myself, to develop myself—this is my true duty in life. An integral and responsible part of the great system of society, I owe it to society and to its Author not to degrade or destroy either my body, mind, or instincts. On the contrary, I am bound to the best of my power to give to those parts of my constitution the highest degree of perfection possible. I am not only to suppress the evil, but to evoke the good elements in my nature. And as I respect myself, so am I equally bound to respect others, as they on their part are bound to respect me." Hence mutual respect, justice, and order, of which law becomes the written record and guarantee.

Self-respect is the noblest garment with which a man

* 'Saturday Review.'

may clothe himself—the most elevating feeling with which the mind can be inspired. One of Pythagoras's wisest maxims, in his 'Golden Verses,' is that with which he enjoins the pupil to "reverence himself." Borne up by this high idea, he will not defile his body by sensuality, nor his mind by servile thoughts. This sentiment, carried into daily life, will be found at the root of all the virtues—cleanliness, sobriety, chastity, morality, and religion. "The pious and just honouring of ourselves," said Milton, "may be thought the radical moisture and fountain-head from whence every laudable and worthy enterprise issues forth." To think meanly of one's self, is to sink in one's own estimation as well as in the estimation of others. And as the thoughts are, so will the acts be. Man cannot aspire if he look down ; if he will rise, he must look up. The very humblest may be sustained by the proper indulgence of this feeling. Poverty itself may be lifted and lighted up by self-respect ; and it is truly a noble sight to see a poor man hold himself upright amidst his temptations, and refuse to demean himself by low actions.

One way in which self-culture may be degraded is by regarding it too exclusively as a means of "getting on." Viewed in this light, it is unquestionable that education is one of the best investments of time and labour. In any line of life, intelligence will enable a man to adapt himself more readily to circumstances, suggest improved methods of working, and render him more apt, skilled and effective in all respects. He who works with his head as well as his hands, will come to look at his business with a clearer eye ; and he will become conscious of increasing power—perhaps the most cheering consciousness the human mind can cherish. The power of self-help will gradually grow ; and in proportion to a man's self-respect, will he be armed against the temptation of low indulgences. Society and its action will be regarded with quite a new interest, his sympathies will widen and enlarge, and he will thus be attracted to work for others as well as for himself.

Self-culture may not, however end in eminence, as in the numerous instances above cited. The great majority of men, in all times, however enlightened, must necessarily be engaged in the ordinary avocations of industry; and no degree of culture which can be conferred upon the community at large will ever enable them—even were it desirable, which it is not—to get rid of the daily work of society, which must be done. But this, we think, may also be accomplished. We can elevate the condition of labour by allying it to noble thoughts, which confer a grace upon the lowliest as well as the highest rank. For no matter how poor or humble a man may be, the great thinker of this and other days may come in and sit down with him, and be his companion for the time, though his dwelling be the meanest hut. It is thus that the habit of well-directed reading may become a source of the greatest pleasure and self-improvement, and exercise a gentle coercion, with the most beneficial results, over the whole tenour of a man's character and conduct. And even though self-culture may not bring wealth, it will at all events give one the companionship of elevated thoughts. A nobleman once contemptuously asked of a sage, "What have you got by all your philosophy?" "At least I have got society in myself," was the wise man's reply.

But many are apt to feel despondent, and become discouraged in the work of self-culture, because they do not "get on" in the world so fast as they think they deserve to do. Having planted their acorn, they expect to see it grow into an oak at once. They have perhaps looked upon knowledge in the light of a marketable commodity, and are consequently mortified because it does not sell as they expected it would do. Mr. Tremenheere, in one of his 'Education Reports' (for 1840-1) states that a schoolmaster in Norfork, finding his school rapidly falling off, made inquiry into the cause, and ascertained that the reason given by the majority of the parents for withdrawing their children was, that they had expected "education was to make them better off than they were before," but that having found it had "done them no good," they had taken their children from school, and would give themselves no further trouble about education !

The same low idea of self-culture is but too prevalent in other classes, and is encouraged by the false views of life which are always more or less current in society. But to regard self-culture either as a means of getting past others in the world, or of intellectual dissipation and amusement, rather than as a power to elevate the character and expand the spiritual nature, is to place it on a very low level. To use the words of Bacon, "Knowledge is not a shop for profit or sale, but a rich storehouse for the glory of the Creator and the relief of man's estate." It is doubtless most honourable for a man to labour to elevate himself, and to better his condition in society, but this is not to be done at the sacrifice of himself. To make the mind the mere drudge of the body, is putting it to a very servile use ; and to go about whining and bemoaning our pitiful lot because we fail in achieving that success in life which, after all, depends rather upon habits of industry and attention to business details than upon knowledge, is the mark of a small, and often of a sour mind. Such a temper cannot better be reproved than in the words of Robert Southey, who thus wrote to a friend who sought his counsel : " I would give you advice if it could be of use ; but there is no curing those who choose to be diseased. A good man and a wise man may at times be angry with the world, at times grieved for it ; but be sure no man was ever discontented with the world if he did his duty in it. If a man of education, who has health, eyes, hands, and leisure, wants an object, it is only because God Almighty has bestowed all those blessings upon a man who does not deserve them."

Another way in which education may be prostituted is by employing it as a mere means of intellectual dissipation and amusement. Many are the ministers to this taste in our time. There is almost a mania for frivolity and excitement, which exhibits itself in many forms in our popular literature. To meet the public taste, our books and periodicals must now be highly spiced, amusing, and comic, not disdaining slang, and illustrative of breaches of all laws, human and divine. Douglas Jerrold once observed of this tendency, " I am convinced the world will get tired (at least I hope so) of this eternal guffaw about all things. After all, life has something serious in it. It cannot be all a comic history of humanity. Some men, would, I believe, write a Comic Sermon on the Mount. Think of a Comic History of England, the drollery of Alfred, the fun of Sir Thomas More, the farce of his daughter begging the dead head and clasping it in her coffin on her bosom. Surely the world will be sick of this blasphemy." John Sterling, in a like spirit, said :— " Periodicals and novels are to all in this generation, but more especially to those whose minds are still unformed and in the process of formation, a new and more effectual substitute for the plagues of Egypt, vermin that corrupt the wholesome waters and infest our chambers."

As a rest from toil and a relaxation from graver pursuits, the perusal of a well-written story, by a writer of genius, is a high intellectual pleasure ; and it is a description of literature to which all classes of readers, old and young, are attracted as by a powerful instinct ; nor would we have any of them debarred from its enjoyment in a reasonable degree. But to make it the exclusive literary diet, as some do,—to devour the garbage with which the shelves of circulating libraries are filled,—and to occupy the greater portion of the leisure hours in studying the preposterous pictures of human life which so many of them present, is worse than waste of time : it is positively pernicious. The habitual novel-reader indulges in fictitious feelings so much, that there is great risk of sound and healthy feeling becoming perverted or benumbed. " I never go to hear a tragedy," said a gay man once to the Archbishop of York, "it wears my heart out." The literary pity evoked by fiction leads to no corresponding action ; the susceptibilities which it excites involve neither inconvenience nor self-sacrifice ; so that the heart that is touched too often by the fiction may at length become insensible to the reality. The steel is gradually rubbed out of the character, and it insensibly loses its vital spring. "Drawing fine pictures of virtue in one's mind," said Bishop Butler, " is so far from necessarily or certainly conducive to form a *habit* of it in him who thus employs himself, that it may even harden the mind in a contrary course, and render it gradually more insensible."

Amusement in moderation is wholesome, and to be com mended ; but amusement in excess vitiates the whole nature, and is a thing to be carefully guarded against. The maxim is often quoted of " All work and no play makes Jack a dull boy ; " but all play and no work makes him something greatly worse. Nothing can be more hurtful to a youth than to have his soul sodden with pleasure. The best qualities of his mind are impaired ; common enjoyments become taste-less ; his appetite for the higher kind of pleasures is vitiated ; and when he comes to face the work and the duties of life, the result is usually aversion and disgust. " Fast" men waste and exhaust the powers of life, and dry up the sources of true happiness. Having forestalled their spring, they can produce no healthy growth of either character or intellect. A child without simplicity, a maiden without innocence, a boy without truthfulness, are not more piteous sights than the man who has wasted and thrown away his youth in self-indulgence. Mirabeau said of himself, " My early years' have already in a great measure disinherited the succeeding ones, and dissipated a great part of my vital powers." As the wrong done to another to-day returns upon ourselves to-morrow, so the sins of our youth rise up in our age to scourge us. When Lord Bacon says that "strength of nature in youth passeth over many excesses which are owing a man until he is old," he exposes a physical as well as a moral fact which cannot be too well weighed in the conduct of life. "I assure you," wrote Giusti the Italian to a friend, "I pay a heavy price for existence. It is true that our lives are not at our own disposal. Nature pretends to give them gratis at the beginning, and then sends in her account." The worst of youthful indiscretions is, not that they destroy health, so much as that they sully manhood. The dissipated youth becomes a tainted man; and often he cannot be pure, even if he would. If cure there be, it is only to be found in inoculating the mind with a fervent spirit of duty, and in energetic application to useful work.

One of the most gifted of Frenchmen, in point of great intellectual endowments, was Benjamin Constant; but, *blasé* at twenty, his life was only a prolonged wail, instead of a harvest of the great deeds which he was capable of accomplishing with ordinary diligence and self-control. He resolved upon doing so many things, which he never did, that people came to speak of him as Constant the Inconstant. He was a fluent and brilliant writer, and cherished the ambition of writing works, "which the world would not willingly let die." But whilst Constant affected the highest thinking, unhappily he practised the lowest living; nor did the transcendentalism of his books atone for the meanness of his life. He frequented the gaming-tables while engaged in preparing his work upon religion, and carried on a disreputable intrigue while writing his 'Adolphe.' With all his powers of intellect, he was powerless, because he had no faith in virtue. "Bah!" said he, "what are honour and dignity?

The longer I live, the more clearly I see there is nothing in them." It was the howl of a miserable man. He described himself as but "ashes and dust." "I pass," said he, "like a shadow over the earth, accompanied by misery and *ennui.*" He wished for Voltaire's energy, which he would rather have possessed than his genius. But he had no strength of purpose—nothing but wishes: his life, prematurely exhausted, had become but a heap of broken links. He spoke of himself as a person with one foot in the air. He admitted that he had no principles, and no moral consistency. Hence, with his splendid talents, he contrived to do nothing ; and, after living many years miserable, he died worn out and wretched.

The career of Augustin Thierry, the author of the ' History of the Norman Conquest,' affords an admirable contrast to that of Constant. His entire life presented a striking example of perseverance, diligence, self-culture, and untiring devotion to knowledge. In the pursuit he lost his eyesight, lost his health, but never lost his love of truth. When so feeble that he was carried from room to room, like a helpless infant, in the arms of a nurse, his brave spirit never failed him ; and blind and helpless though he was, he concluded his literary career in the following noble words :—" If, as I think, the interest of science is counted in the number of great national interests, I have given my country all that the soldier, mutilated on the field of battle, gives her. Whatever may be the fate of my labours, this example, I hope, will not be lost. I would wish it to serve to combat the species of moral weakness which is *the disease* of our present generation ; to bring back into the straight road of life some of those enervated souls that complain of wanting faith, that know not what to do, and seek everywhere, without finding it, an object of worship and admiration. Why say, with so much bitterness, that in the world, constituted as it is, there is no air for all lungs—no employment for all minds? Is not calm and serious study there? and is not that a refuge, a hope, a field within the reach of all of us? With it, evil days are passed over without their weight being felt. Every one can make his own destiny—every one employ his life nobly. This is what I have done, and would do again if I had to recommence my career; I would choose that which has brought me where I am. Blind, and suffering without hope, and almost without intermission, I may give this testimony, which from me will not appear suspicious. There *is* something in the world better than sensual enjoyments, better than fortune, better than health itself—it is devotion to knowledge."

Coleridge, in many respects, resembled Constant. He possessed equally brilliant powers, but was similarly infirm of purpose. With all his great intellectual gifts, he wanted the gift of industry, and was averse to continuous labour. He wanted also the sense of independence, and thought it no degradation to leave his wife and children to be maintained by the brain-work of the noble Southey, while he himself retired to Highgate Grove to discourse transcendentalism to his disciples, looking down contemptuously upon the honest work going forward beneath him amidst the din and smoke of London. With remunerative employment at his command he stooped to accept the charity of friends; and, notwithstanding his lofty ideas of philosophy, he condescended to humiliations from which many a day-labourer would have shrunk. How different in spirit was Southey! labouring not merely at work of his own choice, and at taskwork often tedious and distasteful, but also unremittingly and with the utmost eagerness seeking and storing knowledge purely for the love of it. Every day, every hour had its allotted employment: engagements to publishers requiring punctual fulfilment; the current expenses of a large household duly to provide for: Southey had no crop growing while his pen was idle. " My ways," he used to say, " are

z

as broad as the king's high-road, and my means lie in an inkstand."

Robert Nicoll wrote to a friend, after reading the 'Recollections of Coleridge,' "What a mighty intellect was lost in that man for want of a little energy—a little determination !" Nicoll himself was a true and brave spirit, who died young, but not before he had encountered and overcome great difficulties in life. At his outset, while carrying on a small business as a bookseller, he found himself weighed down with a debt of only twenty pounds, which he said he felt " weighing like a millstone round his neck," and that " if he had it paid he never would borrow again from mortal man." Writing to his mother at the time he said, " Fear not for me, dear mother, for I feel myself daily growing firmer and more hopeful in spirit. The more I think and reflect—and thinking, not reading, is now my occupation—I feel that, whether I be growing richer or not, I am growing a wiser man, which is far better. Pain, poverty, and all the other wild beasts of life which so affrighten others, I am so bold as to think I could look in the face without shrinking, without losing respect for myself, faith in man's high destinies, or trust in God. There is a point which it costs much mental toil and struggling to gain, but which, when once gained, a man can look down from, as a traveller from a lofty mountain, on storms raging below, while he is walking in sunshine. That I have yet gained this point in life I will not say, but I feel myself daily nearer to it."

It is not ease, but effort—not facility, but difficulty, that makes men. There is, perhaps, no station in life, in which difficulties have not to be encountered and overcome before any decided measure of success can be achieved. Those difficulties are, however, our best instructors, as our mistakes often form our best experience. Charles James Fox was accustomed to say that he hoped more from a man who failed, and yet went on in spite of his failure, than from the buoyant career of the successful. " It is all very well," said he, " to tell me that a young man has distinguished himself by a brilliant first speech. He may go on, or he may be satisfied with his first triumph ; but show me a young man who has *not* succeeded at first, and nevertheless has gone on, and I will back that young man to do better than most of those who have succeeded at the first trial."

We learn wisdom from failure much more than from success. We often discover what *will* do, by finding out what will not do; and probably he who never made a mistake never made a discovery. It was the failure in the attempt to make a sucking-pump act, when the working bucket was more than thirty-three feet above the surface of the water to be raised, that led observant men to study the law of atmospheric pressure, and opened a new field of research to the genius of Galileo, Torrecelli, and Boyle. John Hunter used to remark that the art of surgery would not advance until professional men had the courage to publish their failures as well as their successes. Watt the engineer said, of all things most wanted in mechanical engineering was a history of failures : " We want," he said, " a book of blots." When Sir Humphry Davy was once shown a dexterously manipulated experiment, he said—" I thank God I was not made a dexterous manipulator, for the most important of my discoveries have been suggested to me by failures." Another distinguished investigator in physical science has left it on record that, whenever in the course of his researches he encountered an apparently insuperable obstacle, he generally found himself on the brink of some discovery. The very greatest things—great thoughts, discoveries, inventions—have usually been nurtured in hardship, often pondered over in sorrow, and at length established with difficulty.

Beethoven said of Rossini, that he had in him the stuff

Z 2

to have made a good musician if he had only, when a boy, been well flogged ; but that he had been spoilt by the facility with which he produced. Men who feel their strength within them need not fear to encounter adverse opinions ; they have far greater reason to fear undue praise and too friendly criticism. When Mendelssohn was about to enter the orchestra at Birmingham, on the first performance of his ' Elijah,' he said laughingly to one of his friends and critics, " Stick your claws into me ! Don't tell me what you like, but what you don't like !"

It has been said, and truly, that it is the defeat that tries the general more than the victory. Washington lost more battles than he gained ; but he succeeded in the end. The Romans, in their most victorious campaigns, almost invariably began with defeats. Moreau used to be compared by his companions to a drum, which nobody hears of except it be beaten. Wellington's military genius was perfected by encounter with difficulties of apparently the most overwhelming character, but which only served to nerve his resolution, and bring out more prominently his great qualities as a man and a general. So the skilful mariner obtains his best experience amidst storms and tempests, which train him to self-reliance, courage, and the highest discipline ; and we probably owe to rough seas and wintry nights the best training of our race of British seamen, who are, certainly, not surpassed by any in the world.

Necessity may be a hard schoolmistress, but she is generally found the best. Though the ordeal of adversity is one from which we naturally shrink, yet, when it comes, we must bravely and manfully encounter it. Burns says truly,

> " Though losses and crosses
> Be lessons right severe,
> There's wit there, you'll get there,
> You'll find no other where."

"Sweet indeed are the uses of adversity." They reveal to us our powers, and call forth our energies. If there be real worth in the character, like sweet herbs, it will give forth its finest fragrance when pressed. " Crosses," says the old proverb, " are the ladders that lead to heaven." " What is even poverty itself," asks Richter, "that a man should murmur under it? It is but as the pain of piercing a maiden's ear, and you hang precious jewels in the wound." In the experience of life it is found that the wholesome discipline of adversity in strong natures usually carries with it a self-preserving influence. Many are found capable of bravely bearing up under privations, and cheerfully encountering obstructions, who are afterwards found unable to withstand the more dangerous influences of prosperity. It is only a weak man whom the wind deprives of his cloak : a man of average strength is more in danger of losing it when assailed by the beams of a too genial sun. Thus it often needs a higher discipline and a stronger character to bear up under good fortune than under adverse. Some generous natures kindle and warm with prosperity, but there are many on whom wealth has no such influence. Base hearts it only hardens, making those who were mean and servile, mean and proud. But while prosperity is apt to harden the heart to pride, adversity in a man of resolution will serve to ripen it into fortitude. To use the words of Burke, " Difficulty is a severe instructor, set over us by the supreme ordinance of a parental guardian and instructor, who knows us better than we know ourselves, as He loves us better too. He that wrestles with us strengthens our nerves, and sharpens our skill : our antagonist is thus our helper." Without the necessity of encountering difficulty, life might be easier, but men would be worth less. For trials, wisely improved, train the character, and teach self-help ; thus hardship itself may often prove the wholesomest discipline for us, though we recognise it not. When the gallant young Hodson, unjustly removed from his Indian command, felt himself sore pressed down by unmerited calumny and reproach, he yet preserved the courage to say to a friend, "I strive to look the worst boldly in the face, as I would an enemy in the field, and to do my appointed work resolutely and to the best of my ability, satisfied that there is a reason for all ; and that even irksome duties well done bring their own reward, and that, if not, still they *are* duties."

The battle of life is, in most cases, fought up-hill ; and to win it without a struggle were perhaps to win it without honour. If there were no difficulties there would be no success; if there were nothing to struggle for, there would be nothing to be achieved. Difficulties may intimidate the weak, but they act only as a wholesome stimulus to men of resolution and valour. All experience of life indeed serves to prove that the impediments thrown in the way of human advancement may for the most part be overcome by steady good conduct, honest zeal, activity, perseverance, and above all by a determined resolution to surmount difficulties, and stand up manfully against misfortune.

The school of Difficulty is the best school of moral discipline, for nations as for individuals. Indeed, the history of difficulty would be but a history of all the great and good things that have yet been accomplished by men. It is hard to say how much northern nations owe to their encounter with a comparatively rude and changeable climate and an originally sterile soil, which is one of the necessities of their condition,—involving a perennial struggle with difficulties such as the natives of sunnier climes know nothing of. And thus it may be, that though our finest products are exotic, the skill and industry which

have been necessary to rear them, have issued in the production of a native growth of men not surpassed on the
globe.

Wherever there is difficulty, the individual man must
come out for better for worse. Encounter with it will
train his strength, and discipline his skill ; heartening him
for future effort, as the racer, by being trained to run
against the hill, at length courses with facility. The road
to success may be steep to climb, and it puts to the proof
the energies of him who would reach the summit. But
by experience a man soon learns that obstacles are to be
overcome by grappling with them,—that the nettle feels as
soft as silk when it is boldly grasped,—and that the most
effective help towards realizing the object proposed is the
moral conviction that we can and will accomplish it. Thus
difficulties often fall away of themselves before the determination to overcome them.

Much will be done if we do but try. Nobody knows
what he can do till he has tried ; and few try their best
till they have been forced to do it. "*If* I could do such and
such a thing," sighs the desponding youth. But nothing
will be done if he only wishes. The desire must ripen into
purpose and effort ; and one energetic attempt is worth a
thousand aspirations. It is these thorny " ifs "—the mutter-
ings of impotence and despair—which so often hedge round
the field of possibility, and prevent anything being done
or even attempted. "A difficulty," said Lord Lyndhurst,
"is a thing to be overcome ;" grapple with it at once ;
facility will come with practice, and strength and fortitude
with repeated effort. Thus the mind and character may
be trained to an almost perfect discipline, and enabled to
act with a grace, spirit, and liberty, almost incomprehen-
sible to those who have not passed through a similar experience.

Everything that we learn is the mastery of a difficulty ;

and the mastery of one helps to the mastery of others. Things which may at first sight appear comparatively valueless in education—such as the study of the dead languages, and the relations of lines and surfaces which we call mathematics—are really of the greatest practical value, not so much because of the information which they yield, as because of the development which they compel. The mastery of these studies evokes effort, and cultivates powers of application, which otherwise might have lain dormant. Thus one thing leads to another, and so the work goes on through life—encounter with difficulty ending only when life and culture end. But indulging in the feeling of discouragement never helped any one over a difficulty, and never will. D'Alembert's advice to the student who complained to him about his want of success in mastering the first elements of mathematics was the right one—"Go on, sir, and faith and strength will come to you."

The danseuse who turns a pirouette, the violinist who plays a sonata, have acquired their dexterity by patient repetition and after many failures. Carissimi, when praised for the ease and grace of his melodies, exclaimed, "Ah! you little know with what difficulty this ease has been acquired." Sir Joshua Reynolds, when once asked how long it had taken him to paint a certain picture, replied, "All my life." Henry Clay, the American orator, when giving advice to young men, thus described to them the secret of his success in the cultivation of his art : "I owe my success in life," said he, "chiefly to one circumstance—that at the age of twenty-seven I commenced, and continued for years, the process of daily reading and speaking upon the contents of some historical or scientific book. These off-hand efforts were made, sometimes in a corn-field, at others in the forest, and not unfrequently in some distant barn, with the horse and the ox for my auditors. It is to this early practice of the art of all arts that I am indebted for the primary and leading impulses that stimulated me onward and have shaped and moulded my whole subsequent destiny."

Curran, the Irish orator, when a youth, had a strong defect in his articulation, and at school he was known as "stuttering Jack Curran." While he was engaged in the study of the law, and still struggling to overcome his defect, he was stung into eloquence by the sarcasms of a member of a debating club, who characterised him as "Orator Mum;" for, like Cowper, when he stood up to speak on a previous occasion, Curran had not been able to utter a word. The taunt stung him and he replied in a triumphant speech. This accidental discovery in himself of the gift of eloquence encouraged him to proceed in his studies with renewed energy. He corrected his enunciation by reading aloud, emphatically and distinctly, the best passages in literature, for several hours every day, studying his features before a mirror, and adopting a method of gesticulation suited to his rather awkward and ungraceful figure. He also proposed cases to himself, which he argued with as much care as if he had been addressing a jury. Curran began business with the qualification which Lord Eldon stated to be the first requisite for distinction, that is, "to be not worth a shilling." While working his way laboriously at the bar, still oppressed by the diffidence which had overcome him in his debating club, he was on one occasion provoked by the Judge (Robinson) into making a very severe retort. In the case under discussion, Curran observed "that he had never met the law as laid down by his lordship in any book in his library." "That may be, sir," said the judge, in a contemptuous tone, "but I suspect that *your* library is very small." His lordship was notoriously a furious political partisan, the author of several anonymous pamphlets characterised by unusual violence and dogmatism. Curran, roused by the allusion to his straitened circumstances, replied thus: "It is very true, my lord, that I am poor, and the circumstance has certainly curtailed my library; my books are not numerous, but they are select, and I hope they have been perused with proper dispositions. I have prepared myself for this high profession by the study of a few good works, rather than by the composition of a great many bad ones. I am not ashamed of my poverty; but I should be ashamed of my wealth, could I have stooped to acquire it by servility and corruption. If I rise not to rank, I shall at least be honest; and should I ever cease to be so, many an example shows me that an ill-gained elevation, by making me the more conspicuous, would only make me the more universally and the more notoriously contemptible."

The extremest poverty has been no obstacle in the way of men devoted to the duty of self-culture. Professor Alexander Murray, the linguist, learnt to write by scribbling his letters on an old wool-card with the end of a burnt heather stem. The only book which his father, who was a poor shepherd, possessed, was a penny Shorter Catechism; but that, being thought too valuable for common use, was carefully preserved in a cupboard for the Sunday catechisings. Professor Moor, when a young man, being too poor to purchase Newton's ' Principia,' borrowed the book, and copied the whole of it with his own hand. Many poor students, while labouring daily for their living, have only been able to snatch an atom of knowledge here and there at intervals, as birds do their food in winter time when the fields are covered with snow. They have struggled on, and faith and hope have come to them. A well-known author and publisher, William Chambers, of Edinburgh, speaking before an assemblage of young men in that city, thus briefly described to them his humble beginnings, for their encouragement: " I stand before you," he said, " a self-educated man. My education was that which is supplied at the humble parish schools of Scotland; and it was only when I went to Edin-

burgh, a poor boy, that I devoted my evenings, after the
labours of the day, to the cultivation of that intellect which
the Almighty has given me. From seven or eight in the
morning till nine or ten at night was I at my business as a
bookseller's apprentice, and it was only during hours after
these, stolen from sleep, that I could devote myself to study.
I did not read novels : my attention was devoted to physical
science, and other useful matters. I also taught myself
French. I look back to those times with great pleasure,
and am almost sorry I have not to go through the same
experience again ; for I reaped more pleasure when I had
not a sixpence in my pocket, studying in a garret in
Edinburgh, than I now find when sitting amidst all the
elegancies and comforts of a parlour."

William Cobbett's account of how he learnt English
Grammar is full of interest and instruction for all students
labouring under difficulties. "I learned grammar," said he,
"when I was a private soldier on the pay of sixpence a day.
The edge of my berth, or that of my guard-bed, was my seat
to study in ; my knapsack was my book-case ; a bit of board
lying on my lap was my writing-table ; and the task did not
demand anything like a year of my life. I had no money
to purchase candle or oil ; in winter time it was rarely that
I could get any evening light but that of the fire, and only
my turn even of that. And if I, under such circumstances,
and without parent or friend to advise or encourage me,
accomplished this undertaking, what excuse can there be for
any youth, however poor, however pressed with business,
or however circumstanced as to room or other conveniences?
To buy a pen or a sheet of paper I was compelled to forego
some portion of food, though in a state of half-starvation :
I had no moment of time that I could call my own ; and I
had to read and to write amidst the talking, laughing, singing,
whistling, and brawling of at least half a score of the most
thoughtless of men, and that, too, in the hours of their

freedom from all control. Think not lightly of the farthing that I had to give, now and then, for ink, pen, or paper! That farthing was, alas! a great sum to me! I was as tall as I am now; I had great health and great exercise. The whole of the money, not expended for us at market, was two-pence a week for each man. I remember, and well I may! that on one occasion I, after all necessary expenses, had, on a Friday, made shifts to have a halfpenny in reserve, which I had destined for the purchase of a redherring in the morning; but, when I pulled off my clothes at night, so hungry then as to be hardly able to endure life, I found that I had lost my halfpenny! I buried my head under the miserable sheet and rug, and cried like a child! And again I say, if, I, under circumstances like these, could encounter and overcome this task, is there, can there be, in the whole world, a youth to find an excuse for the non-performance?"

We have been informed of an equally striking instance of perseverance and application in learning on the part of a French political exile in London. His original occupation was that of a stonemason, at which he found employment for some time; but work becoming slack, he lost his place, and poverty stared him in the face. In his dilemma he called upon a fellow exile profitably engaged in teaching French, and consulted him what he ought to do to earn a living. The answer was, "Become a professor!" A professor?" answered the mason—"I, who am only a workman, speaking but a patois! Surely you are jesting?" "On the contrary, I am quite serious," said the other, "and again I advise you—become a professor; place yourself under me, and I will undertake to teach you how to teach others." "No, no!" replied the mason, "it is impossible; I am too old to learn; I am too little of a scholar; I cannot be a professor." He went away, and again he tried to obtain employment at his trade. From London he went into the provinces, and travelled several hundred miles in vain; he could not find a master. Returning to London, he went direct to his former adviser, and said, " I have tried everywhere for work, and failed ; I will now try to be a professor !" He immediately placed himself under instruction ; and being a man of close application, of quick apprehension, and vigorous intelligence, he speedily mastered the elements of grammar, the rules of construction and composition, and (what he had still in a great measure to learn) the correct pronunciation of classical French. When his friend and instructor thought him sufficiently competent to undertake the teaching of others, an appointment, advertised as vacant, was applied for and obtained ; and behold our artisan at length become professor! It so happened, that the seminary to which he was appointed was situated in a suburb of London where he had formerly worked as a stonemason ; and every morning the first thing which met his eyes on looking out of his dressing-room window was a stack of cottage chimneys which he had himself built ! He feared for a time lest he should be recognised in the village as the quondam workman, and thus bring discredit on his seminary, which was of high standing. But he need have been under no such apprehension, as he proved a most efficient teacher, and his pupils were on more than one occasion publicly complimented for their knowledge of French. Meanwhile, he secured the respect and friendship of all who knew him —fellow-professors as well as pupils ; and when the story of his struggles, his difficulties, and his past history, became known to them, they admired him more than ever.

Sir Samuel Romilly was not less indefatigable as a self-cultivator. The son of a jeweller, descended from a French refugee, he received little education in his early years, but overcame all his disadvantages by unwearied application, and by efforts constantly directed towards the same end. " I determined," he says, in his autobiography, " when I was between fifteen and sixteen years of age, to apply myself seriously to learning Latin, of which I, at that time, knew little more than some of the most familiar rules of grammar. In the course of three or four years, during which I thus applied myself, I had read almost every prose writer of the age of pure Latinity, except those who have treated merely of technical subjects, such as Varro, Columella, and Celsus. I had gone three times through the whole of Livy, Sallust, and Tacitus. I had studied the most celebrated orations of Cicero, and translated a great deal of Homer. Terence, Virgil, Horace, Ovid, and Juvenal, I had read over and over again." He also studied geography, natural history, and natural philosophy, and obtained a considerable acquaintance with general knowledge. At sixteen he was articled to a clerk in Chancery; worked hard; was admitted to the bar; and his industry and perseverance ensured success. He became Solicitor-General under the Fox administration in 1806, and steadily worked his way to the highest celebrity in his profession. Yet he was always haunted by a painful and almost oppressive sense of his own disqualifications, and never ceased labouring to remedy them. His autobiography is a lesson of instructive facts, worth volumes of sentiment, and well deserves a careful perusal.

Sir Walter Scott was accustomed to cite the case of his young friend John Leyden as one of the most remarkable illustrations of the power of perseverance which he had ever known. The son of a shepherd in one of the wildest valleys of Roxburghshire, he was almost entirely self-educated. Like many Scotch shepherds' sons—like Hogg, who taught himself to write by copying the letters of a printed book as he lay watching his flock on the hill-side—like Cairns, who from tending sheep on the Lammermoors, raised himself by dint of application and industry to the professor's chair which he now so worthily holds—like Murray, Ferguson, and many more, Leyden was early inspired by a thirst for knowledge. When a poor barefooted boy, he walked six or eight miles across the moors daily to learn reading at the little village schoolhouse of Kirkton; and this was all the education he received; the rest he acquired for himself. He found his way to Edinburgh to attend the college there, setting the extremest penury at defiance. He was first discovered as the frequenter of a small bookseller's shop kept by Archibald Constable, afterwards so well known as a publisher. He would pass hour after hour perched on a ladder in mid-air, with some great folio in his hand, forgetful of the scanty meal of bread and water which awaited him at his miserable lodging. Access to books and lectures comprised all within the bounds of his wishes. Thus he toiled and battled at the gates of science until his unconquerable perseverance carried everything before it. Before he had attained his nineteenth year he had astonished all the professors in Edinburgh by his profound knowledge of Greek and Latin, and the general mass of information he had acquired. Having turned his views to India, he sought employment in the civil service, but failed. He was however informed that a surgeon's assistant's commission was open to him. But he was no surgeon, and knew no more of the profession than a child. He could however learn. Then he was told that he must be ready to pass in six months! Nothing daunted, he set to work, to acquire in six months what usually required three years. At the end of six months he took his degree with honour. Scott and a few friends helped to fit him out; and he sailed for India, after publishing his beautiful poem 'The Scenes of Infancy.' In India he promised to become one of the greatest of oriental scholars, but was unhappily cut off by fever caught by exposure, and died at an early age.

The life of the late Dr. Lee, Professor of Hebrew at Cambridge, furnishes one of the most remarkable instances in modern times of the power of patient perseverance and resolute purpose in working out an honourable career in literature. He received his education at a charity school at Lognor, near Shrewsbury, but so little distinguished himself there, that his master pronounced him one of the dullest boys that ever passed through his hands. He was put apprentice to a carpenter, and worked at that trade until he arrived at manhood. To occupy his leisure hours he took to reading; and, some of the books containing Latin quotations, he became desirous of ascertaining what they meant. He bought a Latin grammar, and proceeded to learn Latin. As Stone, the Duke of Argyle's gardener, said, long before, "Does one need to know anything more than the twenty-four letters in order to learn everything else that one wishes?" Lee rose early and sat up late, and he succeeded in mastering the Latin before his apprenticeship was out. Whilst working one day in some place of worship, a copy of a Greek Testament fell in his way, and he was immediately filled with the desire to learn that language. He accordingly sold some of his Latin books, and purchased a Greek Grammar and Lexicon. Taking pleasure in learning, he soon mastered the language. Then he sold his Greek books, and bought Hebrew ones, and learnt that language, unassisted by any instructor, without any hope of fame or reward, but simply following the bent of his genius. He next proceeded to learn the Chaldee, Syriac, and Samaritan dialects. But his studies began to tell upon his health, and brought on disease in his eyes through his long night watchings with his books. Having laid them aside for a time and recovered his health, he went on with his daily work. His character as a tradesman being excellent, his business improved, and his means enabled him to marry, which he did when twenty-eight years old. He determined now to devote himself to the maintenance of his family, and to renounce the luxury of literature; accordingly he sold all his books. He might have continued a working carpenter all his life, had not the chest of tools upon which he depended for subsistence been destroyed by fire, and destitution stared him in the face. He was too poor to buy new tools, so he bethought him of teaching children their letters,—a profession requiring the least possible capital. But though he had mastered many languages, he was so defective in the common branches of knowledge, that at first he could not teach them. Resolute of purpose, however, he assiduously set to work, and taught himself arithmetic and writing to such a degree as to be able to impart the knowledge of these branches to little children. His unaffected, simple, and beautiful character gradually attracted friends, and the acquirements of the "learned carpenter" became bruited abroad. Dr. Scott, a neighbouring clergyman, obtained for him the appointment of master of a charity school in Shrewsbury, and introduced him to a distinguished Oriental scholar. These friends supplied him with books, and Lee successively mastered Arabic, Persic, and Hindostanee. He continued to pursue his studies while on duty as a private in the local militia of the county; gradually acquiring greater proficiency in languages. At length his kind patron, Dr. Scott, enabled Lee to enter Queen's College, Cambridge; and after a course of study, in which he distinguished himself by his mathematical acquirements, a vacancy occurring in the professorship of Arabic and Hebrew, he was worthily elected to fill the honourable office. Besides ably performing his duties as a professor, he voluntarily gave much of his time to the instruction of missionaries going forth to preach the Gospel to eastern tribes in their own tongue. He also made translations of the Bible into several Asiatic dialects ; and having mastered the New Zealand language, he arranged a. grammar and vocabulary for two New Zealand chiefs who were then in England, which books are now in daily use in the New Zealand schools. Such, in brief, is the remarkable history of Dr. Samuel Lee ; and it is but the counterpart of numerous similarly instructive examples of the power of perseverance in self-culture, as displayed in the lives of many of the most distinguished of our literary and scientific men.*

There are many other illustrious names which might be cited to prove the truth of the common saying that " it is never too late to learn." Even at advanced years men can do much, if they will determine on making a beginning. Sir Henry Spelman did not begin the study of science until he was between fifty and sixty years of age. Franklin was fifty before he fully entered upon the study of Natural Philosophy. Dryden and Scott were not known as authors until each was in his fortieth year. Boccaccio was thirty-five when he commenced his literary career, and Alfieri was forty-six when he began the study of Greek. Dr. Arnold learnt German at an advanced age, for the purpose of reading Niebuhr in the original ; and in like manner James Watt, when about forty, while working at his trade of an instrument maker in Glasgow, learnt French, German, and Italian, to enable himself to peruse the valuable works on mechanical philosophy which existed in those languages. Thomas Scott was fifty-six before he began to learn Hebrew. Robert Hall was once found lying upon the floor, racked by pain, learning Italian in his old age, to enable him to judge of the parallel drawn by Macaulay between Milton and Dante. Handel was forty-eight before he published any of his great works. Indeed hundreds of instances might be given of men who struck out an entirely new path, and successfully entered on new studies, at a comparatively advanced time of life. None but the frivolous or the indolent will say, " I am too old to learn."

And here we would repeat what we have said before, that it is not men of genius who move the world and take the

* See the admirable and well-known book, 'The Pursuit of Knowledge under Difficulties.'

lead in it, so much as men of steadfastness, purpose, and indefatigable industry. Notwithstanding the many undeniable instances of the precocity of men of genius, it is nevertheless true that early cleverness gives no indication of the height to which the grown man will reach. Precocity is sometimes a symptom of disease rather than of intellectual vigour. What becomes of all the " remarkably clever children?" Where are the duxes and prize boys? Trace them through life, and it will frequently be found that the dull boys, who were beaten at school, have shot ahead of them. The clever boys are rewarded, but the prizes which they gain by their greater quickness and facility do not always prove of use to them. What ought rather to be rewarded is the endeavour, the struggle, and the obedience ; for it is the youth who does his best, though endowed with an inferiority of natural powers, that ought above all others to be encouraged.

An interesting chapter might be written on the subject of illustrious dunces—dull boys, but brilliant men. We have room, however, for only a few instances. Pietro di Cortona, the painter, was thought so stupid that he was nicknamed " Ass's Head" when a boy ; and Tomaso Guidi was generally known as " Heavy Tom" (Massaccio Tomasaccio), though by diligence he afterwards raised himself to the highest eminence. Newton, when at school, stood at the bottom of the lowest form but one. The boy above Newton having kicked him, the dunce showed his pluck by challenging him to a fight, and beat him. Then he set to work with a will, and determined also to vanquish his antagonist as a scholar, which he did, rising to the top of his class. Many of our greatest divines have been anything but precocious. Isaac Barrow, when a boy at the Charterhouse School, was notorious chiefly for his strong temper, pugnacious habits, and proverbial idleness as a scholar ; and he caused such grief to his parents that his father used to say

2 A 2

that, if it pleased God to take from him any of his children, he hoped it might be Isaac, the least promising of them all. Adam Clarke, when a boy, was proclaimed by his father to be "a grievous dunce;" though he could roll large stones about. Dean Swift was "plucked" at Dublin University, and only obtained his recommendation to Oxford "speciali gratia." The well-known Dr. Chalmers and Dr. Cook* were boys together at the parish school of St. Andrew's; and they were found so stupid and mischievous, that the master, irritated beyond measure, dismissed them both as incorrigible dunces.

The brilliant Sheridan showed so little capacity as a boy, that he was presented to a tutor by his mother with the complimentary accompaniment that he was an incorrigible dunce. Walter Scott was all but a dunce when a boy, always much readier for a "bicker," than apt at his lessons. At the Edinburgh University, Professor Dalzell pronounced upon him the sentence that "Dunce he was, and dunce he would remain." Chatterton was returned on his mother's nands as "a fool, of whom nothing could be made." Burns was a dull boy, good only at athletic exercises. Goldsmith spoke of himself as a plant that flowered late. Alfieri left college no wiser than he entered it, and did not begin the studies by which he distinguished himself, until he had run half over Europe. Robert Clive was a dunce, if not a reprobate, when a youth; but always full of energy, even in badness. His family, glad to get rid of him, shipped him off to Madras; and he lived to lay the foundations of the British power in India. Napoleon and Wellington were both dull boys, not distinguishing themselves in any way at school.† Of the former the Duchess d'Abrantes says, "he had good health, but was in other respects like other boys."

* Late Professor of Moral Philosophy at St. Andrew's.

† A writer in the 'Edinburgh Review' (July, 1859) observes that "the Duke's talents seem never to have developed themselves until

Ulysses Grant, the Commander-in-Chief of the United States, was called "Useless Grant" by his mother—he was so dull and unhandy when a boy; and Stonewall Jackson, Lee's greatest lieutenant, was, in his youth, chiefly noted for his slowness. While a pupil at West Point Military Academy he was, however, equally remarkable for his indefatigable application and perseverance. When a task was set him, he never left it until he had mastered it; nor did he ever feign to possess knowledge which he had not entirely acquired. "Again and again," wrote one who knew him, "when called upon to answer questions in the recitation of the day, he would reply, 'I have not yet looked at it; I have been engaged in mastering the recitation of yesterday or the day before.' The result was that he graduated seventeenth in a class of seventy. There was probably in the whole class not a boy to whom Jackson at the outset was not inferior in knowledge and attainments; but at the end of the race he had only sixteen before him, and had outstripped no fewer than fifty-three. It used to be said of him by his contemporaries, that if the course had been for ten years instead of four, Jackson would have graduated at the head of his class." *

John Howard, the philanthropist, was another illustrious dunce, learning next to nothing during the seven years that he was at school. Stephenson, as a youth, was distinguished chiefly for his skill at putting and wrestling, and attention to his work. The brilliant Sir Humphry Davy was no cleverer than other boys: his teacher, Dr. Cardew, once said of him, " While he was with me I could not discern the faculties by

some active and practical field for their display was placed immediately before him. He was long described by his Spartan mother, who thought him a dunce, as only 'food for powder.' He gained no sort of distinction, either at Eton or at the French Military College of Angers." It is not improbable that a competitive examination, at this day, might have excluded him from the army.

* Correspondent of 'The Times,' 11th June, 1863.

which he was so much distinguished." Indeed, Davy himself
in after life considered it fortunate that he had been left to
" enjoy so much idleness" at school.   Watt was a dull
scholar, notwithstanding the stories told about his precocity ;
but he was, what was better, patient and perseverant, and it
was by such qualities, and by his carefully cultivated inventiveness, that he was enabled to perfect his steam-engine.

What Dr. Arnold said of boys is equally true of men—
that the difference between one boy and another consists
not so much in talent as in energy.   Given perseverance
and energy soon becomes habitual.   Provided the dunce
has persistency and application he will inevitably head the
cleverer fellow without those qualities.   Slow but sure
wins the race.   It is perseverance that explains how the
position of boys at school is so often reversed in real life ;
and it is curious to note how some who were then so
clever have since become so commonplace ; whilst others,
dull boys, of whom nothing was expected, slow in their
faculties but sure in their pace, have assumed the position
of leaders of men.   The author of this book, when a boy,
stood in the same class with one of the greatest of dunces.
One teacher after another had tried his skill upon him and
failed.   Corporal punishment, the fool's cap, coaxing, and
earnest entreaty, proved alike fruitless.   Sometimes the
experiment was tried of putting him at the top of his class,
and it was curious to note the rapidity with which he
gravitated to the inevitable bottom.   The youth was given
up by his teachers as an incorrigible dunce—one of them
pronouncing him to be a " stupendous booby."   Yet, slow
though he was, this dunce had a sort of dull energy of
purpose in him, which grew with his muscles and his
manhood ; and, strange to say, when he at length came
to take part in the practical business of life, he was found
heading most of his school companions, and eventually left
the greater number of them far behind.   The last time the

author heard of him, he was chief magistrate of his native town.

The tortoise in the right road will beat a racer in the wrong. It matters not though a youth be slow, if he be but diligent. Quickness of parts may even prove a defect, inasmuch as the boy who learns readily will often forget as readily; and also because he finds no need of cultivating that quality of application and perseverance which the slower youth is compelled to exercise, and which proves so valuable an element in the formation of every character. Davy said "What I am I have made myself;" and the same holds true universally.

To conclude: the best culture is not obtained from teachers when at school or college, so much as by our own diligent self-education when we have become men. Hence parents need not be in too great haste to see their children's talents forced into bloom. Let them watch and wait patiently, letting good example and quiet training do their work, and leave the rest to Providence. Let them see to it that the youth is provided, by free exercise of his bodily powers, with a full stock of physical health; set him fairly on the road of self-culture; carefully train his habits of application and perseverance; and as he grows older, if the right stuff be in him, he will be enabled vigorously and effectively to cultivate himself.

CHAPTER XII.

EXAMPLE—MODELS.

" Ever their phantoms rise before us,
Our loftier brothers, but one in blood;
By bed and table they lord it o'er us,
With looks of beauty and words of good."—*John Sterling.*

" Children may be strangled, but Deeds never : they have an indestructible life, both in and out of our consciousness."—*George Eliot.*

" There is no action of man in this life, which is not the beginning of so long a chain of consequences, as that no human providence is high enough to give us a prospect to the end."—*Thomas of Malmesbury.*

XAMPLE is one of the most potent of instructors, though it teaches without a tongue. It is the practical school of mankind, working by action, which is always more forcible than words. Precept may point to us the way, but it is silent continuous example, conveyed to us by habits, and living with us in fact, that carries us along. Good advice has its weight: but without the accompaniment of a good example it is of comparatively small influence ; and it will be found that the common saying of " Do as I say, not as I do," is usually reversed in the actual experience of life.

All persons are more or less apt to learn through the eye rather than the ear ; and, whatever is seen in fact, makes a far deeper impression than anything that is merely read or heard. This is especially the case in early youth, when the eye is the chief inlet of knowledge. Whatever children see they unconsciously imitate. They insensibly come to resemble those who are about them—as insects take the colour of the leaves they feed on. Hence the vast importance of domestic training. For whatever may be the efficiency of schools, the examples set in our Homes must always be of vastly greater influence in forming the characters of our future men and women. The Home is the crystal of society—the nucleus of national character; and from that source, be it pure or tainted, issue the habits, principles and maxims, which govern public as well as private life. The nation comes from the nursery. Public opinion itself is for the most part the outgrowth of the home; and the best philanthropy comes from the fireside. "To love the little platoon we belong to in society," says Burke, "is the germ of all public affections." From this little central spot, the human sympathies may extend in an ever widening circle, until the world is embraced; for, though true philanthropy, like charity, begins at home, assuredly it does not end there.

Example in conduct, therefore, even in apparently trivial matters, is of no light moment, inasmuch as it is constantly becoming inwoven with the lives of others, and contributing to form their natures for better or for worse. The characters of parents are thus constantly repeated in their children; and the acts of affection, discipline, industry, and self-control, which they daily exemplify, live and act when all else which may have been learned through the ear has long been forgotten. Hence a wise man was accustomed to speak of his children as his "future state." Even the mute action and unconscious look of a parent may give a stamp to the character which is never effaced; and who can tell how much evil act has been stayed by the thought of some good parent, whose memory their children may not sully by the commission of an unworthy deed, or the indulgence of an impure thought?

The veriest trifles thus become of importance in influencing the characters of men. "A kiss from my mother," said West, "made me a painter." It is on the direction of such seeming trifles when children that the future happiness and success of men mainly depend. Fowell Buxton, when occupying an eminent and influential station in life, wrote to his mother, "I constantly feel, especially in action and exertion for others, the effects of principles early implanted by you in my mind." Buxton was also accustomed to remember with gratitude the obligations which he owed to an illiterate man, a gamekeeper, named Abraham Plastow, with whom he played, and rode, and sported—a man who could neither read nor write, but was full of natural good sense and mother-wit. "What made him particularly valuable," says Buxton, "were his principles of integrity and honour. He never said or did a thing in the absence of my mother of which she would have disapproved. He always held up the highest standard of integrity, and filled our youthful minds with sentiments as pure and as generous as could be found in the writings of Seneca or Cicero. Such was my first instructor, and, I must add, my best."

Lord Langdale, looking back upon the admirable example set him by his mother, declared, "If the whole world were put into one scale, and my mother into the other, the world would kick the beam." Mrs. Schimmel Penninck, in her old age, was accustomed to call to mind the personal influence exercised by her mother upon the society amidst which she moved. When she entered a room it had the effect of immediately raising the tone of the conversation, and as if purifying the moral atmosphere—all seeming to breathe more freely, and stand more erectly. "In her presence," says the daughter, "I became for the time transformed into another person." So much does the moral health depend upon the moral atmosphere that is breathed, and so great is the influence daily exercised by parents over their children.

by living a life before their eyes, that perhaps the best system of parental instruction might be summed up in these two words : " Improve thyself."

There is something solemn and awful in the thought that there is not an act done or a word uttered by a human being but carries with it a train of consequences, the end of which we may never trace. Not one but, to a certain extent, gives a colour to our life, and insensibly influences the lives of those about us. The good deed or word will live, even though we may not see it fructify, but so will the bad ; and no person is so insignificant as to be sure that his example will not do good on the one hand, or evil on the other. The spirits of men do not die : they still live and walk abroad among us. It was a fine and a. true thought uttered by Mr. Disraeli in the House of Commons on the death of Richard Cobden, that " he was one of those men who, though not present, were still members of that House, who were independent of dissolutions, of the caprices of constituencies, and even of the course of time."

There is, indeed, an essence of immortality in the life of man, even in this world. No individual in the universe stands alone ; he is a component part of a system of mutual dependencies ; and by his several acts he either increases or diminishes the sum of human good now and for ever. As the present is rooted in the past, and the lives and examples of our forefathers still to a great extent influence us, so are we by our daily acts contributing to form the condition and character of the future. Man is a fruit formed and ripened by the culture of all the foregoing centuries ; and the living generation continues the magnetic current of action and example destined to bind the remotest past with the most distant future. No man's acts die utterly ; and though his body may resolve into dust and air, his good or his bad deeds will still be bringing forth fruit after their kind, and influencing future generations for all time to come. It is in this momentous and solemn fact that the great peril and responsibility of human existence lies.

Mr. Babbage has so powerfully expressed this idea in a noble passage in one of his writings that we here venture to quote his words: " Every atom," he says, " impressed with good or ill, retains at once the motions which philosophers and sages have imparted to it, mixed and combined in ten thousand ways with all that is worthless and base ; the air itself is one vast library, on whose pages are written *for ever* all that man has ever said or whispered. There, in their immutable but unerring characters, mixed with the earliest as well as the latest sighs of mortality, stand for ever recorded vows unredeemed, promises unfulfilled ; perpetuating, in the united movements of each particle, the testimony of man's changeful will. But, if the air we breathe is the never-failing historian of the sentiments we have uttered, earth, air, and ocean, are, in like manner, the eternal witnesses of the acts we have done ; the same principle of the equality of action and reaction applies to them. No motion impressed by natural causes, or by human agency, is ever obliterated. . . . If the Almighty stamped on the brow of the first murderer the indelible and visible mark of his guilt, He has also established laws by which every succeeding criminal is not less irrevocably chained to the testimony of his crime ; for every atom of his mortal frame, through whatever changes its severed particles may migrate, will still retain adhering to it, through every combination, some movement derived from that very muscular effort by which the crime itself was perpetrated."

Thus, every act we do or word we utter, as well as every act we witness or word we hear, carries with it an influence which extends over, and gives a colour, not only to the whole of our future life, but makes itself felt upon the whole frame of society. We may not, and indeed cannot, possibly, trace the influence working itself into action in its various ramifications amongst our children, our friends, or associates ;. yet there it is assuredly, working on for ever. And herein lies the great significance of setting forth a good example,— a silent teaching which even the poorest and least significant person can practise in his daily life. There is no one so humble, but that he owes to others this simple but priceless instruction. Even the meanest condition may thus be made useful ; for the light set in a low place shines as faithfully as that set upon a hill. Everywhere, and under almost all. circumstances, however externally adverse—in moorland shielings, in cottage hamlets, in the close alleys of great towns—the true man may grow. He who tills a space of earth scarce bigger than is needed for his grave, may work as faithfully, and to as good purpose, as the heir to thousands.. The commonest workshop may thus be a school of industry, science, and good morals, on the one hand ; or of idleness, folly, and depravity, on the other. It all depends on the individual men, and the use they make of the opportunities. for good which offer themselves.

A life well spent, a character uprightly sustained, is no slight legacy to leave to one's children, and to the world ; for it is the most eloquent lesson of virtue and the severest reproof of vice, while it continues an enduring source of the best kind of riches. Well for those who can say, as Pope did, in rejoinder to the sarcasm of Lord Hervey, " I think it enough that my parents, such as they were, never cost me a blush, and that their son, such as he is, never cost them a tear."

It is not enough to *tell* others what they are to do, but to exhibit the actual example of doing. What Mrs. Chisholm described to Mrs. Stowe as the secret of her success, applies. to all life. " I found," she said, " that if we want anything. *done*, we must go to work and *do :* it is of no use merely to talk—none whatever." It is poor eloquence that only shows. how a person can talk. Had Mrs. Chisholm rested satisfied with lecturing, her project, she was persuaded, would never have got beyond the region of talk; but when people saw what she was doing and had actually accomplished, they fell in with her views and came forward to help her. Hence the most beneficent worker is not he who says the most eloquent things, or even who thinks the most loftily, but he who does the most eloquent acts.

True-hearted persons, even in the humblest station in life, who are energetic doers, may thus give an impulse to good works out of all proportion, apparently, to their actual station in society. Thomas Wright might have talked about the reclamation of criminals, and John Pounds about the necessity for Ragged Schools, and yet done nothing; instead of which they simply set to work without any other idea in their minds than that of doing, not talking. And how the example of even the poorest man may tell upon society, hear what Dr. Guthrie, the apostle of the Ragged School movement, says of the influence which the example of John Pounds, the humble Portsmouth cobbler, exercised upon his own working career:—

"The interest I have been led to take in this cause is an example of how, in Providence, a man's destiny—his course of life, like that of a river—may be determined and affected by very trivial circumstances. It is rather curious—at least it is interesting to me to remember—that it was by a picture I was first led to take an interest in ragged schools—by a picture in an old, obscure, decaying burgh that stands on the shores of the Frith of Forth, the birthplace of Thomas Chalmers. I went to see this place many years ago; and, going into an inn for refreshment, I found the room covered with pictures of shepherdesses with their crooks, and sailors in holiday attire, not particularly interesting. But above the chimney-piece there was a large print, more respectable than its neighbours, which represented a cobbler's room. The cobbler was there himself, spectacles on nose, an old shoe between his knees—-the massive forehead and firm mouth indicating great determination of character, and, beneath his bushy eyebrows, benevolence gleamed out on a number of poor ragged boys and girls who stood at their lessons round the busy cobbler. My curiosity was awakened ; and in the inscription I read how this man, John Pounds, a cobbler in Portsmouth, taking pity on the multitude of poor ragged children left by ministers and magistrates, and ladies and gentlemen, to go to ruin on the streets—how, like a good shepherd, he gathered in these wretched outcasts—how he had trained them to God and to the world—and how, while earning his daily bread by the sweat of his brow, he had rescued from misery and saved to society not less than five hundred of these children. I felt ashamed of myself. I felt reproved for the little I had done. My feelings were touched. I was astonished at this man's achievements ; and I well remember, in the enthusiasm of the moment, saying to my companion (and I have seen in my cooler and calmer moments no reason for unsaying the saying)—'That man is an honour to humanity, and deserves the tallest monument ever raised within the shores of Britain.' I took up that man's history, and I found it animated by the spirit of Him who 'had compassion on the multitude.' John Pounds was a clever man besides ; and, like Paul, if he could not win a poor boy any other way, he won him by art. He would be seen chasing a ragged boy along the quays, and compelling him to come to school, not by the power of a policeman, but by the power of a hot potato. He knew the love an Irishman had for a potato ; and John Pounds might be seen running holding under the boy's nose a potato, like an Irishman, very hot, and with a coat as ragged as himself. When the day comes when honour will be done to whom honour is due, I can fancy the crowd of those whose fame poets have sung, and to whose memory monuments have been raised, dividing like the wave, and, passing the great, and the noble, and the mighty of the land, this poor, obscure old man stepping forward and receiving the especial notice of Him who said 'Inasmuch as ye did it to one of the least of these, ye did it also to Me.'"

The education of character is very much a question of models; we mould ourselves so unconsciously after the characters, manners, habits, and opinions of those who are about us. Good rules may do much, but good models far more; for in the latter we have instruction in action— wisdom at work. Good admonition and bad example only build with one hand to pull down with the other. Hence the vast importance of exercising great care in the selection of companions, especially in youth. There is a magnetic affinity in young persons which insensibly tends to assimilate them to each other's likeness. Mr. Edgeworth was so strongly convinced that from sympathy they involuntarily imitated or caught the tone of the company they frequented, that he held it to be of the most essential importance that they should be taught to select the very best models. "No company, or good company," was his motto. Lord Collingwood, writing to a young friend, said, "Hold it as a maxim that you had better be alone than in mean company. Let your companions be such as yourself, or superior; for the worth of a man will always be ruled by that of his company." It was a remark of the famous Dr. Sydenham that everybody some time or other would be the better or the worse for having but spoken to a good or a bad man. As Sir Peter Lely made it a rule never to look at a bad picture if he could help it, believing that whenever he did so his pencil caught a taint from it, so, whoever chooses to gaze often upon a debased specimen of humanity and to frequent his society, cannot help gradually assimilating himself to that sort of model.

It is therefore advisable for young men to seek the fellowship of the good, and always to aim at a higher standard than themselves. Francis Horner, speaking of the advantages to himself of direct personal intercourse with high-minded, intelligent men, said, "I cannot hesitate to decide that I have derived more intellectual improvement from them than from all the books I have turned over." Lord Shelburne (afterwards Marquis of Lansdowne), when a young man, paid a visit to the venerable Malesherbes, and was so much impressed by it, that he said,—"I have travelled much, but I have never been so influenced by personal contact with any man; and if I ever accomplish any good in the course of my life, I am certain that the recollection of M. de Malesherbes will animate my soul." So Fowell Buxton was always ready to acknowledge the powerful influence exercised upon the formation of his character in early life by the example of the Gurney family: "It has given a colour to my life," he used to say. Speaking of his success at the Dublin University, he confessed, "I can ascribe it to nothing but my Earlham visits." It was from the Gurneys he "caught the infection" of self-improvement.

Contact with the good never fails to impart good, and we carry away with us some of the blessing, as travellers' garments retain the odour of the flowers and shrubs through which they have passed. Those who knew the late John Sterling intimately, have spoken of the beneficial influence which he exercised on all with whom he came into personal contact. Many owed to him their first awakening to a higher being; from him they learnt what they were, and what they ought to be. Mr. Trench says of him :—"It was impossible to come in contact with his noble nature without feeling one's self in some measure *ennobled* and *lifted up*, as I ever felt when I left him, into a higher region of objects and aims than that in which one is tempted habitually to dwell." It is thus that the noble character always acts; we become insensibly elevated by him, and cannot help feeling as he does and acquiring the habit of looking at things in the same light. Such is the magical action and reaction of minds upon each other.

Artists, also, feel themselves elevated by contact with artists greater than themselves. Thus Haydn's genius was first fired by Handel. Hearing him play, Haydn's ardour for musical composition was at once excited, and but for this circumstance, he himself believed that he would never have written the 'Creation.' Speaking of Handel, he said, "When he chooses, he strikes like the thunderbolt;" and at another time, "There is not a note of him but draws blood." Scarlatti was another of Handel's ardent admirers, following him all over Italy; afterwards, when speaking of the great master, he would cross himself in token of admiration. True artists never fail generously to recognise each other's greatness. Thus Beethoven's admiration for Cherubini was regal: and he ardently hailed the genius of Schubert: "Truly," said he, "in Schubert dwells a divine fire." When Northcote was a mere youth he had such an admiration for Reynolds that, when the great painter was once attending a public meeting down in Devonshire, the boy pushed through the crowd, and got so near Reynolds as to touch the skirt of his coat, "which I did," says Northcote, "with great satisfaction to my mind,"—a true touch of youthful enthusiasm in its admiration of genius.

The example of the brave is an inspiration to the timid, their presence thrilling through every fibre. Hence the miracles of valour so often performed by ordinary men under the leadership of the heroic. The very recollection of the deeds of the valiant stirs men's blood like the sound of a trumpet. Ziska bequeathed his skin to be used as a drum to inspire the valour of the Bohemians. When Scanderbeg, prince of Epirus, was dead, the Turks wished to possess his bones, that each might wear a piece next his heart, hoping thus to secure some portion of the courage he had displayed while living, and which they had so often experienced in battle. When the gallant Douglas, bearing the heart of Bruce to the Holy Land, saw one of his knights surrounded and sorely pressed by the Saracens, he took from his neck the silver case containing the hero's bequest, and throwing it amidst the thickest press of his foes, cried, "Pass first in fight, as thou wert wont to do, and Douglas will follow thee, or die;" and so saying, he rushed forward to the place where it fell, and was there slain.

The chief use of biography consists in the noble models of character in which it abounds. Our great forefathers still live among us in the records of their lives, as well as in the acts they have done, which live also; still sit by us at table, and hold us by the hand; furnishing examples for our benefit, which we may still study, admire and imitate. Indeed, whoever has left behind him the record of a noble life, has bequeathed to posterity an enduring source of good, for it serves as a model for others to form themselves by in all time to come; still breathing fresh life into men, helping them to reproduce his life anew, and to illustrate his character in other forms. Hence a book containing the life of a true man is full of precious seed. It is a still living voice : it is an intellect. To use Milton's words, "it is the precious life-blood of a master spirit, embalmed and treasured up on purpose to a life beyond life." Such a book never ceases to exercise an elevating and ennobling influence. But, above all, there is the Book containing the very highest Example set before us to shape our lives by in this world—the most suitable for all the necessities of our mind and heart—an example which we can only follow afar off and feel after,

> "Like plants or vines which never saw the sun,
> But dream of him and guess where he may be,
> And do their best to climb and get to him."

Again, no young man can rise from the perusal of such lives as those of Buxton and Arnold, without feeling his mind and heart made better, and his best resolves invigorated. Such biographies increase a man's self-reliance by demonstrating what men can be, and what they can do ; fortifying his hopes and elevating his aims in life. Sometimes a young man discovers himself in a biography, as Correggio felt within him the risings of genius on contemplating the works of Michael Angelo : "And I too, am a painter," he exclaimed. Sir Samuel Romilly, in his autobiography, confessed himself to have been powerfully influenced by the life of the great and noble-minded French Chancellor Daguesseau :—"The works of Thomas," says he, "had fallen into my hands, and I had read with admiration his ' Eloge of Daguesseau ;' and the career of honour which he represented that illustrious magistrate to have run, excited to a great degree my ardour and ambition, and opened to my imagination new paths of glory."

Franklin was accustomed to attribute his usefulness and eminence to his having early read Cotton Mather's ' Essays to do Good '—a book which grew out of Mather's own life. And see how good example draws other men after it, and propagates itself through future generations in all lands. For Samuel Drew avers that he framed his own life, and especially his business habits, after the model left on record by Benjamin Franklin. Thus it is impossible to say where a good example may not reach, or where it will end, if indeed it have an end. Hence the advantage, in literature as in life, of keeping the best society, reading the best books, and wisely admiring and imitating the best things we find in them. "In literature," said Lord Dudley, "I am fond of confining myself to the best company, which consists chiefly of my old acquaintance, with whom I am desirous of becoming more intimate ; and I suspect that nine times out of ten it is more profitable, if not more agreeable, to read an old book over again, than to read a new one for the first time."

Sometimes a book containing a noble exemplar of life, taken up at random, merely with the object of reading it as a pastime, has been known to call forth energies whose existence had not before been suspected. Alfieri was first drawn with passion to literature by reading 'Plutarch's Lives.' Loyola, when a soldier serving at the siege of Pampeluna, and laid up by a dangerous wound in his leg, asked for a book to divert his thoughts: the 'Lives of the Saints' was brought to him, and its perusal so inflamed his mind, that he determined thenceforth to devote himself to the founding of a religious order. Luther, in like manner, was inspired to undertake the great labours of his life by a perusal of the 'Life and Writings of John Huss.' Dr. Wolff was stimulated to enter upon his missionary career by reading the 'Life of Francis Xavier;' and the book fired his youthful bosom with a passion the most sincere and ardent to devote himself to the enterprise of his life. William Carey, also, got the first idea of entering upon his sublime labours as a missionary from a perusal of the Voyages of Captain Cook.

Francis Horner was accustomed to note in his diary and letters the books by which he was most improved and influenced. Amongst these were Condorcet's 'Eloge of Haller,' Sir Joshua Reynolds' 'Discourses,' the writings of Bacon, and 'Burnet's Account of Sir Matthew Hale.' The perusal of the last-mentioned book—the portrait of a prodigy of labour—Horner says, filled him with enthusiasm. Of Condorcet's 'Eloge of Haller,' he said: "I never rise from the account of such men without a sort of thrilling palpitation about me, which I know not whether I should call admiration, ambition, or despair." And speaking of the 'Discourses' of Sir Joshua Reynolds, he said: "Next to the writings of Bacon, there is no book which has more powerfully impelled me to self-culture. He is one of the first men of genius who has condescended to inform the world of the steps by which greatness is attained. The confidence with which he asserts the omnipotence of human labour has the effect of familiarising his reader with the idea that genius is an acquisition rather than a gift; whilst with all there is blended so naturally and eloquently the most elevated and passionate admiration of excellence, that upon the whole there is no book of a more *inflammatory* effect." It is remarkable that Reynolds himself attributed his first passionate impulse towards the study of art, to reading Richardson's account of a great painter; and Haydon was in like manner afterwards inflamed to follow the same pursuit by reading of the career of Reynolds. Thus the brave and aspiring life of one man lights a flame in the minds of others of like faculties and impulse ; and where there is equally vigorous effort, like distinction and success will almost surely follow. Thus the chain of example is carried down through time in an endless succession of links,—admiration exciting imitation, and perpetuating the true aristocracy of genius.

One of the most valuable, and one of the most infectious examples which can be set before the young, is that of cheerful working. Cheerfulness gives elasticity to the spirit. Spectres fly before it ; difficulties cause no despair, for they are encountered with hope, and the mind acquires that happy disposition to improve opportunities which rarely fails of success. The fervent spirit is always a healthy and happy spirit; working cheerfully itself, and stimulating others to work. It confers a dignity on even the most ordinary occupations. The most effective work, also, is usually the full-hearted work—that which passes through the hands or the head of him whose heart is glad. Hume was accustomed to say that he would rather possess a cheerful disposition—inclined always to look at the bright side of things—than with a gloomy mind to be the master of an estate of ten thousand a year. Granville

Sharp, amidst his indefatigable labours on behalf of the slave, solaced himself in the evenings by taking part in glees and instrumental concerts at his brother's house, singing, or playing on the flute, the clarionet, or the oboe; and, at the Sunday evening oratorios, when Handel was played, he beat the kettle-drums. He also indulged, though sparingly, in caricature drawing. Fowell Buxton also was an eminently cheerful man; taking special pleasure in field sports, in riding about the country with his children, and in mixing in all their domestic amusements.

In another sphere of action, Dr. Arnold was a noble and a cheerful worker, throwing himself into the great business of his life, the training and teaching of young men, with his whole heart and soul. It is stated in his admirable biography, that "the most remarkable thing in the Laleham circle was the wonderful healthiness of tone which prevailed there. It was a place where a new comer at once felt that a great and earnest work was going forward. Every pupil was made to feel that there was a work for him to do; that his happiness, as well as his duty, lay in doing that work well. Hence an indescribable zest was communicated to a young man's feeling about life; a strange joy came over him on discerning that he had the means of being useful, and thus of being happy; and a deep respect and ardent attachment sprang up towards him who had taught him thus to value life and his own self, and his work and mission in the world. All this was founded on the breadth and comprehensiveness of Arnold's character, as well as its striking truth and reality; on the unfeigned regard he had for work of all kinds, and the sense he had of its value, both for the complex aggregate of society and the growth and protection of the individual. In all this there was no excitement; no predilection for one class of work above another; no enthusiasm for any one-sided object: but a humble, profound, and most religious consciousness that work is the appointed calling of man on earth ; the end for which his various faculties were given ; the element in which his nature is ordained to develop itself, and in which his progressive advance towards heaven is to lie." Among the many valuable men trained for public life and usefulness by Arnold, was the gallant Hodson, of Hodson's Horse, who, writing home from India, many years after, thus spoke of his revered master : " The influence he produced has been most lasting and striking in its effects. It is felt even in India ; I cannot say more than *that.*"

The useful influence which a right-hearted man of energy and industry may exercise amongst his neighbours and dependants, and accomplish for his country, cannot, perhaps, be better illustrated than by the career of Sir John Sinclair; characterized by the Abbé Gregoire as "the most indefatigable man in Europe." He was originally a country laird, born to a considerable estate situated near John o' Groat's House, almost beyond the beat of civilization, in a bare wild country fronting the stormy North Sea. His father dying while he was a youth of sixteen, the management of the family property thus early devolved upon him ; and at eighteen he began a course of vigorous improvement in the county of Caithness, which eventually spread all over Scotland. Agriculture then was in a most backward state ; the fields were unenclosed, the lands undrained ; the small farmers of Caithness were so poor that they could scarcely afford to keep a horse or shelty ; the hard work was chiefly done, and the burdens borne, by the women ; and if a cottier lost a horse it was not unusual for him to marry a wife as the cheapest substitute. The country was without roads or bridges ; and drovers driving their cattle south had to swim the rivers along with their beasts. The chief track leading into Caithness lay along a high shelf on a mountain side, the road being some

hundred feet of clear perpendicular height above the sea
which dashed below.   Sir John, though a mere youth,
determined to make a new road over the hill of Ben
Cheilt, the old let-alone proprietors, however, regarding his
scheme with incredulity and derision.   But he himself laid
out the road, assembled some twelve hundred workmen
early one summer's morning, set them simultaneously to
work, superintending their labours, and stimulating them
by his presence and example ; and before night, what had
been a dangerous sheep track, six miles in length, hardly
passable for led horses, was made practicable for wheel-
carriages as if by the power of magic.   It was an admirable example of energy and well-directed labour, which
could not fail to have a most salutary influence upon the
surrounding population.   He then proceeded to make more
roads, to erect mills, to build bridges, and to enclose and
cultivate the waste lands.   He introduced improved methods of culture, and regular rotation of crops, distri-
buting small premiums to encourage industry ; and he thus
soon quickened the whole frame of society within reach of
his influence, and infused an entirely new spirit into the
cultivators of the soil.   From being one of the most inaccessible districts of the north—the very *ultima Thule* of
civilization—Caithness became a pattern county for its
roads, its agriculture, and its fisheries.   In Sinclair's youth,
the post was carried by a runner only once a week, and the
young baronet then declared that he would never rest till
a coach drove daily to Thurso.   The people of the neighbourhood could not believe in any such thing, and it
became a proverb in the county to say of any utterly impossible scheme, "Ou, ay, that will come to pass when Sir
John sees the daily mail at Thurso !"   But Sir John lived
to see his dream realized, and the daily mail established to
Thurso.

The circle of his benevolent operations gradually widened.

Observing the serious deterioration which had taken place in the quality of British wool,—one of the staple commodities of the country,—he forthwith, though but a private and little-known country gentleman, devoted himself to its improvement. By his personal exertions he established the British Wool Society for the purpose, and himself led the way to practical improvement by importing 800 sheep from all countries, at his own expense. The result was, the introduction into Scotland of the celebrated Cheviot breed. Sheep farmers scouted the idea of south country flocks being able to thrive in the far north. But Sir John persevered ; and in a few years there were not fewer than 300,000 Cheviots diffused over the four northern counties alone. The value of all grazing land was thus enormously increased ; and Scotch estates, which before were comparatively worthless, began to yield large rentals.

Returned by Caithness to Parliament, in which he remained for thirty years, rarely missing a division, his position gave him farther opportunities of usefulness, which he did not neglect to employ. Mr. Pitt, observing his persevering energy in all useful public projects, sent for him to Downing Street, and voluntarily proposed his assistance in any object he might have in view. Another man might have thought of himself and his own promotion ; but Sir John characteristically replied, that he desired no favour for himself, but intimated that the reward most gratifying to his feelings would be Mr. Pitt's assistance in the establishment of a National Board of Agriculture. Arthur Young laid a bet with the baronet that his scheme would never be established, adding, " Your Board of Agriculture will be in the moon ! " But vigorously setting to work, he roused public attention to the subject, enlisted a majority of Parliament on his side, and eventually established the Board, of which he was appointed President. The result of its action need not be described, but the stimulus which it gave to agriculture and stock-raising was shortly felt throughout the whole United Kingdom, and tens of thousands of acres were redeemed from barrenness by its operation. He was equally indefatigable in encouraging the establishment of fisheries; and the successful founding of these great branches of British industry at Thurso and Wick was mainly due to his exertions. He urged for long years, and at length succeeded in obtaining the enclosure of a harbour for the latter place, which is perhaps the greatest and most prosperous fishing town in the world.

Sir John threw his personal energy into every work in which he engaged, rousing the inert, stimulating the idle, encouraging the hopeful, and working with all. When a French invasion was threatened, he offered to Mr. Pitt to raise a regiment on his own estate, and he was as good as his word. He went down to the north, and raised a battalion of 600 men, afterwards increased to 1000; and it was admitted to be one of the finest volunteer regiments ever raised, inspired throughout by his own noble and patriotic spirit. While commanding officer of the camp at Aberdeen he held the offices of a Director of the Bank of Scotland, Chairman of the British Wool Society, Provost of Wick, Director of the British Fishery Society, Commissioner for issuing Exchequer Bills, Member of Parliament for Caithness, and President of the Board of Agriculture. Amidst all this multifarious and self-imposed work, he even found time to write books, enough of themselves to establish a reputation. When Mr. Rush, the American Ambassador, arrived in England, he relates that he inquired of Mr. Coke of Holkham, what was the best work on Agriculture, and was referred to Sir John Sinclair's; and when he further asked of Mr. Vansittart, Chancellor of the Exchequer, what was the best work on British Finance, he was again referred to a work by Sir John Sinclair, his 'History of the Public Revenue.' But the great monument of his inde-

fatigable industry, a work that would have appalled other
men, but only served to rouse and sustain his energy, was
his 'Statistical Account of Scotland,' in twenty-one volumes,
one of the most valuable practical works ever published in
any age or country. Amid a host of other pursuits it occupied him nearly eight years of hard labour, during which he
received, and attended to, upwards of 20,000 letters on the
subject. It was a thoroughly patriotic undertaking, from
which he derived no personal advantage whatever, beyond
the honour of having completed it. The whole of the profits
were assigned by him to the Society for the Sons of the
Clergy in Scotland. The publication of the book led to
great public improvements; it was followed by the immediate
abolition of several oppressive feudal rights, to which it called
attention; the salaries of schoolmasters and clergyman in
many parishes were increased; and an increased stimulus
was given to agriculture throughout Scotland. Sir John then
publicly offered to undertake the much greater labour of
collecting and publishing a similar Statistical Account of
England; but unhappily the then Archbishop of Canterbury
refused to sanction it, lest it should interfere with the tithes
of the clergy, and the idea was abandoned.

A remarkable illustration of his energetic promptitude
was the manner in which he once provided, on a great
emergency, for the relief of the manufacturing districts.
In 1793 the stagnation produced by the war led to an unusual number of bankruptcies, and many of the first houses
in Manchester and Glasgow were tottering, not so much
from want of property, but because the usual sources of
trade and credit were for the time closed up. A period of
intense distress amongst the labouring classes seemed imminent, when Sir John urged, in Parliament, that Exchequer
notes to the amount of five millions should be issued immediately as a loan to such merchants as could give security,
This suggestion was adopted, and his offer to carry out his

plan, in conjunction with certain members named by him, was also accepted. The vote was passed late at night, and early next morning Sir John, anticipating the delays of officialism and red tape, proceeded to bankers in the city, and borrowed of them, on his own personal security, the sum of 70,000*l.*, which he despatched the same evening to those merchants who were in the most urgent need of assistance. Pitt meeting Sir John in the House, expressed his great regret that the pressing wants of Manchester and Glagsow could not be supplied so soon as was desirable, adding, " The money cannot be raised for some days." " It is already gone ! it left London by to-night's mail ! " was Sir John's triumphant reply ; and in afterwards relating the anecdote he added, with a smile of pleasure, " Pitt was as much startled as if I had stabbed him." To the last this great, good man worked on usefully and cheerfully, setting a great example for his family and for his country. In so laboriously seeking others' good, it might be said that he found his own—not wealth, for his generosity seriously impaired his private fortune, but happiness, and self-satisfaction, and the peace that passes knowledge. A great patriot, with magnificent powers of work, he nobly did his duty to his country ; yet he was not neglectful of his own household and home. His sons and daughters grew up to honour and usefulness ; and it was one of the proudest things Sir John could say, when verging on his eightieth year, that he had lived to see seven sons grown up, not one of whom had incurred a debt he could not pay, or caused him a sorrow that could have been avoided.

CHAPTER XIII.

CHARACTER—THE TRUE GENTLEMAN.

> " For who can always act ? but he,
> To whom a thousand memories call,
> Not being less but more than all
> The gentleness he seemed to be,
>
> But seemed the thing he was, and join'd
> Each office of the social hour
> To noble manners, as the flower
> And native growth of noble mind;
>
> And thus he bore without abuse
> The grand old name of Gentleman."—*Tennyson.*

> " Es bildet ein Talent sich in der Stille,
> Sich ein Charakter in dem Strom der Welt."—*Goethe.*

"That which raises a country, that which strengthens a country, and that which lignifies a country,—that which spreads her power, creates her moral influence, and makes her respected and submitted to, bends the heart of millions, and bows down the pride of nations to her—the instrument of obedience, the fountain of supremacy, the true throne, crown, and sceptre of a nation;—this aristocracy is not an aristocracy or blood, not an aristocracy of fashion, not an aristocracy of talent only; it is an aristocracy of Character. That is the true heraldry of man."—*The Times.*

THE crown and glory of life is Character. It is the noblest possession of a man, constituting a rank in itself, and an estate in the general goodwill; dignifying every station, and exalting every position in society. It exercises a greater power than wealth, and secures all the honour without the jealousies of fame. It carries with it an influence which always tells; for it is the result of proved honour, rectitude, and consistency—qualities which, perhaps more than any other, command the general confidence and respect of mankind.

Character is human nature in its best form. It is moral order embodied in the individual. Men of character are not only the conscience of society, but in every well-governed State they are its best motive power; for it is moral qualities in the main which rule the world. Even in war, Napoleon said the moral is to the physical as ten to one. The strength, the industry, and the civilisation of nations—all depend upon individual character; and the very foundations of civil security rest upon it. Laws and institutions are but its outgrowth. In the just balance of nature, individuals, nations, and races, will obtain just so much as they deserve, and no more. And as effect finds its cause, so surely does quality of character amongst a people produce its befitting results.

Though a man have comparatively little culture, slender abilities, and but small wealth, yet, if his character be of sterling worth, he will always command an influence, whether it be in the workshop, the counting-house, the mart, or the senate. Canning wisely wrote in 1801, " My road must be through Character to power; I will try no other course; and I am sanguine enough to believe that this course, though not perhaps the quickest, is the surest." You may admire men of intellect; but something more is necessary before you will trust them. Hence Lord John Russell once observed in a sentence full of truth, " It is the nature of party in England to ask the assistance of men of genius, but to follow the guidance of men of character." This was strikingly illustrated in the career of the late Francis Horner—a man of whom Sydney Smith said that the Ten Commandments were stamped upon his countenance. " The valuable and peculiar light," says Lord Cockburn, " in which his history is calculated to inspire every right-minded youth, is this. He died at the age of thirty-eight; possessed of greater public influence than any other private man; and admired, beloved, trusted, and deplored

by all, except the heartless or the base. No greater homage
was ever paid in Parliament to any deceased member. Now
let every young man ask—how was this attained? By rank?
He was the son of an Edinburgh merchant. By wealth?
Neither he, nor any of his relations, ever had a superfluous
sixpence. By office? He held but one, and only for a
few years, of no influence, and with very little pay. By
talents? His were not splendid, and he had no genius.
Cautious and slow, his only ambition was to be right. By
eloquence? He spoke in calm, good taste, without any
of the oratory that either terrifies or seduces. By any fasci-
nation of manner? His was only correct and agreeable.
By what, then, was it? Merely by sense, industry, good
principles, and a good heart—qualities which no well-con-
stituted mind need ever despair of attaining. It was the
force of his character that raised him ; and this character
not impressed upon him by nature, but formed, out of no
peculiarly fine elements, by himself. There were many in
the House of Commons of far greater ability and eloquence.
But no one surpassed him in the combination of an adequate
portion of these with moral worth. Horner was born to
show what moderate powers, unaided by anything whatever
except culture and goodness, may achieve, even when these
powers are displayed amidst the competition and jealousy of
public life."

Franklin, also, attributed his success as a public man,
not to his talents or his powers of speaking—for these
were but moderate—but to his known integrity of character
Hence it was, he says, " that I had so much weight with my
fellow citizens. I was but a bad speaker, never eloquent,
subject to much hesitation in my choice of words, hardly
correct in language, and yet I generally carried my point."
Character creates confidence in men in high station as well
as in humble life. It was said of the first Emperor Alexander of Russia, that his personal character was equivalent

to a constitution. During the wars of the Fronde, Montaigne was the only man amongst the French gentry who kept his castle gates unbarred; and it was said of him, that his personal character was a better protection for him than a regiment of horse would have been.

That character is power, is true in a much higher sense than that knowledge is power. Mind without heart, intelligence without conduct, cleverness without goodness, are powers in their way, but they may be powers only for mischief. We may be instructed or amused by them; but it is sometimes as difficult to admire them as it would be to admire the dexterity of a pickpocket or the horsemanship of a highwayman.

Truthfulness, integrity, and goodness—qualities that hang not on any man's breath—form the essence of manly character, or, as one of our old writers has it, "that inbred loyalty unto Virtue which can serve her without a livery." He who possesses these qualities, united with strength of purpose, carries with him a power which is irresistible. He is strong to do good, strong to resist evil, and strong to bear up under difficulty and misfortune. When Stephen of Colonna fell into the hands of his base assailants, and they asked him in derision, "Where is now your fortress?" "Here," was his bold reply, placing his hand upon his heart. It is in misfortune that the character of the upright man shines forth with the greatest lustre; and when all else fails, he takes stand upon his integrity and his courage.

The rules of conduct followed by Lord Erskine—a man of sterling independence of principle and scrupulous adherence to truth—are worthy of being engraven on every young man's heart. "It was a first command and counsel of my earliest youth," he said, "always to do what my conscience told me to be a duty, and to leave the consequence to God. I shall carry with me the memory, and

2 C

I trust the practice, of this parental lesson to the grave. I have hitherto followed it, and I have no reason to complain that my obedience to it has been a temporal sacrifice. I have found it, on the contrary, the road to prosperity and wealth, and I shall point out the same path to my children for their pursuit."

Every man is bound to aim at the possession of a good character as one of the highest objects of life. The very effort to secure it by worthy means will furnish him with a motive for exertion; and his idea of manhood, in proportion as it is elevated, will steady and animate his motive. It is well to have a high standard of life, even though we may not be able altogether to realize it. "The youth," says Mr. Disraeli, "who does not look up will look down; and the spirit that does not soar is destined perhaps to grovel." George Herbert wisely writes,

> " Pitch thy behaviour low, thy projects high,
>   So shall thou humble and magnanimous be.
> Sink not in spirit ; who aimeth at the sky
>   Shoots higher much than he that means a tree."

He who has a high standard of living and thinking will certainly do better than he who has none at all. " Pluck at a gown of gold," says the Scotch proverb, "and you may get a sleeve o't." Whoever tries for the highest results cannot fail to reach a point far in advance of that from which he started; and though the end attained may fall short of that proposed, still, the very effort to rise, of itself cannot fail to prove permanently beneficial.

There are many counterfeits of character, but the genuine article is difficult to be mistaken. Some, knowing its money value, would assume its disguise for the purpose of imposing upon the unwary. Colonel Charteris said to a man distinguished for his honesty, " I would give a thousand pounds for your good name." " Why?" "Because I could make ten thousand by it," was the knave's reply.

Integrity in word and deed is the backbone of character; and loyal adherence to veracity its most prominent characteristic. One of the finest testimonies to the character of the late Sir Robert Peel was that borne by the Duke of Wellington in the House of Lords, a few days after the great statesman's death. " Your lordships," he said, " must all feel the high and honourable character of the late Sir Robert Peel. I was long connected with him in public life. We were both in the councils of our Sovereign together, and I had long the honour to enjoy his private friendship. In all the course of my acquaintance with him I never knew a man in whose truth and justice I had greater confidence, or in whom I saw a more invariable desire to promote the public service. In the whole course of my communication with him, I never knew an instance in which he did not show the strongest attachment to truth; and I never saw in the whole course of my life the smallest reason for suspecting that he stated anything which he did not firmly believe to be the fact." And this high-minded truthfulness of the statesman was no doubt the secret of no small part of his influence and power.

There is a truthfulness in action as well as in words, which is essential to uprightness of character. A man must really be what he seems or purposes to be. When an American gentleman wrote to Granville Sharp, that from respect for his great virtues he had named one of his sons after him, Sharp replied : " I must request you to teach him a favourite maxim of the family whose name you have given him—*Always endeavour to be really what you would wish to appear.* This maxim, as my father informed me, was carefully and humbly practised by *his* father, whose sincerity, as a plain and honest man, thereby became the principal feature of his character, both in public and private life." Every man who respects himself, and values the respect of others, will carry out the maxim in act—doing honestly what he proposes to do—putting the highest character into his work, scamping nothing, but priding himself upon his integrity and conscientiousness. Once Cromwell said to Bernard,—a clever but somewhat unscrupulous lawyer, " I understand that you have lately been vastly wary in your conduct ; do not be too confident of this ; subtlety may deceive you, integrity never will." Men whose acts are at direct variance with their words, command no respect, and what they say has but little weight ; even truths, when uttered by them, seem to come blasted from their lips.

The true character acts rightly, whether in secret or in the sight of men. That boy was well trained who, when asked why he did not pocket some pears, for nobody was there to see, replied, "Yes, there was : I was there to see myself ; and I don't intend ever to see myself do a dishonest thing." This is a simple but not inappropriate illustration of principle, or conscience, dominating in the character, and exercising a noble protectorate over it ; not merely a passive influence, but an active power regulating the life. Such a principle goes on moulding the character hourly and daily, growing with a force that operates every moment. Without this dominating influence, character has no protection, but is constantly liable to fall away before temptation ; and every such temptation succumbed to, every act of meanness or dishonesty, however slight, causes self-degradation. It matters not whether the act be successful or not, discovered or concealed ; the culprit is no longer the same, but another person ; and he is pursued by a secret uneasiness, by self-reproach, or the workings of what we call conscience, which is the inevitable doom of the guilty.

And here it may be observed how greatly the character may be strengthened and supported by the cultivation of good habits. Man, it has been said, is a bundle of habits ; and habit is second nature. Metastasio entertained so strong an opinion as to the power of repetition in act and thought, that he said, " All is habit in mankind, even virtue itself." Butler, in his 'Analogy,' impresses the importance of careful self-discipline and firm resistance to temptation, as tending to make virtue habitual, so that at length it may become more easy to be good than to give way to sin. " As habits belonging to the body," he says, " are produced by external acts, so habits of the mind are produced by the execution of inward practical purposes, *i. e.*, carrying them into act, or acting upon them—the principles of obedience, veracity, justice, and charity." And again, Lord Brougham says, when enforcing the immense importance of training and example in youth, " I trust everything under God to habit, on which, in all ages, the lawgiver, as well as the schoolmaster, has mainly placed his reliance ; habit, which makes everything easy, and casts the difficulties upon the deviation from a wonted course." Thus, make sobriety a habit, and intemperance will be hateful ; make prudence a habit, and reckless profligacy will become revolting to every principle of conduct which regulates the life of the individual. Hence the necessity for the greatest care and watchfulness against the inroad of any evil habit; for the character is always weakest at that point at which it has once given way ; and it is long before a principle restored can become so firm as one that has never been moved.   It is a fine remark of a Russian writer, that " Habits are a necklace of pearls : untie the knot, and the whole unthreads."

Wherever formed, habit acts involuntarily, and without effort ; and, it is only when you oppose it, that you find how powerful it has become.   What is done once and again, soon gives facility and proneness.   The habit at first may seem to have no more strength than a spider's web; but, once formed, it binds as with a chain of iron.   The small events of life, taken singly, may seem exceedingly unimportant, like snow that falls silently, flake by flake ; yet accumulated, these snow-flakes form the avalanche.

Self-respect, self-help, application, industry, integrity—all are of the nature of habits, not beliefs. Principles, in fact, are but the names which we assign to habits; for the principles are words, but the habits are the things themselves: benefactors or tyrants, according as they are good or evil. It thus happens that as we grow older, a portion of our free activity and individuality becomes suspended in habit; our actions become of the nature of fate; and we are bound by the chains which we have woven around ourselves.

It is indeed scarcely possible to over-estimate the importance of training the young to virtuous habits. In them they are the easiest formed, and when formed they last for life; like letters cut on the bark of a tree they grow and widen with age. " Train up a child in the way he should go, and when he is old he will not depart from it." The beginning holds within it the end; the first start on the road of life determines the direction and the destination of the journey; *ce n'est que le premier pas qui coûte.* " Remember," said Lord Collingwood to a young man whom he loved, " before you are five-and-twenty you must establish a character that will serve you all your life." As habit strengthens with age, and character becomes formed, any turning into a new path becomes more and more difficult. Hence, it is often harder to unlearn than to learn; and for this reason the Grecian flute-player was justified who charged double fees to those pupils who had been taught by an inferior master. To uproot an old habit is sometimes a more painful thing, and vastly more difficult, than to wrench out a tooth. Try and reform a habitually indolent, or improvident, or drunken person, and in a large majority of cases you will fail. For the habit in each case has wound itself in and through the life until it has become an integral part of it, and cannot be uprooted. Hence, as Mr. Lynch observes, " the wisest habit of all is the habit of care in the formation of good habits."

Even happiness itself may become habitual. There is a habit of looking at the bright side of things, and also of looking at the dark side. Dr. Johnson has said that the habit of looking at the best side of a thing is worth more to a man than a thousand pounds a year. And we possess the power, to a great extent, of so exercising the will as to direct the thoughts upon objects calculated to yield happiness and improvement rather than their opposites. In this way the habit of happy thought may be made to spring up like any other habit. And to bring up men or women with a genial nature of this sort, a good temper, and a happy frame of mind, is perhaps of even more importance, in many cases, than to perfect them in much knowledge and many accomplishments.

As daylight can be seen through very small holes, so little things will illustrate a person's character. Indeed character consists in little acts, well and honourably performed; daily life being the quarry from which we build it up, and rough-hew the habits which form it. One of the most marked tests of character is the manner in which we conduct ourselves towards others. A graceful behaviour towards superiors, inferiors, and equals, is a constant source of pleasure. It pleases others because it indicates respect for their personality; but it gives tenfold more pleasure to ourselves. Every man may to a large extent be a self-educator in good behaviour, as in everything else; he can be civil and kind, if he will, though he have not a penny in his purse. Gentleness in society is like the silent influence of light, which gives colour to all nature; it is far more powerful than loudness or force, and far more fruitful. It pushes its way quietly and persistently, like the tiniest daffodil in spring, which raises the clod and thrusts it aside by the simple persistency of growing.

Even a kind look will give pleasure and confer happiness. In one of Robertson of Brighton's letters, he tells of a lady

who related to him "the delight, the tears of gratitude, which
she had witnessed in a poor girl to whom, in passing, I
gave a kind look on going out of church on Sunday.
What a lesson! How cheaply happiness can be given!
What opportunities we miss of doing an angel's work! I
remember doing it, full of sad feelings, passing on, and
thinking no more about it; and it gave an hour's sunshine
to a human life, and lightened the load of life to a human
heart for a time!" *

Morals and manners, which give colour to life, are of
much greater importance than laws, which are but their
manifestations. The law touches us here and there, but
manners are about us everywhere, pervading society like
the air we breathe. Good manners, as we call them, are
neither more nor less than good behaviour; consisting of
courtesy and kindness; benevolence being the prepon-
derating element in all kinds of mutually beneficial and
pleasant intercourse amongst human beings. "Civility,"
said Lady Montague, "costs nothing and buys everything." The cheapest of all things is kindness, its exercise requiring the least possible trouble and self-sacrifice.
"Win hearts," said Burleigh to Queen Elizabeth, "and
you have all men's hearts and purses." If we would only
let nature act kindly, free from affectation and artifice, the
results on social good humour and happiness would be in-
calculable. The little courtesies which form the small
change of life, may separately appear of little intrinsic
value, but they acquire their importance from repetition
and accumulation. They are like the spare minutes, or the
groat a day, which proverbially produce such momentous
results in the course of a twelvemonth, or in a lifetime.

Manners are the ornament of action; and there is a
way of speaking a kind word, or of doing a kind thing,
which greatly enhances their value. What seems to be done

* Robertson's 'Life and Letters,' i. 258.

with a grudge, or as an act of condescension, is scarcely accepted as a favour. Yet there are men who pride themselves upon their gruffness; and though they may possess virtue and capacity, their manner is often such as to render them almost insupportable. It is difficult to like a man who, though he may not pull your nose, habitually wounds your self-respect, and takes a pride in saying disagreeable things to you. There are others who are dreadfully condescending, and cannot avoid seizing upon every small opportunity of making their greatness felt. When Abernethy was canvassing for the office of surgeon to St. Bartholomew Hospital, he called upon such a person—a rich grocer, one of the governors. The great man behind the counter seeing the great surgeon enter, immediately assumed the grand air towards the supposed suppliant for his vote. "I presume, Sir, you want my vote and interest at this momentous epoch of your life." Abernethy, who hated humbugs, and felt nettled at the tone, replied: "No, I don't: I want a pennyworth of figs; come, look sharp and wrap them up; I want to be off!"

The cultivation of manner—though in excess it is foppish and foolish—is highly necessary in a person who has occasion to negociate with others in matters of business. Affability and good breeding may even be regarded as essential to the success of a man in any eminent station and enlarged sphere of life; for the want of it has not unfrequently been found in a great measure to neutralise the results of much industry, integrity, and honesty of character. There are, no doubt, a few strong tolerant minds which can bear with defects and angularities of manner, and look only to the more genuine qualities; but the world at large is not so forbearant, and cannot help forming its judgments and likings mainly according to outward conduct.

Another mode of displaying true politeness is consideration for the opinions of others. It has been said of dogmatism, that it is only puppyism come to its full growth ; and certainly the worst form this quality can assume, is that of opinionativeness and arrogance. Let men agree to differ, and, when they do differ, bear and forbear. Principles and opinions may be maintained with perfect suavity, without coming to blows or uttering hard words ; and there are circumstances in which words are blows, and inflict wounds far less easy to heal. As bearing upon this point, we quote an instructive little parable spoken some time since by an itinerant preacher of the Evangelical Alliance on the borders of Wales :—"As I was going to the hills," said he, "early one misty morning, I saw something moving on a mountain side, so strange looking that I took it for a monster. When I came nearer to it I found it was a man. When I came up to him I found he was my brother."

The inbred politeness which springs from right-heartedness and kindly feelings, is of no exclusive rank or station. The mechanic who works at the bench may possess it, as well as the clergyman or the peer. It is by no means a necessary condition of labour that it should, in any respect, be either rough or coarse. The politeness and refinement which distinguish all classes of the people in many continental countries show that those qualities might become ours too—as doubtless they will become with increased culture and more general social intercourse—without sacrificing any of our more genuine qualities as men. From the highest to the lowest, the richest to the poorest, to no rank or condition in life has nature denied her highest boon—the great heart. There never yet existed a gentleman but was lord of a great heart. And this may exhibit itself under the hodden grey of the peasant as well as under the laced coat of the noble. Robert Burns was once taken to task by a young Edinburgh blood, with whom he was walking, for recog-

nising an honest farmer in the open street. "Why you
fantastic gomeral," exclaimed Burns, " it was not the great
coat, the scone bonnet, and the saunders-boot hose that I
spoke to, but *the man* that was in them ; and the man, sir,
for true worth, would weigh down you and me, and ten
more such, any day." There may be a homeliness in ex-
ternals, which may seem vulgar to those who cannot discern
the heart beneath ; but, to the right-minded, character will
always have its clear insignia.

William and Charles Grant were the sons of a farmer in
Inverness-shire, whom a sudden flood stripped of everything,
even to the very soil which he tilled. The farmer and his
sons, with the world before them where to choose, made
their way southward in search of employment until they
arrived in the neighbourhood of Bury in Lancashire. From
the crown of the hill near Walmesley they surveyed the wide
extent of country which lay before them, the river Irwell
making its circuitous course through the valley. They were
utter strangers in the neighbourhood, and knew not which
way to turn. To decide their course they put up a stick,
and agreed to pursue the direction in which it fell. Thus
their decision was made, and they journeyed on accordingly
until they reached the village of Ramsbotham, not far distant.
They found employment in a print-work, in which William
served his apprenticeship ; and they commended themselves
to their employers by their diligence, sobriety, and strict
integrity. They plodded on, rising from one station to
another, until at length the two men themselves became employers, and after many long years of industry, enterprise,
and benevolence, they became rich, honoured, and respected
by all who knew them. Their cotton-mills and print-works
gave employment to a large population. Their well-directed
diligence made the valley teem with activity, joy, health, and
opulence. Out of their abundant wealth they gave liberally
to all worthy objects, erecting churches, founding schools,

and in all ways promoting the well-being of the class of working-men from which they had sprung. They afterwards erected, on the top of the hill above Walmesley, a lofty tower in commemoration of the early event in their history which had determined the place of their settlement. The brothers Grant became widely celebrated for their benevolence and their various goodness, and it is said that Mr. Dickens had them in his mind's eye when delineating the character of the brothers Cheeryble. One amongst many anecdotes of a similar kind may be cited to show that the character was by no means exaggerated. A Manchester warehouseman published an exceedingly scurrilous pamphlet against the firm of Grant Brothers, holding up the elder partner to ridicule as "Billy Button." William was informed by some one of the nature of the pamphlet, and his observation was that the man would live to repent of it. "Oh!" said the libeller, when informed of the remark, "he thinks that some time or other I shall be in his debt; but I will take good care of that." It happens, however, that men in business do not always foresee who shall be their creditor, and it so turned out that the Grants' libeller became a bankrupt, and could not complete his certificate and begin business again without obtaining their signature. It seemed to him a hopeless case to call upon that firm for any favour, but the pressing claims of his family forced him to make the application. He appeared before the man whom he had ridiculed as "Billy Button" accordingly. He told his tale and produced his certificate. "You wrote a pamphlet against us once?" said Mr. Grant. The supplicant expected to see his document thrown into the fire; instead of which Grant signed the name of the firm, and thus completed the necessary certificate. "We make it a rule," said he, handing it back, "never to refuse signing the certificate of an honest tradesman, and we have never heard that you were anything else." The tears started into the man's eyes. "Ah," continued Mr. Grant, "you see my saying was true, that you would live to repent writing that pamphlet. I did not mean it as a threat—I only meant that some day you would know us better, and repent having tried to injure us." "I do, I do, indeed, repent it." "Well, well, you know us now. But how do you get on—what are you going to do?" The poor man stated that he had friends who would assist him when his certificate was obtained. "But how are you off in the mean time?" The answer was, that, having given up every farthing to his creditors, he had been compelled to stint his family in even the common necessaries of life, that he might be enabled to pay for his certificate. "My good fellow, this will never do; your wife and family must not suffer in this way; be kind enough to take this ten-pound note to your wife from me: there, there, now—don't cry, it will be all well with you yet; keep up your spirits, set to work like a man, and you will raise your head among the best of us yet." The overpowered man endeavoured with choking utterance to express his gratitude, but in vain; and putting his hand to his face, he went out of the room sobbing like a child.

The True Gentleman is one whose nature has been fashioned after the highest models. It is a grand old name, that of Gentleman, and has been recognized as a rank and power in all stages of society. "The Gentleman is always the Gentleman," said the old French General to his regiment of Scottish gentry at Rousillon, "and invariably proves himself such in need and in danger." To possess this character is a dignity of itself, commanding the instinctive homage of every generous mind, and those who will not bow to titular rank, will yet do homage to the gentleman. His qualities depend not upon fashion or manners, but upon moral worth—not on personal possessions, but on personal qualities. The Psalmist briefly describes him as one "that walketh uprightly, and worketh righteousness, and speaketh the truth in his heart."

The gentleman is eminently distinguished for his self-respect. He values his character,—not so much of it only as can be seen of others, but as he sees it himself; having regard for the approval of his inward monitor. And, as he respects himself, so, by the same law, does he respect others. Humanity is sacred in his eyes : and thence proceed politeness and forbearance, kindness and charity. It is related of Lord Edward Fitzgerald that, while travelling in Canada, in company with the Indians, he was shocked by the sight of a poor squaw trudging along laden with her husband's trappings, while the chief himself walked on unencumbered. Lord Edward at once relieved the squaw of her pack by placing it upon his own shoulders,—a beautiful instance of what the French call *politesse de cœur*—the inbred politeness of the true gentleman.

The true gentleman has a keen sense of honour,—scrupulously avoiding mean actions. His standard of probity in word and action is high. He does not shuffle or prevaricate, dodge or skulk; but is honest, upright, and straightforward. His law is rectitude—action in right lines. When he says *yes*, it is a law: and he dares to say the valiant *no* at the fitting season. The gentleman will not be bribed; only the low-minded and unprincipled will sell themselves to those who are interested in buying them. When the upright Jonas Hanway officiated as commissioner in the victualling department, he declined to receive a present of any kind from a contractor; refusing thus to be biassed in the performance of his public duty. A fine trait of the same kind is to be noted in the life of the Duke of Wellington. Shortly after the battle of Assaye, one morning the Prime Minister of the Court of Hyderabad waited upon him for the purpose of privately ascertaining what territory and what advantages had been reserved for his master in the treaty of peace between the Mahratta princes and the Nizam. To obtain this information the minister offered the general a very large sum—considerably above 100,000*l.* Looking at him quietly for a few seconds, Sir Arthur said, "It appears, then, that you are capable of keeping a secret?" "Yes, certainly," replied the minister. "*Then so am I,*" said the English general, smiling, and bowed the minister out. It was to Wellington's great honour, that though uniformly successful in India, and with the power of earning in such modes as this enormous wealth, he did not add a farthing to his fortune, and returned to England a comparatively poor man.

A similar sensitiveness and high-mindedness characterised his noble relative, the Marquis of Wellesley, who, on one occasion, positively refused a present of 100,000*l.* proposed to be given him by the Directors of the East India Company on the conquest of Mysore. "It is not necessary," said he, "for me to allude to the independence of my character, and the proper dignity attaching to my office; other reasons besides these important considerations lead me to decline this testimony, which is not suitable to me. *I think of nothing but our army.* I should be much distressed to curtail the share of those brave soldiers." And the Marquis's resolution to refuse the present remained unalterable.

Sir Charles Napier exhibited the same noble self-denial in the course of his Indian career. He rejected all the costly gifts which barbaric princes were ready to lay at his feet, and said with truth, 'Certainly I could have got 30,000*l.* since my coming to Scinde, but my hands do not want washing yet. Our dear father's sword which I wore in both battles (Meanee and Hyderabad) is unstained."

Riches and rank have no necessary connexion with genuine gentlemanly qualities. The poor man may be a true gentleman,—in spirit and in daily life. He may be honest, truthful, upright, polite, temperate, courageous, self-respecting, and self-helping,—that is, be a true gentleman. The poor man with a rich spirit is in all ways superior to the rich man with a poor spirit. To borrow St. Paul's words, the former is as " having nothing, yet possessing all things," while the other, though possessing all things, has nothing. The first hopes everything, and fears nothing; the last hopes nothing, and fears everything. Only the poor in spirit are really poor. He who has lost all, but retains his courage, cheerfulness, hope, virtue, and self-respect, is still rich. For such a man, the world is, as it were, held in trust; his spirit dominating over its grosser cares, he can still walk erect, a true gentleman.

Occasionally, the brave and gentle character may be found under the humblest garb. Here is an old illustration, but a fine one. Once on a time, when the Adige suddenly over-flowed its banks, the bridge of Verona was carried away, with the exception. of the centre arch, on which stood a house, whose inhabitants supplicated help from the windows, while the foundations were visibly giving way. " I will give a hundred French louis," said the Count Spolverini, who stood by, " to any person who will venture to deliver these unfortunate people." A young peasant came forth from the crowd, seized a boat, and pushed into the stream. He gained the pier, received the whole family into the boat, and made for the shore, where he landed them in safety. " Here is your money, my brave young fellow," said the count. " No," was the answer of the young man, " I do not sell my life; give the money to this poor family, who have need of it." Here spoke the true spirit of the gentle-man, though he was but in the garb of a peasant.

Not less touching was the heroic conduct of a party of Deal boatmen in rescuing the crew of a collier-brig in the Downs but a short time ago.* A sudden storm which set in

* On the 11th January, 1866.

from the north-east drove several ships from their anchors, and it being low water, one of them struck the ground at a considerable distance from the shore, when the sea made a clean breach over her. There was not a vestige of hope for the vessel, such was the fury of the wind and the violence of the waves. There was nothing to tempt the boatmen on shore to risk their lives in saving either ship or crew, for not a farthing of salvage was to be looked for. But the daring intrepidity of the Deal boatmen was not wanting at this critical moment. No sooner had the brig grounded than Simon Pritchard, one of the many persons assembled along the beach, threw off his coat and called out, " Who will come with me and try to save that crew." Instantly twenty men sprang forward, with " I will," " and I." But seven only were wanted ; and running down a galley punt into the surf, they leaped in and dashed through the breakers, amidst the cheers of those on shore. How the boat lived in such a sea seemed a miracle ; but in a few minutes, impelled by the strong arms of these gallant men, she flew on and reached the stranded ship, " catching her on the top of a wave " ; and in less than a quarter of an hour from the time the boat left the shore, the six men who composed the crew of the collier were landed safe on Walmer Beach. A nobler instance of indomitable courage and disinterested heroism on the part of the Deal boatmen—brave though they are always known to be—perhaps cannot be cited ; and we have pleasure in here placing it on record.

Mr. Turnbull, in his work on ' Austria,' relates an anecdote of the late Emperor Francis, in illustration of the manner in which the Government of that country has been indebted, for its hold upon the people, to the personal qualities of its princes. " At the time when the cholera was raging at Vienna, the emperor, with an aide-de-camp, was strolling about the streets of the city and suburbs, when a corpse was dragged past on a litter unaccompanied by a

single mourner. The · unusual circumstance attracted his
attention, and he learnt, on inquiry, that the deceased was a
poor person who had died of cholera, and that the relatives
had not ventured on what was then considered the very
dangerous office of attending the body to the grave. ' Then,'
said Francis, 'we will supply their place, for none of my
poor people should go to the grave without that last mark of
respect; and he followed the body to the distant place of
interment, and bare-headed, stood to see every rite and
observance respectfully performed."

Fine though this illustration may be of the qualities of
the gentleman, we can match it by another equally good,
of two English navvies in Paris, as related in a morning
paper a few years ago. "One day a hearse was observed
ascending the steep Rue de Clichy on its way to Montmartre, bearing a coffin of poplar wood with its cold
corpse. Not a soul followed—not ·even the living dog of
the dead man, if he had one. The day was rainy and
dismal; passers by lifted the hat as is usual when a funeral
passes, and that was all. At length it passed two English
navvies, who found themselves in Paris on their way from
Spain. A right feeling spoke from beneath their serge
jackets. ' Poor wretch!' said the one to the other, 'no
one follows him; let us two follow!' And the two took
off their hats, and walked bare-headed after the corpse ·of a
stranger to the cemetery of Montmartre."

Above all, the gentleman is truthful. He feels that truth
is the "summit of being," and the soul of rectitude in human affairs. Lord Chesterfield declared that Truth made
the success of a gentleman. The Duke of Wellington,
writing to Kellerman, on the subject of prisoners on parole,
when opposed to that general in the peninsula, told him
that if there was one thing on which an English officer
prided himself more than another, excepting his courage,
it was his truthfulness. "When English officers," said he,

"have given their parole of honour not to escape, be sure
they will not break it. Believe me—trust to their word;
the word of an English officer is a surer guarantee than the
vigilance of sentinels."

True courage and gentleness go hand in hand. The
brave man is generous and forbearant, never unforgiving
and cruel. It was finely said of Sir John Franklin by his
friend Parry, that "he was a man who never turned his
back upon a danger, yet of that tenderness that he would
not brush away a mosquito." A fine trait of character—
truly gentle, and worthy of the spirit of Bayard—was displayed by a French officer in the cavalry combat of El
Bodon in Spain. He had raised his sword to strike Sir
Felton Harvey, but perceiving his antagonist had only one
arm, he instantly stopped, brought down his sword before
Sir Felton in the usual salute, and rode past. To this may
be added a noble and gentle deed of Ney during the same
Peninsular War. Charles Napier was taken prisoner at
Corunna, desperately wounded; and his friends at home
did not know whether he was alive or dead. A special
messenger was sent out from England with a frigate to
ascertain his fate. Baron Clouet received the flag, and
informed Ney of the arrival. "Let the prisoner see his
friends," said Ney, "and tell them he is well, and well
treated." Clouet lingered, and Ney asked, smiling, "what
more he wanted"? "He has an old mother, a widow, and
blind." "Has he? then let him go himself and tell her he
is alive." As the exchange of prisoners between the countries
was not then allowed, Ney knew that he risked the dis-
pleasure of the Emperor by setting the young officer at
liberty; but Napoleon approved the generous act.

Notwithstanding the wail which we occasionally hear
for the chivalry that is gone, our own age has witnessed
deeds of bravery and gentleness—of heroic self denial and
manly tenderness—which are unsurpassed in history. The

events of the last few years have shown that our countrymen are as yet an undegenerate race. On the bleak
plateau of Sebastopol, in the dripping perilous trenches
of that twelvemonth's leaguer, men of all classes proved
themselves worthy of the noble inheritance of character
which their forefathers have bequeathed to them. But it
was in the hour of the great trial in India that the qualities
of our countrymen shone forth the brightest. The march of
Neill on Cawnpore, of Havelock on Lucknow—officers and
men alike urged on by the hope of rescuing the women
and the children—are events which the whole history of
chivalry cannot equal. Outram's conduct to Havelock, in
resigning to him, though his inferior officer, the honour of
leading the attack on Lucknow, was a trait worthy of Sydney,
and alone justifies the title which has been awarded to him
of, "the Bayard of India." The death of Henry Lawrence
—that brave and gentle spirit—his last words before dying,
" Let there be no fuss about me ; let me be buried *with the
men,*"—the anxious solicitude of Sir Colin Campbell to rescue
the beleaguered of Lucknow, and to conduct his long train
of women and children by night from thence to Cawnpore,
which he reached amidst the all but overpowering assault
of the enemy,—the care with which he led them across the
perilous bridge, never ceasing his charge over them until he
had seen the precious convoy safe on the road to Allahabad,
and then burst upon the Gwalior contingent like a thunder-
clap ;—such things make us feel proud of our countrymen
and inspire the conviction that the best and purest glow
of chivalry is not dead, but vigorously lives among us yet.

Even the common soldiers proved themselves gentlemen
under their trials. At Agra, where so many poor fellows
had been scorched and wounded in their encounter with
the enemy, they were brought into the fort, and tenderly
nursed by the ladies ; and the rough, gallant fellows proved
gentle as any children. During the weeks that the ladies

watched over their charge, never a word was said by any soldier that could shock the ear of the gentlest. And when all was over—when the mortally-wounded had died, and the sick and maimed who survived were able to demonstrate their gratitude—they invited their nurses and the chief people of Agra to an entertainment in the beautiful gardens of the Taj, where, amidst flowers and music, the rough veterans, all scarred and mutilated as they were, stood up to thank their gentle countrywomen who had clothed and fed them, and ministered to their wants during their time of sore distress. In the hospitals at Scutari, too, many wounded and sick blessed the kind English ladies who nursed them; and nothing can be finer than the thought of the poor sufferers, unable to rest through pain, blessing the shadow of Florence Nightingale as it fell upon their pillow in the night watches.

The wreck of the *Birkenhead* off the coast of Africa on the 27th of February, 1852, affords another memorable illustration of the chivalrous spirit of common men acting in this nineteenth century, of which any age might be proud. The vessel was steaming along the African coast with 472 men and 166 women and children on board. The men belonged to several regiments then serving at the Cape, and consisted principally of recruits who had been only a short time in the service. At two o'clock in the morning, while all were asleep below, the ship struck with violence upon a hidden rock which penetrated her bottom; and it was at once felt that she must go down. The roll of the drums called the soldiers to arms on the upper deck, and the men mustered as if on parade. The word was passed to *save the women and children;* and the helpless creatures were brought from below, mostly undressed, and handed silently into the boats. When they had all left the ship's side, the commander of the vessel thoughtlessly called out,

" All those that can swim, jump overboard and make for the boats." But Captain Wright, of the 91st Highlanders, said, " No! if you do that, *the boats with the women must be swamped;*" and the brave men stood motionless. There was no boat remaining, and no hope of safety; but not a heart quailed; no one flinched from his duty in that trying moment. " There was not a murmur nor a cry amongst them," said Captain Wright, a survivor, "until the vessel made her final plunge." Down went the ship, and down went the heroic band, firing a *feu de joie* as they sank beneath the waves. Glory and honour to the gentle and the brave ! The examples of such men never die, but, like their memories, are immortal.

There are many tests by which a gentleman may be known; but there is one that never fails—How does he *exercise power* over those subordinate to him? How does he conduct himself towards women and children? How does the officer treat his men, the employer his servants, the master his pupils, and man in every station those who are weaker than himself? The discretion, forbearance, and kindliness, with which power in such cases is used, may indeed be regarded as the crucial test of gentlemanly character. When La Motte was one day passing through a crowd, he accidentally trod upon the foot of a young fellow, who forthwith struck him on the face: " Ah, sire, said La Motte, you will surely be sorry for what you have done, when you know that *I am blind.*" He who bullies those who are not in a position to resist may be a snob, but cannot be a gentleman. He who tyrannizes over the weak and helpless may be a coward, but no true man. The tyrant, it has been said, is but a slave turned inside out. Strength, and the consciousness of strength, in a right-hearted man, imparts a nobleness to his character; but he will be most careful how he uses it; for

> " It is excellent
> To have a giant's strength ; but it is tyrannous
> To use it like a giant."

Gentleness is indeed the best test of gentlemanliness. A consideration for the feelings of others, for his inferiors and dependants as well as his equals, and respect for their self-respect, will pervade the true gentleman's whole conduct. He will rather himself suffer a small injury, than by an uncharitable construction of another's behaviour, incur the risk of committing a great wrong. He will be forbearant of the weaknesses, the failings, and the errors, of those whose advantages in life have not been equal to his own. He will be merciful even to his beast. He will not boast of his wealth, or his strength, or his gifts. He will not be puffed up by success, or unduly depressed by failure. He will not obtrude his views on others, but speak his mind freely when occasion calls for it. He will not confer favours with a patronizing air. Sir Walter Scott once said of Lord Lothian, "He is a man from whom one may receive a favour, and that's saying a great deal in these days."

Lord Chatham has said that the gentleman is characterised by his sacrifice of self and preference of others to himself in the little daily occurrences of life. In illustration of this ruling spirit of considerateness in a noble character, we may cite the anecdote of the gallant Sir Ralph Abercromby, of whom it is related, that when mortally wounded in the battle of Aboukir, he was carried in a litter on board the ' Foudroyant ;' and, to ease his pain, a soldier's blanket was placed under his head, from which he experienced considerable relief. He asked what it was. " It's only a soldier's blanket," was the reply. " *Whose* blanket is it?" said he, half lifting himself up. " Only one of the men's." "I wish to know the name of the man whose blanket this is." " It is Duncan Roy's, of the 42nd, Sir Ralph." " Then see that

Dur.can Roy gets his blanket this very night." * Even to ease his dying agony the general would not deprive the private soldier of his blanket for one night. The incident is as good in its way as that of the dying Sydney handing his cup of water to the private soldier on the field of Zutphen.

The quaint old Fuller sums up in a few words the character of the true gentleman and man of action in describing that of the great admiral, Sir Francis Drake : " Chaste in his life, just in his dealings, true of his word ; merciful to those that were under him, and hating nothing so much as idlenesse ; in matters especially of moment, he was never wont to rely on other men's care, how trusty or skilful soever they might seem to be, but, always contemning danger, and refusing no toyl, he was wont himself to be one (whoever was a second) at every turn, where courage, skill, or industry, was to be employed."

* Brown's ' Horæ Subsecivæ.'

INDEX.

THE END

LONDON:
PRINTED BY W. CLOWES AND SONS, STAMFORD STREET
AND CHARING CROSS.

MAG (815,930)

www.ingramcontent.com/pod-product-compliance
Lightning Source LLC
Chambersburg PA
CBHW032303280326
41932CB00009B/685